KANGAROO KAY

Robert Gordon "Chip" Cathcart Kay
25 September 1931 – 24 January 2020

FROM JUNGLE TO TEAPOT
An historical biography of Triumph and Tragedy in central Africa

Sharlene Hayton

First Edition Printed by Amazon Books – Kindle Direct Publishing
www.amazon.com

Book designed by Sharlene Hayton

Maps: Velhagen & Klafing 1922, Directorate of Colonial Surveys 1948, Anette Kay 2020
Photographs: courtesy of the Cathcart Kay family, Anette Kay, Danika Thomas, Malamulo Archives, and the author.

ISBN: 9798698334774

To my humble, unfaltering parents Kevin and Marian de Berg

Introduction

Chip and Sharlene at House Number One, Satemwa circa 2017

Kangaroo Kay is a biography about Chip Cathcart Kay, a tea planter from British Central Africa. Born in Nyasaland to Scottish pioneers in 1931, Chip's life has spanned the historic changes of the British Protectorate, from colonial roots through independence to current day Malawi. Chip's life was one of adventure. He was educated in Cape Town and England as a young child, catching trains and ships alone at a young age and then taking care of his little sister along the journey. When he returned to Nyasaland to help his father run the tea estate, Satemwa, he began to develop hobbies and interests outside of agriculture.

By the mid 1950's he was an expert bush pilot, trained on Tiger Moths and Cessnas, he flew all over Africa for business and pleasure. He was the heart and soul of the local flying club and famous in Africa's interior as the pilot with the "yellow tail." His nickname, "Kangaroo Kay" was coined after his bouncing attempts at landing his first tiger moth on the runway. "You look like a Kangaroo!" his flying buddies had teased. And the name stuck. He ran rescue missions for downed pilots, arriving days too late to rescue one from the jaws of hyena.

As Chip grew up, the country he loved so much grew along with him. He witnessed the 'winds of change' as Malawi gained independence. He fought to maintain his estate under changing conditions. He lost a marriage and close family members who died tragically from accidents. He battled the wild African bush and animals as he sought to domesticate a corner of Malawi for his family.

He loved deeply and he lost more than he thought he could bear at times. The family tensions he felt growing up along with the white and black tensions in his beloved home country are central themes of this book. Chip never thought of himself as different from his African childhood friends on the estate until his 21st birthday party when he realized his stark privilege. He loved the Malawian people in ways that outsiders could not fathom.

As Chip aged, he became an avid storyteller, and could be found on a Sunday afternoon on the lawn of the home he built when he was 18 years old. An eager group of visitors would circle around him and the abundant tea trolley with all its nibbles and dribbles, would be in the center of the crowd. He would relish retelling his life stories, the Iceland plane confiscation, his mother's religious obsession, his father's passion to grow tea, and how he and his wife Dawn overbooked the kitchen on a Sunday morning with the horse and flying clubs accidentally invited on the same day.

People always told him to write a book so this important part of Malawi history could be preserved. Many travel magazines and articles have been written on Chip's life, but this book is the complete edition of stories told from Chip himself to me, every Monday afternoon for two years. A pristine collection of newspapers, journals and photographs kept in Blantyre and loaned to me by friends allowed me to piece Chip's story together with added historical interests that corresponded with Chip's life. His life is really a depiction of Malawi's last Colonial. A story of human endeavor, of triumph and tragedy.

Africa – circa 1922

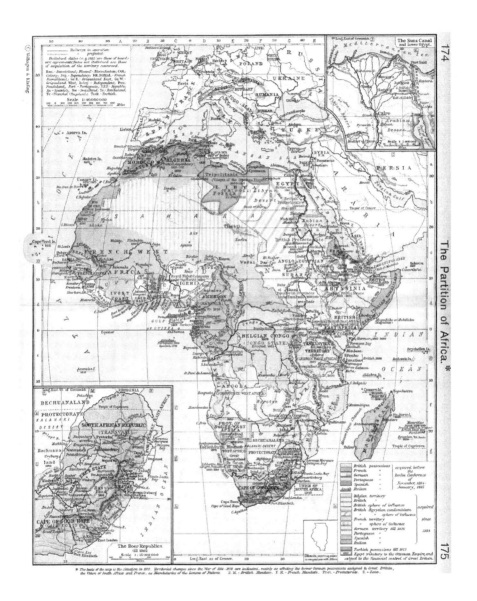

Nyasaland, Northern Rhodesia and Southern Rhodesia federated 1953-1963

1948

Nyasaland 1948

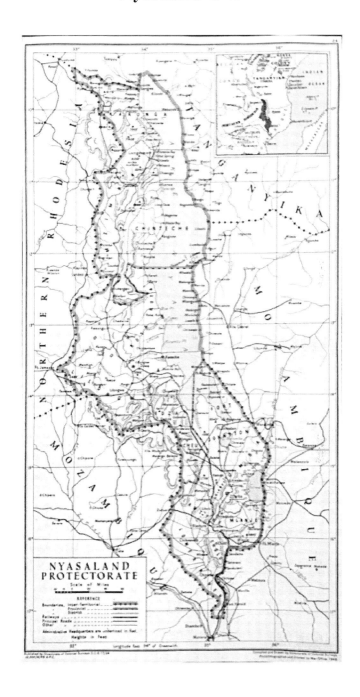

Satemwa Tea and Coffee Estate 2020

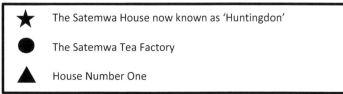

★ The Satemwa House now known as 'Huntingdon'

● The Satemwa Tea Factory

▲ House Number One

The Satemwa House known as Huntingdon from 2007 circa 2015

House Number One – Chip and Dawn's home circa 2016

Brief Historical Background to the Story

Political Events

From the 15th century European countries were intent on expanding their interests over the globe to enhance their economies by trade and their civilizing influence through Christian belief. In the 15th century Portugal was a major sea-faring nation and was first involved in trade on the west coast of Africa and later on the east coast of Africa. Trading proved profitable through the use of slave labor, a brutal and dehumanizing system of oppression. By the 19th century Portugal's influence as a sea-faring nation was declining and Portuguese East Africa was largely restricted to Mozambique. From 1859 to 1891 the area now known as Malawi was classified as the 'interior' of Portuguese East Africa. Great Britain, Germany and France were significant world powers in the 19th century with Great Britain having the supreme naval force and dominance in its colonial activities. This resulted in the annexation of Malawi as "The British Central Africa Protectorate" from 1891 to 1907. In 1892 Consul General Sir Harry Johnston commenced a process of 'land settlement' or 'certificates of claim' to restrict 'land grabs' by greedy Europeans and to ensure that the local people were receiving appropriate prices for their land. This process saw a decrease of the land 'grabbed' by Europeans from 15% to 2% by its conclusion. In 1894 it was estimated 3,691,767 acres of land had been taken from the Nyasa people. Through a process of Crown acquisitions, buy-backs, take-overs, forced sales, and legal sales, only 422,000 acres of European-owned estates remained by Independence in 1964.[a,b,c,d,e,f]

From 1907 to 1953 Malawi was known as the British Nyasaland Protectorate. By 1953 the British colony of Southern Rhodesia and the two British Protectorates of Nyasaland and Northern Rhodesia saw advantages economically in forming a Federation known as the Central African Federation (CAF). The fact that many African countries were seeking independence from their European Protectors by the 1960's led to the Federation dissolving in 1963 and Nyasaland achieved independence in 1964 becoming known as Malawi. The ensuing black majority rule with its corruption and 'rule for life' scenario has proved perplexing and worrying to the private land owners who received their legitimate land claims during the time of British supervision.[g]

Christian Missionaries

Central to Malawi's history is the Christian Scottish explorer David Livingstone (1813-1873) who, after having visited Africa as a missionary, was sent by the British Government to find the source of the Nile River. The city of Blantyre in Malawi is named after Livingstone's birthplace in Scotland. Livingstone, steeped in Christian traditions and judgements, believed that if the primitive peoples on the 'dark continent' were educated and taught about Christ, the inter-tribal skirmishes, the tribal wars and hostile take-overs, and above all, the cruel traffic in black humanity would cease. Representatives from the Catholic and Protestant faiths established missions within Malawi and across Africa. These missions were associated in most cases with providing healthcare and education for the local people.[h]

The slave trade was lucrative, and it had brought Arab merchants in droves to the interior. Setting themselves up as petty Chieftains, they were often conspiring with the local chiefs who began to act as the Arab's lieutenants. They had no moral qualms about stealing humans from their neighboring village to supply the Arab's caravans, as they marched the pilfered lives, ram-shackled in manacles, to the coast. The slaves provided the Arabs with free porterage for their second commodity, ivory, the transport of which relied heavily on the burdened slave. If they failed to bear the mass of their loads -the tusks weighing an average of 30kg - they were abandoned, tied to a tree, and left to starve, or shot dead on the path - blood pooling beneath their wasted bodies. Great Britain had passed legislation against the practice of slavery in 1834 but it was not until 1895 that the fall of the Arab Chieftain, Mlozi, marked the end of slavery in Nyasaland.[i,j,k,l]

Commerce and Trade

Livingstone had dreamed of establishing a thriving cotton industry to compete with that in the USA as one means of challenging their practice of slavery. However cotton could not rival the production of tobacco and tea. Unlike other African nations like Nigeria (oil), Botswana (diamonds), and Zambia (copper), Malawi has practically no natural resources and so relies very much on the produce of its plantations. With the establishment of a number of trading companies, some as private companies and some as the off-shoots of Christian missions, Nyasaland's exports grew from 7,000 pounds in 1891 to 100,000 pounds by 1909. By the early 1900's, Nyasaland was exporting ivory, tobacco, coffee, cotton, tea, rubber, sisal, among other commodities to an awaiting world. However, the growth of exports has not been able to finance a nation with an exploding population. The population of 1,187,631 in 1922 would expand to greater than 18,000,000 by 2020, a strain that would burden existing governments, necessitate a boom in foreign aid, and increase the tensions over land ownership. Today, Malawi is one of the poorest nations on earth.[m,n]

Current Context

In 1892, when Johnston was granting 'certificates of claim' for deeds to land in Nyasaland, estates had a difficult time recruiting labor, often resorting to importing workers from surrounding countries. In 2020, planters are tested in a different way – how are they going to support the multitude that come to their plantations seeking employment? How are they going to produce an export crop when the internal veins of the country are imploding? Previously, the challenge was fighting slave-hunters, creating a fair base for an infant country to grow, and recruiting labor in a country with few people.[o]

Today, Malawi is splitting at the sides, schools are filled with more bodies than space to sit, the healthcare system so burdened that women give birth at home or in the corridors of its hospitals, deforestation is rapidly wiping out the ecosystem, and floods and droughts spell death for thousands. Now planters who survive Chip Kay, born in Nyasaland to a father who dreamed to live under the African sun and create a monument to human endeavor (Satemwa), somberly contemplate Malawi's future and how her people can survive and dream to thrive.

CONTENTS

Kangaroo Kay
From Jungle to Teapot

And now, the end is near
And so I face the final curtain
My friends, I'll say it clear
I'll state my case of which I'm certain
I've lived a life that's full
I traveled each and every highway
But more, much more than this
I did it my way…

I've loved, laughed and cried
I've had my fill, my share of losing
And now, as tears subside
I find it all so amusing
To think I did all that
And may I say, not in a shy way
Oh no, no, not me
I did it my way.

-Paul Anka

A Colonial Childhood 1931-1945

Robert Gordon "Chip" Cathcart Kay 1938

PART ONE

On the war-weary deck of the Cunard Liner, RMS Mauretania, 4,000 servicemen and 1,000 civilian passengers waited patiently, bobbing in the North Atlantic inlet just outside of their destination, the Princes Landing Stage in Liverpool. Due into port on the 23rd of September 1945, RMS Mauretania had made a record-breaking voyage, sailing 28,662 miles from New Zealand in 81 days and 18 hours, but was unavoidably held up in the grip of the cold ocean, poor docking conditions preventing her punctuality and placing her into port two days late on the 25th of September 1945.

It was a somber day for some whose loved ones never made the journey home from war, yet for others, cheering on the dock, the day was a giddy reunion, heaven-sent with rain-wet embraces and booming chatter that echoed around the dock as family and friends found each other in the crowds.

Among the kaleidoscope of passengers, there was a young boy from Central Africa, traveling solo, with a sea-sick stomach that could barely tolerate the cafeteria-style food on board the ship. RMS Mauretania's pre-war advertisements, "Getting There is Half the Fun," certainly did not resonate with the nauseated teenager. He stepped off the ship as a chilly wind swirled through the one meter gap with the dock, the end of fall in England, a spitting cold reminder of the distance between his warm African home and his new surroundings on a continent which he had visited twice before, once as a small boy of three and another time at seven years of age.

The day he set foot on the dock in Liverpool was his fourteenth birthday, and he felt as much like celebrating as the people who sat disappointed on the steel beams alongside the dock, whose family and friends had become ghosts of the horrible war.

The English rain was incessant; it bore into his body, past his skin, and through his bones if it were possible. It certainly was different from his African home, where he would wake, already sweaty, doused in the heat of the day. In Africa, reprieve would come by afternoon when the rains roared out of the sky, full, heavy and reckless. He thought for a moment about how he would run out into the rain, hands raised, laughing with his friends as they stomped in the 'made in a minute puddles' on his parent's tea estate, Satemwa, his beloved home.

Indignantly, he wiped the foreign, cold rain of Liverpool off his brow. He narrowed his eyes to read the street signs, looking for the Adelphi Hotel, his destination for the night. He found it easily, past the docks, and several city blocks, but through a flood of tears that embarrassed him.

Along with the majority of British colonials in the outskirts of the Empire, his father, a tea planter from Nyasaland, and his mother, an able wife and farmer in her own capacity, had sent him away to attend school. Initially the plan of an English education was thwarted by the imminent War of 1939, and he spent the war years in Cape Town, two thousand miles away from Satemwa. At age nine, he had learned to travel alone, roving by rail between Nyasaland and Cape Town for school holidays. At fourteen, he considered himself experienced in negotiating travel and was disgusted with himself for the ragged state he had allowed himself to manifest upon his arrival, the beginning of his 'sentence' to the drab, dreary country of England, where he was doomed to reside for the remainder of his education.

He closed the door to his room at the Adelphi, and mumbled in between stifled sobs, trying to lift his gloomy mood as he found the mirror which hung above the ornate bureau and forced himself to look into it. He pulled faces at his image, drying his tears and stiffening his neck. He nodded to his reflection, "Happy birthday," and began to remember happier times, memories from a 'million miles away.' He shook the thoughts and returned to the strange room.

He turned back towards the mirror; his hazel green eyes grew round as he stared hard at his appearance. His dusty brown hair was coated in the salty spray that skimmed over the decks of the Mauretania and the

English rain which had unwelcomed him to Liverpool and done its best to tangle the strands of hair further. He inspected his undone self in the hotel mirror. His tan cotton shirt was soaked through, and his woolen woven shorts spattered with water, absorbing the drips from his shirt and hair like a sponge. It was no matter, for a bath and fresh clothes could morph his ratted image, but something that would not change was the way his nose began to resemble his father's. He scrunched it up, wiggling it, wondering if there really was such a likeness as he imagined. It would be an honor to be just like his father. He was an average height for a boy of fourteen but considered himself no average teenager.

Ordinarily, he was proud to be a boy who could travel by train, or car, or ship – an independent child. He was the boy, who on his parent's tea plantation in the African interior, was seldom found at the family breakfast table, having escaped through his bedroom window when the first rays of sunlight crept in. Occasionally, the garden boys arrived at work to catch a fleeting glimpse of Chip as he ran – barefoot and carefree – over the manicured lawns that sprawled before 'The Satemwa House' (his parent's house) like a putting green. He remembered swimming through the tea fields to the sound of pluckers nipping – two leaves and a bud – and hurling the fresh tips of tea into their woven baskets which were perched high on their backs. He remembered skittering, past the blue gum forest, which stretched towards the vast blue sky, through a patch of virgin jungle with wild date palms and chisoso weeds scratching at his naked ankles.

He thought for a moment about the shifting sands of his life, about his colonial childhood, which pushed him outside of his comfort zone, out into other countries, making him feel, at times, a little transient. Even his name, Robert Gordon, was only a name of momentary holding. Within minutes of his first breath of life, Nurse Melville, who had ridden her bicycle nine miles from Malamulo Mission Hospital to the Cathcart's 'Namireme' thatch-roofed house to deliver the baby, declared, "Well, isn't he a Chip off the old block!" looking directly at Maclean, who beamed with fatherly pride. "Chip," repeated his mother, Flora Jean. And so it was, from his first day on, he was no longer Robert Gordon, he was Chip Cathcart Kay. [1]

PART TWO

Chip and Juliet circa 1938

Alarmed at fourteen to find himself away from his beloved Africa, Chip settled his thoughts back to happier times, and imagined himself years earlier in the post-dawn hours putting distance between himself and his neatly organized bedroom at 'The Satemwa House'. After passing through the scrappy jungle he remembered arriving only mildly puffed at the estate homes, where tea pluckers and their families resided. His two best friends, John Humbiani and Nelson Nagoli emerged from behind their mother's three-stone village fire, where a bubbling porridge simmered, the steam cutting through the humid morning air like an intense fog.

"Madzuka, Chippy," (good morning) John would say prompting Chip's reply, "Dadzuka iwe, kaya inu?" (I am well and how are you?). Nelson liked to sing to Chip in his very best 'English' voice, "London breedge is foe-ling do-wen, foe-ling do-wen," and "tweenkel, tweenkel, leetel star…" It was obvious to Chip that Nelson hoped to sound properly English, but with his long-drawn vowels and thick African accent, he sounded more African after speaking English than he had when he stuck to Chi'Nyanja, Nyasaland's vernacular.

"Tingapite kumtsinje lero?" (shall we go to the river today?) the friends asked each other. "Eya, tikawedze kusodza." (yes, let's go catch fish). The three boys slurped hot phala (porridge) from Nelson's steaming pot and disappeared behind the housing compound, padding quietly through the jungle, always watching for leopard tracks and listening to the running water of the Nswadzi River.

Sometimes, when the children were drawn back to the 'big house' by their rumbling tummies, or the setting sun, or the familiar call of the nightjar, they left behind the adventure of the day and reluctantly drew near to the family pet, hopeful he would engage in their games. The pet was a blue vervet monkey with old-man eyebrows knotted in wispy charm. His cheeky grin and quick sharp movement put him at an advantage against the loping youngsters who sought his company. One day, the monkey took off from his roosting post and flew in the air, like sudden gunfire, towards Chip, John and Nelson. A wild second later without time to react Chip found the family pet clamped ferociously onto his forearm, where instant pain heated and spread. John rushed to a three-stone fire burning nearby and extracted a hot coal which he pressed into the monkey's side. He squawked and released his grip and Chip was free from the vervet's jaws at last. "Eh, John, coma zanzero zimenizo." (That's a clever idea you had). "Chonde kwambiri." (thank you very much). [2]

The monkey suffered a fatal blow from the charcoal on that day, and a funeral was arranged, with an orderly ceremony in which Chip's father, Maclean, was the presiding Reverend. Chip and his sister, Juliet, (who was three years younger than Chip), solemnly said their farewells to their pet, although Chip had mixed emotions about the animal since his forearm was still aching. They buried the monkey under an ant hill, so the ants could consume the flesh and leave the bones. Raised in the Scottish Kirk the children believed that just as Christ rose from the dead after three days, so our dead must rise and go to heaven. Four days after the monkey burial, Juliet dug up the termite mound, and to her dismay found their monkey still underground. He had not gone to heaven, and Chip, nursing his hurt arm, was not surprised.

A more sensible pet for the children proved to be the goldfish that their mother, Flora Jean, acquired from Rhodesia. As an outreach to troubled souls Jean and her bridge club friends visited the local prison to play bridge with the prisoners. Among the incarcerated she found a white man whose hobby was breeding goldfish. Jean requested some for her pond at 'The Satemwa House' in Nyasaland. When she brought the fish home the children were delighted to watch them swim between the reeds and lily pads, lighting up the cement pond with their ginger-carroty scales. Every so often the Africans would peer into the pond, spreading the papyrus where it grew thick in parts, and comment in Chi'Nyanja, "The white folks must be waiting for them to get big, like in the river, then they will eat them."[3]

One day, Juliet came sobbing into the house. "Winston, my fish, he's on the very top of the water, Mummy – please come quickly!" Winnie the goldfish, (named after Winston Churchill) was dead. Just as they had given the monkey a funeral, so Winnie required a ceremony. Juliet chose to bury Winnie in "Mandalay", her mother's exotic garden, brimming with plants that Jean had smuggled into Nyasaland in her sponge bag, past the wary eye of customs officers who looked down on undocumented arrivals. Jean deferred the job of Reverend to the manager of their tea factory, 'Old Hutchinson', who was known never to change the oil in his Ford V8 pick-up because "once you start changing the oil in your car, you have to do it all the time." Hutchinson called everyone to attention and solemnly stated, "Here lies Winnie the fish, if he'd lived any longer he'd have ended up on a dish."[4]

Juliet and her best friend, an African girl called Maggie, joined Chip, John and Nelson on their adventures around the estate. They spoke Chi'Nyanja amongst themselves and the estate workers ululated when the children passed, enjoying the sight of the Bwana's (Boss') children growing up with theirs. The five close friends scouted the tea fields, forests, rivers and open spaces for new games. Barefooted, they created puffs of red smoke as they ran along the dry estate roads. They whittled the hours away and the long, hot days in the Shire Highland at the foot of Cholo mountain were among the happiest of Chip's and Juliet's young lives. Between Chip's nanny, 'Chelima', who was a tall, strong man from the Yao tribe, the garden boys who hailed from Mozambique - Portuguese East Africa (PEA) and his plantation friends, Chip was more proficient in the local dialects than in the King's English, a fact that his family had yet to discover.[5]

In June 1938, Maclean took his son on an ocean-crossing to Scotland, boarding the Stirling Castle in Cape Town. The ship was built for the purpose of carrying mail from Southampton to South Africa. Maclean and Chip sailed two weeks to arrive at Macleans' family home at 221 Nithsdale Rd in Glasgow, Scotland. It was the second time Chip's grandparents had seen him and for Chip it was the first time he remembered meeting them. Afraid of creating a poor first impression and possibly being accused of 'going native' – a term given to describe settlers from the Dominion losing their fine manners in the outskirts of the Empire – Maclean had briefed Chip on what to say and how to act. But it soon became clear to Maclean that his son spoke better African dialects (Llomwe, Yao, Ngoni, Nyanja, Chewa) than English and under family pressures he resolved to 'fix it' when they returned to Nyasaland. Maclean wrote letters home to Jean mentioning Chip's occasional 'rudeness' but described the meeting overall as a 'general success.' He wrote, "Alex (Maclean's brother) is very fond of Chip and Chip thinks he is the very best thing. You see, he plays trains with Chip for hours. His granny and Aunt are still very much taken up with the kid. They think he is so well-bred and has fine manners, so they say they are pals. But they also admit he can be very rude unless kept down by me…"[6]

Having learned of Chip's English deficiency while abroad in 1938, Maclean sought information regarding schooling options for both his children. In a letter home to Jean he spoke of "Whitecraigs Belmont School," and inspected "Tauntons" in London upon the suggestion of his mother-in-law. Neither school fitted their needs. His trip fast became burdened with financial concerns. Jean wrote that there was a shortage of maize for their workers in Nyasaland. He had to interview and hire an engineer from England, supply Satemwa with food, and find an appropriate school for his children. He wrote to Jean, "I shall take a run down (to London) to discuss the matter, and by then perhaps the finance may have been fixed up OK. These folk regard us as people of wealth and that is that."[7]

Maclean, Jean, Chip and Juliet Kay circa 1938

Colonial families were under extreme pressures associated with education for their growing children. Education in the Protectorate of Nyasaland was partitioned by race, as were employment options and hospital facilities – falling into one of three main categories: European, Asiatic, or African. The Nyasaland Government stated that for European children of school age, "Cultural and climatic conditions render it unwise to keep children in Nyasaland after the age of 11 years." In fact, during 1938 not one European child over the age of 13 attended school in Nyasaland.[8]

When Maclean returned with Chip to Nyasaland, he and Jean decided to enroll Chip, aged 8, in the Salisbury Correspondence course under the tutelage of a new white nanny, Barbara Buchanan. Buchanan came from Goodwin in the Cape of South Africa and promised the family she could sort out Chip's English problems in short order, which she did. [9]

Begrudgingly Chip plodded through his correspondence course and inhaled Buchanan's instructions in the same way a dog takes deworming tablets- poorly. But he was learning and the family were pleased with his progress. However, if Chip had his way - which he often did – he spent his hours on mechanical projects honing his desire to figure out how things worked. One day he decided to turn his bicycle upside down to fix a clanking chain. He spun the rickety wheels and poked at the stubborn gears, trying to find the source of the screeching noise. Suddenly, without warning, the ring finger on his right hand became stuck between cogs and blood instantly gushed from a wound. To quell the intense throbbing, his father made a tea-leaf poultice and placed it on the bleeder. Chip held the bandage tightly as they drove to Malamulo Mission Hospital, past a pride of lazy lions lounging on the grass by the Nyasa Mission, their young cubs imploring the adult lions to play. Once at the mission, Dr Morell put Chip's finger right again, rendering it "bulletproof", or so Chip liked to think.[10]

Despite Buchanan's tremendous efforts, Maclean and Jean knew they needed to send Chip away for school. Since the war seethed by 1940, children were denied travel to England for education, 'safety' being a primary concern. Children were told to remain in the colonies and Chip, along with thousands of other colonials, had to find alternative solutions on the African continent. He was enrolled in Bishops – the Diocesan College Preparatory School for Boys in Cape Town – mockingly named "Dead Cats Pea Soup," by those in attendance, a cruel nickname for a school whose objective was "to give a sound education to the youth of the colony."

Bishops school for boys had walls painted stark white, occasionally muted by sandstone cornices, and softened by the meticulously kept garden beds and clipped trees. Rugby fields neatly marked the center of the campus and were lined by bushes and hedges tidily pruned. It was different from the wild jungles of Satemwa, but the same as the sweeping tea fields, where order and precision ruled the day. Chip felt both out of place and at home at the same time. His mother stayed in a flat in Cape Town, close to Bishops, and signed on to become one of 180,000 women in the Women's Auxiliary Air Force (WAAF). She was the daughter of Captain Moffat-Baily and she was determined to help the war effort, packing parachutes, performing aircraft maintenance, intelligence operations, and communications duties on wireless telephonic and telegraphic devices. Jean was never a woman to be idle.[11]

Chip's favorite person at Bishops was his Rossall housemaster, Kerry Keeble. The boys his age just didn't compare to John and Nelson, his Nyasaland friends. He often dreamed of the long, warm days on Satemwa, chasing the sun and rolling Nsima (staple maize starch) on his palm before dipping it in Ndiwo (relish) and sucking it off his fingers.

Holidays came slowly and the return to school came annoyingly quickly. When he left to go back to Bishops after his first holiday, he was placed in charge of his sister, Juliet aged 6, who had been enrolled in St James' Convent Star of the Sea just thirty minutes down the track from Bishops for Boys. Juliet was a pretty young girl, with strawberry blonde curls framing her bright green eyes and innocent face. She was often described by her father as "wee wig" or "jewel".

Chip was a robust 9 years old when he was given the reigns for independent travel. His father would drive them from Satemwa in his blue Studebaker Commander, forty-five minutes down the road to Luchenza Railway Station where, after some brief instructions, Maclean would watch as his 9 year-old son and 6 year-old daughter slipped out of sight on the sleek rails. John Humbiani often heard the rumble of the Studebaker and rushed along the Satemwa road to wave Chip off, shouting, "Chippy – eh you are so smart in your car. When you come home, you must teach me to drive, ok?"[12]

Luchenza Railway Station was close to the main Cholo – Mlanje road, and was the bustling epicenter connecting the cities of Nyasaland to the outside world. Among other things, Luchenza was a mail-sorting depot where customs officers pored over packages and boxes to determine their contents and allocate fees. Behind the warehouse opposite the station platform was the tea association warehouse, where Maclean sent tonnes of Satemwa tea every month destined for England.

Often the trains came late. Nyasaland railway engines burnt wood for fuel, which resulted in "frequent halts" as the engine drivers and firemen had to re-load the tenders at intervals of 50 miles. An African fireman was tasked to find ganyu (pieceworkers) to help sharpen axes and chop trees to load the train boilers so the engine could continue up the track. The process could take several hours. It was noted that this practice resulted in "de-forestation of rail-side forests near re-fueling points."[13]

Jean stayed in Cape Town to aid the WAAF and Maclean waved his children off from Luchenza alone. He gave Chip 4 pounds sterling, enough to provide food and bedding (at 7 shillings and 6 pence per segment) for him and Juliet on their five-day trip to Cape Town[14]. Chip studied the train in some detail. It's convex roof gleamed under the hot sun and the dark brown exterior of the carriage hid the African dirt well. There were twelve box-shaped windows on each side of the carriage and each had wooden flaps attached outside to deflect any embers which might escape the engine fire and settle on an unsuspecting passenger.[15] Chip and Juliet were not first-class customers, but they found a modest cabin with a bunk bed and clean amenities.

After Luchenza the train pulled into Kongeni Station and Juliet tugged at Chip's arm. She had seen a small blue waxbill, tweeting, behind his chiwale palm jail. She begged Chip to buy it, which he did, bargaining with the young African boy who demanded 6 pence for his efforts. Chip looked down at the 4 pounds he had in his pocket and told the boy authoritatively, "Ndikupadtsa tickey." (I'll take it for 3 pence). The boy shoved his morning catch and the cage towards Chip, "Tenga," (take it) and disappeared into the swath of people who had come to gawk at the strange white people and their puffing train. "We're releasing him at the next stop," Chip told Juliet, hoping she wouldn't set her mind to keep him.

But she had, and Chip spent 2 pounds of their allowance on a fancy bird-cage from a shifty salesman at the Portuguese Emporium in Beira. His father had organized friends to meet the children at the railway in Beira, and DeSuza, his father's Indian friend just rolled his eyes half back in their sockets when he saw Chip carrying a silver bird-cage to meet the 6pm Rhodesian Railways train bound for Umtali.[16]

The best part about the 8am arrival at Umtali was the sumptuous breakfast at Brown's Hotel. There was no restraint on the crispy bacon, poached eggs with runny yellow centers, white toast with thick slabs of butter, baked beans cooked with grizzly sausage, and bottomless juice to wash it all down. With skinny pre-breakfast tummies now swollen from the buffet, Chip and Juliet hardly took much notice of the 11am rail stop at Headlands where the train picked up the restaurant carriage, equipped to feed the passengers for most of the remaining trip to Cape Town. Bypassing the food on menu, Chip ordered cigarettes and blew the pale green smoke with prodigious delight. Juliet, who had snuck a few draughts from her father's pipe was not allowed to participate because she was "much too young" for such a "grown up" habit.[17]

The Southern Rhodesian Railways joined the South African Railways after a night train took the passengers from Salisbury (now Harare) (where an ex-Nyasaland friend, Mrs Saunders had found the two Cathcart children and stuffed them with cake and tea) to Bulawayo. Northern Rhodesian school children also bound for the Cape had joined the train and Chip was befriended by the Wilkin brothers, Dougie and his "terribly naughty younger brother." It was Dougie, Chip and Dougie's "terribly naughty younger brother" who snuck between carriages uncoupling the wagons and returned to their cabins straight-faced with just a hint of mischief in their boyish eyes. When the undone wagons were found, the train master roared through the carriages, shouting "Who did this!?" No one owned up.[18]

Chip had other problems to worry about. The train was rapidly approaching the entry port between Rhodesia and the Protectorate of

Bechuanaland at Mafeking (now Mahikeng). The train had passed by Fig Tree and Chip had moments to act, since transporting animals was illegal without a permit. He had to conceal his sister's bird. She helped by throwing her bedding over the cage, while Chip tucked it behind his teal trunk. The plan worked and the bird passed undetected.

But the night approaching Cape Town was cold, and they had run out of money to buy bedding for the last leg of the journey for two, so they shared a bed that night, as well as the bedding and furry warm blanket. Neither cared, since they knew that when the morning came they might not see each other again for weeks, possibly months.[18]

Before Chip left the train at Rondebosch Station he asked some decent-looking people seated near them to make certain Juliet got off the train at St James Station, just thirty minutes down the track. "When you see the nuns on the platform, please hand my sister over to them," Chip said. He watched the train puff away from Rondebosch and waved confidently to Juliet as she pressed her nose against the smudged glass pane. He was in charge and they had just made it – Luchenza to Cape Town.

PART THREE

Jean with Chip and Juliet at the Satemwa House circa 1938

Several years passed with the same travel routine repeated many times, the Cathcart Kay children peripatetic between the Cape and Satemwa, Jean dedicated to the WAAF in Cape Town, and Maclean tirelessly keeping their tea estate out of crisis and providing processed tea to a profitable market in England whose population were begging for a cup of that "hot grateful beverage" to make it through the awful war.

After some time, and probably a greater exposure to the shenanigans of Dougie, Chip and Dougie's "terribly naughty younger brother," the Railway companies decided to segregate travel for school children by gender. There was a well-mannered girls' carriage, full of natter and nail polish, and an energetic boys' carriage, bursting with pre-pubescent hormones and mischief enough to write a book of tales.[19]

On one occasion Chip purchased a "Gilbert's Chemistry Set"[20] from the same emporium where he had bought the bird-cage but for half the price. He took his one-pound bargain back to the lolling boys on the train and under the cover of darkness, they snuck over the sleeping guards up onto the convex roof of the carriage, arriving with a roguish thud on the girls' wagon. They shook the Gilbert's test tube solutions and poured them onto sulfide cards that had come with the kit. One by one, they pushed the rank smelling papers under the doors of the girls' cabins and waited to ambush them in a teasing embrace when they rushed from their rooms to escape the foul odors. Despite a few sullen scowls from the rudely awakened girls, the boys considered the night a roaring success.[21]

Chip was a young, unimpeded, cigarette-smoking boy on the wild edges of adolescence and he sometimes forgot his place as a junior boy on the school train which he shared with much older, much burlier boys than himself. One time John Ness, a hulk of a sixteen year-old, rugby-playing, weight-crushing, seeming giant was assigned to Chip's cabin as his bunk mate. They got in an altercation about the top or lower bunk, and John pulled a Smith & Wesson on Chip, enjoying how the cocked gun made Chip's eyes fearful. It was loaded and Ness shot out the window, emptying the six bullets with a crack, and staring at Chip wordless, watching him quiver. Chip decided he would always hold that moment against John, because it just wasn't a nice thing to do.[22]

The bang of John's revolver often echoed in Chip's head, and sudden, loud pops of noise took his mind back to that terrible day on the train. In March of 1942, Cape Town underwent an air raid drill. Designed to keep the citizens alert and prepare a city for war, the drill sent school children at Bishops across the street to lie flat in a ditch near the main road. Their teacher, Miss Wolf, walked up and down the line of boys, some with their bums sticking up too high above the ditch and others with mouths that would not quieten. She admonished them and corrected their behaviors, earning her the title of "Regimental Sergeant Major."[23]

When school broke for term end, Juliet and Chip reunited and gushed over stories from their schools, each often trying to outdo the other, or tell an account of something terrifically brave or mischievous. Juliet often burst first, itching to share her stories with her brother. She asked Chip, "Do you know if nuns have hair or not?" And Chip shrugged, unsure of the answer. "Well I know because I spied it out."[24]

She launched into "the night of the dead nun", whose body lay in the Church at St James Convent for the first stage of burial. The nun's feet were turned eastward, her habit neatly pressed and her wimple and veil tucked into place. There were dark curtains tied back around the four-post structure which held the lifeless body. The church was quiet and the misty night air drifted in and out of the open back doors. Alone, Juliet snuck out of her dormitory and raced across the cold wet grass to the Chapel where the dead nun lay. She peeked inside the church and, believing it empty, she tiptoed down the aisle towards the lifeless body. She peered over the structure and boldly peeled back the wimple on the nun's head. The nun on guard duty suddenly awoke and chased Juliet around the curtained bed, back down the aisle, out the large back doors and across the wet grass back to her dormitory.

"So…?" Chip asked. "So, what?" Juliet said. "So…do nuns have hair?" "Oh yes, they certainly do."

Chip admired her courage and told her so, admitting that he also had been earmarked for discipline during the term and he was rather mad about the way in which it happened. Some of the boys from his class had observed his indifference to rules which made no common sense and waited for the perfect moment to tattle on him to Rossall Housemaster, Kerry Keeble. When Mr Keeble summoned Chip to his office, the sniping laughter from the other boys in class was barely muffled when they stuffed their delighted faces into their sweaters in dizzy victory. Chip slung a half-eye, "watch it" look at them as he left the room. Upon arrival at Kerry Keeble's office, Chip was asked to sit and explain the vegetable patch he had illegally grown in between Rossall House and the main administration block. Chip expressed to Keeble, "For as long as I can remember, Sir, I've always had this terrible desire to grow things." He beamed when he told the Housemaster the satisfaction of growing something from seed, "Ninety days to harvest from seed." He explained how the produce from his patch went to Nooki in the Cafeteria. Nooki was an old African chef-help who Chip later mused was "five feet high and five feet wide." Nooki, in exchange for Chip's vegetables, would allow him an extra helping of brown bread and dripping.[25]

To compound Chip's compliance issues, a cat – Chip's cat – which he also wasn't allowed, ran to the vegetable patch to greet Chip and Kerry Keeble. "Who's this?" Keeble asked. "Kerry," Chip spoke shyly, knowing now that he had two offences to explain: the vegetable patch and the cat. "He's named after you, if that wasn't obvious," Chip said.

Kerry Keeble could not fault Chip's garden and was flattered to have a scraggly cat named after him. He told Chip not to worry and advised him to "keep on planting."

That evening, with the fading light of day streaming softly onto his paper, Chip took his lead and colored pencils and penned a letter to his father.

SATEMWA TEA ESTATE
P.O. BOX 6
CHOLO, NYASALAND

My dear daddy,
Thank you very much for the
letter.
I am having lovly time at sckool,
I don't think you no what kind
of badje I weer on my cap
I am showing it to you on
the side of the page what
it looks like.
I hope my dam is not washed away and the
bridje I want you to tell me
what it looks like and I want
you to dram a plan of it.
I hope you are all right.
Love from
Chip Kay.[26]

****

Chip often felt far away from home, just as he had when a boy in Cape Town. So now, at fourteen in cold, rainy Liverpool, all he could think of was his father and Satemwa. He yearned for home, the rolling tea fields bursting in bud-break, and his father's warm smile behind the smoke from his pipe. But it would be years before he would see it all again, before he would smell the three-stone village fires and run wild through the Satemwa jungles with his African friends. In the English city he thought mostly of his father, Maclean Kay, a child raised in Scotland, a pioneer rubber planter in Malaya, and now, a tea planter in Nyasaland. To Chip, his father was a pioneering hero, and he knew if his father could make a life in the British colonies, then he could surely survive education in England.

Maclean Kay, the Early Days 1892 - 1922

Maclean Kay in the 'wavy navy' 1914-1918

"Sa-Tem-Ah," the African boy paused, pointing at the bango stems which formed a dense, tall reed-swamp around the river; he peered into the probing face of the new white man, wondering if he understood. The bango reeds were a sacred stalk used to make sleeping mats and shroud the dead. The reeds were "not to be cut" – "Satema" – do not cut, except by order of the local chief. "Satemah?" the stranger repeated with inquisitive tone, scanning the river that cut through his new purchase of land. He motioned to the small child who was desperately trying to be helpful, although neither understood the other's language. Maclean thought "Sa-Tem-Ah" was the native name for the river that carved through the forested boundaries. He checked with the boy again, signaling the expanse of water that spilled before them both. "Satema – river is it not?" Maclean wanted to be precise. "Ndi, Bwana, Sa-Tem-Ah," the boy repeated, wanting to be sure the newcomer did not cut their 'holy' reeds. "Satema - it's a good name for a river and a fine one for my plantation," thought the young Scottish pioneer.

He crossed the river, gently brushing the 'holy' reeds as he passed, battling a tangle of gristly vines that groped the rivers edge as he ascended the other side. Maclean sliced a track as he pushed through the dense jungle and rested at the foot of the Pterocarpus tree whose large yellow flowers had mostly fallen to the ground, the intoxicating odor of honey pervading from the trees blossoms caught lingering in the morning air. Looking down at his mud-covered leather boots, Maclean swept the bracken ferns to clear a view from their wispy fronds and unveiled the cause of his sudden discomfort marching around the trodden earth in a hard line three or four thick in parts-Safari ants- 'Soldier' ants. Maclean shook them off his feet, aware now of several outliers who had made it past his belt buckle undetected; he hastily sought them out and scraped their toughened bodies off his skin, leaving their pinchers behind.[27]

Owning a 'piece of Africa' was not part of Maclean's original plan. Maclean Kay was the youngest boy born to a middle class family in Glasgow, Scotland, on July 4, 1892.[28] His family had acquired the name "Cathcart" through a murky history involving a Mary Maclean and her sister who emigrated back to Scotland from Canada where Mary married a guy called Mr Kay. Mr Kay came from the island of Mull, but through favor of the Laird of Cathcart became unequivocally attached to the village. His children from that point would inherit the name, if they chose, Cathcart Kay, "Cath-Cart" meaning "a river winding through a narrow channel."[29]

The eldest boy was Gordon Cathcart who migrated to Canada. Next was Alexander who became one of Scotland's leading trust lawyers. Robert Kay followed him and became known as Jack, the general manager of the Clydesdale Bank. Maclean was the youngest of the brothers and the 'baby' of the family after his parent's last-born child, his sister Victoria, took ill and died. During his school days at the Glasgow Academy, Maclean, wondering what direction to take with his life, and poised with a sense of national pride, signed with the British military and joined the Sea Cadets. He was accredited to the Royal Navy Volunteer Reserve, (RNVR), which was colloquially addressed as the 'Wavy Navy', owing to the unique stripes of interwoven lace that was stitched to their uniforms. In 1910, upon completion of his schooling at the Academy, young Maclean signed a four-year contract with Guthrie Group Limited, and sailed to Malaya joining the labors of the first British Trading company in Southeast Asia, and learning the skills of planting rubber and the ethics of hard toil.[30]

Four years later, the world watched, partly with disbelief, partly with consternation, as the Kaiser war broke out in 1914. Maclean Kay, along with 30,000 RNVR compatriots, received his service orders, and taking leave from Guthries in Malaya found himself stationed in the Seychelles. The islands, which had long fallen under French rule, were now conjoined to the Empire. For the greater portion of the 18th century, the wary eye of Britain had been monitoring activities of frigates and slavery, supported, or at least not prevented, by the authorities in the

Seychelles. With their push for anti-slavery, Britain acquired the Seychelles as a colony in 1903, seizing the opportunity to curtail the slave trade through control of the African islands. While countries had been raging against each other for centuries, the First World War bore new intonations for a changing world. The British Empire, which had been slowly adding territories and spheres of influence, was now under the microscope of world politics.[31]

The war had changed the world. For one, "Before the war" or "After the war" were now common pretexts for beginning a sentence, and provided clarity to a way of life that once existed but could no longer be reconciled with the present. Moreover, the war had altered everything for young Maclean. He returned to Malaya, to his job with Guthries, and planted rubber as he had done before the war. He noticed that the plantation, the trees that he had pressed earth around as seedlings, had taken grip and dove into the soil; some were even ready for 'tapping'. He assisted the Malayans as they made incisions beneath the bark on the mature trees, collecting the milky colloid in vessels. The latex was then refined into rubber ready for commercial processing. Walking around the plantation, he felt uneasy, an outsider who once belonged but belonged now to somewhere else. He was a subordinate of men who had chosen not to fight for the Empire, and having given up promotions in order to serve the King, he felt resentful of those who now held superior offices over him but had not fought in the war. He also suffered recurrently from ravaging fevers and relentless body aches associated with malaria, the only part of tropical living that made him yearn for home.

The company systems were still functioning, but the labor force was scattered in thought and several took hold of communist ideas that trickled down from the north. Maclean found the Malayan workers to be lazy, requiring micromanagement to complete a task. If he had a choice, he opted to hire the 'Chinamen', who exhibited good work ethics and a teachable nature. With no pressure for appearing 'politically correct', "John Chinaman" was the nickname planters gave men from China. The workplace climate was delicate after the war and Malayans began organizing strikes, seeking to disrupt the British Trading Company. One morning, several Malayans arrived at Maclean's doorstep wielding knives and threatening his physical safety. The men lurched forward, grabbing Maclean by his shirt scruff and pitching him hard to the ground. His neck snapped on impact and his body lay motionless on the stony earth. Maclean's 'Gungadene' (water carrier) was a 'John Chinaman' and witnessing the fight as he rushed through the house, he picked up Maclean and threw his boss over his shoulder. With men in chase, he stepped nimbly over the rocky path that led down to the river, where, glancing behind him, he saw the angry men and promptly hurled Maclean into the river, telling him to stay under the water. The dissatisfied employees retreated, leaving Maclean to drift downstream among the reeds and rapids. Perhaps an hour or more passed before Maclean clambered to the edge of the bank and scratched his way out. His Gungadene had saved his life, but his neck was fractured, not where it would paralyze him, but certain to cause him frequent discomfort for the rest of his life.[32]

Pasci Jinghi (left) and Maclean Kay (right) in Malaya circa 1916

His contract with Guthrie's was ending, and Maclean knew his time as a planter in Malaya was over. He had been patient to learn the skill of planting, the finesse of product perfection, and the fragility of the employment relationship, especially in handling a disgruntled mob. He had success in as much as he had experienced failures, yet he would always be grateful for the foundation that his time with Guthries had given him. He arrived in Malaya as a student graduate and he would leave, a challenged young man, knowledgeable in planting, employment and war. His years spent working for an organization in a foreign land would be more useful for his future than he could have imagined on the day that he boarded the Pennisular and Orient (P&O), heading home to Glasgow, the past flapping behind him, and a future which he couldn't conceive, just days ahead.

The P&O was en route to Aden, the port city of Yemen located on the Eastern approach to the Red Sea. Four miles from the busiest East-

West trade route, rulers had fought each other for centuries to conquer the port city, considered one of the top five natural ports in the world. In 1839, the British East India Company sent Royal Marines to Aden, occupying the territory with ambition to stop pirate raids on British ships traveling through the region. Aden was an important transit point for coal, water and fuel and its significance intensified with the opening of the Suez Canal in 1869. Entering the Yemeni coastal plains, Maclean's boat docked at 'steamer point' and he disembarked onto the "Prince of Wales" pier, built in 1919 to accommodate the increase in activity at the Port[33]. He had been fortunate to purchase a "Port Out, Starboard Home" (POSH) ticket[34] yet he was sure he did not resemble the typecast, opulent and swanky POSH simply because he could afford the premium ticketing on the P&O, which provided shade on the Eastern Journey and shade coming home. Momentarily lost among the other passengers who were trundling off the gangway, and wandering aimlessly for the first time in years, Maclean paused and circled around himself, taking in the vistas of the turquoise water that bumped into the pier where he was fixed to his feet, lost in thought. His Trilby hat, immovable on his head, except to tip it slightly in the presence of an attractive woman, Maclean tucked his thick, wavy hair behind his ear, and found his way back to the crowds and into the town.

"Where are you coming from, son?" A voice directed towards Maclean caused him to glance up, withdrawing his lips from the brandy snifter[35]. "Malaya," he responded, with an upwards nod of his chin. He placed his glass on the table in front and motioned to the empty seat opposite, "Take it, if you like." The man removed his coat and laid it over the arm of the available chair before settling into it. They examined each other with the curiosity of two Europeans who had stories to tell beyond their homeland, and each wondered what brought the other to Aden. The man opposite Maclean had leathered skin, sun scorched in parts, and a callused handshake revealed he was used to hard work. He spoke again, "Malaya? And where are you going now?" Maclean's face softened with an unsure smile, a half-hearted, lop-sided grin that indicated he had no firm plans. He lifted his shoulders slightly and feeling released of burden from work and contracts, he replied, "I'm going home to Glasgow, and then I don't know."

His new acquaintance was John Scott, a rubber planter from Makwasa, Nyasaland. Bonded in the comradery of planters, the two men became easy friends, conversing into the night, and clinking their glasses to toast the ideas that were spilling from their heads. They discussed methods of planting, obstacles in harvesting, and the frustrations of working cross-culturally, how the war had changed things, the perils of tropical disease, the pangs of loneliness, and the delight of the humid climate. "Back to the dreary grey of Scotland, hey?" John teased after a few hours of banter. "Why don't you just sign off from that gloomy place and come work for me in Nyasaland?" The pair leaned in towards each other, the lightness of the moment fell away, and their eyes locked as their glasses met in the middle. Maclean, realizing he had just been offered a job, took stock, and declared, "Now, that is a positive idea."

One year later, having reunited with family in Glasgow and signing off permanently from Guthries, Maclean embarked on a new adventure. His family, knowing he was determined to leave, decided to support him and gathered the necessary funds that the Government of Nyasaland required Europeans to possess in order to enter the country without a Crown job. The rationale was designed to ensure that outsiders would not increase the burden on the recently formed Protectorate; therefore, subjects of the Empire, without Government employ, must be able to provide for themselves. Maclean decided he wouldn't require the money once he started working for John Scott. He could preserve the funds and return it to his brothers when he went home on leave. Thanking them for their faithfulness, love and provision, Maclean departed, anxious to meet up with the planter from Makwasa and begin work.

Maclean Kay (left) with brother Jack and parents in Glasglow circa 1919

He sailed; Liverpool to Cape Town, Cape Town to Beira and took the railroad from Beira to Muraca, where the train terminated[36]. The mighty Zambezi, effectively splitting Mozambique in half, prevented a single line from reaching Nyasaland and had previously caused delays in mails and goods[37] which took two to three weeks to reach the coast, and after three transshipments, exposed the commodities to a risk of water damage[38]. After the war, the British knew the isolation of their land-locked protectorate mandated better access to the rim of Africa. With a concession granted from the Portuguese in 1894 for such a rail line, the Trans-Zambezia Railway was realized in 1922; a line was constructed from Dondo junction to Muraca – opposite Chindio, allowing travelers to reach the Zambezi in 24hours, an overnight trip. Maclean, who had been shifting in his seat, desperate to find a position which relieved the ache in his back, was thankful when the train pulled up 174 miles from Beira, arriving at Muraca[39]. He was also glad that the engine master had thrown out caution in regard to the gossip that the journey would be too dangerous owing to wild animals at night[40].

He stepped off the train, the humid air cloaking his unprotected forearms, the lack of breeze slowing even the tsetse flies to a hover, while the rust tinted African earth clung to his already moist skin. Carrying what he could, he motioned to a porter at the river junction to load the remainder of his goods, and happily stood on the deck of the ferry for the short crossing to Chindio where as a rule, passengers had to spend the night[41,42]. The Trans-Zambezi portion of his journey was complete. The next day he continued northbound, 61 miles to Nsanje aboard Central African Railways (C.A.R.), a journey which was only passable during the "low water period."[43]

At Nsanje, Nyasaland Railways took the passengers the last 113 miles to Limbe, passing through the lower Shire and up to the Highlands. He strained to view the territory, the wagons of the train lumbering along. Sometimes the only sound was the clickety-clack of the steel wheels as they rolled through the British sphere of influence known among many as the "Cinderella" of the Protectorates[44]. The enigmatic countryside was swaying with barren, dry grass, thirsty for rain that hadn't fallen in months. The drought of 1921-22, that proved disastrous for native foodstuffs, was palpable. The crackling earth was dehydrated and the subsistence farmers, who relied on a robust crop of millet from their ridged plots of land, were hungry. The population, estimated at around 1,187,631, suffered during the famine, and relief measures rendered necessary. Consequently, the government had imported 1,500 tons of maize to distribute throughout the Protectorate.[45]

Maclean noticed the embers from the wood-burning engine, as they escaped past the funnel through the trap designed to catch the sparks, and down the side of the carriage; occasionally searing a sight-seeing passenger standing on the balcony. Maclean had to draw his breath inward in the cabin, dodging the ash that blew in from the window flaps. The train was moseying through the lower Shire, dambos welling up from the otherwise parched land, and he hoped an ember from the train would not suffice to ignite a fire, which if it did, would no doubt spread so quickly that the entire lower plains would be enveloped. Further along as the train began an ascent up the escarpment of the Great Rift Valley, the desolate landscape was slowly contradicted by full-breasted forests of Albizzia, Borassu's palms, and Mbawa, reaching high above the scraggly sansevieria plants which "ordinarily look as though they had forgotten where they came from and what they were doing." The Macuna bean, 'buffalo bean', was diligently aiming to strangle the prosperous plants in the jungle, creeping along bushes and trees, tempting a traveler to touch her silky reddish brown seed pods which upon contact leave the skin covered in white weals and irritation and heat so intense that only "stripping and rubbing oneself with a cooling lotion (would) afford relief."[46]

Maclean, experiencing the bush of Africa from the train, longed for an opportunity to explore it, to trace his fingers around its details, perhaps not as Livingstone had done, but in his own way. The landscapes and the animals that roamed before him were entrancing. Sometimes, water- buck, a white circle dominating their rear like a target for a predator, would wander beside a river. There were kudus, whose faces were as if painted for battle, their antlers reaching an impressive height as they curled upward from their heads. Families of wart-hogs darted through the long grass, detected only because their tails, erect, acted like a flag waving as they ran.

He looked out at the miles of untouched land, occasional fires drifting heavenward from three-stone village plumes. There was promise in the vast expanse that trolled before him and there was opportunity too, an opportunity he had not yet counted on.

Stopping every 50 miles to re-fuel was wearisome, but like travelers before him, Maclean believed his troubles settled after the Zambezi crossing, and the remainder of the trip was surely slow but quite leisurely. They made it to the Shire Highlands, passing Kongeni and Luchenza until they rambled into Railway Headquarters at Limbe Station, where several other engines had retired for the night, their carriages resting in the yard.[47] "Bwana, tikakusiyeni mtouni?" a voice probed in the dwindling day. "He wants to know if you need a ride to town...," another man interpreted. "Yes, thank you. I'm heading to Blantyre, Ryall's Hotel," young Maclean responded, shuffling a paper with his scribbled notes back into his pocket. "Everybody is," the man huffed back, helping Maclean with his boxes and opening the door to his 'Tin Lizzie', which was parked on the street.

The transporter was correct; it seemed that all 300 of the Europeans who lived in Blantyre had descended on the newly opened Ryall's Hotel[48]. There was nothing available for the young planter when he stood at the counter, ragged from his journey, and desperate for a bath.

"Try down the road, Victoria Avenue, B&EA (Blantyre and East Africa), the annex," the lady behind the desk spoke softly, kindness in her tone. She felt sorry she didn't have space for the newcomer. The annex was Blantyre and East Africa's head office, and they had thought to open it for lodging as the demand for Ryall's was so pressing that several foreigners had wound up with nowhere to stay. Thanking the lady for her assistance, Maclean gathered his belongings and departed. He found B&EA, who provided a room for him, and after checking in at their annex, he relished a much-desired bath. The red earth of Africa disappeared from his body and settled on the base of the ceramic tub.

The next day Maclean awoke with renewed purpose. He was going to make his way to 'Makwasa' and seek out John Scott, his Aden consociate, and upon receiving directions for his anticipated employment, he would swiftly get to work. He walked up Victoria Ave, past the pedestrians who stared long and speculating at his very new face. He found Hays Garage Ltd, on the corner of Victoria Ave and Glynn Jones Street and he browsed the inventory of vehicles and cycles on offer.[49]

The salesman, eager to please his prospective customer, began asking questions – trying to figure out what mode of transport would best suit this 'Johnny-come-lately'. Maclean, although confident and capable beyond his 30 years of age, humbly inquired about the infrastructure of the roads, and how the seasons might affect his connection to the towns, since he was planning on living past Cholo in Makwasa. The man flattened out a map. It was slightly dated and therefore failed to show the newly formed and drained road to Cholo[50]. "It's just been completed this year," the salesman acknowledged, speaking directly of the road from Blantyre to Cholo. "Any of these vehicles will pass on it, with little trouble," he added, sweeping his hand around the showroom, indicating that any choice might be a good one. Maclean walked around the stock options on the floor, not settled by anything he saw, until lined up by the wall, he found it; the machine he had to have. Cherry-red paint, beaming beside fattened white tires, a black shiny bell light fastened on the handlebars, fenders wide enough to catch the mud - which he anticipated would come once the rains arrived - and a gearbox bolted to the 42-degree V-twin engine, it was – the Indian Scout Motorcycle.[51,52]

The advertisement posted beside the Motorcycles boldly asserted, "Once you own an Indian the spirit of life tingles in your veins – the exhilaration of power thrills you – the world lies before you to explore…"

The slogan resonated with the young Scottish planter, and he dipped into his funds, laying down the money needed to purchase his first motorcycle in Africa. After organizing his personal effects, Maclean found himself the proud owner of a sparkling Indian Scout, revving out of

Blantyre and down the newly formed road to Cholo. What had been known as the 'elephant track' was now a road wide enough for vehicles to pass, and the only hindrances for a motorcycle were the wild animals that had discovered the road or passed quickly over it as they searched for water. He saw a solitary bushbuck flick over the dirt track, so skittish; he barely recognized the tiny spots that dotted his coat. There were elephant prints, but no sign of the pachyderms. Even over the engine rumble, he could hear the bellows of a pair of silvery-cheeked hornbills as they swooped between the palms. "How lucky I am," thought Maclean, enjoying the miles of thick forests, which grew steadfast beside the road, time passing, with not a soul in sight.

He arrived at the turn-off from the main road, and stopping to clarify, he found a native and inquired, "Makwasa?" pointing in the direction he assumed was correct after chartering his map. "Ndi, Bwana," said the man with smooth, chocolate skin, "Ndi Namireme, Ndi Timcke Town, Ndi Ntumbynyama, Ndi Makwasa," he repeated, confirming the direction. If it was possible, the road at the junction was more primitive than the one he just left, but he managed to navigate it, passing the old Nyasaland Mission in Ntumbynyama, the midday sun bouncing off it's white painted walls so that he had to squint as he rode. He let himself feel excited as he neared Makwasa, enthusiastic to find Scott, keen to get to work.

A few people gathered near where John had told him they would meet. There were pale faces in the group, looking more quizzically at Maclean than the natives; and after minutes one inquired, "Who are you looking for? You've come a long way…" "Scott, John Scott" Maclean began, "We met in Aden a year ago, and I've come to plant rubber with him." He could tell by their sullen expression something was amiss, and he wondered for a moment if he was even in the right place. "Sorry, chap, Scott's not here, and nobody's planting rubber," one man spoke up. "That's ok, I can wait," Maclean noted, thinking it might take a few hours. "What I mean, is that John Scott, he's not in Nyasaland. He's taken leave to England," the man clarified, his arms crossing on his chest as he spoke.

John Scott was one of Shire Highlands' last rubber planters, and had been fighting a decline in rubber cultivation country-wide. The marked decrease during the war, 1914-1915, saw the area of rubber agronomy decrease from 10,562 acres to just 5,936. The rubber industry would never recover from the low prices experienced during these years. Wild and commercial rubber trees were left untapped, or cultivation abandoned completely.[53] John, perhaps an optimist, was most likely hoping to revive the industry, but miscalculated his own enthusiasm for the reality of the situation which left Maclean caught in John's dream and in a new country with no job.

The past year, and in particular the last 3 weeks of travel, bearable only because it was necessary for his dream to plant rubber again, swirled around in Maclean's head, as he tried to absorb the reality that the life he intended to live was ending before it had begun. He thanked the men and returned to his bike, disappointed, let down, lost beyond words.

Nyasaland's planters had been reeling in the boom year of 1920, and the reaction from that year continued to affect the country. Stocks, shipped to the United Kingdom, were still lying unsold on the auction floors, which proved to be the planters' chief difficulty. As a result, they lacked the capital for carrying on planting operations, and by 1922 many planters found themselves, "seriously embarrassed financially." Their position was worsened by the banks who had been "optimistic during the period of prosperity following the conclusion of hostilities" but imposed restrictions on the planters' operations when the depression set in.[54] While this may have been the impetus for Scott to take leave, it was also possibly responsible for the 'crack in the fabric of good fortune' that Maclean urgently needed.

Unsure of what to do, he started back down the road, as aimless as he had found himself when he stepped off the P&O at Aden over a year ago. He even contemplated returning his 'new' motorcycle to Hays in Blantyre, and saying, "Well, it just didn't work out," as he reversed his trip back to Scotland. He left Makwasa, past Malamulo Mission – where lepers received hope and help – retracing his tire marks through Ntunbayama until he found himself at the river, Nswadzi. He took the northwesterly track, hardly pressed for time anymore; in fact, he considered he was now sightseeing, on holiday, if you will. The terrain was mostly as he had found it coming in, thick jungles, roped with vines, reaching out beyond the forest edges, grabbing whatever grew outside the brink and consuming it. He crossed over Namireme and beyond Mianga, where tea grew in patches, little more than a trial crop which had not taken root. Further down, having crossed the river he saw squares of earth, ploughed into ridges, ready for tobacco planting, timed to take root at first rain. Realizing he was on a private estate, he was not surprised when another pale face flagged him down; obviously taken back by his presence and possibly his cherry red 'Indian Scout'. "Hunter," the man threw out his hand, enquiring as Maclean reciprocated, "Kay."

Hunter, perhaps having been caught in the 'financial embarrassment' of the 1922 era, suffering from the effects of a depressed market and consequently a "shortage of floating capital", or perhaps wanting to decrease his share in land ownership in the Shire Highlands, was looking to sell part of his portfolio[55]. Their providential meeting resulted in multiple telegraphs communicated by the African Transcontinental Telegraph Company, through the trunk line telegraphs in Nyasaland to Glasgow, Scotland, where Maclean's brother, Alexander, using his proficiency and expertise as a trust lawyer, helped Maclean sign the deeds to the property of Hunter[56]. During the months of discussion concerning the Nyasaland property, Maclean mastered the art of communication over the telegraph to his brother, his business sense guiding his carefully chosen words which were billed to him at, 1s. 7d. and 9 ½ d. per word[57].

It took over six months for the property to officially become Maclean Kay's right of deed, signing for it on June 26th, 1923 and registering the deed with the Blantyre Lands Office on July 4th, 1923, an appropriate way to celebrate his 31st birthday. He had effectively purchased one of 75 land certificates of claim granted by Sir Harry Johnston's government of the Protectorate in 1892-1894.

With soldier ant remnants pricking his skin, and a prospective name for his purchase at the tip of his tongue, he meandered from the river where the bango reeds remained, awaiting the local chief, towards the site of his pitch and daub house. The thatched roof was golden in the afternoon rays, the clearing around the house pedantically swept with a bundled broom of twigs, and a few seedlings showed signs of life as they poked out of the potties where Maclean had planted them. He slipped off his boots as he entered the dwelling, searching for his tattered mattress in which he sat; it was firm yet inviting, and he reclined his body onto it. He would no longer be a rubber planter, working for somebody else. He had just bought a 'piece of Africa'. He had invested his family's savings, and his life, into the privileges and challenges of the African continent.

His ability to adapt to the harsh environment, to the experimental crops of a minor territory, to drought, depression, and a desolate workforce, would determine whether Satema would succeed or fail. One thing was certain, he was now ready to get to work.

From Jungle to Teapot, 1923-1945

Maclean Kay plants Satemwa tobacco 'seed at stake' 1926

"Sa-Tem-Ah" Maclean repeated continuously under breath, as he surveyed the fibrous hessian wrapped bundles of tobacco at his feet. He wrote it, more curiously, with crinkled brow on a paper beside him, "Satema," he scrawled, in almost indecipherable penmanship. It did not sound "nice" anymore. Not to him, anyway. He pursed his lips, adding "Wa" to the ending, and felt pleased with the result. "Sa-Tem-Wah," he regurgitated the newly added consonant with growing satisfaction. "Sa-Tem-Wah, Satem-Wa, Satemwa!" He put a bold line through the previous notes, and in capitals wrote, SATEMWA, attaching the paper to the tobacco bales that were destined for export to England through the Imperial Tobacco Company headquartered in Limbe.[58]

Tobacco had emerged as the premier European crop of Nyasaland, even after a slump in 1923 when 5,158,326 lbs were exported, short by over one million lbs from 1922. It was still well above the next highest yielding crop, which was cotton exported at 2,182,537 lbs. Cholo, home to Satemwa, was the country's sixth largest producer of tobacco, falling behind Lilongwe, Blantyre, Dowa, Mlanje, and Zomba in production.[59]

Nyasa's natives had been growing tobacco and cotton long before Livingstone trekked through in 1859. However, Livingstone searched for ways to end the slave trade and consequently promoted cotton to the natives, hoping that establishing a flourishing cotton industry in Nyasa would undermine the American market and reduce the need for slaves as an upshot. "Christianity, Commerce and Cotton," were the original three C's promoted by the lion-hearted British missionary-explorer, and it is noted that Livingstone handed out cotton seed wherever he traveled in the country.

The natives took to cotton planting, but they continued also to grow tobacco, which some suggest they had been doing for centuries. African grown tobacco would continue to bolster the industry in Nyasaland, proving important for exports as well as stimulating the local economies. The European government in Nyasaland used resources and initiatives to improve the tobacco industry, decreasing primitive cultivation and establishing flue-curing and varieties of tobacco not yet cultivated in the country. In 1902-1903, two Americans from Virginia were commissioned to instruct the growers on expert curing techniques and they supervised the growing and curing of a flue-curing crop at Songani Estate run by Blantyre and East Africa Ltd. However, Lilongwe's growth in tobacco began eighteen years later, with Barron and Wallace reaping their first crop in 1920. Lilongwe's climate was well suited to tobacco, yet the industry north of Blantyre was not well established. There was no motor road from Limbe to Lilongwe, and in its absence, 1430 porters were hired to carry head-loaded baskets each holding 56 lbs of tobacco the two hundred miles to Limbe. The carriers often reached Limbe within fourteen days, but could take as long as six weeks. However it is recognized that not one basket went missing.[60]

Satemwa was fortunate not to share in the troubles of transport seen from central Nyasaland, but the years demonstrated that nurturing tobacco in the Shire Highlands was tenuous, higher rainfalls and the 'chiperoni' leading to devastating mold in the crops, and frustration among the farmers. Tobacco grows best with 36 inches, (950 mls) of rain per growing annum, and Cholo's 65-70 inches per annum threatened havoc with the crop.[61]

Struggling to maintain the quality needed to export tobacco amid the growing industry in Nyasaland, where farmers established estates in more suitable areas for the annual harvest, Cholo faced a crisis. Planters, like Maclean, had three options. They could slide along with the status quo, wondering if the next rain would wipe out their crops entirely; they could seek an alternate product to produce; or they could sell and admit defeat.

Bred tough and stubborn of character, Maclean looked for alternatives to tobacco. Conferring with his brothers in Scotland, he discovered that Bandanga estate, just 5 miles as the crow flies from Satemwa, had planted an 'experimental' crop of tea with great success. The Colonial Report during the war 1914-1915 highlighted Bandanga's cultivation with a paragraph devoted to the increased demand for commoner tea grades where "excellent prices have been obtained."[62] The

young Scotsman, eager to replace tobacco, seized the opportunity, and
gambling slightly, set his path towards planting tea. He began with
camellia senensis nurseries in 1924, and planted the first field of tea on
Satemwa in 1926. His brother Alexander, a senior partner for the law firm
McClure, Naismith and Brodie, held a special portfolio with Burma Oil.
Burma oil was involved in Assam and Alexander, thinking of his brother in
Central Africa, secured two bags of Assamica tea seed in 1928, and sent
one, on behalf of Burma Oil to Chivangi Tea estate in Tanganyika, and the
other to Satemwa in Cholo. Maclean had acquired the first Assam tea seed
in Africa, and his plantation was slowly transitioning from the cash crop
tobacco, to the 'instant money bush', tea.[63]

However, Maclean had another problem. Saddled alongside the
fickle growing conditions for his primary commodity, and the clear
indicators of the decline of tobacco in Cholo, he was experiencing poor
luck at home. The first house he settled in on the estate was a 'pole and
daggar' abode, modest yet suitable for a bachelor, luxurious by no extent
of the imagination. The white-washed walls of his rounded hut home
comprised of woven lattice wood strips entwined on stakes to make a
fortification, and a sticky mix of dambo sand, soil, animal dung and straw
patted onto the strips until a desired thickness achieved an appropriate
barrier to the outside world. The structure, topped with a dry vegetation
layered so densely it trapped the air and blocked water from entering the
inner roof, also insulated the hut against the tropical climate.[64]

One night, a streak of lightning followed by an explosive clap of
thunder rang in the skies, the clouds hanging over Cholo Mountain barely
holding their bulk before releasing a torrential rain that doused the land in
seconds. He could see the downpour over the forested hills from his house,
yet the land around him remained dry. The lightning cracked close enough
and he could feel it's wrath with each spark. 'Kitchen Boy' who worked
for the planter was near the main house, probably stirring a pot of nsima, or
peeling an onion, when a bolt of fire from the sky struck him down, and he
died instantly. Perhaps with the same vicious crack, a spark ignited the
thatch and before long Maclean was standing outside his house, helplessly
watching hot flames devour it.

A weeping gaggle of women bewailed 'Kitchen Boy', their
screams rolling with anguish as they mourned another loss of life. It
seemed Africa was trying to take everything that came under Maclean's
influence. His crops were adequate but doomed, his house burned flat, and
his worker killed with no remorse. Africa appeared to Maclean like a
dormant volcano. Undercurrents of tropical disease and weather patterns
could foray any man, at any moment, and render him useless or worse - no
more for this world. Europeans were aware of the perils of the tropics

when signing up for the colonial life. As Government hospitals, clinics, and missionary medical outposts increased in number and staffing, survival rates for foreigners and natives also improved. Perhaps it was the present dangers of life in the colonies, the unknown fevers that could take a man's life, suddenly, severely, that led the common colonial to drink, and drink a lot. Imports of spirits fluctuated by year but averaged in the early 1930's between 6,211 and 7,034 proof gallons per year for the Protectorate.[65] Not a teetotaler by nature, but more restrained than the average planter, Maclean was known to write, "I fancy I might have one brandy at the club tonight, but not two."

Resolute, Maclean gritted his teeth and waved his misfortune off as if swatting a fly. He would not be beaten; he would dust off his bad luck and try again. His second house was similar to the first, pitch and daub, and thatch on top. A few modifications made it better than the first, and his siting was near the original homestead, just some fifty meters away, tucked below the burnt foundations of his previous home. He had spent his last wad of money to rebuild and mustered his energies to defy the wilderness and carve out a home from the earth and vegetation that surrounded him. Yet calamity followed the building of his second house when it burned to the ground. He had to hatch another plan, and quick. He had nowhere to live, and no capital to start fresh for the third time. Letters to his brothers in Scotland detailing his woes took weeks to send and replies, weeks to receive. His cash crop, tobacco, had suffered along with other growers in the Shire Highlands, where adverse climatic conditions were not favorable and contributed to the national crop export fetching only 2,289 tons, a decrease of over 1,779 tons from the previous year. The Protectorate took a hit on trade, in particular tobacco and tea, where prices realized were "low."[66] Maclean could not plant the next season's crop with no capital, and perhaps more pressing, he could not live in the jungle with no proper shelter. He needed to sustain his estate, and he couldn't do it while living off the land. There was no other way forward. He had to find a job.[67]

Opposite to "Timcke" town where Bwana Timock had created a trading mall central to planters in the Shire Highlands, was a piece of land owned by a Glasgow based company, Don and Ross Ltd. European numbers had grown significantly since his arrival in 1922, and when the country sank into depression in 1929, he was relieved when he found employment as a tea planter for Don and Ross. He was close enough to Satemwa where he could keep a watch over his estate, and he was employed to plant tea, the crop that would eventually save his own plantation. He was grateful for a house to live in, a house covered in morning glory vines sited on the sloping hill that looked toward Mlanje Mountain. It's thatched roof leaked during heavy rains, a problem which could be resolved with newspaper strategically placed under the holes. It was the Namireme house, a house where he would one day welcome a bride and three children. This was a house where he based his daytime activities, earned a salary, and returned to in the moonlit hours, after planting 'seed at stake' on his Satemwa estate from 6pm to 10pm every night without fail.[68]

A firm believer in quality, Maclean resonated with the sentiments from tea buyers in England, who now had the luxury to pick only the best tea - as quantity on world markets was increasing. Tea, it's cultivation, plucking and processing would become Maclean's passion. Every night, as he left Namireme and putted to his estate, his cherry-red motorcycle scratched with faded paint faithfully transporting him, Maclean would be one plant closer to working for himself once more. He held out his kerosene lamp to light the earth where he stuck tea seed into the soil, tobacco on either side. The tea he planted in 1926 would be ready for harvesting in 1931, five years after the initial planting. For this reason, tea was poised as an 'unpopular' crop with early settlers, "on account of the time which has necessarily to elapse before any return is made on the capital expended."[69] But with the failing tobacco crop, Maclean decided to be patient, knowing that with the green leaf from his first field and the cash from his annual tobacco harvest, he could hold on to Satemwa at least a little longer.

There were several Europeans near his house at Namireme. Timcke, for one, was living at Kasembereka, just a stone's throw from Maclean. He often thought of the woman chief who Kasembereka was named after, Kas-Um-bereka – the woman was barren, and had no children. Surely it was enough shame to be childless in private, but the community made the chief's infertility public, and the whole village was named after her bleak state. Although in the midst of tea pluckers, planters, and villagers who sought to work with him, and an expatriate community from town who he occasionally saw at sporting events or sports clubs, Maclean was lonely. He yearned for companionship, a woman, to share in his reveries, a woman with whom he could partner with in life, and if fortunate enough, raise children together.

Meeting a woman and marrying her transpired quickly, as Maclean's brother writes from Scotland on the 12th of November 1929, "Dear Maclean, just a line, with my present, to wish you and Jean all the happiness and the best of luck in every way. You certainly did not give us much notice so I spread the news in the office on the day your cable arrived. The others were all interested and joined others in good wishes…Yours, Alex."

It was welcome news that the Cathcart family in Scotland were supporting his nuptials to the young daughter of Captain Moffat-Baily, who at the age of 19, was brimming with a zest for life. Her adamant style of communication sometimes earned her a reputation of a young woman with a temper. Maclean teased her in a letter, which stated that he was informed by a certain dame in town that she had a temper, "as if I did not know that."[70] Flora Jean was the kind of woman men noticed. She had a tight figure, and sun-streaked russet hair that dusted her shoulders. Her brown bold eyes sparkled without the need of sunlight to illuminate them. Born with passion and stubbornness, she had the kind of attitude that was appealing to men in the Empire's peripheries. Maclean wrote letters with the maturity of an estate owner and a seasoned planter who had spent 37 years on his own. In one letter he informed Jean – after disagreements between her parents about their engagement, "Tell your father, darling, that I consider they are not signing to the amazement we came to that day (Tuesday 10th) and I shall not forgive it. Anyway Jean after the 26th we shall have our own home....if your people like to keep up these present attitudes they must remain in Blantyre and we shall be in Cholo."[71]

Captain Moffat-Baily, a British officer, was part of the occupying forces that kept Germany under thumb after the Kaiser War. Stationed in Arras, France, he sent his daughter, Flora Jean, to a Catholic Convent for education where she mastered the French language and developed a taste for the fineries of the French culture, which she observed outside the convent walls. Rationing was part and parcel for post-war cities, but remnants of life before the war were scattered around the broken cities, as people worked daily to restore their lives to order, the way it was before the war. In 1919, Captain Moffat-Baily took a post in Nyasaland as an ordinance officer, tasked with marking the boundary of German Tanganyika and other borders. His daughter, Flora Jean, graduated from the convent in France and in 1928 came to find him. She was young, unaccompanied and wildly independent. Independent enough to throw parental caution to the wind, and accept a proposal from a planter in Cholo, an older man, distinct, experienced in the world.

Maclean courted his Blantyre-based fiancé from Cholo where he informed her of the minutiae of his day, tobacco preparations, maize acquisition, supervising brick wall building for Don and Ross. Finishing his day at 11:30pm he wrote, "As you can see I'm up to the neck with work." Jean's letters to Maclean involved sentimental ideas, proposals to organize dates for the two of them, always asking Maclean when he can make time for her. "Don't say I don't want to see you – no patience!" he chided her in one response. "What is this show at Zomba? Never heard of it. Is it a special or just a club stunt? Is the Garden Party at Government house?" he inquired of her proposition for a date. He also wrote about finances, educating "my little girl" as to the state of his banking. "I paid in a draft for £260 last week and I've signed cheques for £270. Accounts is all the time and it's a devil of a job trying to make ends meet….not a bale of the 1926-1927, 1927-1928 crop sold but another 41 pounds in interest charges to be paid." Maclean certainly didn't hesitate to reveal his affairs to his future wife and provided her with intimate details on his finances, his schedule and his worries. Yet, he also made concession for her desire to promenade together when he returns to the idea of the Zomba party near the end of his letter, "To be quite candid Jean I'm not keen on going to a Zomba show. I don't know the people and I can't tolerate the Boma crowd. However if it could be managed I'd go to please you."[72]

There were three sectors of Europeans that settled in Nyasaland; the missionaries, the government workers, and planters - working for themselves or companies. Sir Harry Johnston, the first British Consul to Nyasaland notes in the early 1890's that neither faction really cared for the other. Missionaries often thought "no one ever did any good in Africa but themselves." Government were worried that planters were exploiting the people and land – and that missionaries might go 'rogue', and the planters just wanted to get on with scratching the earth, without having to worry about missionaries or Government criticizing their efforts.

The labor that could have precluded Maclean from attending the Zomba function was his tobacco nurseries, 1000yrds, scheduled to go in on the 20th of September, just six days before their wedding. Lacking the romance of a soon to be married couple, Maclean tells Jean, "I want £300/- to make the end of March. Can you let me have it!!!! It's a great game tobacco planting." But just to be sure the entire letter is not comprised of farming and it's consuming work, he jokes with her to close, "Could I send a boy in with Proverbs for you to read? What would your mother say… Cheerio Jean darling…hope you can read this."[73]

Despite the feigning resignations the couple endured from the bride's family, the pair were resolute to wed. They were married at St Paul's Church in Blantyre on the 26th of September 1929. Maclean brought his "darling young girl" home to the Don and Ross house at Namireme, but they were both envisaging a day when they could build a home together, a home to call their own. He involved Jean in the specifications for their house on Satemwa, asking her opinions about edgings, and reminding her that, "They are for OUR house." Yet, it would be four years before their home was ready, and before Maclean could again work solely for himself. In the meantime, they settled at Namireme, with detail-oriented Maclean telling Jean, "I will arrange about transporting all your worldly belongings out to Cholo….How many boxes. 40???"[74,75]

St. Paul's Church in Blantyre Maclean and Jean's Wedding 1929

Their days at Namireme were bristling with new beginnings. Maclean was navigating his role as a spouse and Jean was figuring out how to run a household and support the work of her husband. She took charge over the family cow, making butter and selling it in the Timcke market place, buying fuel for Maclean's Red Indian motorcycle, and kerosene for the lamps with the proceeds from the dairy. When Jean's father, Captain Moffat-Baily took ill, the newlyweds welcomed him to their home, happily casting aside past hurts and misunderstandings. When he arrived at Namireme, Captain Moffat-Baily purged all the day, for seven straight days, his skin turning yellow as a weaver bird, and his body desperately weak. His urine was tinted 'Coca-Cola' in color, a clear indication that a malarial infection had caused red blood cells to burst in his bloodstream, a condition well known to settlers as 'blackwater fever'. Despite Jean's efforts to administer medicines, whiskey, and water, no exertion she put forth seemed to alter his state. He experienced a brief moment where they hoped for recovery but he quickly relapsed, kidney failure causing a complete shut down on his already tasked body. By morning, on May 9, 1930, he was gone.

Having come to find her father in Nyasaland, only to lose him a few years later, Jean was grateful for the care of her husband who helped arrange for the funeral service and burial of her father. They laid him to rest at Nyasaland's Scottish Church in Blantyre, surrounded by European soldiers who had died in the war, babies who had barely breathed tropical air before succumbing to sickness, mothers who never lived to hold their newborns, and other Europeans who fell victim to the diseases, old age, or the veracities of life in the colonies.

The couple returned to farm and dream at Namireme. When they welcomed a baby boy the year following their marriage, they named him Alexander, a proper gesture to honor Maclean's brother, extending the name in the family for generations. Jean was twenty years old, a wife and a mother, her school girl days in France echoed occasionally in her mind as her daily duties kept her home, sleepless nights, and the demands of a newborn constantly absorbing her, aging her slightly. She hired a male nanny to help her with the baby. His name was Chelima – a strong, tall man from the Yao tribe and he assisted with the mundane duties associated with childcare, changing nappies, washing, and holding the baby. Maclean and Jean, swept up in the bliss of babyhood, were not unhappy to realize another was on the way within the year.

Nurse Melville from Malamulo Mission Hospital pedaled her bicycle to Namirene on the 25th of September, 1931, to assist Jean in her second delivery. Robert Gordon, "a Chip off the old block," was born "blue" and Maclean remedied his condition with alternative submersions into hot and cold buckets of water. Minutes later, "Chip" was no longer a blue baby and the Kays now had a pair of infants under two to watch and love. They were delighted with their robust boys, peppered with Cathcart features, and cries loud enough to seize the attention of their Mother and Nanny simultaneously. Delighted, yet exhausted, the couple fancied futures for young Alexander and Chip, grateful the boys would have each other as playmates. Their imaginary musings and hopes for their children's prospects had barely slipped from their tongues when the unimaginable occurred. The couple would face another funeral, just twenty-three days after Chip was born.

There were 20 deaths recorded amongst the European population in Nyasaland in 1931, a population which was estimated at around 1,905 people, 706 in the Blantyre district, over double the European population when Maclean had arrived in 1922[76]. Among the deaths recorded that year, was Maclean and Jean's baby boy, Alexander, who had succumbed to the quickening and fatal effects of 'black water fever', passing quietly at night, he had fought the tropical fevers for a week when his little body gave out. He was only one year and ten days old when he died, and his young mother and dedicated father were lost in their sorrow. Jean, holding her new born, Chip, and soothing his cries, experienced conflicting emotions of grief and joy, feelings that nestled uncomfortably beside her as she tried to sleep at night.

The couple, numb from loss, could not be consoled. Here was two independent, fierce natures that fought the cogitations of observers implying they should give up and turn their backs on Nyasaland. They resolved to push on, burying their little child in the same cemetery as his grandfather, on a day where dry, dusty winds whipped the earth into funnels, and the relentless squawks of the pied crows ricocheted through their chests. The headstone would read: "In loving memory of Alexander Cathcart Kay, died 18th of October, 1931, aged 1 year and 10 days." They buried their first-born child – the wooden gates that led them out of the cemetery knocked in the wind as they walked towards their car. The freshly dug earth clumped in mounds over Alexander's little body disappeared from their view but not their minds.

Maclean spent the following weeks cabling to Scotland, and breaking the news of his son's death to his family, wondering how Alexander his brother might react to his namesake's passing. He fell into his work, neglecting to return home for supper, unable to face the memories of his son, and his grieving young wife. One thing was certain, the Scottish planter would find a way to continue, a way to provide for his family, and a way out of the misery that plagued his house.

Jean and Maclean waited a few years, carefully watching Chip in his toddler years, as he learned to crawl, sound words, and dig in the dirt, before having their third baby. Juliet Anne Cathcart Kay was born to the couple on the 24th of August 1934. She was three years younger than Chip, but would prove to be a faithful sister, and an invaluable friend for her brother. A year after her birth the family of four moved from the Namireme house to their own home on Satemwa. 'The Satemwa House', built in 1935 on the original site of Maclean's first pitch and daub house, had provided an outlet for the varied sensations that suffused their minds since Alexander's death, as they toiled to build the first three rooms, father's room, the hall and the drawing room. Red clay tiles – essentially hardened bricks - were fitted to the floor in the hall, and their framed photographs, mostly family portraits, strategically placed on the mantle in the drawing room, beside their bed, or on a shelf just out of reach of the robust sun that was sure to fade them. A pressing and life vexing concern for the family was the infirmity of malaria. Constantly worrying about his family's well-being, Maclean searched for ways to evade the common health afflictions that dogged Nyasaland.

The elevation of 'The Satemwa House' on the estate in Cholo is near 1,920 feet. Just 28 miles from Cholo, a multi-lobed plateau rises sharply above the landscape, boasting Mlanje massif, the highest point in south-central Africa.   Planters often sent their families for weeks and sometimes months on end to the expansive plateau on Mlanje Mountain, where wooden cabins provided basic accommodation, and sooty hearths stacked with cedar awaited the families who sought escape from the heat in the Mlanje Boma and Shire Highlands. Built at over 6,000ft elevation, the cabins provided more than a retreat for travelers. At such an altitude, malaria-carrying mosquitos were absent, which meant families were safe from malaria. Complications from the tropical ailment had taken the life of two people close to Jean in recent years, and the devastation caused by losing a child gave both Maclean and Jean impetus to avoid the dreaded illness, even if that meant days, weeks or months living apart.

Nyasaland had improved in transportation methods since the turn of the century, when the most common mode was by 'machila', where a bamboo pole was fitted with a hammock slung around the shaft and a stalwart native man on either end carried a traveler who reclined in the cloth to their destination. Machila transport progressed as the paths widened to two poles and four carriers, a chair structure with canvas curtains forged to the poles maximizing the comfort and protection of the itinerant. Machila teams were chosen based on physical merits and crews of 12 or 16 could cover 15 to 25 miles per day. However, colonials in Nyasaland felt that machila transport needed replacing with more modern and humane methods. The Central African Times (CAT) newspaper in 1900 ran an article under "imperative necessity" stating, "The transport problem has entered upon another stage, that in which the substitution of wheeled vehicles for human beasts of burden is an imperative necessity in the interests of Humanity." The country progressed, obtaining heavy equipment to widen roads and grade new ones for increased access to motor vehicles, which the Protectorate began to import in growing numbers. However, Machila transport did not dissolve completely, especially in the Mlanje district where families took upwards of 100 porters to carry supplies and people from the low-lying town to the plateau where they would happily pass the days. Comforts such as carpet and food items were carried up the mountain for the duration of their stay.

In 1935, when Jean took their two children to the plateau, she hired a machila team to carry Juliet and Chip on either side of the bamboo structure, a cloth chair suspended where a child could sit and freely dangle his or her legs as the machila team ascended the mountain. A hammock was slung in between the two chairs and when needed could hold a grown adult.

Viewed from a distance, with low-level clouds circling the base of Mlanje, the monadnock looked as if 'suspended' in the air, earning the title "the island in the sky". Weather could change dramatically within minutes, and hikers might arrive at their cabins drenched in mountain rain after a ten-minute shower crossed the path on their ascent. The terrain on the mountain was ever changing with each forward step; clogged dry red earth, with thick forests pressing the path, to granite boulder outcrops, exposed to the winds that flew up the steep ravines splitting the lobes of the plateau into segments. When Jean, the children and their porters had reached the plateau and the cabin where they had booked their stay, they settled their belongings and drew deep breaths of the highland air. Looking out beyond the plateau rim, Satemwa seemed a country or two away. Fields of golden grasses glittered as the evening sun fell, leaving the crisp night air to soothe their skin. The glow from the fireplace, where a kettle whistled, welcomed the family to their mountain refuge.

Maclean, inexorable in his dedication to the plantation, stayed at Satemwa to manage the processes and crops, but was glad to send his family to a place where he wrote to his wife, "I'm delighted to hear the children are all so well – the little ones…the change will have had time to enter into your dainty systems." Jean, anything but dainty, in fact, courageously independent asserted to her husband her desire to climb up Sapitwa, Mlanje's highest peak, the grandest in south-central Africa. Perhaps he thought her childish in her whims, yet he inquired if she climbed the 9,849 ft peak, "Or did you just want to?"[77]

The couple communicated with each other by letters. Maclean inquired of Jean, "Letters arriving as desired I trust. I told you I waited so as to send by runner, not my fault if your mail boy is a rotter is it?" He deliberated about the timing further on, speculating as if Jean could hear him instantaneously; "Will this go by runner or by post? Will I wait for the garden boy to bring the fruit? If so, it may be tomorrow." The tone of a young man courting his fiancé all those years ago remains in Maclean's efforts to provide Jean with news of the estate, the weather, "a very cold false chiperoni," and the loans about which his brother Jack cautions him. Maclean would tell Jean that Jack "thinks I'm trying to do too much on loaned money and is quite correct." He enlightened Jean about the brewing unrest in Europe but he believed there would not be a "general war" as pressures rose, but rather that Mussolini would "blame us" for the screw Britain put on him in trade and finance and that would be the end of it.

While Jean and the children passed the days on the sunlit plateau, splashing in the streams that chased run-away leaves across mossy boulders, the responsibilities at home fell on Maclean. Knowing that his young wife and children were enjoying mountain-top cups of tea, the rust colored Satemwa red grounds enhanced by the unalloyed water at high elevation gave Maclean satisfaction. The death of their baby, four years ago to the month, was fresh on his mind as he plugged through wearily long days about the estate. He relieved the perceived worry of a wife far away and comforted Jean by boasting of his domestic accomplishments, "I taught Chelima to make a cup of tea and its quite nice now." Maclean wrote, "I had a bath yesterday afternoon – yes – with soap and I shaved this morning and generally things go on here just the same except for that aching void of loneliness for you all so far away up the mountain top."[78]

Maclean had to find a way to balance his responsibilities on the estate with his domestic lists of to-do's left by Jean; "Your Wednesday's butter has been dispatched and a balance of 3lbs remains to be forwarded to the ALC. As the new cow will be in milk next week you should be able to get at least 5lbs for ALC. These matters have my immediate attention." He bemoaned the fact that Jean fired the cook before she left, but the most bothersome part of his lonely domestic life is the "damned thing you call Mary," he wrote to Jean. The cat is "on heat and makes my nights very unpleasant. I MUST PUT MY FOOT DOWN??????" Mary's incessant "howling" featured in several typed letters that made their way up to the plateau where Jean most likely read the anecdotes with amusement.

Maclean Kay circa 1935

Not wanting to cause Jean anxiety and suggest she descend the mountain prematurely, Maclean only wrote of his back troubles once he was "restored to a straight figure once again." The old injury from Malaya where he was attacked and his neck fractured often flared up, but after describing the kind of aches where it affected his body and what he did to treat it, he assured his young wife, "Well its departed now." He occupied his free time playing bridge at the club. His dislike of "Boma" people was evident when he wrote to Jean about a potential scheduling conflict for the cottage in which she was residing on the mountain and comments about the woman organizing the cabin, "I find her a little grand you know. La Boma all right." Speaking of her husband's occupation in comparison to his own he tells Jean, "I would rather have my 500 acres tea in my own name and £5000 a year safe."

"Let me know day and hour to meet you," his message concluded. "I suppose 10am at the bottom so as to get the children out of the heat before noon." Maclean completed the typed portion and another letter was ready for the 'rotter' mail boy, but as he did with so many of his mails, he added in penned scrawl pertinent thoughts just before posting the papers. "Looking forward to seeing you. Chip will be full of beans, and Juliet will be quite a young woman – waiting – Mick."[79]

Over the years, the Kay family of Jean and the children, sometimes accompanied by Maclean, made several trips to Mlanje Plateau.

Along with Mlanje plateau there were two holiday destinations frequented by the family before the children departed for school; Pebane, in Mozambique, and Cape Town in South Africa. Jean and the children were often in the Cape for months at a time, and Maclean visited them whenever he could manage time away from Satemwa. He was preoccupied during the rainy season, calculating the tonnes of green leaf processed in his factory, anticipating rain fall and bemoaning when it did fall, that it fell too much, or too heavily. He expended his days with monitoring weeding and plucking in all his fields, noting the success or failure of the harvests and cramming accounting functions in between planting duties. He mentioned to Jean that he could spend his entire day in finance, and that "with London buying stores and deducting from sales then all the various things out here, it's getting too big for a planter to do everything. I can spend all day in the office here, yes seven days a week, if records are to be properly kept." [80]

Chip and Juliet in Pebane circa 1938

Jean and the children were between accommodations in Cape Town, and it almost felt as if moving from localities every month extended the feeling of being on vacation. They bounced between a hotel in Muizenberg, the St James Flats and Beach Court, flat number 20. Maclean wrote to them in the Cape constantly, detailing his day, paragraphs punctuated by the time of day and typed letters finished with handwritten scribbles listing corrections or additions that he felt pertinent before posting. Disappointed he wasn't receiving similar correspondence from down south, he underlined in one note, "You never reply to any QUESTION you receive – I think it is due to my long winded letters."[81]

While his family was vacationing in Cape Town, his concern for Juliet, "Wee Wig," heightened if she had spiked a fever or felt unwell, and his worry regarding Chip circled around his inability to swim. "I can see the Shu (Juliet) doing a great swim fishy and I hope Chip is learning to swim. May I suggest you take him to the baths and get him some lessons," he wrote to Jean on January 14, 1939. Chip was seven years old and had developed an aversion to the water. Despite efforts to encourage Chip to swim, he never showed the aptitude for it, and at some point, it just became fact; Chip Cathcart Kay does not swim, ok!

Maclean and Jean were satisfied that all the months spent living apart, sheltering their children from tropical diseases had kept them alive. As the children grew up, Chip and Juliet in Cape Town Schools, and then over to England to continue education once the Second World War had ended, the family experienced extended periods of living apart. Satemwa required Maclean's obsession to detail if it was to succeed, and Jean became a gypsy mother as she trailed the children to Cape Town and then to England.

When Chip arrived in Liverpool on September 25, 1945, his father and Juliet were already in the United Kingdom while his mother was drifting somewhere between the Cape and Cairo. Jane Broughton-Edge joined Jean's journey and together they trekked 'go as you can' across the continent, stopping at Mt Kilimanjaro and hiking up as far as possible before turning back for base as the crater was heavily covered in snow. The ladies walked north, tracing Rhodes' dream line from Cape to Cairo, a railroad that never eventuated, catching whatever mode of transportation wandered their way until they had reached Egypt. Jean and Jane parted ways in Cairo. Jane remained with her husband who worked for the British Embassy and Jean blazed a new trail towards her parent's homeland.[82]

Jean Kay (left) and Cynthia Hind (right) circa 1945

The port city of Alexandria faded behind her as she began the crossing over the Mediterranean Sea and the North Atlantic Ocean where she inhaled the salty air, the taste of independence not just from the war, but also from the responsibilities of a colonial mother disappearing the nearer the ship took her to London. The English coastline was scattered with remnants of battle; her first view of the war effects outside the African continent and her workings for the WAAF in Cape Town. She remembered Maclean's musings about the strife with Mussolini and Hitler "just blowing over" and she wished he had been correct. The war had changed everything.

She was destined for Paddington Borough and a humble two-roomed flat with a dwarfed kitchen and a tikkie meter where a shilling turned on the gas. Of course it was rationed gas that only lighted half-way. Everything was rationed after the war, where tea abounded in great green flushes on Satemwa, tea in England was restricted to 2oz of loose leaf per person per week[83]. Limited gas and electricity were no bother to Jean or Maclean, but limited tea? That was almost unbearable.

Educating Colonial Children 1945-1950

Chip during his English school years circa 1946

By morning on September 26, 1945, the tears that had hydrated Chip's cheeks the previous day had completely dried up, and the confidence he was accustomed to while traveling alone had returned to his countenance. He was fourteen and it was silly to waste time crying about a situation he could not prevent. He traded the marble pillars of the Adelphi Hotel in Liverpool for the luxury of the Glasgow Central Hotel in Scotland, where he was to spend his second night in transit, much relieved that travel by train affected his motion sickness less than a boat at sea.

He lifted the mattress in his room at the Central Hotel and pushed his passport and money under it for safekeeping. He undressed, anticipating a warm bath that would wash away the dust from his travels. Finding no bath or even a washbasin within his room was disappointing. Reluctantly he re-dressed. Then a sudden knock on the door alarmed him, "This is the hotel Manager," came the voice from the other side. Immediately Chip reached the knob and turned it to reveal the man behind the voice, the manager of the Glasgow Central Hotel. Obviously surprised by a teenager registered at the check-in desk, the manager had come to investigate the young boy who was notably alone.

"Laddie, where are your parents?" he inquired, his thick Scottish accent difficult to decipher. "My parents are at home, Sir," Chip responded. "Well, where is home, boy?" the manager probed. "In Africa. Sir." "In Africa? How did you get here?" His right eyebrow lowered while the left one tilted up, his interest in young Chip intensifying. "I came by ship, Sir." "How did you come by Ship?" he asked. "Well, I went first by train; you know it takes five days and nights to get from my home in Central Africa to Cape Town. From there I got on a troop ship." The manager interrupted, "Which ship did you come on?" "The Mauretania, Sir," "And where did it land?" he continued the inquisition, "In Liverpool Sir." Chip was tiring of his questions but they continued, "And how did you get here?" "I came by train Sir." He prodded Chip, finally revealing the main source of his concern, "And why are you here by yourself?" "Well, Sir, I've come to see my Uncle, Alexander Kay." "And where does your Uncle live?" Sensing a near end to the inquisition Chip told the manager, "He lives at Delgarva, number 3 Nithsdale Rd. I have been there before when I was a little boy. My father brought me to be shown to my grandparents, who lived there before the war." The story had come full circle and the manager, satisfied at last, nodded, "Right," and then left.[84]

Within the hour, a Scottish 'Bobbie', complete with his red squared striped uniform appeared at Chip's hotel room door. The presence of Glasgow's police at his room was slightly odd. Yet, because it was pre-empted by the hotel manager's conversation, Chip felt at ease with the giant of a man who stood before him, his height gaining several inches owing to the funny hat he wore on his head. "Pack up your things," the officer instructed Chip. "Where are we going?" Chip asked. "We're going straight to your Uncle Alexander. I've spoken to him on the phone."

Making sure to collect his personals from under the mattress, Chip showed the police his passport, confirming he was a colonial child, and joined the two officers who escorted him to Delgarva. Uncle Ally was waiting to welcome him 'home'. Ally was a tall man, baldly white, his face dominated by a distinguished nose and eyes that could listen to unspoken words. He was one of Scotland's leading trust lawyers, a big bwana, revered and respected among his peers, but to Chip he was simply Uncle Ally, 'a cuddly bear'. At Delgarva, Chip was 'home'. Home, in the third cultural child (TCK) sense of the word.

He stayed several days at Delgarva to connect with his father's family, to reaffirm his Uncle Ally as a warm and affectionate man, and to give his mother time to hitch her way from the Cape to London. When she had secured a flat for the two of them, Chip made his way to Paddington to meet his mother and begin the arduous task of schooling.

Mechanically minded, practically gifted, yet challenged by dyslexia, the thought of school in England was nothing short of disappointing for Chip, where the emphasis of learning was book-based and overseen with rigid uncompromised scrutiny. He was desperate to return to Satemwa, to scratch the earth alongside his father, and to help grow the estate in the Shire highlands. However, the only way to do this with his parent's blessing was to persevere through English education. With his ultimate plan clear in his mind, and return to Nyasaland his motivation, he pushed through failed scores at Crammer schools, musing whether it was Davies, Laing and Dicks' (DLD) job as a crammer school to get him to pass the common entrance exams. Upon his failing, was it really him who failed or them – DLD? He missed the marks required for the Imperial Service College of Haileybury, so an alternate school was required. Under the supervision of R.J.O Meyer at Edgarley Hall at Millfield school, Chip had the opportunity to tuck the Education certificates he needed under his belt.[85]

Still with a desire to grow things, but faced with hostile climatic conditions which were unfamiliar to a colonial child, Chip decided to leave the beds of soil in Africa and start school clubs, involving other students in his ideas, and seeking permission from his house master, R.J.O Meyer who heartily agreed. From inception to creation, Chip spearheaded the school's first Aero Modeling club, Photographic club and Radio Club, and became respected among his teachers who saw that his organized groups were keeping the students out of trouble and occupied with mindful arts. He also joined the Rugby teams, making their first fifteen, and his weekly practices and games boosted his mood. Physical activity he surmised was especially important in England, where the endorphins from sports would offset the grey clouds that menaced depression as they consumed the skies overhead, sometimes for months at a time.

The Speleological Society of Somerset awarded Chip with a prize for a picture of stalactites that he had taken in the Cheddar Caves. He imagined he might find the wife of 'Cheddar Man', Britain's oldest complete human skeleton, as he squeezed down, half-naked, into the narrow shoots of the caverns. The little flash on his box camera exploded in the bowels of the cave, illuminating the stalactites that clung to the roof of the limestone which coursed over his head. The image he captured not only won a prize but also propelled the school club, as their leader had gained notoriety.[86]

During Christmas of 1945 Chip went to a distant Uncle's house in Padstow, Cornwall. His mother and father had returned to Nyasaland, and although the thought of Christmas in Cornwall turned his stomach initially, Padstow soon became a place of dreams during his years in England. Uncle Jack Sleight greeted Chip at the train station. He was a tall man, over 6' 2", a hairy Scot from a town called Leith, the same town from where Jean originated. He had shoes that required polishing, a job that Chip was happy to do, and he marveled at the size of the footwear, thinking how powerful the feet that filled them were.

Uncle Jack Sleight taught Chip how to call for the cattle, bringing them into the paddock with a "ho, ho, ho…" and he learned to scuff the heifer's noses and cuddle with the beef steers.[87] Jack Sleight undoubtedly had one of the best herds in Cornwall and Chip, besotted by life on the farm, fell in love. Not only did he fall in love with the farm, but more importantly, more urgently, with Jack's younger daughter, his somewhat thrice removed cousin, Anne. She had long blonde hair, pinned into a frenzied bun when she worked on the farm, and let loose like a windsock when riding her bicycle, which captivated Chip who rode beside her. The pair jockeyed everywhere together. They attached fishing rods to the seat of their bicycles and went over the hilly coast to a place where they spent the day splashing about the rock pools, catching periwinkles, and digging the little snail out of the shell with one of Anne's hair pins that she had clipped to her blouse. Their journey to the coast went past the Jamaica Inn whose rum smuggling days still echoed in infamy.[88]

Having overheard Chip boasting to her father that he could drive the saloon car parked in their shed, Anne almost dared Chip to take it out one day. "Well, if you could drive it around, how would you get it back in?" she asked with curiosity. Wondering if she really didn't know about the 'reverse' gear of automobiles, Chip stated with puzzled expression, "I'll just reverse it back in." Later that week when Anne's mother was in the dairy and her father in the lower fields, the pair sidled up into the saloon car and went for a drive, Anne nervously clenching the sides of her seat until Chip had managed to, as he said, just reverse the car back in. The term break ended and Chip thanked his extended family for their kindness; then he hesitated, locked eyes with Anne, etching her features for future recall and returned to Millfield.[89]

His excursion to Padstow refreshed him. The farm and climate were different, but it was the closest to Satemwa he had felt since departing Luchenza. He was chuckling to himself about driving Uncle Jack's saloon car and was grateful to know such a basic skill, which impressed Anne. Maclean Kay had all sorts of cars and trucks bobbing about the estate in Nyasaland and Chip had been behind the wheel, although not yet able to reach the pedals, since the age of nine. Now, at fourteen and a half, he resembled an undeveloped adult, thrust into the role by circumstance and a gritty mental capacity. He was an ebbing contradiction of infancy and maturity. Prattling on in Chi'Njanja, which nobody else understood, helped Chip and a fellow Nyasaland student, Patch, to cheat on exams by swapping information in the vernacular, neither of them feeling bad for the habit and both feeling clever having gotten away with it. The few cigarettes he puffed on the trains from Luchenza to Cape Town now compounded into a smoking addiction where Chip mimicked the planters who frequented the bar at Cholo Sports Club in the Shire Highlands, flicking a match to his pipe and taking long draughts of Player's tobacco, exhaling the sweet smolder with growing satisfaction.

The Millfield school was an eclectic mix of students. Some were in their twenties, and had fought in battles, flying planes, and shooting guns. Young men now, aged beyond their years, but desperate for education which the war had interrupted. Chip hoped they would speak of their adventures, and recount their missions of combat, but traumatized by them, their stories remained whispers. Having seen his father in pictures during the First World War in his 'Wavy Navy' coat belonging to the Sea Cadets, Chip signed on with the Army Cadet Force (ACF), becoming a sergeant instructor for Bren guns.[90] But the real perk of admission was the heavy, warm 'great coat' with its lace woven details which came with the job. Chip had never felt so cold; the blustering winters in England which seemed to freeze his body solid were numbing, and he longed again for sunny days on Satemwa where afternoon showers fell to break the heat. There were pupils from neighboring African countries such as John Senior whose father was a minister of mines for Rhodesia and owned the largest goldmine in the country, aptly named, "The Giant." There were Americans, Canadians and Australians. Unlike his school in Cape Town (Bishops for Boys), Millfield educated girls as well and the first appearance of one entering the common room sent Chip leaping out of the window. Not because he didn't like girls, but because he liked girls too much. He was a typical oversexed teenager. Yet when it came to the opposite gender, he suffered for awhile from an overdose of shyness.[91]

Several girls mottled Chip's focus on studies and clubs. For one, he was writing weekly to Anne who was studying in North Devon; their affection for each other emboldened by their inability to be together both owing to distance and to the fact they were somewhat related. There was an Australian girl, Patience, who kept her ash blonde hair in plaits. She was studying to be an engineer, a fact that excited Chip, and when her bicycle was broken down he swept in to fix it and gain her attentions. There was a French girl, Jacqueline Bertrand, who Chip told at term's end, "I'm coming to see you." "You are?" she sounded surprised. "And how will you get to my house in Pau?" she inquired. Chip pulled out a map of France and said, "Mark it here, and I'll make a way to you."

And so, in 1947, at the age of sixteen, Chip crossed the English Channel, marked map in hand to find Jacqueline Bertrand. Chip had a long trip ahead of him; Pau at the foot of the Pyrenees in the South of France was just 85km from the Spanish border. He swung his khaki colored rucksack over his shoulders; the metal rods that framed the pack fitted neatly to the curve in his back and slipped the YMCA (Young Men's

Christian Association) card he had recently acquired into his wallet. With his limited French that he had learned from his mother and Jacqueline, he flagged passing trucks that were southbound, edging closer to Pau with each ride. He was short on cash, so he told the truck drivers to drop him outside of town where he would secure a bush bed for the night, often in a forest or on a farm. One morning, after settling into the ridged earth just after sundown, he awoke to find himself surrounded by tobacco. "I thought this only grew in Nyasaland," he mused to himself, rubbing one of the ripening yellow leaves at the base of the stalk. He thought for a moment about Satemwa, and how once, tobacco had grown as the estate's main crop. He didn't understand at the time why his father had switched to tea, but he was grateful for it, because tea kept the landscape green year-long, whereas tobacco allowed the parched earth to blaze red after harvest.[92]

He wandered to the farmhouse, found the woman of the grange and requested, "Can I feed your chickens? Can I clean your sties?" The lady looked at Chip, up and down, observing his rucksack, his un-brushed hair and the little whips of dirt that had settled on his shorts, indicating he had slept somewhere nearby. He understood her French when she inquired where he was coming from and going to, and after she was satisfied with his answers, she gave him work, food and a bed. He only stayed a few days, enough to work and enjoy the gumbo, tomato, fromage and tumbler wine that she served to him for breakfast, before he pushed forward further south to find Jacqueline.

It was just after dusk when Chip arrived in Pau. His Rhodesian shorts, Rugger stockings and canvas rucksack advertised that he was a foreigner; he was clearly not from Pau at any rate, and Jacqueline, who was in town with her father, spotted him immediately. "Salut! Chip, tu l'as fait, je suis content de te voir," she called to him before her father's car had come to a complete stop. "And I am happy to see you too, Jacqueline," Chip returned, a slight blush detected on his cheeks. He stayed with Jacqueline and her family for three happy days, embraced by his friend's French relatives; they were some of the most pleasant days he had experienced, certainly in the past few weeks. Then, Jacqueline watched as her school friend waved and left Pau, now wayfaring to Paris, where he pre-arranged to meet his parents under the Arc de Triomphe.[93]

Alongside other young men who were traveling 'go as you can', Chip discovered a quicker, more efficient route to Paris. He dodged the armed guards at railway stations and flung himself under the tarpaulin of covered bogies, riding the train for an hour or so, jumping off only to check the direction of the ride by finding the nearest station and then sneaking onto another northbound carriage.[94]

The 6-penny air letter mails that had passed between Chip and his parents predestined them to be in Paris on a certain day, at a decided hour, past the Champs-Élysée, beside the Unknown French Soldier entombed at the base of the Arc de Triomphe. Despite the unpredictable methods of transportation used to bring him from the south of France to the central-north, Chip had arrived in Paris on the exact day he had scheduled a rendezvous with his parents. He bustled down the Champs-Élysée, eyes strained ahead to decipher the crowd and he recognized his father and mother immediately. They were idling about the foot of the Arc de Triomphe as if waiting for engagement, a characteristic Trilby hat mounted on his father's head, and his mother balancing a large grey Ascot fedora, glamorously clad in Parisian couture.[95]

"Chip! My darling, you look positively starving!" his mother greeted him, with accustomed distance in her stride. His parents lacked physical affections and although he felt an urge to embrace them, smothering their cheeks with lost kisses, he refrained and answered, "Yes mother, quite hungry." They shared a momentary hug and Maclean grasped Chip under the chin, and squared up to him, "Son, you have done well, and we have much to talk about." With that, the three of them ambled down Avenue De Wagram, finding "Au Rendez Vous Des Chauffeurs" where a hearty meal, complete with Biff steak, awaited them. Jean, fluent in French, took the lead for ordering, and the waiter responded to her with supreme service, amusing Chip with his scribbles on the paper tablecloth to designate not only the order but also the bill. When Maclean had paid, the waiter tore off the piece of tablecloth, which displayed the totals and threw it onto the floor, joining the sawdust below their chairs.[96]

Maclean, allotted 10 pounds for travel to Europe due to restrictions after the war forbidding foreign currency in excess of 5 pounds per person into Europe, knew it was enough for a few days in Paris with his wife and son. Being with his parents, even in Paris, reminded Chip of his home on Satemwa. He asked for news on the estate, "Have you seen John or Nelson lately? Please tell me what they are doing." He inquired about developments, hoping one day to be a part of them. When he crossed the channel back to England, and arrived at Millfield, he told himself, "Not long now, Chip, and then you can go home for good."

By early 1950 Chip had succeeded in completing his higher school certificate, free now to leave England. The only hesitancy in his departure circled around his affections for Anne, their letters between North Devon and Millfield, and their excursions by the sea in Padstow, reverberating in his head as he packed up his room at school. Although they had talked about a future, imagining the reality was somewhat hopeless because their families, in any case, would surely disapprove.

Just as he had sailed from Cape Town in 1945, he now returned to it by boat, and suffered similarly with an instant case of sea-sickness as soon as the string was untied from the dock. The passengers were a disparate group, but the soldiers he had remembered from the Mauretania, along with their bunks and mess tables were gone. From the age of 11 to 14, the war was central to his life, and every function became altered as a result. Now, people were pressing forward, and the environment was starting to take shape apart from the war, despite the war.

Chip arrived, albeit green in the face, to Cape Town, tracked down a Bishops' friend called John Scott who he barely recognized since John had completed a Charles Atlas course during Chip's absence and stood before him, not a meagre boy of pre-puberty, but a strapping hulk, with muscles that made Chip feel weak just at their sheer sight.[97] A few years certainly had changed things. He recovered from his ocean journey, leaving John and his muscles in Cape Town and then departed by train for Nyasaland. He had lived abroad from ages 14 to 17 and although he was no Charles Atlas, his physique had changed, he was handsome; the wavy locks of his father, bristles of facial hair on his sculpted jaw, and his hazel green eyes glittering with the unmet passions of a boy morphing into a man. The tears of a tender child discovering a new land abandoned and a rugged confidence, a colonial swagger had blossomed.

He had five long days to travel before arrival to Satemwa, and unlike his train trips to Bishops, there was no girls' carriage to cast experiments on, and no childish crushes to occupy his thoughts. They were five impatient days, where he wished the train could travel faster or that it would suddenly grow wings and soar over the mighty Zambezi, up the Great Rift Valley and touchdown on the rambling green lawn outside 'The Satemwa House'. He dreamed his father would be waiting on the khondi, pipe in hand and greeting Chip, they would immediately set to work.

When A Boy Becomes A Man 1950-1954

Chip Kay circa 1950

PART ONE

Eventually, the train pulled into Luchenza, the screech from the brakes and the loud bellows of steam escaping the funnels announced to the passengers who had fallen asleep on the voyage that the train had arrived. Standing on the platform, just under the eaves where LUCHENZA hung in capital letters, was Maclean and Jean. It seemed to Chip that his interactions with his parents, at least for the past ten years centered around arrivals and departures. Now, it was different. He was returning home, with no plans to live elsewhere and he was anxious, just as his father had been in 1922, to be productive.[98]

He imagined beginning work on the estate straightaway, even the very afternoon he had arrived into Luchenza. However, he had not accounted for the childhood nostalgia nor the weariness of travel to arch over him upon arrival home. Besides, his father had told him to rest and plan for something to do on Satemwa, a personal interest project, before diving head first into the tea. Chip, lacking the callused feet of his childhood, donned rugged boots and rather than sneaking out the nursery window at first light, he strolled down the hallway, past his father's room, through the entrance hall and out onto the khondi where he could see the tea factory roofs northwest ahead. His father was already on estate rounds, so Chip meandered over the grass, greeting the garden boys in Llomwe dialect, pleased that the words rolled off his tongue as if he was speaking it yesterday, through the tea, to the sound of the pluckers cutting, and over to the workers compound where he fancied he might find his friends.

He had barely crept around the corner of the workers village when a familiar voice spat into the air, "Chip!! Chippy!! Ehhhhh, Takulandirani, you are back." It was John Humbiani, and he took little time to prompt Chip about the promise he had made to him when they were small boys. "First, I have to get my license," Chip told John, "and probably we will need a car too." John seemed disappointed not to be behind the wheel immediately, and sensing it, Chip assured him, "Osa opha (do not worry) John – first the car, then I will teach you to drive."[99]

Before Chip could buy a car he needed to earn a salary. He needed a job. That night over dinner Maclean asked Chip, "Well, son, what do you want to do? Do you want to learn how to build roads?" The next day, Chip was assigned to Benson who was to teach him to build roads. Benson was an ex-public works department capitao (PWD) who was now a Maclean employee. As a commentary on the state of the roads in Nyasaland PWD was often jokingly referred to as 'Potholes Widened and Deepened'. Jokes aside, it only took a week for Chip to grow tired of maintaining existing roads and so announced to his father, "I want to build a new road." Grateful for his son's enthusiasm, Maclean took Chip to the Chawani office the following day and said, "There is a special place on the mountain that I'd like to be able to drive to. If you go into the forest you can walk that way and go see what you think."[100]

The forest behind Chawani looked impenetrable, even finding a gap to enter its dark, wooded bounds seemed improbable. It was a thick canopy where Mbawa trees plunged towards the sultry sky, and the red, sticky sap of the Mlombwa threatened discomfort to passersby. Preceding the dense jungle was a line of Stipa grass whose barbed seeds had ripened and sought distribution by methods painful to a human. Just beyond the Stipa, the reddish-brown pods of the Macuna bean waited in ambush, presenting a menacing irritation so severe that nothing short of cooling lotion could remedy the sensation.[101] Once inside the forest, the carnivora, well represented on Satemwa, were hiding, watchful, in their lairs. Chip remembered the leopard tracks from his childhood which he, John and Nelson traced by the Nswadsi River. He remembered the beautiful servals, which despite colonial attempts to domesticate, proved too wild to tame. And he remembered too well the growls of the lions searching for their mates which resonated from the foot of Cholo mountain to the walls of his nursery room at 'The Satemwa House'.

There were many animals who found a home on Satemwa, safe within her virgin forests, viewed only when they desired to be seen. However, the population of Nyasaland was increasing, now near 2,400,000 people, over double the census from 1922 of 1,187,631 when Maclean had first set foot in the Protectorate. The impact of wild animals on the growing population, particularly on Native agricultural gardens became paramount.[102,103] On April 17, 1950 the Nyasaland Times ran an article on the "War Against Wild Animals" which was aimed at Crop Protection and financed by the Native Development and Welfare Fund. "The public enemies of the animal world are raiding Elephant, Hippopotmami, Buffalo, Water-buck, and some of the larger antelopes like Roan, Eland and Kudu, Baboons, Wild Pig and Carnivora." Beginning in 1948, a team of approximately 92 hunters spread out over the entire Protectorate of Nyasaland, tasked with bringing these 'crop pests' to justice. The hunters became excellent shots and required only 1 to 1.5 rounds of ammunition for each animal killed. The Southern Province, where Satemwa was located, returned principal numbers for decimation where each hunter averaged 290 kills apiece.[104]

"Wild animals shot in 1949 included 79 Elephant, 106 Hippopotami, 163 Water-buck, 187 larger Antelopes, 357 other Buck, 8,892 Baboons, and 469 Wild Pig." The bag also included 79 Carnivora where numbers of stock raiding Lions, Leopard and Hyena were undifferentiated. Additionally, methods such as nets and poison further protected native gardens and the rationale of saving African food seemed to justify the carnages. The article surmised, "When it is realized that these animals destroy more food than they actually eat themselves and all of the animals shot, netted or poisoned were a pressing danger to African crops, the amount of food saved is considerable."

The 'pest control' that took place while Chip was in England, would only intensify over the years, and he did not know at that time how special his sightings of the Carnivora on his parent's estate were, nor how rare they would become.

Chip saw that the daunting forest, although overgrown and sprinkled with matted acacia bushes which had no room to stretch to a mature height, was not in fact impassable; there was rumor that a peculiar American researcher had studied snakes from the very spot Maclean had demarcated. As he slashed through the undergrowth, cutting creepers off their prey and discarding them to tread underfoot, he forged a trail to the edge of the mountain where he laid the vision for a new access road. He anticipated the reward for his effort would not only be a magnificent vista that spilled around the edge of the highland, where, once cleared, would show Mount Mulanje rising like an island in the sky, but also the approval of his father which he unswervingly desired.

It was his first special project on the estate, and he was determined to carve a road out of the mountainside and provide his father a 'room with a view'. He struck his foot to the pedal of his BSA motorbike and chugged to the worksite at Chawani, where 25 men with hoes and 50 children with old plucking baskets awaited his arrival. The men swung their hoes into the clay-laced earth and filled the awaiting child's basket with soil. The children, in between giggling about their new bwana and his funny habit of breathing fire from a stick, (his pipe) were marveling how if they closed their eyes and listened to him jangle in Chi'Nyanja they would swear he was a black man, perhaps a village chief as he spoke with such authority. The youngsters eagerly transported the soil dug by the men to an allocated spot until after about three days of soil redistribution, Chip realized a dam was forming. Not only was a dam emerging, but just beyond it there was a bulky wedge of mountain that would be very challenging to remove. [105]

Reporting to his father in the dining room that night, Chip conveyed information about the new dam and the wall that confronted his project and proposed that the access road was still a possibility, despite the obstruction, and that all was going as planned besides. Maclean, leaning back on his chair so only two pegs touched the ground, rocked for a moment and then lurched forward with sudden laughter, warm deep larks, contagious enough to set Chip chuckling too. "We'll call it 'Chip's FOLLY' and that will be the end of it. I suppose you'll never make it through." He patted Chip on the back, the kind of touch that was affectionate and yet chiding at the same time. Despite his father's amusement upon hearing of the dam, and the joke that transpired as a result, Chip harbored the same breed of stubbornness and told Maclean, "Oh no, father, you'll see, I will sort it out. You will have your road and your room soon enough."[106]

Making the road to the picnic spot circa 1950

After a lot more digging and earth shifting, the day came, with great delight, where Chip drove his father up to the new 'room with a view'. They passed by 'Chip's Folly' and as they drove through the cut-out foothill, Chip glanced sideways at his father as if to put a checkmate on the topic. They arrived at the opening where work was still underway to clear the land for a view, and they inspected the old campsite that Chip had uncovered while shaping the new road. "Yes, that's where the American based his research," Maclean said satisfactorily, squinting through the vines that hung like rope ladders from the forest awning, "I can tell by the view." This puzzled Chip, as he strained to see the 'view' but then he realized that his father had walked every inch of the estate and knew not only the tea fields but the jungles too. Chip enrolled his mother to help beautify the clearing and asked her to source hydrangeas for the perimeter because he thought of the purple, white and blue flowers as Satemwa's national plant. It was not long before this new secret road was their family's preferred picnic spot and they spent many afternoons watching the sun fall away over the Great Rift Valley, eventually melting into the Shire River thousands of feet below.[107]

PART TWO

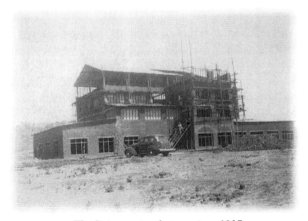

The Satemwa tea factory circa 1937

Soon Chip began to wonder what his father was preparing for his future, or if he had any plans at all. He was apprenticed from one department to the next. One week, alongside the labor force, he learned how to pick tea. Frederick Nahua, the head Caiptao, made sure he was not favored in the process, critiquing his efforts to precisely clip two leaves and a bud, all the while commenting on the speed at which he was able to fill the woven basket strapped to his back. Chip rotated between his father's head Capitaos and each leader was tasked with teaching young Chip about the running of the estate, the details of the jobs which fell into their respective departments, and to groom Chip about the business of tea, so one day he could manage the estate, perhaps even take it over from his father.

The year before Chip returned home, Nyasaland experienced a severe 'Njala' (hunger) where thousands of people died of starvation. The Protectorate had braced for such a disaster, aware years prior that "Nyasaland could no longer rely on surpluses from subsistence farming to provide supplies of staple foodstuffs, particularly maize." The 1948 Colonial Report attributed this problem to the "steadily increasing pressure of a growing population upon a soil of dwindling fertility, which in many areas undergoes continuous cultivation with no rest."[108] Colonial Governments were active in conducting research programs and making recommendations to avoid future distress, and the Maize Control Board, along with the Land Planning Committee reported, "Soil conservation work proceeded uneventfully, and there appears to be a growing realization among African cultivators of the need to abandon traditional harmful methods of cultivation."[109] However, this marked decrease in maize production "led to an increasingly heavy demand for secondary foodstuffs." Partnered with an "abnormal shortage of rain," the prospects of a good harvest for the 1948-1949 growing season were "poor."[110]

During the height of the 1949 Njala episode, Maclean's European manager, Mr Saunderson, surrounded by estate labor, whistled for his German Shepherds to appear at his feet where he ordered the canines to sit at attention. It was the end of a long working day and the employees and dogs were equally ravenous, drooling in chorus as Mr Saunderson reached into his meat box and threw tender morsels of beef into the mouths of the expecting hounds. It was a difficult sight for the estate labor whose unemployed friends and families were sharing a meal made for five with eighteen mouths. The estate labor had lost friends to starvation, and now they watched in complete repulsion as animals ate superior food. It was a poorly miscalculated error and Saunderson paid for it, almost with his very life. Following an uprising he left Nyasaland voluntarily and never returned.

His actions grated against the fibers of what Maclean believed to be supremely important. The labor force must have proper food in adequate amounts. Sustenance was a vital commodity for Satemwa employees, and Maclean commented how his estate labor preferred to take 4d for a day with increased phoso (food rations) and a hot feed than the neighboring estates 6d with only a cup of beans. While in England, in

1938, Maclean wrote to Jean and told her he could not possibly hire the new engineer unless Jean could confirm she had been able to secure the additional 70 tonnes of maize needed to stock the Satemwa warehouse for the laborer's rations. "Can we in view of the maize position afford to hire the engineer," his letter queried. Jean, in the process of building Magara house, overseeing thousands of bricks in the kiln, and shuffling working orders for carpenters, builders and day labor, sent untimely replies which left Maclean to ponder the maize crisis, reflecting on bits of news from other planters who were also having difficulty securing enough tonnage. He closed his letter by imploring Jean to "mention how maize and labour is next time you write."[111]

It remained an important issue, even when Chip took over the running of Mwalunthunzi estate from the recently departed Mr Saunderson. "You need to fix that estate, Chip," his father told him, expecting that even at the fresh age of 18 Chip would be up for the challenge. Mwalunthunzi estate was in chaos, with a dozen agitated watchmen tasked to subdue the inflamed Saunderson situation. Chip, sensing their nervousness, dismissed all twelve men shortly after accepting the assignment. If he was to 'fix the estate' he was going to do it with his own employees, ones that he hired personally, people he could trust.

"I expect you will require between 500 and 1,000 people to clear the estate," Maclean proposed to Chip as they surveyed the grounds of Mwalunthunzi. The estate that fell under Satemwa's control was now known as 'plot remaining Mwalunthunzi' after Dr I Conforzi (Conforzi Estates) and Sir Malcolm Barrow (Namingomba) had both purchased large sections from the original owners, Blantyre and East Africa (B&EA). The name, 'Mwalunthunzi' became famous in Cholo after a meteorite fell from the heavens to land on earth; the meteorite believed to be a stone that holds mysterious 'charms'. The legend of the meteoritic Mwalunthunzi stone says travelers are compelled to whistle while circling the stone three times, tapping the rock with a small stone, and then proceeding onward with the blessings of safe travels. 'Mwala' (stone) and 'Thunzi' (the vapor that rises) were a typical occurrence when the morning sun heated the dawn's dew, thereby creating the 'magic' of the Mwalunthunzi stone.[112]

As he began the process of establishing Mwalunthunzi estate, Chip realized that female laborers were particularly hard working, accomplishing their tasks efficiently and effectively, excelling their male counterparts in almost every function. Farmers growing tobacco concurred and the year after Chip began recruiting a predominantly female workforce the tobacco growers in Southern Rhodesia stated, "The women reap very much more quickly and cleanly than the men and appear to have a much better eye for the color when it comes to selecting ripe leaf."[113] Chip wasted no time in hiring 500 females and 300 males for Mwalunthunzi estate, remarking to his father one afternoon as the chiperoni winds stroked their faces, "It is the women who have done most of the clearing, you know. I find them to be excellent workers."[114]

Yet in Nyasaland, an abandoned woman with a child was without hope. And it seemed to Chip that there were too many women with small children who had nothing to do and no man to care for them or the child. "Getting a woman pregnant and then leaving! Who does that?" Chip mused to himself, under breath, resolving to build the first Mbeta Compound Nyasaland had seen, establishing homes for neglected women and children. He told his father, "The men 'nyenga' a girl. 'Kunyenga' – they cheat her and I can tell you it's the woman who suffers the results of pregnancy...." "Then you are right to build the Mbeta Chip, and we will support it anyhow we can," Maclean assured his son.[115]

Considering the recent 'njala' of 1949, the Nyasaland Government issued a verdict to farmers to propagate any unplanted fields with sweet potato and cassava. They wanted to ensure there were enough secondary foodstuffs to prevent a future hunger crisis. This was a setback to Chip's plans. He had managed to plant one field of tea before the restrictions but following them, he had to comply with the government orders and abandoned his tea nurseries that were ready for insertion on the recently cleared Mwalunthunzi land and instead planted sweet potato and cassava.[116]

"Moni, Chimwemwe, Mwana Chifundo Ali Bwanji?" Chip greeted a female laborer, inquiring about her child as well. "Chifundo Ali Bwino, Ndili Bwino, kaya inu?" she responded, indicating both she and her child were in good health. Chip moved from worker to worker, calling to each one by name, "Thokosani, Nasingo, Chisali, Mwai, Madalitso, Madzuka Bwanji?" In a row, the workers looked up from their duties, and respectfully greeted their boss. "Dazuka, Bwana Chippy, kaya inu?" "Bwino, Bwino," Chip replied, nodding to each one and making further inquiries as needed about their task, or their families at home. Often the labor would be murmuring once Chip had left, "He knows us by name, even our children, he asks after them. This is a good Bwana."

PART THREE

A balding landscape emerged as the forests of 'plot remaining Mwalunthunzi' fell to the axes, saws and hoes of Chip's labor force. One day, Chip walked to the edge of the newest clearing and decided to strain further inside the lashed jungle. He whacked the straggling vines with his machete and pressed through the tangled underbrush to a clearing where he found five houses but no people. There was smoke escaping the thatched roof of one hut, and he called out, "Odi, Odi, Eya?" But no one answered. The crackling sound of the fire in the dwelling echoed off the jungle which was pressing in on all sides. There was a serval skin, drying on the eave, and the smell of msamba simmering in the pot that was causing the smoke to drift toward the forest canopy. Intrigued, and still alone, he retreated to where he had come from, retracing his steps all the way out of the jungle, and back onto the familiar land where his workers were toiling.

"Mr Nahua, do you know of this place in the jungle, a place of five homes and no people?" Chip asked, intent on an answer. Frederick Nahua, the Capitao who had taught Chip to pluck tea, had been with Maclean since 1926. It was likely if anybody knew what that five-hutted place was, it would be Nahua. "Oh Master Chip, Bwana Chippy, you must not go there. It is a bad place. Mavuto Kwambiri," he assured Chip, scolding him enough with a deep, parent-like tone so to persuade him not to return to the huts. Chip, wondering if it had to do with 'witch craft', the 'black magic', challenged Nahua, "Don't come to me with stories of witches and magic, you know Mr Nahua, I just don't believe in them." But he actually did only because he knew from his childhood with John and Nelson that such things existed. At least the believing in witchcraft existed. Nahua evaded Chip's questioning, and simply demanded that Chip "not go back there."[117]

"Dr Hodges?" Chip had found their male nurse, who worked on the estate in the medical clinic. "Eya, Bwana Chippy, how are you today?" He spoke strangely, the American accent he picked up from his training at Malamulo Mission somehow out of place in the clinic. "Dr Hodges, you have to help me," Chip insisted. "I've been told not to go to the five huts in the clearing, but I just have to know what's going on there. Won't you come with me, please?" If there was one thing Chip was very good at by now, it was getting his own way. Dr Hodges looked at young Bwana Chippy and instantly softened, striding alongside the young boss to Mr Nahua, whose previous resistance was now hopeless, and together, all three went to visit the mysterious huts. On the way, Mr Nahua spoke of people who occupied the houses. "Lepers, you know," his voice softened empathetically, and he continued, "You're not allowed to touch them, do you hear me Bwana Chippy?"

Approximately 30,000 cases of leprosy were documented in Nyasaland in 1950, of which 6,600 were severe lepromatous infections. Leprosy carried with it social stigma where, if left untreated or was too advanced, rendered the afflicted a village outcast. However, 82% of the identified leper cases "lived in close contact with an average of four healthy children each: a tragic situation demanding the supply as soon as possible of available preventative methods." By 1950, there were thirteen mission stations within the Protectorate, working together with Government hospitals and clinics where lepers received treatments in varying stages of the disease. "Admissions were (for) the more advanced and crippled cases in which treatment was "disheartening" but at the Center of Malamulo early cases were treated with 'considerable success'." The Nyasaland Government had increased funding for leprosy control from £1500 to £7000 and hoped to "put leprosy control measures on a sound footing in the near future", despite the war. The 'Njala' of 1949 had affected lepers where "owing to food shortages only infective and early cases were admitted for treatment, and sulphetrone was first supplied to a few centers for trial." By the end of 1950, sulphones were available to all patients who had registered under a medical practitioner, but regrettably, many lepers never registered, and never received treatment.[118]

"Modern anti-leprosy measures in a backward and poor country," mounted challenges for the Hospitals and clinics throughout the Protectorate. With less than 2% of the infected lepers receiving treatment, the "enormity of the problem facing Nyasaland" centered on the quantity of drugs available and the willingness of the afflicted to pursue treatment.[118]

Entering the clearing where the leper huts stood clumped like Meer Kat observation hills, Chip, Dr Hodges, and Mr Nahua called to the residents, "Odi, Odi, Mulipo?" Their words fell in silence until a slight shuffling sound, a scratching of twigs on dry dirt, preceded the man who dragged the broom behind him as he walked out to face the intruders. The earth around the huts meticulously swept, and the chimbuzi (toilet) smells often pungent in a confined space such as this one were only noticeable because of their absence. "Lowani…," the man's voice was low and crackled. He stepped into the shaft of light that shone like a column into the cleared space where Chip was able to view him properly for the first time. He was missing four fingers from his right hand, and two from his left. His face was stippled with swollen bumps as if stung repeatedly by the wild bees. He had a cloth haphazardly tied around his hips, and a string made from torn bits of cotton, strangling his wrist. He frowned at the strangers, the one pale face and his two dark companions, and then somehow deciding to approve of their presence, he lifted his arms peacefully after which women, children and more men trickled out from their hiding place behind the great big Mbawas that guarded their huts. Satemwa, whether consensual or not, housed a leper colony. "What should we do, Bwana Chippy?" the Doctor asked. "We should feed them," Chip stated in a manner that would suggest it was the only thing to consider. "We'll give them metal plates that can be decontaminated by fire and we will send food for them, every day."

Shortly after Chip's discovery, Satemwa purchased enamel plates for the leper colony and just as Chip had proposed, food arrived for them every day. With the help of Dr Hodges and the clinical team at Satemwa, the lepers received regular medical aid, checking for new cases among the children who were born to the colony and sending them, if caught early, for treatment to Malamulo.[119]

Satemwa shared in the challenges that faced the Protectorate with care for the growing leper population. Despite the free treatments offered, it was difficult to encourage everyone to accept medical care, and yet by 1957, Malamulo Mission had discharged the first patient from their Leprosarium. When Ruth Kafere walked out of the Leprosarium, shaking the hand of her liberator, Dr Jack Harvey, she left behind 30 years of life as an admitted leper.[120] Progress had come. And a decade after uncovering the hidden community on Mwalunthunzi, those five little huts which captivated Chip's attention and assistance, disappeared. Just like a drop of rain from the sky, the huts blackened by owner-arson, seethed to the ground and the lepers, cured in droves, vanished.

Dr Jack Harvey with Ruth Kafere circa 1957

PART FOUR

The Leper colony was among many of Chip's concerns during his early days on assignment to the Mwalunthunzi portion of his parent's estate. Once the forced secondary food crops of cassava and sweet potato were harvested, Chip, free from obligation, was now able to plant his first fields with tea. He had 800 laborers toiling the estate, but he needed more. Cholo was scarcely populated and those who had relocated had done so for work, and now there were more jobs than there were people seeking attachments. The business of tea farming was among the most labour intensive in the country, and it was estimated that in the early 1950's over one million lbs of tea was "lost each year as a result of the shortage of pluckers."[121] Pacing the halls of 'The Satemwa House' after a long day on the Mwalunthunzi project Chip muttered to the walls, "How do I find more labour?" He brushed his hair to one side and threw the question into the air, not expecting a response. Maclean, nearby, heard him ponder and offered, "Mozambique, son. You have to poach labour from Mozambique." "Isn't that illegal?" Chip inquired. "There are ways to do it right, and then you will be successful." His father began to guide him through the process of 'creative' labour acquisition.[122]

Friday following the discussion with his father, Chip readied the old diesel truck, stocking maize flour, Canadian Wonder Beans and salt, which he carried in large gunnysacks as trading goods. Then he covered the truck tray with a tarpaulin and constricted the rope around the metal latches to hold it down. The colors of twilight sprayed beside Cholo Mountain indicated it was time to depart, and he revved up the engine, small puffs of smoke fleeing the exhaust pipes as he rolled off the estate. He was driving approximately 55 miles northeast to Gurue, a Nyasaland town 14 miles past the post office in Phalombe, edging the border with Mozambique. Gurue, unlike most little villages in Nyasaland, was bustling with people. The loud hum of the diesel engine approaching, and the clouds of dust that hovered like a permanent appendage behind the truck, alerted the villagers to an impending arrival, long before they could see who had come to visit. When Chip slowed the truck to a walking speed, the road, even in the dark night, was dotted with people who began waving excitedly with shouts of "Mzungu" once they saw Chip's pale skin illuminated in the moonlight. Chip enjoyed this undercover operation and nodded to the people, occasionally raising his hand with a friendly wave.

He stopped the truck when he arrived in the Boma of Gurue and stepped out of the cab. "How is the evening?" he greeted an elderly man, who looked like he had been sleeping for hours, and was now abruptly awake. "Bwino, Bwana," the man replied, clapping his hands together to show respect. "Where might I find your Chief, your Bwana Wonkulu?" Chip asked. "I'll take you to him now. He will be expecting news of the truck." The man lowered his head and shuffled his feet, motioning Chip to follow. When he was presented before the village headman Chip made sure to apologize for the late arrival and said, "I hope the reason for my untimeliness will please you all." They agreed not to discuss business until the following day, and Chip was given a mat and a hut where he spent the remainder of the night.

The morning squawk of the village rooster just outside of Chip's hut woke him suddenly. The familiar smell of porridge bubbling over a three-stone fire wafted into the hut and he rose to find a dozen faces peeking in between the cracks in the mud hut, inquisitively watching his every motion. The process of discussions with the village chief took the entire day, because employing the men from Gurue was an important matter that could not be rushed or resolved urgently. Besides, Chip was a stranger, and the Chief had to decide if he could be trusted. The fact that Chip was fluent in their Llomwe dialect immediately gave him an advantage, and the Chief knew his negotiations had to be accurate; there could be no cheating a white man who spoke Llomwe with such perfection. Chip presented the Chief with his barter goods, telling him, "You've never tasted such delicious beans." Then he satisfied the Chief's requests that his men should have proper wages, time to build a grass hut upon arrival at Satemwa, and leave to return to Gurue to be with their families as needed.[123]

By Sunday night, Chip had hired 30 men with the Chief's blessing, driving them back to Satemwa under the cover of darkness. This process of labour recruitment continued every month and the relationship between Chip and the Gurue Chief thrived. The town started to wonder every Friday night if this was the weekend when the Llomwe-speaking pale face from Cholo would appear with his old, smelly diesel truck, laden with all kinds of goods for their Headman. By his third visit to Gurue, Chip's appointment was not only highly anticipated; he was designated a hut for his personal use, and special provisions, even a roasted chicken upon arrival.

The days of acquiring labour had just begun, and when Chip realized that, as a general rule, people from the Yao tribes were the best pluckers in the tea industry, he took his diesel truck up to Lake Nyasa and befriended the Chief of the Yao's, making similar trade agreements before bringing Yao men back to work on Satemwa. His childhood nanny, Nchilma, a tall Yao man, who he had spent many hours beside, learning how to stuff mud into brick molds and burn the play-stacks with tiny bits of kuni (firewood) was not a typical Yao as he would discover. While the Yao tribe were excellent pluckers, their downfall was gambling. They were horrific gamblers, jousting winnings in the game of Juga, which kept them up all night, rendering them useless for dawn plucking.[124]

Then there were the Nguru tribes that trickled in from Mozambique. They were excellent manual workers, digging large tree stumps out of hard packed earth with little effort. Their tough physique was matched by a fastidious attitude which was apparent at first sighting. The Nguru decided where they wanted to work. Groups of ten or more men

walked into Nyasaland, past Mulanje, trekking all the way to the 12th mile
on the Cholo-Blantyre Road, and then moseying down to Makwasa and
back up to Cholo. At some point along the way, they would stop at an
estate and say, "We have chosen to work for you." Maclean had warned
Chip, "You must observe these people. They are not stupid you know.
They are looking at you to figure out whether you're a good Bwana or
not." Chip wasn't sure he understood this idea, so queried, "How do they
find out whether I'm a good Bwana?" The answer was very circular, "If
there are no weeds in your tea fields, then your estate has plenty of labour,
and if your estate has plenty of labour it's because you are a good Bwana,
and how can you tell if you're a good Bwana?" Maclean was amused by
this round-about way of thinking or circular reasoning. His eyes were
smiling as he finished, and then he lifted his glass to salute Chip, "And you
son, have found plenty of labour, you must be a good Bwana."[125]

PART FIVE

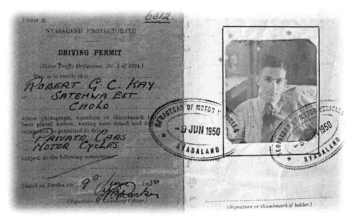

Chip Kay driver's license circa 1950

Chip was pleased that his father thought he was performing well.
He was also satisfied to be earning a salary, £20 per month. He had been
saving since his first pay period and now he had money to purchase a car.
In his pocket he carried his first official Driver's Permit. He had qualified
on the 9th of June, 1950, and the black and white picture glued to the blue
cardboard booklet showed his youth. He looked his age, all of 18, thick
brown hair, parted sharply on the left, a thin black tie falling from his white
collared long sleeve shirt which bunched over his slouching shoulders. The
tight, flat smile that pulled on his face made him appear more serious than
he felt. But he didn't really care how the picture looked. He was legal and
all he needed now was a car.

On a neighboring estate there was an old KWV, which wobbled a little, and appeared to have been caught in a cross fire of hail and sleet at the same time. The paint was peeling off, and rusty spots grew like mold on the surface where metal adjoined the wooden panels. After initial spluttering, the 2 stroke engine settled to a hum and the KWV screamed with potential. Watching Chip inspecting the car, Steve Tweedy, the manager of Sambankanga estate and the owner of the KWV said, "I'll swap you the car for a 6 Volt battery, but it has to be a new battery, ok?" Chip took no time to respond, "That Sir is a DEAL!" The next week Chip went to town to purchase a new 6 Volt battery, and eagerly took it to Mr Tweedy. "Brand spanking new," Chip said, handing the battery over with anticipation. He eagerly took the keys to the KWV and began making plans to fix it.[126]

Chip wasn't sure how John found out about his purchase, but when he got home, John Humbiani was waiting by the driveway, eyebrows raised in approval. "Eya, Chippy! Look at that beautiful thing, Wokongola!" By beautiful John meant that it actually worked. And a working thing in Nyasaland certainly qualified as beautiful. "Wokongola…. maybe," Chip responded, "But it has potential and it will be useful. John, I have an idea, but you've got to help me, ok?" Chip got out of the KWV and walked around to where John was waiting. "We're going to cut it in half," he stated, looking directly at John to see if he was up for the challenge. "Half, Chippy? And still it will drive?" John looked lost. "The back half John, we'll make it into a box body." Chip glanced over to see if that information would settle the matter. "Ok, so we just have to saw it off from here?" John asked. "Yes, and I think we should start right away," Chip replied, already moving towards the carpenter's shed where he retrieved a 6ft Sawyers knife. The pair worked on the KWV until the back end fell off, like timber crashing in the forest. Delighted, they plopped into the newly formed cab and drove to the factory to show off their handiwork.[127]

"Ok, John." Chip looked over to where John sat in the passenger's seat, looking back with keen eyes. "I think I must teach you to drive now." John Humbiani was a big man. He was built like a rugby player, broad shoulders, muscular arms, and strong legs that could run a mile at quick speed. He never wore shoes, revealing the largest toes Chip had ever seen in his life. "I never noticed your toes, John, until you put your foot on the accelerator. Your big toe almost covers the entire pedal." The friends chuckled and John exaggerated the size of his big toe by tucking the four others under the pedal.

It wasn't long before Chip managed to upgrade the KWV with an 800cc, side valve Morris Minor. The Morris Minor, later known as a

'British Icon', typified "Englishness", a matter that usually would have girded the Scottish Catchcart Kay's, but viewing the Morris Minor's classic grille and neat metal bands that ran over the bonnet giving contour to an already shapely car seemed to nullify it's Britishness. The split windshield with shiny metal banding lining the edges, the round headlights that stoutly flanked the grille, the tube tires that shone as much as the hubcaps they surrounded made the Minor a vehicle worthy of admiration. "Wokongooooooola….," John spurted, drawing the "O" out long for effect. "Yes, this one really is beautiful," Chip agreed. "I think this is the car you should take your driving test in. Let's go to the District Commissioner and see if we can get you a license."

Mr. Illingsworth was the Assistant District Commissioner in Cholo, and happened to be in charge of new driving licenses when Chip and John showed up at the office. "Ah, Chip. What can I do for you today?" Mr. Illingsworth inquired. "Oh, well, not for me today, Sir, but my friend here, John. I have brought him to sit for his driving license," Chip replied. "Well, can he drive?" Illingsworth asked. "Oh yes, he can. His English isn't good. But if I come with you I can help to translate," Chip offered.

John sat behind the wheel of Chip's Morris Minor and clasped the thin steering circle with a nervous grip. Mr. Illingsworth, sitting beside John, glanced over his shoulder at Chip who was in the back, as if to ask again, "Can this man really drive?" He cleared his throat, perhaps equally as nervous as John and caught a glimpse of John's big toe, which entirely covered the square accelerator pedal of the Morris Minor. He squinted to see if his passing view was accurate, then trying not to look at the toe, but obviously having a hard time avoiding the sight, he asked John, "Can you reverse?"[128]

John replied with a "Humpf" having caught onto the word "reverse" and promptly flicked the gears and reversed out, stopped, pushed the gearbox to first and motored forward. Mr Illingsworth, having not taken his eye off John's big toe, hardly noticed that he had successfully reversed. "Chip, please can you tell him to drive around the flagpole twice and then park." Chip repeated the instructions in Chi'Njanga so John could precisely do as required. And when John brought the MM into a perfect park, he smiled, looked over to his instructor who was still focused on his big toe, and then exited the vehicle.[129]

John received his driver's license and his big toe had the reputation of being the largest big toe in Nyasaland. "The natives certainly do have large toes," Mr Illingsworth commented to Chip as he handed over the stamped cardboard booklet with John's license. Chip replied, "Yes, sir – this one in particular."

On the way back to Satemwa, John and Chip were laughing, considering if it was skill or an unusually large toe that had awarded John his driver's license.

PART SIX

Juliet and Maclean during the school years circa 1950

Chip's learning curve on Satemwa was steep. He had many job functions to absorb, and the responsibilities he held were immense, especially for an 18 year-old. Yet, he took to each role with enthusiasm and enjoyed the process, even when he made mistakes. He was working, but he was having fun too.

"Juliet comes home this week," his mother announced as they read the CAT newspaper on the khondi, watching the colors of the lawn change as the light of day lessened. Immediately Chip grew excited. Juliet was not only the 'jewel' in her father's eyes, she was a delight in Chip's life, and he longed for his sister to join them on the estate. "She's flying on the BOAC, and arrives in Cape Maclear on Wednesday," Flora Jean stated matter-of-factly. "Chip, I suppose you're too busy with Mwanlunthunzi to come pick her up?" his mother said barely looking up, absorbed in the newspaper. "Oh no, mother, I'm quite ok to settle the work here. I am coming," Chip responded, already imagining all the fun he and Juliet would have catching up about school, the estate, the boys in England and the girls in Nyasaland. "It's settled then," Maclean observed, "We will leave together, all three of us, after breakfast on Wednesday."

The British Overseas Airways Corporation (BOAC) ran a 3 ½ day service on their Solent 'flying boat' from England to Cape Maclear. The Solent monoplane was built from Aluminium, with a broad rudder for its base and two flotation torpedoes set underneath each high wing, where four Bristol Hercules Engines provided power to lift the 34 passenger, 7 crew plane.[130] It was touted to be "all too short for such a pleasurable cruise, and that includes touching down every night when you stay at the best hotels." The advertisement stated, "On wings of luxury", and promised "the accommodation is spacious, the comfort truly luxurious, with everything to make life enjoyable, even to a cocktail bar."[131] Yet, the BOAC was a strange sight at Cape Maclear where native people had only seen canoes and steamboats plying the lake. Now this large metal 'boat' fell out of the sky and rested on top of the water. If it's landing, splashing through the ripples of Cape Maclear's fresh water was not a peculiar sight, it's take-off certainly was. The engines would engage with a rumble, sending sound waves bouncing along the surface of the lake, reaching every village within earshot. Then, slowly at first, but gaining speed, it would rise from the water and disappear into the clouds. In a land brimming with witchcraft, the BOAC was part of "the white man's magic."

BOAC often ran 'special feature' tickets where "scholars from the age of 12 to 21 years can visit their homes from University or school at single fare for the return journey." [132] Juliet, on board the BOAC Solent Springbok service to Cape Maclear, was now on her way home. Her parents and brother drove from Cholo to meet her, putting the whole family back together once she arrived. Maclean, behind the wheel of his long-based, high-winged Citroen found the journey to be pleasant, with good roads and a dry breeze gushing through the opened windows, reprieving the morning heat which was otherwise unbearable. The Citroen was a revolutionary masterpiece, boasting four-wheel independent suspension, a unitary body with no separate frame, and front-wheel drive.[133] The road leading to Cape Maclear had deteriorated, and when the family began ascending a hill nearly half-way from the main road turn-off to the lake, the Citroen started spinning in the sand.

"Ah, front wheel drive vehicles! No problem," Maclean said, easing the worried look on his wife's face. "If you and Chip get out and sit on the wings, I'll reverse us up the hill."
Chip and his mother obliged and sat like weighted logs on the front wings of the Citroen. The metal wings arched around the tires like a swan covering her babies while Chip and Jean sat holding onto the immense headlamps. With the car in reverse Maclean backed them up over the hill. Successfully at the ridge, Maclean waited until his family gracefully slid off the arms of the Citroen and returned to their seats. When they arrived

at Cape Maclear they checked into the Cape Maclear Hotel.[135] "You're lucky we have space for you," the clerk suggested, adding, "We've been booked out from April to October."[134] It was the end of October now, and Juliet was coming home for the holidays. She was on one of the very last flights that BOAC booked into Cape Maclear.[136]

The BOAC plane on the water at Cape Maclear circa 1950

Chip heard the plane as it approached Cape Maclear, it's engines filling the bay with an unmistakable thunder and when it splashed onto the liquid runway, Chip, suddenly unaware of the magnificent Solent before him, was preoccupied searching for the face of his sister. She found his gaze immediately and they both sprang into the air a few inches. Chip's arm was raised high, waving while shouting, "Juliet!" She was the picture of sophistication as she stepped off the BOAC in her Scottish tartan skirt, a neat cardigan overtop her undershirt, and her strawberry blonde hair bobbing above her shoulders. She preferred the impractical styles of Paris with exaggerated puffs and pleats to the streamlined tailoring of British designers, who in her opinion - took all the fun out of fashion.[137] But she chose to arrive in Scottish tartan because she knew it would please her father. She was becoming a lady, a demure young woman and even though Chip still viewed her as his little sister with whom he charged around Satemwa catching fish in the stream, it was clear now that others saw her quite differently. Young men took long glances at young Juliet, and although Chip didn't like it, he knew he would have to get used to it.

Juliet's time at home on Satemwa was not unlike Chip had imagined it would be. They spent hours teasing each other, recounting stories of what they had been doing, Juliet in England and Chip in Nyasaland. Chip showed Juliet the road to the new picnic spot, the Mwalunthunzi estate that he managed, the dairy herd that came under his control, the leper colony, and his new Morris Minor - washed every morning to take the dust of the estate roads off its otherwise shiny paint. "I can't believe you are naming all the Heifers after your girlfriends," Juliet teased Chip, adding, "How do you think Anne would feel if she finds out you named a cow after her?" She winked at Chip as he blazed with satisfaction about his dairy herd and their titles.

He showed her the old foundations, covered by creepers and brush, where he proposed to build his own home. The view from the siting showed promise, although the estate, still swarming with forests and scrub, clogged the scene and would require clearing before a real vista materialized. "I'm very proud of you, Chippy, you have really done good things for father and mother, the estate is growing," she told him, reaching her arms around his chest and hugging him tightly from his side. "I'm just having fun," Chip replied, not sure how to take the compliment and not wanting to jinx his progress. "Perhaps one day, after your school, you will come back too?" Chip looked at Juliet, knowing she aspired for modeling in Europe and fancied more of a city life, just like his mother. "It can't hurt to hope," he thought to himself, imagining that somehow they would all be together again once England had played her role and education was complete. "Maybe," Juliet said rolling her eyes slightly with a half-smile. She was lost in bigger dreams than the tea estate she was born to in Central Africa.

PART SEVEN

For now, Juliet returned to England and Chip dove back into his work on Mwalunthunzi with a full heart. The months since her departure raced by and soon it was the middle of 1951 and Chip had been working for his father for a full year. One day Maclean found Chip and said, "Son, you know the rules I have for my managers. They apply to you as well." Unsure what his father was angling at Chip just shrugged his shoulders prompting his father to be more specific, "Holiday, Chip, annual leave - you have to take at least ten days leave. Everyone needs a break from their work and you are no exception."[138]

The idea of a few weeks cessation from managing the estate, dealing with the labor force, beating around the tea fields on foot in the heat of summer, sounded appealing so Chip loaded his Morris Minor with a few necessary supplies and motored off Satemwa for his first official annual leave. The weight of his responsibilities fell away as the Minor turned onto the Cholo Blantyre road, bound for Monkey Bay along Lake Nyasa.

Gleaming in the bay, the large and newly appointed Ilala II Motor Vessel (MV) floated like a beacon of pride for Nyasaland Railways Ltd., who, despite not making a profit on lake services, believed that expansion was necessary to provide a future for developments in the lake basin. Before the ship's launch, the General Manager for Nyasaland Railways stated, "It is my sincere hope that our good ship about to be launched will bring much prosperity and well-being to thousands who to date have been living on the fringe of civilization. Livingstone and other early pioneers had one aim, 'to promote the welfare of the African, every plan and purpose was subordinate to that single aim.' Let us hope that the Ilala II will do much to perpetuate the ideals of the man we honor in her name."[139]

Named after the place of Livingstone's death, the first Ilala was the earliest steamboat to sit on Lake Nyasa. The original Ilala arrived in 1875, in pieces, having sailed stowed on the Walmer Castle from London to Cape Town, then the German Hara which transported the undone Ilala to the mouth of the Zambezi where her parts were assembled on the beach.[140] It was difficult to send a large steamer to Lake Nyasa, where a series of inland rivers and tributaries posed problems for navigation due to areas where falls and rapids were too great to tackle. When the original 'Ilala' made her way to Lake Nyasa the crew was held up at Murchinson Falls, where they "took her to pieces, cleaned and packed up the sections, boilers and fittings in five and a half days, and sent off the first loads (by native carriers) on September 12, up the right bank of the Shire, reaching Pimba on the upper side of the Falls on September 22. Here again, as at Kongoni, we made sheds, shelters and a slip, and then re-built the steamer, completing her and launching her in two weeks after our arrival." They reached Lake Nyasa on October 12, 1875 and successfully launched the first steamboat, the Ilala on the freshwater. Those who had journeyed with the steamer to the lake were "thankful to the Creator for all things thus giving us success."[141]

Stormy weather had delayed the inauguration of the MV Ilala II but when the weather cleared slightly on January 28, 1951, Lady Colby smashed a bottle of champagne over the bow declaring, "I name this ship the Ilala – may God bless all who sail in it." Whistles and cheers from a patient crowd rose to the sky. National flags from around the globe decorated the ship from bow to stern and flapped in the inclement weather. When the great baulks of timber that formed the launching triggers were knocked away, the 620 ton vessel paused before "sliding swiftly into the blue waters of the lake in a great foaming wave." Four motorized 24ft aluminum life boats hung from the railings of the MV Ilala II. There were First Class Cabins for 12 passengers, six placements for Second Class accommodation, and 16 men and 12 women could occupy the Third Class Saloon. In addition, the ship could accommodate 350 passengers in Third

Class for short journeys. There were dining saloons, flush bathrooms, galleys and a sick bay.[142]

Outclassing her predecessor in size and function, the MV Illala could accommodate over 350 passengers and 100 tons of cargo. It had taken over five months for the MV Ilala II to begin passenger transport since her launch in January. Chip drove onto the rocky sands of Monkey Bay in his Morris Minor seeking passage to the north of the country for both himself and his car. It took several minutes to sort out the logistics for boarding the Morris Minor, as it was the first motor vehicle the MV Illala had transported. Equipped with an 8 ton derrick and two 10-cwt electric cranes, the 38 crew members soon negotiated the loading of the Morris Minor while Chip navigated his way to the dining room, and an ice-cold beverage. Once on board the motion sickness that was all too familiar to Chip passed through his body like the waves they emulated on the lake, and he questioned his decision to travel by boat voluntarily. However, the time passed quickly and he enjoyed the view from the deck as it pulled into ports at Chipoka, Chinteche and Nhkata Bay before arriving in the north at Mwyer, a small port in the Kyela region of Tanganyika.

Awkwardly the cranes dropped the Minor prematurely off the Ilala at Kyela. With the effort of several men bursting under the weight, Chip's Morris Minor[143] off-loaded into a foot of water, was heaved out of the dipping sands, and onto the beach where dry pebbles topped the strand, just firm enough to prevent the Minor from sinking. With a small crowd gathering on the fringes of the shore, Chip realized his appearance and disappearance respectively was a unique sighting for villages. As his Morris Minor churned through the sand and onto the main road, he watched in the rear-view mirror as daring little children ran after his car, close to the bumper at first, but then quickly fading once his tires left the sand.[144].

He headed north from the port into Tanganyika through the rice paddies that grew more abundantly than maize, and the banana plants that swayed beside them. The road joining Nyasaland and Tanganyika sat on top of a mountain ridge, where the left side fell away to the valley below and the other side revealed far-reaching mats of green tea, methodically pruned, with neat rows, a foot wide, cutting perfect lines through the fields. There were acres of organized blue gums patched throughout the property and Chip, a planter at heart, thought, "The most attractive place to spend the night is here surrounded by tea." He motored onto Chivangi Tea Estate, searching for a guesthouse where he could spend the night. He found the Guesthouse manager who obliged him with boarding upon his request. It was getting dark, and he was settling into his room, marveling how good it felt to be on vacation but still wrapped in tea. As he was settling into the bath he noticed lights approaching, and soon heard the roll of a motor engine draw near. He quickly dressed and opened the door of the cottage, revealing a man with distinctive red hair, his face, strangely familiar to Chip even in the dimly lit night. "Have you come from Nyasaland?" the man asked Chip. "Yes, I have – on the Illala, just this afternoon," Chip said. "From Cholo?" the man pressed. "Yes," Chip replied. "Are you related to Satemwa Tea Estates?" "That's my father." Chip had now placed this stranger beside his past and when the man asked, "Do you know me?" Chip surprised him, "Yes, sir, I recognize you; you used to be an engineer on Satemwa when I was little."[145]

Chip did not recount the story of how he remembered the engineer from years ago before he went away for school. He remembered the red-headed man up high on a ladder in his mother's kitchen, fixing a lightbulb, when an earthquake struck, shaking the Wedgwood in the pantry. Jean had chased the cook and the kitchen boy outside to safety while the engineer, still up the ladder, could not figure out what had caused the commotion.

"What are you doing here, at Chivangi?" the engineer probed, to which Chip replied, "I'm on a mandatory annual leave from Satemwa, and thought it might be nice to drive to Dar Es Salaam." "Well, perhaps get a bit more dressed up and let me take you to a party at the club tonight," he said, looking at Chip's half-clad, hurriedly dressed body and down at his feet where a small puddle of bath water pooled around his toes.

The 'club' was the Tukuyu Sports Club, a typical outpost for Empirical settlers. A sports club was imperative to a growing colonial town, with cricket pitches, rugby fields, squash courts, tennis courts, golf courses, swimming facilities, and a ballroom with an attached bar where community functions could be hosted. The sports club was central to life for colonialists who gathered to play mid-week bridge or billiards, cheer for their local rugby team on the weekend, or meet a friend for a Johnnie Red Label whiskey at the bar. The Sports club in Tukuyu was hosting a function the night Chip arrived and inadvertently he had become an honored guest. "Let me present to you our visitor from Nyasaland." Chip held out his hand to greet his new acquaintance, "Chip, meet our District Commissioner (DC)." With that the engineer left Chip and the DC and meandered to the bar to fetch some drinks. Quickly, Chip hurdled his shyness and formed friendships, earning him a private tour of the factory and the estate the day following the party. Satemwa's ties to Chivangi ran deeper than an ex-employee. Chip discovered during the tour that in 1928 his Uncle Alexander, through the Burma Oil portfolio, had sent Assam tea seeds to two estates in Africa, Satemwa was one, the other was Chivangi.

Annual leave was disappearing fast and he wanted to get across to Dar Es Salaam and feel the ocean breeze, salty against his skin. He left the charm of Chivangi and made his way, 36 miles north to Mbeya, then 510 miles east over dusty, broken roads to Dar Es Salaam. The sun had been sleeping for many hours by the time he arrived in Dar Es Salaam, and yet even without it, the night was hot as day. A wet, humid air shrouded Chip's body, and his clothes stuck immediately to the sweaty skin they hid. His feet, suffocated by his socks and loafers, felt like hot coals, the slow burn inching up his legs. His head was dripping, and wiping his brow was useless as the sweat instantly reappeared the moment his hand left his forehead. What a difference to his previous night, where the cool air at 5,000ft elevation on the Chivangi Tea Estate had made his sleep comfortable. He now tossed all night, unable to get reprieve from the heat which by morning had only increased.[147]

Chip, already weary from the temperature in Dar Es Salaam where the heat blanketed the city, crossed the Indian Ocean by ferry to Zanzibar, a straight course, twenty miles northeast from Dar Es Salaam to the city of Stone Town where he disembarked to find a hotel for a few nights. Stone Town, the old part of Zanzibar City had narrow, cobbled streets, leading to foot traffic and the odd bicycle. Once past the perimeter of town, Chip found himself lost in a maze of plastered mud walls stretching high on both sides, and rusty window frames sprayed by ocean mist streaking the walls red. Chip wandered around the labyrinth of cobblestoned paths, sniffing the cinnamon, vanilla, saffron, and nutmeg at the vendors' make-shift stalls. He found the old slave market where the Anglican Church now stood in place of the slave auction, a predominantly Arab-run slave auction that the British dismantled in 1873, the same year David Livingstone, who fought vehemently against the trade, died.

Despite his mother's efforts early in his life to help him swim, including lessons in Cape Town, and encouragement to join swim squads in school, Chip still disliked immersion in water anything more than three inches as he drew in his bath. He was content to find a decent restaurant and look out from the rooftop dining over the Indian Ocean, where wooden boats, tied at anchor, clung to the shore. He had little more than a week left of annual leave. Watching the drifting vessels tug at their anchors, he tucked a napkin between his shirt and his neck, spreading it wide like a sail over his torso, dipped a prawn into the cocktail sauce accompanying the dish, and plotted a course home to Satemwa. He left Zanzibar the following morning, tacked around the north of Nyasaland into Northern Rhodesia, and down into Southern Rhodesia, where he happily found Salisbury - a modern city, teeming with luxury.

Chip met his Rhodesian girlfriend at Meikles Hotel at a moment's notice. He had many girlfriends at the time, but no long-term dates or friendships. He mostly took girls out to the movies at the Limbe Club in

Nyasaland on a Wednesday night, and rarely at this point did he take the same girl twice.

Meikles Hotel was in the epicenter of Salisbury overlooking Cecil Square where many years ago British Settlers had first raised the Union Jack for the King.[147] Chip threw on his sports coat, a little scruffy after a week on the road, but he still looked sharp, neatly combed hair, a splash of cologne on his neck, and his shoes freshly polished for a tikkie by the man outside the hotel door. His girlfriend arrived with long, white gloves gliding over her fingers, and a felt hat with a lace ribbon dangling at the back. The Meikles morning high tea came complete with mannequins - models beautifully dressed by Parisian Courtiers parading through the tearoom as customers sipped from Wedgwood porcelain the finest tea in Rhodesia. Chip felt transported to the streets of London, momentarily, until the blaze of the African sun beamed through the large glass windows and onto his saucer, catching his eye the same way it did when it bounced off his motorbike on Satemwa. He parted with his girlfriend, a simple kiss on the lips and then suddenly, as if morning tea had taken two minutes too long, it was time to go home.

PART EIGHT

He trundled back to Nyasaland in his Morris Minor, bringing with him the memories of the past few weeks on the road and also a set of 'King's Pattern Dining Service' which he purchased with part of his £50 Christmas bonus. Although he did not yet have a house of his own, he was making plans to build one, and when he returned to Satemwa he took his father to the site he had chosen, hoping Maclean would find it satisfactory.[148]

The bush fires had run through a portion of the Mwalunthunzi estate, and he told his father, "I want to build a house here. I've already found a site and I've discovered foundations of a previous house."[149] "I think we should get Jim Harper to come check this site, Chip. I wonder who had a house here before now?" Maclean made plans to bring Jim to Satemwa and when he arrived he told the Cathcart Kays, "Ah! This is the site of McKinnon's old house." McKinnon, a renowned name in the coffee world making wet pulper machines and coffee processing machines, was also incidentally famous for his club, where planters gathered to drink whiskey and gamble their estates. In the early 1900's at the McKinnon Club, the Chawani portfolio which Maclean had purchased, notoriously changed hands three times in one night. One of the gamblers mischievously switched the boundary markers for Chawani, which should have run West/East, and for years the planter who 'won' the north side drowned in rainfall, and the planter who 'won' the south side suffered draught. When Maclean purchased the estate, he bought both pieces, evening out the rainfall distribution and meteorologically setting himself up for improved outcomes.[150]

After the fires had burned the underbrush and clipped the ends of the large Mbawas, the site of the old McKinnon house and the new location for Chip's house bragged a view. Across the virgin forests immediately in front of the foundations and the tea in field 6 that his mother had planted in 1945, Cholo Mountain framed the horizon. The tree tops, thick along the ridge, looked like marching ants on procession.[151]

He decided to build it right there and imagined a teacart stocked with freshly brewed tea, biscuits and sandwiches, rolled out beside him while he watched the sun dipping behind the rim of Cholo Mountain. "Then, you better get to work, son." Maclean left Chip to daydream, knowing the nursery room at 'The Satemwa House' would soon be empty, a matter that left him mixed with emotions.[152]

In between the running of Mwalunthunzi, Chip started a brick-building project just below the site for his house. The labourers cut out sections of earth, creating flattened terraces by removing trees and digging out soil for the brick molds. This inadvertently increased the beauty of the vista. When the thousands of bricks were sufficiently fired and tested strong to the 'drop' check, Chip began to build his home. Once the partitions were erect, Turner's Big 6 asbestos roofing brought into Nyasaland from Salisbury capped the walls.[153]

Not unlike his father's home, 'The Satemwa House', Chip's house also began modestly with three main rooms; the bedroom, the hall and the drawing room. The kitchen was outside with a temperamental wood stove, and inside, the house was lit with Tilley paraffin lamps, pressure lamps that needed pumping in order to work[154]. Although missing some of the conveniences of 'The Satemwa House', such as running electricity off the generator that powered the factory, Chip liked the independence from his parents just 3 miles away. It was not until 1955 that a main line for electricity ran from Blantyre to Cholo, providing a "tremendous benefit to the tea industry as a whole."[155] To see the line realized, Satemwa provided the electric company with all the blue gum poles needed from Blantyre to Makwasa. At that time, individuals could buy lead-off lines from the main road, to electrify their homes and estates, reducing their operating costs significantly.[156]

In typical bachelor fashion, it was not long before Chip's house resembled a warehouse of goods. His office was located centrally in the drawing room and a drum of petrol was stashed in the corner of the hall alongside his motorbike. When he built the fourth room, the second bedroom attached to the drawing room, it became the main storeroom, filled with timber, Indian cotton, and military battledress, tunics, great coats and boots. The timber was kept for building frames and furniture and the cotton and military gear was for his labor force.

There was a mail boy who was given a Great Coat, the same kind of coat that kept Chip warm during the English winters at Millfield, and every day, whether it was summer or winter, he wore his coat to walk to the Boma to collect the mail. He was simply known as the mail boy in the winter Coat because he was always arrayed in it. He told Chip, "It keeps the heat in when winter comes, and it keeps the heat out when it's summer."[157]

Chip always found the Africans amusing, yet since he had grown up around them his whole life, he accepted their unusual habits and ways of doing things because he too had strange, unorthodox ways of accomplishing tasks. Despite the obvious disparities of class and color, he never thought of himself much different to his friends, John and Nelson. They were the boys whom he spent his childhood besides, the boys who liked the same things, the boys who were equally amused at finding leopard tracks in the jungle, calling out to Chip, "Chenjerani Nyaglugwe!" (Beware Leopard!) and pouncing on him from behind a wild date palm, pretending to be one.

PART NINE

The Satemwa House circa 1952

On the day of his twenty-first birthday, Chip woke earlier than usual, arriving before the garden boys to his vegetable patch where he surveyed the onions, leeks, carrots, potatoes, peppers, and sweet potato growing abundantly, and designed a menu in his head for his birthday dinner that night. When the garden boy arrived, Chip gave him directions for which vegetables to pick and told him, "Pitisani masamba Nyumba, Zikomo." (Please take this food to the house) "Inde, Bwana, Zikomo," (Yes, boss, thank you) the garden boy responded, already beginning to prepare the vegetables for delivery to Chip's house.

The day was passing as most days, except Chip was pleased with the feeling that accompanied turning twenty-one, the official growing-out of his teenage years and the formal start of his adulthood. This was a turning point; everything he had been doing up until now seemed childish. He was on the cusp of new beginnings; he could feel beating like the African night drums inside his chest. Life loomed before him, and all he had to do was grasp it. He could accomplish anything.

His father arrived early just as Chip was walking back to the house from his vegetable patch and bid his son good morning. He presented Chip with a radiogram styled by leading designers. It was an expensive instrument of entertainment for the house. It housed a larger speaker than the domestic radio and, fitting into a polished wooden cabinet, boasted design features that made it a unique piece of functional furniture.[158] Chip was delighted at the sight of the radiogram, the most beautiful one he had ever seen. He cleared space in the drawing room, which had become an office, and enthusiastically directed the placement of the radiogram against the shared wall with the hall. The day had begun so well.

Chip left his kitchen boy with directions regarding the vegetable haul from the garden, and then took his motorbike to the dairy where he perused the herd, looking for the suitable heifer to make beef stew. There was 'Patience', 'Jacqueline', 'Anne' and several others who came plodding to the fence when they heard Chip's bike. "Hello, my dear cows, now, which one of you will celebrate with me tonight?" he whispered to the animals, not wanting to frighten them. He stepped away from the herd and whistled to the cattle boy who was leaning on the fence with his whip in hand, "Pitisani Maria nyumba." "Inde Bwana Chippy," the cattle boy responded, flicking the whip towards Maria and corralling her to the corner.

It was still early morning, the mist from the night's dew on the grass slowly evaporating and the warmth of the morning sun just starting to smolder. Chip found a 44 gallon drum capable of holding up to 200 liters of stew. It was the perfect 'pot' for his party and he instructed the cook to clean it properly and start simmering 'Maria' along with all the vegetables from the morning picking. He left the cook and the drum and went about estate rounds checking in the nursery at the tea seeds which grew now as little trees, and over to the stumping grounds where more land was being cleared for planting.[159]

By evening, Chip had gathered his labour together, centered around the 44 gallon drum, where the flavors from the vegetables and the tender meat had been simmering all day. He announced to them, "Lelo ndi tsiku langa lokumbukira kubadwa! (It is my birthday today) Ndili ndi zaka twenty-one tsopano (I am twenty-one years old). Kwawo kwa makolo anga timakondwe lela ndi nzathu zakudya zabwino. (Where my parents come from, we celebrate such days with our friends and with good food)." He dipped his cup into the drum to show the workers what the drum contained, and sipped it immediately to demonstrate its goodness. The vegetables from his garden, mingling with the tender beef from his personal herd, created a delightful stew, mild flavors with a hearty texture. By now, the labour force had become interested in the drum of stew, and they wondered if they would get to taste it. "Ndikufuna ndikondwelele pamodzi ndi inu (I want to celebrate tonight with all of you)." Chip spoke to the crowd, sweeping his hand around to acknowledge all the faces, which were keenly watching him. "Mumagwila mulimbika nchito (You have worked hard). Tiyeni tidyere limodzi chakudya ichi (Let us enjoy this tasty stew together)." Chip, along with the help of his house staff, stood by the drum, ready to hand out plastic cups to his employees. "Tengani cup yanu indi ku tenga chakudya, ndipo khalani pansi ndi kudya (You take your cup and dip it in the drum, sit down and eat)." Chip instructed the group by modeling again how to perform the stew collection and then motioned for the meal to begin.

One by one, the workers stood to their feet, accepting a cup, dipping it into the drum, drawing out hot aromatic beef stew then returning to their roost on the ground. About twenty men had passed through, for they always ate before the women, when the strangest thing happened. Chip could barely believe what he was witnessing, as one by one the men poured the stew onto the ground, their lips puckering in disgust, "Ayi, sitimadya chonchi (we don't' eat this sort of food)." They sat, arms crossed, as if waiting for the next course, a course that would satisfy them.

Puzzled and offended, Chip confronted them, "Ndi chifukwa chani mukutaya chakudya chimene ndakukonzerani inu (Why do you throw out this meal that I have prepared for you)?" The man who was the first to tip the stew out of his cup told Chip, "Chakudyachi sichabwino, timadya Nsima osati izi (It is not good, we eat Nsima, not stew)," a look of contempt on his face as he spoke. Chip nodded to the group of men who sat beside their spoiled stew, walked over to the 44 gallon drum which was teetering on a three-stone fire, placed his foot up on the cylinders side, and pushed it over. The drum split when it hit the ground, and the birthday stew that Chip had been preparing all day ran like a river of rocks over the ground. He didn't have the heart to speak to the crowd as dissension was growing in their ranks with those who had missed the stew now angry at the few who had ruined their meal.[160]

Chip took his motorbike and went home. It was a disappointing ending to his twenty-first birthday. Where he imagined celebrating with his labour force, he now felt scorned by them. He was irritated, reacting in haste and fury that ran counter to his nature. He had allowed the stew tippers to rattle his usually calm exterior. He realized that even though he was born in the same country as those he managed, he was different to them, very different. At the age of seven, he never felt unlike John or Nelson, apart from the obvious skin variances. As children, they had the same interests. As adults, the birthplace of their fathers and their respective cultures divided them.

Elladale 1947-1953

Jean and Maclean Kay in Salisbury circa 1948

The long drawn-out jingle of the family's Model 302 disc-dial telephone always brought the house staff at 'The Satemwa House' to a mid-work halt, staring at the little black machine with curious eyes until the master of the house responded to the persistent ringing. The Kay's were reached in Cholo at number 3 on the telephone dial, behind Dr I Conforzi who rang at number 2, and Sir Malcolm Barrow of Namingomba assigned to the number 1. Maclean had barely lifted the handset when his friend Tim Thorburn bellowed through the cables, "Mick! Is that you old chap?", "Oh Tim! Yes, I can hear you just fine. How are things these days in Rhodesia?" Maclean, favorably called 'Mick' by his friends answered. "Well, Mick, that's why I'm calling. I've just bought the farm next door for you. Can you come down and organize the papers?" Tim's words faded away to silence as Mick struggled to absorb the news. "You've done what Tim?" Maclean blurted out, still shocked by the rapidity of the information transpiring and wondering if his 'speculations' about one day owning a farm in Rhodesia were taken more seriously by his friend Tim than by himself. Feeling the pressure to commit on the spot Maclean stated, "But I don't want another farm and not in Southern Rhodesia." However, after a few more minutes on the wire with Tim, his inertia at accepting the deal flipped upside down. Within a week he was motoring to Salisbury in his Hudson Straight 8 American motorcar, license BT 1007, crossing the border from Nyasaland, where it was registered, to Rhodesia and a farm called Elladale, 1,347 meters above sea level; an hour south-west of Salisbury.[161,162]

The war had ended two years before Tim Thorburn's phone call, and the uncertainty that followed the world battles saw multiple pieces of land in the colonies for sale. It was either abdicators who left after the war, disillusioned by dreams in the colonies, or a reshuffling of order and expansion driven by colonial development that resulted in previously unopened property now available for purchase. Upon inspection of Elladale Farm the Cathcart family realistically viewed it to be less than ideal, a little 'clapped out', but nonetheless a foothold into the farming community of the flourishing Southern Rhodesian economy. Diversification had to prove beneficial, even if the farm itself was nothing to boast about and with growing talks of a Federation between Nyasaland and Northern and Southern Rhodesia, such an expansion seemed to make sense.[163]

With Chip and Juliet both at school in England, Maclean and Jean again made the decision to live apart, Jean moving to Rhodesia to manage Elladale and Maclean remaining in Cholo with Satemwa.

In 1950 when Chip joined the Satemwa Company, he also took on the responsibility of helping his mother on Elladale. He considered himself a bush mechanic and fixed her Fordson Major paraffin-run tractor, and other farm equipment that needed maintenance. After the war, each farm was rationed with one tractor so it was imperative that the tractor be in good working order. He made the journey from Cholo to Salisbury every six weeks and took two Satemwa trucks in his convoy. Sometimes the trucks were loaded with Satemwa tea which fetched higher prices in Rhodesia than in Nyasaland. Other times, they carried 60 men. Flora Jean, the 'newcomer' to Rhodesia found slim pickings for labour. Many of the well-established farmers were hiring well in advance of seasonal needs and knew how to manipulate a diminished labour force. Since Satemwa owned Elladale, employees from Nyasaland could work across the border in Rhodesia under a 'transfer of labour' agreement.[164] In addition, the minimum wages in Rhodesia fetched over 10 shillings more per ticket than in Nyasaland, which meant many Nyasa men willingly signed up for work on the Elladale Farm.[165]

Chip's 5 tonne Dodge and 5 tonne Commer trucks steadily rumbled from Cholo to Salisbury every six weeks, encountering enough challenges along the way to make their arrival unpredictable. First, the road between Cholo and Blantyre was experiencing "ever increasing drops between the tarmac and those rough bits of open country known as verges." One reader from The Nyasaland Times Newspaper thought the garages were "in league" with the Public Works Department who had failed to maintain the road properly, causing severe damage to the vehicles trying to navigate it.[166] Secondly, there were the Tsetse fly stops where travelers sat in a dark room on a sofa tented with mosquito netting, while a worker went around the vehicle with a flit gun, collecting the insects. The Tsetse flys, caught and recorded, were placed into a jam jar along with the offending car's license plate number. Third, along the main Blantyre to Salisbury road, there was a section during the dry season where the common bush fires licked at the tar, menacing the traffic that had no alternative route. Fourth, after passing through the gauntlet of bush fires, checking to make sure the trucks hadn't carried any flames with them, came the River Ruvugwe.[167]

Unpassable, except for pontoons poled by Africans, the 'Snag at Ruvugwe' was often called a "fantastic state of affairs," not because there was anything fanciful about it, but because it's swift waters were quite impossible and the pontoons were not safe enough to carry both lorry and load simultaneously.[168] Convoys would wait on either bank, off-load their goods, and send first the lorry across and then the supplies it carried on a separate pontoon. Sometimes Chip waited days at the River Ruvugwe, his trucks giving way to sedans that pass quicker on the pontoons, and stuck behind others with lorry loads, each waiting patiently for the next raft crossing. Chip battled this process of removing the tea chests and sending the trucks and loads separately for many years. The frustration for travelers only ceased in 1957 when the new Tete-Benga ferry was established, capable of carrying the fully laden lorry negating the old 'Ruvugwe Snag'.[169]

After the sluggish crossing of the man-poled pontoon at the Ruvugwe, the passage at the Zambezi River seemed a modern delight. The Zambezi ferry was drawn by a Portugeuse tug boat attached to a floating pontoon that could carry both a lorry and it's load at the same time. One time, after several days delay at the Ruvugwe, Chip anxiously arrived to the Zambezi only to meet a grim- faced tugboat captain. "Eh, Mr Kay, I am glad to see you again," the Captain said between shoulder shrugs. "It's my engine, it's having some old trouble." He looked at Chip, hoping for assistance. Chip noticed the line-up of cars and trucks waiting to cross the Zambezi, and said to the Captain, "Causing some grief, the old diesel huh?" looking at the tugboat that sat depressed at the river's edge. "Ok, I'll lend you some parts from my engine and we can all cross today," Chip asserted, heading towards his truck and banging on the sides to signal his driver, "Million", to open the bonnet. He took his tools out from the truck cab and began to disassemble the injectors from his engine. Fortunately, the Portuguese tugboat ran on a Perkins P-6 Diesel Engine, the same kind as Chip's trucks, so Chip was able to install his injectors onto the tugboat and his convoy could cross the Zambezi without further delay. Once his fleet had successfully passed to the other side, Chip sent the Captain back and offered to get the parts necessary to fix the tugboat engine from Stansfields in Salisbury and bring it back the following week.

Roads in Nyasaland crossing circa 1950

Before arriving at Elladale, Chip made one additional stop to visit his father's 'brother' in Mtoko. Knowing that they were not true relatives, Chip asked Bernie, the lovely Jewish man he had called upon, "Why do you call my father your brother?" to which Bernie replied, "We're both Scottish," and Chip retorted, "But you're NOT Scottish!" which prompted Bernie to tap his skull in the area where doctors had used a tin plate to mend his head wound years ago. Chip looked at the grafted bald spot on his skull, shining under the swept away hair. "I've had many pints of blood after the accident that caused this gash in my head – and it was done in the best hospital in the world, the Edinburgh Royal Infirmary. It's a Scot's hospital, with Scot's blood, so now I'm half Scottish," Bernie laughed, tapping the tin on his head. Chip rolled his eyes and chuckled along, "Well, then, my father's brother – how about a drink?"[170]

He had spent many days on the road when he finally made it to his mother's farm at Elladale, and she was pleased to see he had arrived safely, bringing mementos of Satemwa with him. Often a long-typed letter from Maclean was sent detailing the business of Satemwa and the social buzz of Cholo and in turn inquiring about Elladale. "Chip, did you hear that the government is giving everybody £50 for each dam they build that is at least 100ft wide by 6ft deep?" Jean looked at her son, as if to request that he build one or two but without actually asking if he would. "I did hear talk of such an arrangement," Chip replied, brushing the dust from the truck off his khaki cotton shirt. His mother's eyes widened as she spun around, dashing to inspect the convoy from Cholo, her blue awning striped shirt coming untucked from her tapered skirt as she hastened away. Whatever effect she meant to have on Chip by bringing up the dams for pounds scheme was not known, but over the course of the next few years Chip built twelve such structures on his mother's farm, contributing £600 towards the running costs of Elladale.

Flora Jean spent six years working the farm with every resource she could assemble. The tobacco crop, one of Southern Rhodesia's finest exports, proved easy enough to grow, even on their 'clapped out' property. She was a woman in a predominantly male industry, aware of the strengths and weaknesses of her male counterparts. She hired managers who ran parcels of the estate, and when their wives were particularly sweet upon the eye, she strategically positioned them beside her bales at the auction floor, with noticeable price increases on her tobacco as a result.[171] Chip was uncertain how his mother felt when six years after opening up the farm at Elladale, and all the elbow grease she had plowed into its growth, the government built Hunyani dam, which became Lake McIlwaine which consequently flooded the bottom portion of the Elladale estate, leading to a Government buyout offer to the family in the amount of £3,000.[172]

Flora Jean's Southern Rhodesian property was gone, and she returned to Satemwa where her husband waited, proud of her efforts, yet also glad to have her home. With £3,000 as a showing for the last six years toil, Maclean and Jean took the money and went to find Chip. "Do something with this, won't you? You go fix it," Maclean instructed his son, handing the buy-back money to him. "You know Dad, I'm not going to grow tea. I'm going to stick it in a packet and make a million." The boyish grin that preceded his bluster appeared and Chip took the £3,000 and set off to make it flourish.

The Wonder of £85: From 1953

PTA "Three Leaves tea packet circa 1953-1963

The proposed alliance between Nyasaland and Southern and Northern Rhodesia, known as 'Federation', came on the cusp of growing tensions surrounding White Rule over a Black majority, sparked by the newly formed ideas on "Nationalism". Not just within the continent of Africa, where Apartheid in South Africa was widely viewed by Nyasaland Settlers as a "doomed policy", but throughout the watchful world where the very word 'Colonialism' had developed an "almost sinister meaning."[173] As countries within the African continent gained their 'independence', those countries who were still under Colonial Rule were subject to greater inspection by the vigilant eye of the world. African Nationalists began lobbying in England for an immediate end to Colonial Rule, and colonialists opposed them, believing that their colonial policies around 'gradualism' were not yet exhausted and that overall Africa was not ready to self-govern. In 1951, Britain's Rt. Hon. A. Creech Jones addressed the mounting pressures and commented, "It would be a calamity for Britain to break her treaty and moral obligations to the African and renounce her burden. Our experience and technical resources, the financial aid and educational facilities required are an enormous asset to the Colonial peoples which cannot be replaced by any international authority." He continued to assure the public that colonials did not wish to leave the work undone in Africa, and that "Economies and social standards of the territories continue to be built up to serve and enrich the people, and exploitary practices are controlled."[173]

By 1953 the ties between Southern and Northern Rhodesia and Nyasaland strengthened. After the Second World War and the great boom that followed, the idea of a closer union between Southern and Northern Rhodesia and Nyasaland transpired with the hope of providing a "hard core of political stability, and a great source of common wealth, in the heart of Africa." A scheme for Federation, drafted following the 1949 and 1951 conferences between Britain and the three territory governments in Africa, concluded that Federation would be "a much needed stabilizing factor in a continent which is in such a state of flux." The Prime Minister of Southern Rhodesia had declared on the wings of Federation, "It is up to us to save Central Africa by our exertions and Africa by our example."[174] Yet, the people had to agree and in 1953 the Nyasaland newspaper was inundated with advertisements to "Vote Federal – and Win the World's Confidence," promising that a vote for Federation would open the door "to great opportunity" and that by voting for the Federal party on the December 15, 1953 election Nyasaland would be electing a "Government that will win world confidence by it's realism, commonsense and moderation."[175] While some voters in Nyasaland remained skeptical of Federation probing such questions as, "What does Federation want out of Nyasaland? What can Nyasaland contribute to the economy?" The Nyasaland vote passed in a landslide, favoring an amalgamation of the three states and joining Nyasaland to Southern and Northern Rhodesia as a Federation in the December vote of 1953. One of the four elected members for Nyasaland's federal government was Maclean and Jean's neighbor, Sir Malcolm Barrow of Namingomba Tea Estate in Cholo, who won the seat for Minister of Commerce and Industry.[176]

Despite the concerns with Nyasaland's involvement in the Federation, there were certain advantages to opening the doors between the countries for commerce. Nyasaland, by all accounts, the smaller contributor to Federation, later enjoyed newspaper headlines such as, "Lake Nyasa again the Playground of Federation, " where by road, rail and plane, the hotels along the lakeshore were booked out for the 1955 Easter holidays, with people streaming across the borders from the two Rhodesia's to the Calendar lake.[177] Chip, for one, was grateful for the Federation as it created smooth transitions between Cholo, and his new business endeavors in Southern Rhodesia. He had £3,000 burning a hole in his pocket and he was looking for a sound investment. When the Planters Tea and Agency in Southern Rhodesia went up for tender, Chip took his £3,000, added £85 to it, and beat out the English Tea Company, Brooke Bonds, in the bid. He offered £85 more than his competitor's bid and when he was awarded the company, Planters Tea and Agency, a new future began to blossom.

One day he met a Dutchman by the name of Juul Felderhof who ran an operation called 'The Capital Tea and Coffee Company'. "Juul," Chip began, inquisitively searching the Dutchman's face as if to look for character flaws, "You already packet coffee and tea, don't you?" Juul, with a broad smile and still clutching Chip's hand stated, "You know I do. And I suspect you want to know more?" Chip said, "I grow tea and I can make the tea come here. You can packet it and we'll form a partnership – any objections?" With their hands already clasped, the deal was easy and they shook heartily, both recognizing that something special had just transpired, but neither knowing that it would be the longest, most rewarding working partnership of their lives.

Chip returned to Satemwa, formulating his plans as he traversed the Salisbury to Blantyre road, over the pontoon crossings of the Zambezi and Ruvugwe, back to the Shire Highlands and his three-roomed house which kept growing extensions. Every now and then, he would instruct the builders to add a new room, or enlarge the khondi, or lay a rock patio with creeper vines overhead. It was part of the reason he loved living in Africa – anything was possible. He couldn't wait to bring his father into his ideas, and the next day he saw Maclean, he challenged, "Father, I want to buy tea." Maclean wanted to know what Chip had designed, and after hearing of his plan to packet tea in Southern Rhodesia, he not only sold Chip Satemwa tea, but he gave him a 9 month running credit to buy it. Additionally, he granted Chip permission to tailor the tea to the intended market by experimenting with the drying processes in the Satemwa factory and packing it into returnable kit bags for the fortnightly trip to Southern Rhodesia. Their main customers were Africans, concentrated around Salisbury, but eventually their base spread throughout the Federation.[178]

"We're not going to spend a shilling on advertising," Chip told Juul one day as they discussed how to grow the business. "Then how are we going to get people to buy it?" Juul inquired. "We'll put any available money into the quality of the tea and upgrade it," Chip replied. That was the secret. The tea was such good value people could hardly keep their hands off it. The company grew, and as the packeted tea rolled out of the factory, the money began to float in.[179]

Fortunately, for Planters Tea and Agency (PTA), most of their sales were on the Continent, unaffected by the fluctuating prices for tea in London. Tea prices rose and fell at the auctions in England where the brew's reputation remained "a cup that really cheers." A principal import crop for Britain, the mother country still held the apron strings for tea farmers in the Colonies. Following a post-war shortage of tea, and tea rationing in England, which prevailed for 12 years - ending in 1952, tea farmers were experiencing increased prices for their product.[180] However, to protest the upsurges, a "solid wall of British Housewives" boycotted the tea industry who they thought were realizing "record profits" at the housewife's expense.[181] They fought this price increase by using "less tea; the custom of one teaspoonful per person and one for the pot went into suspension."[182] The auctions at Mincing Lane could not uphold the posted price increases, forcing the "already printed price labels" to be returned to storage. This was considered an unusual 'win' against the supply and demand economics. It would not last long, but its effects would be felt in the Federation whose tea drinking population was not large enough to bolster the gap. Several small tea estates sold out to larger Companies, ending proprietary small tea planter holdings in Nyasaland.[183] With increased African consumption of Chip's tea – packeted as Three Leaves Tea, his business - Planters Tea Agency Pty Ltd grew steadily despite the housewife strike.

It grew so steadily that expansion became necessary, and Chip decided to move a branch of PTA to Nyasaland, calling it Planters Tea Agency Nyasaland Limited, mainly to keep him occupied when he wasn't in Southern Rhodesia. Mwalunthunzi Estate now ran smoothly with less input from Chip, and he had to find outlets for the ideas that were jumping around in his head. These ideas involved business growth, not just for PTA but also for Satemwa.

PTA in Nyasaland ran a different kind of business from PTA in Southern Rhodesia. In Nyasaland PTA specialized in non-expiring products, introducing tea troughs into the country through a connection with Monsieur De San from Kivu in the Congo. Because the troughs required fans to run, Chip made a trip to Europe to acquire the parts needed for sale in Nyasaland. He was still a proficient international traveler and had previously returned to England for the Coronation of Queen Elizabeth on June 2, 1953 and a sneaky visit with his old Cornish girlfriend, Anne, their mutual affections unperturbed by their years apart. These early trips marked the beginning of extensive business travel for Chip, and he began to think of ways to reduce his travel cost and time.[184]

Advertisements for Rhodesian Building Societies dotted the newspapers, with more and more societies emerging until there was a total of seventeen in the country. The Building Societies were designed as money safe houses, where you could deposit 10% of your salary and earn interest. The First Rhodesian Permanent Building Society boasted a 3 ½% per annum Savings Account, and a 6% per annum on Investment Shares. The Society was growing rapidly, doubling their assets and membership biannually, reaching 8,571 members and £3,221,803 by 1954. Most of these societies had a rule that a maximum contribution per investor could not exceed 60,000 Rhodesian dollars.[185]

One day as Juul was running over the business details of PTA with Chip, he casually looked up from the paperwork scattered on his desk and reported, "Well, we've got 17 accounts of 60,000 dollars, what are we going to do with this darn stuff?" They both sat down at the desk where Juul had spread out the accounting, and then Juul said, "You know, I know a guy over here who makes fantastic products, but he is a lousy businessman." They both pondered this statement for a few moments, and

Chip added, "And I heard of another chap who lost his business last year, but I don't understand it because he made the best shoes in the Empire." They looked down at the papers of their accounts, brimming with Rhodesian dollars, and with no more opportunities to invest in the already maxed-out Building Societies, the pair decided to become backers for failing businesses with good products.[186]

They structured business partnerships, setting themselves as the primary financiers and 30% owners, 30% for the manufacturer, 10% for the workers, and 30% split between three farmers who were looking for ways to invest but lacked the business mindset. The farmers agreed to each front 10% with no dividends for three years, but when their money inevitably doubled at year 5, PTA's reputation as a sound investment saw farmers lining up to make contributions. Eventually, Chip and Juul ran five very successful companies, essentially as bankers, and the money, that £3,000 from Elladale, thrived, and PTA it seemed could not help but make money out of money.

With the spontaneous excitement of a schoolboy, Chip purchased a Cessna Skylark 175 Airplane given there was enough cash flow for this purpose. He walked around the Skylark and paused under the high wing, looking into the four-seater cabin. He savored the smell of the brand-new plane as he opened the door. He fell in love, not with a woman, but with a plane. It was not the first airplane he had bought, but it was his first new plane, and his passion for flying, born years earlier, was now more fired up than ever.[187]

1954 – The Intoxication of Flying

Des Tennett and Chip Kay with Tiger Moth "Oscar Charlie" circa 1954

Unlike his father who was preoccupied with work from sun-up to sunset, Chip – since he was a little boy – enjoyed pursuing hobbies. Whether it was photography, aero modeling, radio fixing, playing rugby, converting a rusty car into a box body, or simply entertaining his mind with something mechanical, his was constantly occupied. After he returned to Nyasaland in 1950, his work about the estate consumed most of his time, but his vacant attentions turned not towards photography or radios, but towards the opposite sex. Along with at least 8-10 other young men, recently returned from school, Chip waited at the Luchenza Railway Station during school breaks to see who was coming home for the holidays. The young schoolgirls, unaware of 'predators', giggled instantly when they saw the young men at the station. By the weekend, everybody had secured a date, and the Limbe Club Theatre was full of couples who paid more attention to each other than the film on show. Occasionally married couples who had come to view the flick would have to "Shhhh" the young people, who were fervently whispering in the dark.[188]

It was difficult to have a regular girlfriend. For starters, Chip didn't feel like being 'serious' or settling down just yet. He was transiting between Southern Rhodesia and Cholo on such a consistent basis that he felt a steady relationship was simply out of the question. Secondly, he enjoyed being a bachelor, able to float with the wind and take any girl he liked out for a date. "The blonder the better," he joked with his friends, poking fun at his own dating record. His parents encouraged his friendships, but when his mother started questioning him in detail he told her, "It's all very innocent," placating her worries as she seemed to grow more religious every day, frowning on the idea that her son was gallivanting around Nyasaland or Rhodesia with 'just any old girl.'

But it wasn't his mother's religiosity that curtailed his chasing of girls. It was a hobby. A hobby that grew out of the Malborough Flying Club in Southern Rhodesia where John Senior, his school friend from England, dangled a carrot under Chip's nose.[189] John organized for Chip to be a passenger in a De Havilland "Tiger Moth", the biplane commonly used for training by the Royal Air Force during WWII[190], which despite overseas competitors such as the "Cornell" and the "Harvard", "never lost the affection of those who believed in it."[191] From take-off to landing, the Tiger Moth and the skillful maneuvers of the pilot at the helm, captivated Chip and he told John when his two feet were back on solid ground, "That is the closest to heaven anyone could ever get." His entire visage was a picture of happiness, and the smile that the Tiger Moth put on his face that day never quite disappeared.

Aviation history in Nyasaland was relatively undeveloped. A handful of airlines offered services since 1933, when Christowitz Air Service boasted two Puss Moths and one Gypsy Moth in its fleet, and the Nyasaland Aero Club held one Auster. When the main airport switched from BCA Hill in Limbe to the newly cleared Chileka in May 1933, the future for Nyasaland Flying expanded.[192] An amalgamation between Christowitz and a Rhodesian Aviation Syndicate formed RANA (Rhodesian and Nyasaland Aviation) which dominated air service up until the Second World War. Just before the war, RANA closed and gave way to SRAS (Southern Rhodesian Air Services) which operated throughout the war until 1946 when CAA (Central African Airways) was established. There were a few charter companies offering limited services, such as Chileka to Cape Maclear, to meet the flying Solent BOAC during it's operations between 1949-1950. By the time Chip caught the flying bug, aviation in Nyasaland was on the rise.

Opened in 1952, "The Prop and Tail Wheel Restaurant" was Chileka's catering service, with a bar on site, and instructions to serve the general public without partiality to air travelers and crews.[193] It was the chosen location for meetings of flying enthusiasts who rallied together around Captain J.A.C. Florence who on April 2, 1955 successfully started the Nyasaland Flying Club.[194] The club had timed it's opening to coincide with the Rhodesian Air Force Association's (RAFA) jet display over Chileka. The "High Whine" of the four 'Vampires' and one 'Dakota' aircraft impressed an awaiting crowd who swelled behind the barriers to view the high-speed take-offs and formation flying of the RAFA. For a land-locked country, flight provided opportunities not yet realized and individuals who sensed this were eager to join the Flying club and learn how to pilot an aircraft. Club membership was "open to all, with an entrance fee of £5 5s. and a yearly subscription fee of £3 3s." Clearly, there was an interest in flying. The club put forth goals for members to achieve their Private Pilot's License (PPL) and although no aircraft yet belonged to the club, the era of chartered flight in Nyasaland looked promising.

Fifteen miles from Cholo, the town of Luchenza still bustled around the arrivals and departures of the trains. There was a mail-sorting depot where custom's officers viewed arriving packages, and there was a tea warehouse where planters stored chests of tea waiting for export. There was also a parcel of land where an old emergency airstrip lay buried under long grasses. The occasional sapling, allowed to grow into an immature tree haphazardly dotted the old runway.

Close by the old airfield lived the Tennett family who immigrated to Nyasaland in the early 1900's when John Tennett captained the paddle steamboats up the Shire.[195] After six years on the boats, he bought property in Luchenza and began "Tennett & Sons" transport and farming business, growing tobacco and oranges.[196] His sons Basil and Des Tennett, born in Nyasaland, were contemporaries of Chip. Des, also pricked by the flying bug, became a close friend to Chip. He was five years older but just as thin and wiry. His colorings were like Chip with brown hair; Des had blue eyes while Chip's were hazel green, and Des was only a few inches shorter. It was not uncommon for the two men to be confused for the other. But most importantly Des harbored the same burn as Chip, the same restless desire to take his feet off the ground; the longing to fly. Between Chip's first flight in a Tiger Moth just years previous, and Des' first exposure when as a 6 year-old boy he had been 'flipped' in a Gypsy Moth during the celebrations at the Chileka Airport opening in 1933[197], the two men were flying captives. "It's completely intoxicating," Chip remarked to Des one night, "Better than anything I can imagine," to which Des inquired, "Better than anything?" Chip paused, it was a difficult decision given the fact that he had not yet achieved his PPL, but he knew in his heart, "Yes, better than anything."[198]

"We'll clear the old airstrip, build a hangar and a club house, and maybe even a swimming pool?" Chip responded, casting his dreams out as he spoke. "Sunday could be the special club day – after the work week is through on Saturday, we will all want to relax and some of us can fly," Des suggested and then the pair split in laughter, "I guess first we will need a plane, and then somebody will have to learn how to fly it."

Soon, The Nyasaland Flying Club that began at Chileka decided to move it's operations to Luchenza, remaining "The Nyasaland Flying Club" but headed by Chip and Des whose efforts saw preparations for the old airfield achieved for a new generation of flyers.[199]

Planes were rarely advertised in the 'for sale' section of the Nyasaland Times Newspaper, so in the meantime, while 'searching' for their newly formed club's first plane, they got to work on the airfield, clearing the runway and tidying the pitch. Other keen flying fans had joined "The Nyasaland Flying Club" and formed what Des and Chip called the 'debating society' – where all talk and no action transpired, but where the appetite for flying was kept buoyant until a suitable plane could be found.[200]

Before they could entertain buying a plane Des, Chip, and their helpers spent six hard months clearing the runway, grading the surface, laying runway markers and erecting buildings.[201] They constructed a concrete-floored hangar made from blue gum poles and topped with corrugated iron. It was only a single hangar but seemed sufficient in the absence of a plane. They threw up a clubhouse, somewhat hastily, using poles and thatch. It certainly would not compete with the sports clubs for opulence, but it had adequate shelter and space for the 'debating society' to conjecture 'flying'.

Frequent trips between Salisbury and Cholo had certain advantages for Chip. He had communicated to his friend, John Senior, of the Malborough Flying Club in Rhodesia about his desire to purchase a plane. He asked all his friends who were remotely connected to aviation about planes to purchase. When the Tiger Moth plane, VPY-MY "Mike Yanky" went up for sale, Chip was quick to throw down the £35 requested to secure the Moth, which would also be the first plane The Nyasaland Flying Club had access to. He dialed Des from Salisbury, "Des, are you ready for this?" he asked his friend who was at home in Luchenza. "For what Chip?" Des asked. "I just bought a Tiger Moth. Are you ready to learn to fly?" The excitement was palpable as Chip relayed the events of purchasing the Tiger Moth and the two men knew their aeronautical journey was about to begin.[202]

However, "Mike Yanky" sat in Salisbury for months, and every so often Chip would go to visit it and cut the grass that was growing quickly underneath. Even if all he could do now was to look at "Mike Yanky", owning a 'grounded' plane was better than no plane at all. A closer inspection of the Tiger Moth revealed that the canvas wings were rotten and the wooden propeller full of woodborers. It took over a year for "Mike Yanky" to be overhauled in Bulawayo, achieving its certificate of Airworthiness after Des had purchased another Moth from Salisbury. "Oscar Charlie" – another Tiger Moth was the first to arrive in Nyasaland onto a revitalized runway. Chip and Des both thought there was no more beautiful a sight, its wings catching the sunlight and the drone of its engine sending the mongoose families, which had stood on guard just beyond the clearing, back to their burrows.

Now that the club had access to a functioning plane at Luchenza, they needed a qualified instructor. Chip and Des had been, up until this point, flying enthusiasts of the theoretical kind. They had taken and passed their written PPL test. They had bought aero goggles, suits, sheepskin leather lumberjacks and helmets, but their flying paraphernalia had never been used outside of a grown-up game of 'dress ups'. Their coffee tables, bookshelves and bedside stands were overflowing with books about flying. "Flight Without Formulae" by Kermode was a favourite in which the author argued, "I am going to try to explain how an aeroplane flies. This does not mean that I am going to teach you how to fly an aeroplane – that is a very different matter. Many people who can explain how an aeroplane flies cannot fly one. Still more can fly an aeroplane, but do not know how it flies. A few people can do both." The book was a fixture in Chip's hand and read, cover to cover, by the time an instructor for the Nyasaland Flying Club was discovered. All the aeronautical terms covered in Kermode's book were racing through his head, "lift and drag", "Stalling or Burbling", "Rolling, Pitching and Yawing," when Keith Wadhams, the engineer on Mini Mini Tea Estate in Mlanje, and a certified instructor with the RAF Empire Training scheme out of Salisbury agreed to teach Chip and Des how to fly.[204]

Chip woke early as the Chiperoni mist[205] that wafted over the terraces in front of his home alarmed him for the first time in years. He wondered if the weather would cooperate, if the atmospheric electricity that violently shook the skies the day before would reappear, dashing his plans with Keith, and relegating his flying lessons to the following weekend. He anxiously peered out of his bedroom window towards Cholo mountain where the morning sun was beginning to melt the mist. Breakfast was a formality at this point, and he ate his scrambled eggs, bacon and roasted tomatoes with little thought given to its taste or presentation. He was distracted. He went early to the Luchenza Airfield, the promise of clear weather on the horizon giving hope with each passing mile. He arrived first and anxiously waited.

Casually, Keith showed up at the airport. They spent the first hour performing a 'pre-flight inspection', running through the manuals with an orderly check system and getting to know the plane's details. Even if he didn't know how to act the part of a pilot yet, Chip certainly looked like one, clad in a heavy cotton drill jumpsuit, neck scarf tucked under his open collar, and a leather skull cap, with fitted goggles that rested on top of his head. His ears were covered by large headphones with cable leads that hung low on either side. The headphones were fitted with a jack to connect to the control pit in the plane. Without the earphones and microphone, the student would have no way to hear his instructor in the open-aired Tiger Moth.

Keith walked to the back of the plane where he motioned for Chip to join him. "Hoist the tail up, like this," he instructed Chip throwing the end of the Tiger Moth over his shoulder the way a jockey connects with his horse. Chip took the tail and did as he was coached, guiding the Moth into position while Keith evaluated the direction of the wind and the surface of the runway. Keith dragged large rubber 'chocks' over from the edge of the clearing, telling Chip, "You'd have to be bloody stupid to start a Tiger without chocks." From all his 'reading' about flying, Chip agreed, and wedged the chocks under the Tiger's front wheels. Keith leaned into the cockpit of the plane to ensure the flight controls correctly aligned. He primed the engine by rotating the crankshaft four times, setting the switches to contact.[206] On the next swing of the wooden propeller, the engine fired and burst into life, tugging against the chocks, desperate to surge forward.

Standing on the lower wing, Chip lifted his body into the front cockpit and lowered his frame down into the seat, buckling the four-point harness once settled. Keith took the rear cockpit, and tested the microphones, "Reading, One, Two, and Three. Do you copy, Chip?" Even over the roar of the Tiger's sizeable 130hp engine, Chip, listening intently through his earphones heard Keith and responded, "Roger that. Ready for take-off." The ground aircrew removed the chocks and the Moth was ready to taxi.

"We don't have much visibility over the nose," Keith communicated while sitting in a locked position looking straight ahead to Chip who also had no view over the front. "So we have to 'Waltz' the Tiger, Chip and move it from side to side to negate our blind spots and use the width of the runway to our advantage." "Ok Keith," Chip shouted into his receiver. "And you don't want the plane to topple over so you have to keep the taxi speed low," Keith instructed. "Right, low speed, waltz the tiger, don't topple it over," Chip repeated in his head, clutching the control stick between his legs.

As they taxied down the runway, the prop generated a slipstream that gushed over the cowling into the open cockpit pushing Chip's goggles closer to his skin. The tail-dragging Tiger Moth accelerated, jerking along the turf, until with little coercion it gently lifted off into the upward leg of the climb. With the increased pace of the plane, the wind started whooshing into the cockpit and still grasping the controls, although not yet given them, Chip glanced to either side of the open cockpit, away from the glut of blind spots that dogged his view in front. The hangar roof began to disappear, and the railway tracks leading out of Luchenza were unmistakable from the air. The same railway that took Chip and Juliet to school years previously dominated the landscape from the sky. Clear cuts of civilization coursing through a virgin land, a beacon of hope for the land-locked British Protectorate which was isolated from the coast. Change was coming and Chip could sense it. This flight was the beginning of a new era of exploration, possibilities and freedom.

Once they had levelled off in the clear sky above the Luchenza Airfield, Keith talked to Chip through the controls. "Subtle movements Chip, the Tiger can be a touchy," he warned, "Watch the rudder, give it gentle adjustments, or you'll look like you're fish-tailing in the sky." Chip looked around the bulky controls in his cabin, paying attention to the trim wheel positioned below the throttle. "It's a bit fiddly," he remembered Keith saying on the ground, "but adequate once you learn how to use it."

Thirty airborne minutes seemed to flash by and all too soon Chip heard Keith's voice again, "Let's bring her in for a landing." Using a glide approach, which was the only way Moth's could land, Keith told Chip, "We have to watch the angle of attack carefully and stall her just when the wheels touch the blades of grass." Taking back the controls for the landing, Keith glided the Tiger Moth to a perfect halt. The curious troop of Africans fringed around the airfield ululated when they saw the aircraft float 'magically' from the sky. Unable to process the experience instantaneously, Chip dallied in the cockpit, reliving the flight, simulating the way the Moth dove in the air by stretching his arms out and mimicking the drops.

When Chip finally emerged from under the Tiger Moth Keith asked him, "So, what do you reckon Chip? You want to go again next week?" The question didn't need a response as the euphoric look on Chip's face said what words could only back up. "Next week?" Chip asked. "How about next week and every day thereafter for the rest of my life." He patted the cloth wings of the Tiger Moth, steering her back into the hangar. He stayed for a few hours, pottering around the airfield, treasuring the sensations of the open-aired cockpit and the wind that whipped around his face, the sun that dropped its warmth to a chill as the plane entered the doldrums. He sucked deep breaths of air as he turned the key in his Morris Minor, and rolled out of Luchenza headed for home. Aeronautical hormones pumped through his bloodstream and he couldn't shake the feeling of holding the controls in the cockpit, or sensing the aircraft alter its course at his beckoning. He had two feet back on earth but he was completely intoxicated.

Over time, and having successfully completed his Private Pilot's License, Chip began increasing the fleet at The Nyasaland Flying Club, becoming a proponent for anyone who wanted to learn to fly, encouraging all persons who showed the slightest interest. He built an airstrip in 1956 on Satemwa, close enough so he could taxi his plane from the runway to his home. Chip believed the learning process was a constant evolution and that at no point in time would he know all there was to know, especially about flying.[207]

Chip Kay with his tiger moth outside the hangar at the club circa 1960

Chip always had his flying outfit with him, even if he was just driving his trucks to Rhodesia or taking a car into Blantyre. His brown leather lumberjack folded neatly, his helmet with goggles, his jumpsuit underneath the pile, laid beside him on the passenger seat of his car or truck, even if he had no plans to fly.

Early in the flying days before he had obtained his PPL, he drove the Satemwa 7 tonne Leyland truck loaded with tea bound for Rhodesia, with his flying outfit in an organized heap beside him. The roads were still rough in sections; the verges on the Cholo road provided frequent reader contributions in the newspaper columns from disillusioned motorists who had to navigate the gaping holes. Speculation on when the government was going to fix the road only resulted in more columns from angry citizens who seemed eventually to resign themselves to accept the road for what it was, broken and lousy, but nonetheless a track into the city. It didn't bother Chip, as he spent more time on the Cholo to Luchenza road accessing the Flying Club, and when he did set out in his truck on the Cholo-Blantyre road, he was prepared from the outset for a long and arduous journey.

Crossing through Mozambique on his regular route to Salisbury, Chip encountered a spot of trouble. Because he was sitting high in the cab of the Leyland, he was surprised when a rock from the undercarriage of the car in front of him managed to rise into the air and shatter the windscreen, as if it were flung with great force from a more powerful source. Already weakened from years of wear and tear, the windscreen broke like ice under pressure; at first a slow spread of lines from the epicenter of the hit, and then suddenly, the entire glass panel gave way and Chip had to hold it in place while he pulled the truck off the road. Assessing the damage, he realized he was now without a functional windscreen. He pushed the remaining pieces of glass out of the frame and swept the cabin free from the shards which would surely cause discomfort if he failed to remove them properly. He stood on the ground looking up at the Leyland, the missing windscreen glaringly posing a travel problem, and then remembered his flying kit on the passenger seat. "It will be just like being a Tiger Moth," he thought to himself and he pressed the helmet over his head and adjusted the goggles to shield his eyes. As he returned to the road, the wind gushed through the open windscreen and he was pleased to have his lumberjack providing warmth while he drove.[208]

After off-loading the tea with Juul in Salisbury, he went south to check on Oscar Charlie, revamped by Bob Hyles and ready for transport to Nyasaland. He assessed the Moth and the Leyland simultaneously and concluded that the 7 tonne Leyland would suffice to haul the Tiger Moth back to Nyasaland. He prepared the plane, and himself, dressing in full pilot uniform, lumberjack over the top of the jumpsuit, and his leather helmet covering his head except where his chin poked out underneath his goggles. He began slowly, checking his mirrors and flicking his lights to high beam to illuminate the dark night.

Gradually he increased the pace, the twin speed axle of the Leyland smoothly engaging and propelling the truck and plane forward with momentum. Still on a decent road and keenly making good time towards the border, Chip investigated his rearview mirror and noticed lights, flashing lights. "Police," he thought, glancing down at the speedometer for the first time; 57 miles per hour. He knew it was fast and at 57 mph he was speeding. Pretending not to see the flashing lights, Chip kept driving, bobbing up and down with the truck's suspension. It was an unusual sight for the police, who after passing by the Tiger Moth at the rear of the Leyland, drove up beside the cab, only to see a driver clad in helmet and goggles and the wind spouting freely about the cabin. "STOP, Pull over!" they hollered at Chip, who acknowledged their presence for the first time with a guiltless wave and accentuated nod of his helmet. "PULL OVER," the police repeated. Chip smiled and after some time drew the Leyland to the roadside and looked down on the police who had just exited their car.

There were two white Rhodesian police officers who obviously took their job very seriously. "Good evening Officers. What seems to be the problem?" Chip asked immediately, ignoring his own conspicuousness as he placed his goggles on top of his helmet. The officer, startled by Chip's outfit, and now not sure himself if he had pulled Chip over for speeding or a broken windshield and subsequently indecent motoring attire, asserted, "Speeding. You were doing 57 miles per hour." "57!" Chip exclaimed, sounding very surprised. "You should tell Mr Leyland about that. I think he'd be very impressed that a 7 tonne truck like this could reach those speeds. Are you sure about 57?" He looked at the Officers who were trying not to fume at his remarks. But he was in luck when one of the men lost interest in their speeding accusation and seemed more amused by the plane on the back of the Leyland. "You fly?" he asked, reaching out to touch the wing of the Moth. "Theoretically, yes," Chip stated, ready to change the subject from speeding to planes.[209]

A while later, having not issued a speeding ticket, the officers parted ways with Chip, telling him, "Keep the speed down, and carry on." Chip thanked them for the warning, pulled the goggles down over his eyes and drove onwards to Salisbury.

It was the first Tiger Moth he had towed behind his Leyland, but not the last. John Senior and Chip used to visit the Royal Rhodesian Airforce RRAF base and gawk at the Tiger Moths sitting, unused in the hangars. "I want to buy one of those machines," Chip told the RRAF commander one day, looking at the armada of Moths as they 'rotted' in the hangar. "You can't. They're lease-lend aircrafts not for sale," the commander replied. "Well, what would happen if one went missing at night?" Chip asked to test the waters. The commander, who liked Chip and John, pretended he didn't hear the question, but muttered as he turned away, "It could be a risky thing to do.... if you got caught."

One night, with nothing to lose, and loose 'permission' granted, Chip and John took one of the RRAF planes, "saving her from a life of boredom." John had said, "No plane was built to be grounded."

They disassembled the fan from the nose and towed the plane on the back of Chip's Leyland truck by its wheels, the nose dangerously close to the tarmac because the tray of the Leyland where the tail of the plane was roped was so high. It seemed the Leyland was built for speed, and gathered it quickly, too quickly, turning a corner like a race car, sending the roped Moth at the rear onto her side. Hearing the scrape on the road as the Tiger Moth flipped, Chip and John stopped the truck and ran to the back to check the damage. Douglas Cabidoula, one of the Satemwa drivers, brought along to take shifts, followed Chip and John to view the plane. Moments later, lights appeared, and wishing it would be any other car in

Africa didn't change the fact that the British South Africa Police (BSAP) had found them moments after the crash. "What's going on here?" the BSAP officer inquired, surveying the demised Tiger Moth and the Leyland at once. A small drove of villagers had emerged from the darkness and pressed around the commotion. The BSAP's wondering what to ticket Chip for soon found themselves, along with the villagers and Chip, John and Douglas, hoisting the plane back onto her wheels and assisting Chip in roping the tail more securely to the truck tray. "I think you ought to take it slower," one BSAP suggested, leaving the scene unaware that the RRAF were missing a plane, and oblivious to the fact that it was quite literally just 'under their nose.'[210]

Chasing Crocodiles 1955-1957

Juliet Cathcart Kay circa 1957

Once, when Chip was a teenager enduring the cold winters in England, he told his sister Juliet, "We should never leave Africa, you and I. We weren't made for this kind of weather." She crossed her arms over her tweed coat that held all her body heat inside and replied in a bluster, "Well, stay in Africa if you must. But for me, Africa is just too small."

There wasn't much Chip could do to convince her otherwise, and apart from the occasional trip back to Nyasaland to visit the family, Juliet, after school, was caught up in Spain, modeling in Madrid. Her strawberry blonde hair sat perfectly out of a curler, or bobbed under her chiseled chin, or tied back with a ribbon. Her skin, soft and creamy, with perfect tone could carry off a variety of color pairings. She wore the modern corset, shaving an inch off her already thin waistline. However, her vivid emerald eyes charmed not just the judges, but also the suitors who vied for her attentions. She received gloating reports from the agencies, touting her as "dazzling" and "glamorous", and her talent combined with her penchant for fashion propelled her career forward.

In between high school and modeling, Juliet completed a year in Switzerland at one of their leading 'finishing schools' for young women. Distinctively polished and prepared for entry into society, she graduated with 'upper class' ladies, to a world on the edge of shifting conceptions regarding a woman's role in society. This never bothered her, as her own mother defied the 'role of a woman' and was never caught 'waiting on a man.' The Cathcart Kay's believed in a woman's right to be independent, but they also believed 'ladies should be proper', and that 'manners make a man.'[212]

Juliet in her early twenties - like her mother when she arrived at 18 to Nyasaland - was young, wild and independent. She never lost her childish sense of adventure and she was enthralled with travel. Like her brother, she could go by train, boat, or plane and be perfectly comfortable in new environments. She was a third culture child who had grown into a global lady.

She didn't like to admit it, but despite the opportunities at her fingertips and the affections of a debonair dark-haired Spanish man, she missed her family, and she missed Africa.

One day, Maclean declared, "Chip, I need a girl." Wondering for a moment what his father meant by this, and realizing he was not ready for 'man talk' with his dad, Chip balked, "You need a what?" "Oh! Not for me, silly. For Juliet." Relieved, and embarrassed at the same time Chip responded, "Oh, right, for Juliet." "Well, you have a lot of girls in your Mwalunthunzi division and I just thought you could sort out a ladies maid for Juliet – someone to help her around the house, with her clothes and shoes, and to sort of be a companion if necessary. She'll be here in a week, and she could use some assistance." Maclean put his worn-out farmers hat back on his head and waited for Chip's agreement before leaving.

Below his house, along the road where the estate trucks had gashed ruts into the edges after the last rains had fallen too fast and too heavy, Chip found the sailcloth awning where the Mwalunthunzi estate tea pluckers gathered underneath. The 'sail' flapped in the morning breeze and provided tea workers reprieve from the intensifying heat. Copious leaves of tea were flitting around the rims of the pluckers' baskets and drifting to the ground where they sprinkled the otherwise red-brown earth with patches of green. It was tea break, and some workers perched on roadside rocks, leaning against the sharp cut earth where the tea roots stopped the soil from eroding. Others were lying on the ground, covered by the shade of the large Cassia whose yellow flowers were peeking out in tiny buds before the ample bloom that would surely burst within days. The division manager, seeing Chip approaching, stood to attention, heaving his shoulders forward in the process, while his straight arms, curved slightly at the elbow, were flung in front of his body. His hands were rounded as if they were holding onto a bicycle bar. The 'Satemwa' bicycle salute carried on in the same fashion whether the person was sitting on a bicycle or not. Sometimes Chip imagined a bicycle under the frame of the person performing the formality and wondered if they had actually ever ridden one. Either way, he responded to the manager and told him, "I'm looking for Ruth."

"Ndi Bwana Chippy, Ine ndi Ruthie," came a shy voice from behind the cluster of women under the shade. They knew each other from interactions around the estate and Chip had thought first of her when his father had mentioned a 'ladies' maid' for Juliet. "Ndi ku funa mtsikana," (I need a girl) he told Ruth, making the same mistake as his father evidenced by her reddening cheeks. "Not for me," he promised her, "but for my sister, Juliet; she's coming from England and will need some help."

****

Despite the innocent request for 'a girl' to be a ladies maid for Juliet, the carnal undertone stemmed from colonial reputations for "White Mischief", primarily involving the 'Swingers' of 'Happy Valley' in Kenya and the ensuing question, "Are you married or are you from Kenya?" Lady Myra Idina Sackville, a resident of 'Happy Valley' was known to greet her guests while lying in her green onyx bathtub, dress in front of them, and then proceed to partner them off with feather- blowing, dice-rolling games.[212] However, following the patterns of settler's attitudes from Kenya, Nyasaland was not exempt from moments of organized immorality. A white planter lived in the Shire Highlands and was known for his promiscuity among the Africans. The years proved his fertility and his wanderings, as little colored children, resembling their father, popped up all over the district. On a wider scale, "Top Hat Wyson" was Cholo's version of Kenya's 'White Mischief', where occasionally, settlers would gather for a wife-swapping meet. One of the senior planters walked into the bar at a certain time of night and called out, "Wyson – TOP HAT!" prompting the barman, Wyson, to produce the designated top hat and place it on the wooden counter at the bar. Each man threw his car keys into the hat, and Wyson proceeded to shake the hat and mix the keys. One by one, the men picked out a set of keys and went to find the wife associated with the pick, coyly waiting by her vehicle in the car park. It was part of life in the colonies and settlers cared little of international attentions surrounding their indiscretions.[213]

****

Hesitant to take the promotion for domestic work, Ruth flung up some resistance, but Chip was quick to overt any concerns and soon Ruth was on her way to 'The Satemwa House' to prepare for Juliet's arrival. Minutes before the hum of the Hudson Straight 8 swelled around the lush garden, the staff at the house formed a line on the cobbled pathway to the side of the main steps, dusted their sleeves and straightened their collars, preparing to welcome Juliet home. There was the cook, with his puffy hat askew on his head, the house boys in their black and white livery, mustering up a solemn expression, the garden boys who felt under dressed next to the house staff, and at the end of the line stood Ruth, a little anxious, nervy and excited all at once. She hoped the new Madam would speak Chi'Nyanja as well as her brother because although she knew a few words in English, those few words never sounded right, and she felt foolish every time she tried to speak the foreign tongue.

The car engine gurgled to a halt, and the heavy metal doors of the Hudson creaked when opened. The line of house staff tensed, and Ruth watched down the line for cues as to how she should behave. She stood straighter and held her head equally as high as the garden boy next to her. They were all looking off into the distance at some obscure point, as if it might be rude to stare at the family as they exited the car. Maclean in his single-breasted woolen suit, perspiring under the heat, held his jacket with one finger over his shoulder and shook the hands of the staff in a row. Steps behind him and dressed in the magnificence of European fashion, Juliet whisked along the line of staff, fervently taking the hands of the house workers and telling them in eloquent English, "I'm happy to be home." Her cheeks dusted in warm peach powder, and clear pink lipstick gave her lips added plump. The bold floral print on her circular cotton skirt matched her lipstick and Ruth found herself mesmerized by the fullness of the skirt - how it bounced even on the gentlest movement. A tidy white collared blouse, tapered into Juliet's waist, tucked tightly behind the skirt, and held in place by a matching pink belt. Methodically Ruth's eyes fell away from the new Madam's clothes and fixated on her shoes. She had never seen a pair like it. A strap of leather across the facade of the mule held the foot in place, and her toes peeked out of the hole in the front, pink toes that Ruth squinted to view. The shoes made a strange clacking sound as Juliet walked and Ruth figured it must be owing to the 'spike' that was fitted at the back of the heel.

Some distance behind the procession, Chip realized that Juliet was about to meet Ruth. He shuffled past the lineup murmuring, "Maswela, maswela?" (how is the afternoon) under his breath not wanting to appear discourteous, but clearly distracted as he made a beeline towards Juliet. "Juliet! This is the girl I was telling you about. This is Ruthie." Chip looked at his sister and then changed position to stand nearer to Ruth. Sensing she was nervous he switched to Chi'Nyanja and introduced the two ladies to one another. It was a little awkward at first, especially when Chip realized Juliet's remembrance of the vernacular was limited, then feeling like a third wheel, he left the two women to get acquainted.

Juliet looked at Ruth, wondering why her brother had chosen this woman to be her maid. Ruth was very basic. She wore an old cotton housemaid dress, the kind that made Juliet think of crimes against fashion, a pair of old slippers on her feet and her head was covered in short clusters of curly hair, which on the upside, made her smooth black skin and voluptuous lips stand out. "Come," Juliet motioned to Ruth, who hobbled behind her like a lost puppy. "Ndi, Madam," Ruth responded following Juliet into the nursery room, through the French doors and down the hall, to the very last room on the left wing of the house. Juliet began to unpack her cases and took Ruth beside her, teaching her, "SUITS - these two pieces, they go together, and you hang them over here." Juliet took her jersey brocade olive green skirt and jacket and showed Ruth how to pair it on a coat hanger. "Dresses, the fancy ones go here and the casual ones over here." She began separating the dresses by fabric and style, the glittery evening dresses, full bodied and swanky and the casual town dress, slender and fitted. Standing beside the suitcase that Juliet had abandoned to organize the hangers, Ruth reached in and picked up a small, odd shaped piece of clothing. She held it up and viewed it curiously. "CORSET," Juliet told her, realizing it might need further explanation, "Like underwear, but it sucks you in, like this." Juliet imbibed air dramatically into her lungs and as she did, her chest protruded, and her waist drew smaller. "Voila! The effect of a corset," she stated to Ruth, who was looking on with an expression Juliet thought could be either wonder or horror.

"Well, I guess you don't have to worry about such things in Africa, " Juliet asserted, closing the tin trunk and transferring it to the closet. "And, these Madam?" Ruth was pointing to the case of shoes on the floor. "This, what is it?" Ruth asked, holding up a pair of shoes, similar to the ones Juliet had been wearing at the front of the house. "Oh, high heels, Ruth. Very important but very impractical."

Within a few days Juliet's Chi'Nyanja had improved and she was able to communicate better with Ruth. They did mostly everything together. If Juliet wanted to walk about the estate, Ruth accompanied her. If Juliet wanted to go to town for shopping or a lunch date, Ruth came along. When Juliet needed a companion to read besides, Ruth sat with her. They spent so much time together that Ruth's curiosity at the new Madam's habits peaked. She had watched her paint her nails several times and helped her remove the old polish when it chipped, but she wondered why a person would want to do such a thing. So, one day she asked Juliet, "Why paint?" and Juliet said matter-of-factly, "It's wokongola Ruthy, don't you think?" "Ndi, Madam," Ruth replied, holding a pink polish up with a girlish grin. "Good choice, Ruth. Dior says, 'Pink is for glamor'.

Now, can we paint your nails today?" The two women created their own spa in the bathroom at 'The Satemwa House' and an hour later Ruth emerged with the same pink toes as Juliet had on the day she met her.[214]

"One more thing," Juliet told Ruth, racing to her bedroom and reappearing moments later. She was clutching a pair of black leather pumps with a tidy bow on the ankle and a narrow stiletto heel. "For you, Ruthy," Juliet said, passing the shoes to Ruth who tried them on instantly. They fit well, but sure looked out of place with her cotton maid's uniform. "And, a dress to go with it," she added, smiling wide as she slung a silk garden party dress into Ruth's arms. "Oh Madam!" Ruth exclaimed, eyeing the turquoise dress with admiration. "Zikomo, kwam biri!!" She bent her head with a half curtsy, brushing the dress against her cheek and enjoying the soft, silky fabric.

Months passed and Juliet grew restless. The calm and quiet of Satemwa, the flowing Nswadzi, the hum of the tea factory in the otherwise silent night sky, the picnics with her family at their special place with a view on the side of Cholo mountain, the town trips to see the same people, began to bore her. "I'm going to Rhodesia," she told Chip over dinner at his house. "I've got a job," she added, hoping to smooth the disappointed look on her brother's face. "An architecture firm has hired me because I have a 'good eye'." Chip took in the information, unsurprised by it. He understood her, and felt compelled to support her decision to move. "Good for you, Julie, I think that firm will be lucky to have you," he told her, getting up to go sit near her and put his arm around her shoulder. "I'll miss you. But I'll come see you, when I drive or fly to Rhodesia," he said, winking about the 'flying' comment, remembering his conversation with his sister when he introduced her to the flying club at Luchenza and their Tiger Moths.

They parted, and Juliet left the following week for Salisbury, a city where growth was evident by upscale hotels, new buildings on almost every block, money spilling into the center from the successful tobacco farms in the country, and a variety of entertainment options for the whole family. A compromise between the verdant, edgy life in Spain, and the quiet, work-centered estate in Cholo, Salisbury was a happy medium for Juliet and she enjoyed her work supporting an architecture firm in the heart of the city. As promised, Chip visited her when he made business trips to Southern Rhodesia, taking her along to the Mashonaland Flying Club at Mount Hamton whenever possible, hoping she could enjoy this new Flying community too. Chip introduced his old school friend, John Senior, to his sister one day, recognizing a little spark flew when Juliet and he shook hands. "Pleased to meet you John, I've heard so much…," Juliet began but Chip interrupted, "Well, you'll both have time to get to know each other, but I'm leaving tomorrow, so I'm taking Juliet out to dinner, see you later John," he said, ushering Juliet out of the club and into his car.

"Chippy! That was a bit rude," his sister replied. "Ah! Not trying to be rude, Julie – just not sure how I feel about you and my friend…," he replied, starting the engine. "Chip, we just met – we're not…" She was cut off again, "I know, I know…but…how about Meikles?" He changed the subject and that was the last they spoke of John Senior until the following visit when Juliet and John appeared together at the club, obviously 'going steady'. Shy from their last conversation about John, Juliet declared, "It's nothing serious Chippy."

Chip wasn't sure how he felt about his sister dating John. He was a decent man, and a fellow flyer, so Chip decided to be ok with the romance. John was flying to Luchenza every week on business, and Chip, Des, and The Nyasaland Flying Club had a chance to get to know him better. They could talk about any subject with John, but when the men bordered on female reveries, Chip wanted to stuff little cotton balls in his ears in case he overheard things about his sister, things which he did not want to imagine.

On February 7, 1957, the flying club gathered for a regular meeting at the clubhouse, and one member, recently returned from Salisbury, stirred, "Did you hear that John Senior failed the renewal of his Private Pilot's License?" Chip looked up from the scribbles on his notepad, "Failed? Why?" he asked. "Medicals," the member replied, "John got Type 1 Diabetes and they won't let him fly anymore…" There was a hushed sound through the club and the news breaker asserted, "But we all know he's still flying – and now that we know about his condition, we can't allow him to fly here anymore, or we'd also be breaking some law." He looked directly at Chip, "You're his friend, you need to tell him." It was going to be awkward, given his friendship with John and his sister's attachment to the man, but Chip agreed he was best suited to deliver the club's decision. "I'll do it on Sunday, I'm going there already for business," Chip told the club and they promptly moved on to the next item up for discussion.[215]

Friday, February 8, 1957 John rang Juliet, "I want to take you out today. This afternoon, after work. I'll pick you up?" Sundowners at the end of a workweek had quickly become one of her favorite things to do with John, and she hoped he had plans to go flying before sunset. "Will we go up in the plane today?" she asked. "I think we should, let's go chase some crocodiles…," John laughed thinking of the fun, referring to the route he often flew along the Umfuli river where he could swing the plane so low beside the banks that they could watch the hippopotamus flicking its ears and spinning its tail to break the surface of the water. They might also see little ox-peckers on the hippopotamus' back picking off the blood sucking ticks who didn't know whether to cling tighter to the skin of the hippo or risk flight when the plane swooped overhead. As the aircraft dipped down, the noise from the engine often sent the crocodiles from the rocks, where they were lazily sunning themselves, into the water with a mighty splash, visible momentarily and then lost beneath the murky water.

The afternoon rainstorm fell methodically soft, and lasted long enough to quench the thirsting earth before giving way to the sun and a few scattered clouds. The rain had cooled off the humid morning air, and by the closing of work, the temperature outside was tepid and soothing to the naked skin. "Let's take my car," Juliet said when John arrived to pick her up. He didn't mind, after all the MG Magnette was not only fun to drive, it was a stunning feat of automobile style and function. The silver grill that dominated the bonnet gave the car class and John felt a little like an MI6 agent when he drove it. They parked the car at Mount Hamton Airfield, and John, avoiding other pilots who knew he shouldn't fly, pushed his Luscombe Silvaire out of the hangar and onto the runway. The evening sun was warm, and the air was cooling as they soared into the sky, over the clubhouse, climbing upwards until the huge trunks of the baobabs looked like little tiny blotches on the ground.

There in the distance the Umfuli river ran through the landscape, and the waters gleamed in the sunlight… "Let's go chase those crocodiles," said John as he steadied the plane, preparing to decrease his altitude. He had flown this route so many times, and he was aware that the lower and slower he flew, the more dangerous the flight became because low speed meant that the aeroplane was flying near the stalling angle. He felt for aileron drag and held the wheel tighter, sensing the yawing effect and correcting the rudder to maintain control. They followed the river, mirroring the winding bends, over the sandy beaches where the crocodiles fled, enjoying the ripples they cast when they broke from the bank into the water. Rounding a sharp curve in the river and pulling up slightly over some granite rocks in the center, the shadows that fell from the trees along the banks diminished and the full afternoon sun suddenly leered into the cockpit. Juliet held her hand over her brow, straining to see, and John, squinting hard, was blinded by it.[216]

In Nyasaland, the Friday newspaper lay wrinkled on the desk at 'The Satemwa House'. Maclean had dog-eared page 4, wondering what Juliet would say about Elizabeth Saunders' latest article on the "newest beach coat…styled like an extra-long battle blouse." He was amused by her opinions about fashion, even if he felt completely outdone by the subject.[217]

It was 6:00am on Saturday the 9th of February when the telephone rang at Chip's house. John Senior's brother-in-law was calling from Rhodesia. "Chip, I'm afraid to say, there's been some bad news. John was killed last night in a plane crash…," he paused, unsure how to continue, "And Chip, your sister was with him…" Chip was holding onto the receiver, standing by the console where the telephone resided. The strength in his body drained out, the way water does when a plug is removed from the bath. He crumpled to the concrete floor, still with the receiver pressed to his ear, but not having spoken a word. Disbelief. He listened with mute sadness to the details of the crash, how in the end, there was nothing left of his sister except a sapphire stone, a stone from the gold ring she wore every day, a gift from her father, who thought a 'jewel' for his 'Jewel' was appropriate. The metal had melted, along with everything else, when the plane combusted instantly upon collision with a powerline. Both their bodies were incinerated, and a lump of aluminum, once a flying machine, plopped down onto the sand in a tangled heap. The MG Magnette, parked at the airfield, was waiting for people who never returned.

Chip put the receiver back in place. He had to go now and tell his father. "God, it's going to break him," Chip thought as he kicked his motorbike into gear, and pushed through the morning fog choking the air with a mist so dense, it slowed his motorbike to near walking speed. Along the road to his childhood home, thoughts ran violently through his head. "Was it his fault she died? What if he had called John and told him to quit flying on Thursday night? What if he had called Juliet and told her she was not to fly with John? What if they had waited half an hour more and the sun was less bright?… What if they didn't go foolishly chasing crocodiles? What if she had stayed in Spain with her Spanish man friend?….What if?…"

Chip found his father already dressed for his morning estate rounds, a fresh pot of tea sitting beside him on the small table by his padded sofa. "You mustn't blame yourself," Maclean said, upon hearing the news and sensing Chip's internal struggle. "It's bad enough that Juliet is… gone…" It was the first time he said those words and as he did, he broke down, weeping uncontrollably. His body shook as he tried to breathe between sobs. Heavy tears streamed down his cheeks and dripped off his clothes onto the stamped concrete tiles underfoot. His little girl, "Wee wig", "Jewel", whom he and Jean had protected through childhood, was now dead. His beautiful daughter who caught the eye of every man and the envy of every women was lifeless. It was too much, and if the death of his first baby, Alexander, twenty-six years earlier, had not broken him completely, the news of Juliet's crash did. His countenance shifted, as if a light went out, and there was no switch on the wall to turn it back on.[218]

Jean had gone south to Cape Town just weeks earlier, a trip she often made and one that the pair of them had compromised on, Maclean realizing that everyone needed a break from Nyasaland every so often. "Dad, I have to go," Chip touched his father's drooping shoulder. "Mum doesn't know yet and I should be the one to tell her." Maclean looked up at his son, through swollen eyes and a heaving chest and agreed, "Yes, you should go."

Chip rushed to get a flight organized and departed Chileka that same morning at 10am, passing through Salisbury, Johannesburg and Bloemfontein, where he was so ill, they had to lay him out on the grass near the control tower and wait for his color to return. The combination of air sickness and grief had culminated and hit him like the swift onset of malaria, and he didn't know whether to throw up, cry or do both simultaneously.

The night was falling by the time he arrived into Cape Town, and he found his mother at her Fairmead Court apartment. "Chip! What are you doing here?" She sounded bewildered. "You should have called me, so I could have everything ready for you, a ride from the airport to begin with!" Green from travel, pale with angst, Chip did not look well when his mother ushered him inside and sat beside him on the sofa. "What is it Chip, what's the matter?" she asked, sensing something was terribly awry. He just had to say it. He had to tell her right away. "Mother, Juliet was killed last night in a plane crash in Rhodesia." He hated the news he brought and there was nothing he could do to ease the pain in his mother's eyes or in his own heart. He explained about the crash, the powerlines, and instant burning. A lifetime of sorrow was delivered in a few short sentences.[219]

Jean's cook appeared in the doorway, "Good evening Mrs Kay, is everything alright?" He spoke with an American drawl, which caught Chip off guard. He could see they had been crying, and offered, "I'm going to go and make some tea for you. I'll bring some soup as well."[220]

Both Chip and his mother were lost for words. What could there be left to say anyway? Jean, a mother of three, outliving two of her children, and Chip, a brother twice over, now without a sibling.

The Sunday Mail - The Rhodesian National Newspaper – ran headlines on February 10, 1957, "Two Rhodesians killed in Air Crash – Light Plane Strikes High-Tension Wires," a crash witnessed by a local farmer, Mr Geoffrey Courtney, who "swam across the crocodile infested Umfuli River to try to administer aid." But when he arrived on the scene, he surmised that both passenger and pilot had "died instantly."[221]

On February 15, 1957, the newspaper in Nyasaland ran a notice of DEATH:

"KAY – in a flying accident on February 8th. Juliet Anne Cathcart, only daughter of Mr and Mrs Maclean Kay of Cholo. Aged 22 years."[222]

A week and one day after the crash, the Kay family stood in the cemetery at the Cholo All Saints Church. It was a private ceremony reserved for the family. There were three of them now: Maclean, dressed in his best dark umber tan suit, shoes buffered into a sheen; Jean, in her deep ebony dress, slender fitting, black gloves covering her hands, and a streamlined ascot that allowed pieces of her hair to poke out underneath; and Chip, in his khaki pants, sports coat over his cotton shirt and a brown leather belt that could hold up his pants but not his spirit. Juliet's plot was in the first row just inside the wrought iron gate, and nestled against a cobblestone wall, where the white paint of the quaint English style church glistened in the background. She was alone in the row, with multiple empty plots on either side of her grave, plots reserved by the Kay's in the unfortunate but likely event that more of them would follow.

The Rhodesian National Newspaper The Sunday Mail clipping February 10,

Kangaroo Kay 1955-1957

Chip and his Tiger Moth circa 1957

It was a typical Sunday at The Nyasaland Flying Club: the hum of planes roaring down the runway, and the chatter of children playing on the lawn by the clubhouse watching the planes ascend into the clear blue sky. Pilots from Cholo, Luchenza, Makwasa and Blantyre were all eager to soar. Standing aloof by the hangar of Mike Yanky, Chip scuffed his feet into the dirt and stared blankly, without blinking for seconds, out over the runway towards the immense Mlanje Massif. He was lost, not just in thought, but in grief. How could he fly again and not think of Juliet's last moments? He retreated around the wings towards the back of the hangar where the light was low and dim matching his mood. "Hey, Chip," called Des, who had seen his friend moping in the distance and knew about his family's recent loss. "I know it's hard, but what would you do if a horse bucked you off?" Des was desperate to cheer Chip and get him back in the air. "I don't ride horses, Des….," Chip said gloomily, glancing up at Des and catching the sympathy in Des' eyes. "But if I did…I guess I'd have to get right back on." "Ok then, you better suit up and make this baby purr," Des suggested and helped Chip drag the Moth out of the hangar by its tail.

"I'm riding with you, but you're going to fly it," Des told Chip as he took the copilot cockpit in Mike Yanky. Chip was quietly processing his fear about Juliet and his desire to fly despite her death. He waltzed the Tiger Moth down the runway, Des in his ear offering encouragement, and lifted the plane into the sky. He shook off the nervous energy that had accumulated during his mental struggle on the ground and let the wind blanket his face while he wheeled upwards. Des was right. He felt much better now that he had got back into the cockpit, now that he had been up in the same sky where Juliet breathed her last breath. He did think of her, maybe even more than he had imagined, but it didn't discourage him from flying. In fact it recharged his passion. He muttered into the radio to Des, "Safety first, Des, we should always make sure we are safe pilots." Des knew he was still thinking about the crash but concurred as if it was just a passing remark, "We'll be the safest, best bush pilots in Africa. Now, let's take Mike Yanky down for a landing and Chip – don't bring 'Kangaroo Kay' to the runway, ok?" Chip huffed into the radio and told Des, "'Kangaroo Kay' is why I can now land a Moth on any runway in Africa." The radios were now off but the two men were chortling in the open-aired cockpits thinking about how much they had improved in their skills as pilots.[223]

The two friends had obtained their Private Pilot's License two years earlier, and the hobby that had started small, both in assets and time, had grown. The comradery that centered around the flying club and the fraternity of pilots was palpable and good-natured jeers and jabs gave life to the community of aviators.

One day, a member of the flying club had presented Chip with a cartoon drawing. There was a runway and dust clouds from a recently landed Tiger Moth across the tarmac. Two rabbits sat on the edge of the field watching the landing with a caption that read, "They call him KANGAROO KAY." In reality it was difficult to land a Tiger Moth, and the first few attempts that Chip made he unwittingly entertained the bystanders when the Moth clipped the ground without enough drag, and with too much speed, sending it back to the air momentarily and repeating the process, up and down, until it rested at the runway's end. Onlookers thought his plane imitated the hopping of a kangaroo, and because it was so catchy, it stuck. Chip didn't mind the good-natured fun and decided to frame the cartoon and hang it in the hallway in his house, just outside his master bedroom. Besides, whenever he walked past "Kangaroo Kay" on the wall, he thought not only of his tongue-in-cheek flying mates, but also about the importance of safety in the sky. "For Juliet," he told himself, whenever he resisted the urge to attempt barrel rolls and flips. But he also knew he had a predilection for safety because his parents, after all they had been through, could not survive the loss of another child.

The ground was approaching quickly, and Chip maneuvered Mike Yanky to align with the runway markers on the pitch. Nerves intact and returned confidence at his fingertips, he glided smoothly to a halt on the Luchenza runway. The anxious pre-flight now washed away, and Des, grinning widely from the support cockpit, knew he had just helped his friend 'back on the horse.' "Nicely done, Chip," he beamed, winking, "especially for Kangaroo Kay." Chip shot a look at Des, accepting his chiding because he was grateful Des cared enough to egg him on to his old self. Chip was back in the air, and he was more safety conscious than ever.

However, both he and Des were about to learn that the aeronautical rules protecting them from danger were vastly different from pilot to pilot, and just two months after Juliet's fatal accident in Southern Rhodesia, Chip and Des would experience a crash of their own.

Des Tennett and Chip Kay beside Tiger Moth "Mike Yanky" circa 1957

Red lipstick and the largest Kasamba tree in Africa, April 1957

Chip (right) and friend at the flying club bar circa 1957

News of The Nyasaland Flying Club had spread throughout Nyasaland more effectively than any bush telegraph. Often unknown planes and pilots requested landings on the Luchenza runway, simply because the occupants had heard of the growing club and had in due course come to check it out for themselves. The club was known for its Sundays when wives and girlfriends gathered with their ice-cold gin and tonics at the clubhouse. The little thatched cabanas where the children sought shade while they watched as instructors and students milled around the hangars, and eventually propelled the planes into the sky presented a commanding sight.

One day, a four-seater Cessna 170 dropped out of the sky.[224] Two impressionable young girls and two men desperate to make an impression climbed out of the plane at the end of the runway. The regulars at the Flying Club stood breathless for a moment, analyzing the newcomers and pondering who they were. "Luke Versaghi," said the pilot, offering his hand to Chip for a shake. "Chip Kay, and this is Des Tennett." Formalities aside, Luke asked, "Anyone want to go for a flip – a flight?" Chip and Des had been whispering between themselves as the Cessna had descended, "Looks like the Club Makokola plane, and their pilot, somebody Versaghi…" "Yes, I heard he's quite experienced." "I thought he was getting married next week in Rhodesia, what's he doing here?" "I hope we can go for a flight with him."

Therefore, when Luke offered a 'flip', the pair didn't have to discuss the matter; they both, along with Andy Gray - who worked for

South African Mutual Insurance and was visiting the club -jumped at the proposition. "We'll go," they all said in unison walking enthusiastically to the Cessna. "Here, take my car, go see Likabula Falls in Mlanje," Chip told the one male and two female passengers who now had no seat on the plane. Luke exuded an arrogance about flying as he sauntered to the Cessna, talking the whole way about his accomplishments as a pilot. Chip and Des didn't really care if he wanted to toot his own horn. They were happy to get more flying time with an experienced pilot.[225]

Being in a Cessna was vastly different from a Tiger Moth. For starters, the closed-in cabin was quieter, and four people could sit within arms distance from each other. The visibility over the Cessna's nose was higher, and the power and cruising altitudes increased. Luke wanted a tour of the area surrounding the club, so Chip and Des directed him over the estates. The tea fields looked like great green carpets, interrupted only by virgin forests and blue gum clusters, and of course the harsh separation of agriculture by railway and road lines. Des pointed out his family's farm, where orange tree orchards looked like polka dots and the tobacco, already harvested, left the earth red and ripped. "There's some of our trucks," Des told Luke, pointing to the few lorries in the yard at his father's house. "And look, over there, that's the way to Likabula." "Well, let's go see if my friends have made it to the mountain, hey?" Luke suggested, adding, "We can try to decipher the color of the girl's lipstick from the sky." It seemed like a good idea, at least it added some excitement to the male-dominated plane. "How do I find Likabula?" Luke asked, steering the plane in the general direction of the Massif, but with no clue which end to aim for. "Take it left, and then you'll see to the right of Chambe peak a stream running down the mountain, north-south, and a whole lot of bloody big rocks," Chip told him, motioning as he spoke.[226]

Finding the dirt track that ducked off the main Luchenza to Mlanje road, Luke followed it until he saw the stream, the rocks and Likabula pools, confirmed by Chip's car parked in the clearing. "I see them," he shouted, turning the wings as he yelled. The girls were both in bikinis, sunning themselves on the flat rocks that edged the Likabula pools, and the man was in the water, scooping with his arms like a frog as he swam from side to side. With the turn of the wings, the cabin shifted, and all the men looked over their right shoulder, gaining a view of Luke's three friends, and each straining to see the color of the girl's lipstick. "It's RED!" Chip declared, proud of his hawk-like eyesight. "Clearly, RED, now I think we can go home." "Ok, let's make a few passes, and then we can go, ok?" Luke suggested, levelling off the plane, diving low into a beat up and running the Cessna up the mountain at full speed. He banked hard and brought the plane down turning it again at the base of Likabula and gearing up for a second pass. Des looked at Chip, "He's mad! The fan is too tired to fly up the mountain." Then he turned to Luke, "We ought to go home." But his words fell on deaf ears, and Luke, already determined, flew the Cessna back up the mountain, the propeller laboring as he urged the machine forward.

Beside the rock pools and footpaths that zig-zagged across the streams, the monolith was covered in trees, creepers, and sharp grasses under the canopy. There were Mbawas standing like watchmen, Flame trees scattering scarlet petals, scraggly Acacias flattening the ceiling, and the native Mlanje Cedar whose recent boost in popularity was owing to the Nyasaland Plywood Company who marketed the wood by telling buyers, "No permits of any description are required," and "REMEMBER IT'S ANT PROOF."[227]

Plunging above the jungle foliage, a Kasamba tree reached upwards, with strong limbs and thick knots of leafy clusters teeming from the branches. As the Cessna made a labored approach up the ravine, the altitude dropping under the strain, the passengers aboard lifted their bodies up from their seats as much as their belts would allow, willing the plane up. But the fan was tired, and the plane was too low. The tail of the Cessna caught the canopy, forcing the nose of the plane down. Wildly out of control, there was no hope for Luke to salvage the flight, and the plane collided with the largest Kasamba tree in the forest. The cabin and those inside rested at the very top of the Kasamba, where forked branches balanced the plane as it swayed in the thrust of the accident, even a slight breeze causing alarm as they teetered under the leaves. Pieces of the wings broke free and tumbled to the forest floor. Upon impact, the engine had flown like a small meteorite and landed with a thump some thirty yards away. A limb of the Kasamba punctured the window beside Chip, spraying glass into the cabin, but holding the plane steady as the empty window frame now rested on it.

The four men, hesitant to tumble the plane out of the tree by sudden movement, slowly crawled out of the cabin, clutching branches and leaves until they centered themselves at the trunk of the Kasamba and could visualize a way down. It wasn't until their feet felt the earth that they realized they were going to make it out alive. The De Havilland flying suits that Chip and Des wore were soaked in aviation gas and when Luke reached into his pocket to retrieve a pack of cigarettes and a light Des scolded him, "HOLD IT! Look at all of us! FIRE! We're all doused in gas, you bloody fool."

Luke, unaffected by Des' chiding, nervously broke into laughter. "Hey, man. I've been lucky so long. That's the third one I've walked away from…"

Soon they learned that Versaghi's apparent resumé of great experience included being thrown out of both the Rhodesian Airforce and the South African Airforce for 'cowboying', pranging up. "We need to start checking credentials," Des had told Chip, not caring whether Versaghi could hear him or not.

Moments after they had scampered out of the tree, a European Nyasaland Government Forestry Officer came racing to the scene. "Is anybody alive? Can you hear me? Is anybody there?" Seeing the four survivors stunned by the foot of the Kasamba, he looked around at the very top of the tree where the majority of the plane rested, around the base where broken wing tips and radios lay, and along the trunk where debris had decorated the tree as if readying it for Christmas. "You're all lucky to be alive," he concluded, taking them down to the office. "I suppose you could use a nice hot cup of tea."

Back at the Flying Club, and changed into dry clothes, Chip picked up the phone to make a call. It had only been two months since Juliet's death, and it was urgent that he reach Satemwa. "Father, yeah, it's me. In case you heard any rumors I just thought you should know there's been a little incident down in Mlanje, but I can assure you no one is hurt."[228]

Every time his parents asked him about the 'incident' Chip found a way to change the subject, keeping the details of the crash, and the severity of it to himself for years. Only when he was with Des did they really discuss how close they had come to losing their lives. When a tricky situation surfaced, they would often laugh and quote, "Eh man, I've been lucky so long."

****

Decades later, in a little country pub en route from London to Bangor (near the Welsh border), Chip and his son-in-law, Jim, stopped for lunch. The pub was in the center of town, fenced by a mossy rock wall and a swinging wooden gate which allowed visitors to enter one at a time. The fields to either side were thick with grass and sheep served to mow it down, while the odd, un-milked cow 'mooed' at Chip and Jim as they entered the pub. There were two tables in the establishment, one was already taken, and the bar tender, surprised to have a full house, showed them to the open table. A soft crackling radio spread an eclectic mix of music throughout the pub, so quiet that the sizzle of the deep fryer in the kitchen rose above it. There was no doubt they had chosen a very interesting place for lunch, and without wanting to be rude, Jim spoke to Chip in Chi'Nyanja so they could discuss the remote pub and all its idiosyncrasies without offending its owners or patrons. "It's a two-table pub," Jim joked, Chip adding, "but it's a good sign that beer is in stock."

Across the room, at the only other table in the bar, a man pushed his chair back and rose to his feet, striding across the room towards Chip and Jim. He was near the table when he politely interrupted, "Excuse me, but are you gentlemen from Nyasaland?" "Yes, we certainly are," Chip replied, the face of the stranger looking more familiar by the second. "Are you Chip Kay?" the man continued. "Well, yes, yes I am," Chip said. "Maybe you don't remember me, but you were once in my forest falling out of a tree. I was the Likabula Forestry Officer. Tell me, how are the other survivors?" Chip thought about it for a moment. Des was still his best friend, but he had lost touch with Andy Gray. The pilot, Luke Versaghi, as far as Chip was concerned was like a cat with nine lives, and the day at Likabula was his third. By now, he wondered, had he been lucky nine times? Was he still alive? Chip didn't know.[229]

Soon after the Forestry Officer rendezvous at the little pub by the Welsh border, Chip and his family were in Zimbabwe (formerly Southern Rhodesia). The children, although on school break were taking extra tuition at a reputable school to improve their grades in mathematics. Once they had completed the course, Chip took the family to the Troutbeck Inn, three hours north of Harare (formerly Salisbury). The Nyanga ranges were knitted with ancient pine tree forests and the lake on the property was stocked with so much trout that every visitor left feeling like a top-notch angler. Breakfast was served in the dining room which was past the famous log fire that the owners claimed had never been put out since the hotel's inception in 1947.[230] A champion trout caught by 'Granny Mack's husband' hung in a glass cage on the wall in the dining room. Granny McPherson, a friend of the Kay's liked to tell the children about the fish her husband caught, "A big rainbow trout – this long," she would tell them as she stretched her arms out as wide as they could spread. "Can we see it Dad?" his boys asked, pointing to the prized fishes on the wall. "Of course, let's go closer," Chip replied, taking his two sons over for a better look.

Passing a table of people to get closer to the glass cage, Chip greeted them, "Hello, good morning." One of the men at the table looked up at him, "Oh hello. I know you." "Yes, I know you," said Chip. "You're Des Tennett," the man exclaimed, proud of his recall. "No, I'm the other one. And you – you're alive," Chip returned. "Oh yes, quite. I've been a senior line Captain for Qantas for the past twenty years, a Commodore – five star," he replied, very smug. The men conversed a little longer, but as Chip took his boys back to their table they asked him, "Who's that Daddy?"

Chip told them, "That's Luke Versaghi. Once he flew me into the side of Mount Mulanje and we had to climb out of a tree. I can't believe the Aussies took in a three-times dam buster. Oh well, I guess he has been lucky so long."[231]

For Business and for pleasure 1957-1962

Chip Kay in Red socks circa 1962

Chip and Juul's PTA business expansion prospered, not just because of the Federation, but because Chip had begun to incorporate flying into his work. The use of planes opened up his schedule and increased the services he could offer his clients. The road between Cholo and Salisbury was still frequented by Satemwa trucks, loaded with tea, but if Chip could help it, he no longer drove the distance himself, opting to fly to Salisbury instead. Limited by the Tiger Moth's 103 liter fuel capacity, Chip had to find a way to re-fuel between Luchenza and Salisbury.

In the small Mozambique town of Tsuro an emergency landing strip which was hidden under the grasses provided Chip with an opportunity to create a re-fueling station. His trucks passed by Tsuro on their way to and from Salisbury and his flight route crossed it at an ideal distance for re-fueling. Two 44 gallon drums, filled with aviation gas, were loaded on the tea trucks and taken to the emergency strip where a hired Mlonda (watchman) met the truck. Tasked with the sole job of protecting the drums day-in and day-out, the Mlonda – duty bound – promptly responded to the sound of the approaching trucks. He dug a hole quickly, much faster than Chip had seen any man dig before, and buried the drums in the cool earth, to the side of the runway under the shade of the nearby trees. Once the trucks had departed, the Mlonda waited. Nobody really knew how he occupied his days, whether he waited very close to the buried drums, or at some distance. Then one day, with weeks passing in between, the guard would hear the drone of an engine in the sky and observe the descent of the Tiger Moth, each time marveling at the feat of flight even though he had seen it many times before. Chip could see him from the air, sometimes running through the trees towards the runway, sometimes sitting by the drums, as if he was expecting the plane at just that hour. Then as the Tiger Moth glided to a halt, the Mlonda raced to the buried aviation gas, and madly dug it up.[232]

The Tiger Moth was a marvelous machine and Chip enjoyed its maneuverability, but as his territory expanded, the limitations of the Tiger became clear. Not only was its fuel capacity inadequate, but its maximum speed and elevation were too. Companies such as Cessna and Beechcraft began producing machines that could hold over 55 additional liters of fuel and travel at least 70 kilometers per hour faster than a Moth. Additional seating and load carrying capacity made these newer, modern planes desirable and with PTA thriving, Chip had money to buy one.

He chose the Cessna 175 Skylark boasting an all-metal aluminum alloy airframe, strut-braced high wings, GO-300 engine designed to run at high RPM's, and tricycle landing gear, where the wheels were covered in what looked like cute aeronautical booties.[233] A flying range of 962 kilometers and a maximum take-off weight of over 2,000lbs made the 175 Skylark a sensible option for Chip's growing business.[234]

The Cessna 175 could easily make the journey to Salisbury without re-fueling in Tsuro. He also began flying to the Mozambique coast, making acquaintances with all sorts of people as he traveled, touting his trips as 'business' journeys, but thinking them more worthwhile due to the acquisition of prawns – his favorite seafood – from the coast. "I'm off to chase some prawns, and some girls," he told Des, the pair laughing because the tale was of course, partially true. And with his business partner Juul, he would tease, "I need to fly to Mozambique to see about some prawns, er, I mean diesel parts."[235]

Once, because someone had told him that Mozambique hid a beautiful tea district called Vila Junqueiro at the base of a mountain similar in size to Mlanje, he got in his plane to go find it. There was no clear indication on his map, other than it was in the province of Zambezia, and he was going by the word of his acquaintance in hopes to find Vila Junqueiro. Perhaps feeling a little too bold in his new Cessna with increased flight range, he set off to find it, reaching a point of no return at some stage in his journey and deciding to go forward despite feeling incredibly lost. "You can't miss the mountain," Chip repeated the words that had led him on the hunt, and just when he was about to give in to despondency, he saw it, rising like a mammoth brick out of the earth. At the base of the mountain, the tea district, the promised Vila Junqueiro sprawled outwards, ruling the surrounds. The airfield, easily spotted in amongst the tea, gave Chip a sense of pride. He had made it. He plonked the Cessna onto the runway and a new relationship with the tea planters of Vila Junqueiro began.

The Portuguese tea planters in Mozambique were keen on 'duck' shooting, using clay pigeons for targets. Since Salisbury made the skeets readily and Chip was between Southern Rhodesia and Mozambique bi-weekly, he soon became the primary supplier for the sport. He gained a reputation in parts as the clever chap from Nyasaland who "flys the pigeons in by the plane load."[236]

Every Wednesday Chip flew. One Wednesday he would fly to Mozambique, collecting diesel parts and odd bits that needed fixing. He returned to Nyasaland on Saturday. The following Wednesday he took the parts to Salisbury for Stansfield-Radcliffe to repair, flying back to Luchenza on Saturday. Returning to Mozambique a fortnight later with refurbished diesel spares and parts, he had successfully facilitated a full servicing business. While the Cessna 175 managed the trip, Chip had been checking on the specifications of many aircraft and decided to 'downgrade' to the older Cessna 172 Skyhawk. The 172 was just as fast as the 175 but could travel almost 300 kilometers further per tank. The older and more reliable engine of the 172 overshadowed the finicky GO-300 in the 175. He took out the back seat, which he never used for passengers and put in a chest, to carry all the greasy parts he flew for maintenance and repairs. It was a good switch for Chip and he nicknamed "Fox Echo", the 172, the 'horse-box' owing to its functionality and performance.[237] Over the years, the 172 Skyhawk, originally built as a training plane, would prove to be one of the world's best light aircraft. It's robust design was "so clean and aerodynamic that Cessna's marketing department dubbed it the 'land-o-matic'".[238] It was certainly one of Chip's all-time favorite planes and he hoped he would own "Fox Echo" forever.

Protecting the planes from the wild sometimes seemed a full-time job, if not for Chip, at least for his watchmen. In the absence of a hangar on Satemwa, Chip's planes parked on the terraces in front of his home, where he feared the antlers of grazing antelope. If one should suddenly lift its head beneath his fuel tank, the antler may puncture the tank and ground it for weeks. However, the guards happily chased away the nimble footed creatures, but often lost courage when night fell and predators padded near the planes.

Chip often took tourists on safari to Ngorongoza Game Reserve in Mozambique. Plane and nature clashes were more threatening in Ngorongoza than on Satemwa. For starters, there were 'climbing' lion who liked to sit on top of the cowling, perhaps still drawing heat from a warm engine or the effects of the sun's rays on the body of the plane. Not easily chased off, they were often left alone while the night watchmen huddled behind the rock wall nearby. "What you really have to watch for," Chip told the Londers (the watchmen) one day, "is Hyena. It's one thing to be taken by a lion – that would be quite a manly way to go, but Hyena? No, I wouldn't wish that on anyone." Yet the spotted Hyena, laughing through the night, circling about the planes with sinister grins, often came. Their gnarly sharp teeth often pitted against the tires of Chip's planes, nibbling on the rubber as if it were a tasty morsel of meat. In the morning, Chip would find chunks missing from his tires, or worse, the tires deflated and the rim resting on the ground. Frustrated by his planes' clash with nature, he built a double fenced holding yard, a temporary fix, but a quick solution to the predator problem.[239]

PTA was a flexible service center and Chip thought he could tackle any challenge, "There's not a problem you can throw at me, that I can't resolve," he told Juul one day after they poured over accounts from purchases made in Italy, Germany and the United Kingdom. They were selling Rota vends for the tea factories, and since their packeting business in Southern Rhodesia had taken off, and Three Leaves Tea was everywhere they looked, they struck a deal with the factories. They would sell a Rota vend in exchange for £3,000 worth of tea, which usually equated to about 60 chests of Broken Orange Pekoe (BOP). Eventually PTA was putting 100 tonnes of tea into saleable packets in a single month. Business could not be better.[240]

The Cessnas allowed Chip to reach into Mozambique and Southern Rhodesia, proving reliable and sturdy beyond doubt. However, the Tiger Moths attracted the crowds and entertained the onlookers at the Air Days and Aircraft displays at Chileka Airport. Des had told Chip, "There's more entertainment value for visitors and non-flying members with Tiger Moths, because they are fully aerobatic."[241] On these show days at Chileka, the modern Cessna's took a backseat to the Moths, who danced in the sky at the impulse of their pilots. "What are we going to do for our stunt?" Des asked Chip as they stood beside their Tiger Moths at the Chileka Air Day in the late 1950's. Chip was only 28 and Des in his early thirties when the duo teamed up to regale the crowd with a dare-devil maneuver at the show. They flew the planes directly at each other, crossing precisely in front of the terminal, having estimated that if each one hugged the edge of the tarmac, their wings would pass safely, with the clincher being that one had to go down and the other up just upon meeting. As the parallel was not visible from the crowd, it looked as if one jumped over the other. With speeds of 160 kilometers per hour, and a flurry of air and noise when they crossed, Des and Chip both knew it was a "bit hairy."[242]

The excitement of the Air Day culminated with Des Tennett, dressed now in plain clothes and emulating a drunken spectator, staggered out from the crowd onto the runway. Chip and the announcer on the loudspeaker added to the drama and started yelling, "Hey! Hey! Stop that man!" Des climbed into the cockpit of the nearest plane and opened the taps, which all fell flat and then he lifted the machine over them, proceeding to gyrate like an inebriated pilot. Overexcited, he exceeded the extent of the yawing and skidding and bunting beyond the limits of his rehearsals as the negative "G" caused the fuel to lift to the top of the tank and expose the suction pipe underneath. The engine coughed and spluttered as if also stimulated by the act. Women in the crowd began sheltering their children, moving them behind the terminal building to seek cover. A visiting Rhodesian Airforce Pilot told people he had never seen an aircraft put through those sorts of contortions, which made Des feel proud when he heard the comment after the show. Chip couldn't help but find the entire scenario humorous, especially since his best friend, Des Tennett, the teetotaler, who never touched a drink in his life, played the part of a sozzled spectator so convincingly.[243]

By the late 1950's The Nyasaland Flying Club had graduated from the 'debating' society at the club's commencement, into a full-fledged flying club, where instructor and student numbers increased rapidly. Three Christmas' running, they gathered five of their best pilots and flew in Vic Formation over Blantyre, alternating each year who was at the apex and who tucked en-echelon to the wings.[244] The Africans, startled by the rumbling sky, often remarked, "Ndege Mpamvu" – the bird that flies with power.[245]

By the time his annual leave approached in the early 1960's, Chip was ready to see other parts of the world, having already gained a wide view of Africa through his weekly flying routine. Italy, reveling in the Dolce Vita period in 1960, where the cinematic hit, "The Sweet Life", encouraged self-indulgence and hedonism, and attracted men and women all over the globe to experience what the film promoted. And Chip, having heard rumors of the carefree lifestyle was eager to see for himself what it involved. After several days in Rome, he decided to go find the local Flying Club. A young Italian Airforce Officer was sitting at the bar when Chip arrived and caught Chip's eye as he entered, "You want a drink?" he asked in English, making Chip realize he did look like a foreigner. They had barely begun a conversation when a terrible accident took place. A light aircraft had failed the ascent and crashed back to earth in a flaming mess. Chip stood up to see the wreck and people rushed out towards the smoke. They assumed no one could make it out alive. "There's nothing we can do," said his Italian friend, obviously unattached to the plane and people who perished in it. "Where are you staying?" he asked Chip. "Oh, a small penciona near the terminale," Chip replied still grimacing after the bang. Taking his mind off the accident, the man told Chip, "I'm going to a party tonight, why don't you come along?"[246]

The Italian pilot came that evening to collect Chip, dressed in a dark single-breasted suit, stark white shirt, his black hair slicked into a wave. Outfitted in what had become a little like a uniform for Chip, khaki cotton pants and a matching khaki shirt, with button top pockets, a brown leather belt, and lace up shoes, he immediately felt under-dressed. "Anything goes where we're going," said the Italian, trying to ease the look of discomfort on Chip's face. With wide eyes and a flexible mindset, Chip sat beside his new friend as they whirled through the streets of Rome, bumping around cobbled paths, and leaning into corners with pace, sometimes too close to the small tables where patrons sipped red wine from generous sized glasses. The afternoon was fading and the twilight ignited the Trevi fountain to a peak of beauty catching those who sat around the fountain's ring in the dilemma of staying or leaving.

The sandstone buildings that rose from either side of the street oozed with history, although Chip didn't recognize any of them until the Pantheon with its thick columns holding up the triangular awning fell into view. The people on the steps looked like tiny specs as the height of the columns out-did them, at least ten to one. "The Temple of the Gods!" his friend stated, slowing down so Chip could breathe it in. "We're close now," he said after a few additional city blocks, when a large set of decorated gates, opened in welcome and the man guarding it waved them through. The gates were the fanciest things Chip had seen since coming to Rome, outdoing both the Trevi Fountain and the Pantheon. They slowly drove up the driveway towards the house and Chip wondered if they had arrived at a Palace, manicured gardens framing the drive, and sculpted trees announcing what stood behind them, a magnificent home, towering above the landscape and dripping in wealth. A valet took the pilot's car to park it alongside the Maseratis and Ferraris that lined the lawn, and Chip and his friend walked up the broad staircase, splayed with people who had begun the party quite happily without them.

It was 'Dolce Vita' that had brought Chip all the way from Africa, and now, surrounded by the chicest Italian society with an endless supply of food and drinks, he was completely immersed in it. The Italian women were stunning, dark-haired and elegantly dressed and they thought Chip, with his dusty brown hair and wrapped in khaki, more interesting than the plethora of well-suited Italian men. "Africa?" they asked with amusement, "Tell us what it is like. Are there lion living in your backyard?" They giggled and rubbed his shoulder, each one inching closer to hear his stories from the bush. "We're all very basic," Chip told them, looking around wondering how to compare his mud- bricked home in Cholo to the opulent mansion in Italy. However, the Italian women didn't think he was simple, in fact his stories about flying, including his crash into Mlanje, were thrilling, and he soon realized he could have any of the women who were clustered at his feet. The hours inside the mansion blurred into days, and before he knew it, the sun had set three times before he emerged back onto the driveway, scratching his head and wondering if what had occurred in the house was reality or a sequel to the "It's a Sweet Life" movie.[247]

Madly In Love 1962-1964

Young Juliet and Trysh Kay circa 1968

Flying had consumed Chip and Des the way fire does with a forest in a gusty gale. There was no air left over for other interests, or friends who didn't care for the flying community. If the weather was bad, and they couldn't fly, they spent their time talking about it, or planning new routes and dreaming of exotic destinations. All their social interactions centered around the club and they gave little thought to the fact that neither of them was married, and both were in their early thirties. "Why satisfy one and disappoint many?" Chip joked with Des one day, after they both said goodnight to their dates for the evening. "One thing is certain, whoever does end up marrying me, must not get in the way of my flying." The words were rooted in jest, but the undertone was serious, and Chip was unsure how he could ever find balance in his life, the kind of balance required if he was someday committed enough to take a bride.

Sixty miles from Cholo, Nyasaland's seat of Government in Zomba made the town a bustling center for parties and colonial gatherings not just from within the Federation, but also from the surrounds. Neatly tucked into the slopes at the base of Zomba mountain, the government houses with their wrap-around porches were a beautiful sight. The gardens emulated their English beginnings, with pruned roses ready to bloom and rectangular hedges which ran the lawn, creating boundaries between the vegetable patch and the quiet garden where park benches awaited a visitor with a good book. The tabletop shelf at the rim of the mountain made the plateau itself a desirable place to stay, although the road leading up to it was somewhat precarious, with multiple switchbacks on a steep incline.

Partly owing to the mountain that sheltered the city and partly to the surrounding flatlands, filled with native forests, Zomba held a reputation as one of the most beautiful capitals in the Empire. Queen Elizabeth, the Queen Mother, first visited Zomba in July, 1957, the first of the Royal family to step foot in Nyasaland.[248] Although she was on a short tour of the Federation of the Rhodesias and Nyasaland, she enjoyed Zomba plateau so much that she made a second, unplanned trip up the mountain to the lookout, staying longer than she had the previous day, earning the spot a name after herself, "Queen's lookout". Her tour began in Blantyre at the opening of the Queen Elizabeth Hospital. No longer considered appropriate, European, Asian and African wards now combined under one roof, which prompted the Queen Mother to say, "I feel that the principles of this Hospital are in some way symbolic of the future of the Federation, with all people working together with understanding, and wise tolerance, for those common ideals of progress and prosperity."[249]

Relationships between Nyasaland chiefs and the Colonial Government was exemplified in the extravagant offerings they presented to the Queen Mother during her 1957 visit. Chiefs from all regions throughout Nyasaland, robed in colorful silks, flannels and leopard skins presented a variety of gifts to honor the Royal visitor. She was grateful for her private plane, the Mpika, which allowed her to transport all her gifts without thought to their size or weight. One was from the Central Province, a glorious elephant tusk tipped at either end in silver, the middle of the tusk carved into a map of Nyasaland and the lake and set in silver. The tusk required two messengers to carry it, as it weighed 48lbs and was 4ft, 5 inches long from end to end in a straight line. However, the Queen Mother's cordial visit in 1957, four years after a vote for Federation, did nothing to secure the acceptance of Federation within Nyasaland. In fact, if anything, the African Congress that was seeking Independence was fired up by it, realizing they needed a properly organized outfit if they were to shed Britain of control, and switch to majority rule.

The Boma parties that Chip's mother had requested his father to attend before their wedding in 1929, were still regular occurrences in Zomba, but being neither politically inclined or connected, Chip was seldom invited to those functions, and like his father, would have resisted going anyway. However, if the party had anything to do with the Flying Club, neither Chip nor Des could miss the event. The Nyasaland Flying Club operated with a spirit of abundancy, priding themselves on being the only club in Nyasaland where all the facilities were free, except for flights in aircraft. Their attitudes of inclusivity attracted all kinds of people to the clubhouse on a Sunday, and all kinds of people to their parties, whether they were in Luchenza, Cholo, or Zomba. [250]

The Zomba Sports Club, at the junction of the main road and the route to the plateau was an example of Englishness: the cricket pitch at center stage just below the clubhouse; a squash court in the rear; billiards table in the parlor; and a cocktail bar that could shake and stir with the best saloons in London. It was unsurprising to Chip and Des when they arrived in Zomba for the biggest party of 1962, that amongst the regular flying crowd were several strangers whom they had never seen before. They found the bar, and Chip took his whiskey strong, while Des, along with the underage drinkers present, ordered a lemonade. "Cheers," their glasses met as their eyes began searching the room, looking for acquaintances and friends. A few short seconds passed before Des elbowed Chip who followed his gaze towards three young ladies, slender figures, beautifully dressed and clearly unaccompanied. "It's only polite," Chip said to Des, both on the same wavelength and walking towards the women in unified step. "What are you drinking tonight?" Des asked Peggy, who looked up at him fondly. She was petite, one of the tiniest women in the room, her dark brown hair held behind her ears with a pearled clip. "Sprite please," she responded. Des, lemonade in hand was captivated and together with Peggy left Chip behind in the company of two new female friends.

The two ladies with Chip were the Freeman sisters, their father newly appointed to the Nyasaland Colonial Government as the Director of Education. He had worked in Nairobi, Kenya as the African Education Director, one of three sectors for Education, the other two being European and Asian. One of the sisters, immediately flattered by the men's approach introduced herself with confidence. "I'm Ba," she said, leaning towards Chip in greeting. She was pretty and slim and had obviously spent considerable time taming her thick curly mop of hair that Chip noticed only because it was brown, not blonde. "Chip, sort of my nickname that stuck since birth, and Ba – is that a nickname too?" Chip asked, wondering if he had just met his match.[251]

She was sparky and keen, making good conversation with ears that listened, indicating that she was probably good at her job as a teacher. Soon, the other people present at the party seemed to fade to the edges of the room, and Chip, as if girded with blinders, focused on one woman alone. She was interesting. She had traveled all over the world with her parents, adjusting to the life of a third culture kid, just as Chip had done. Once, because of her exposures she wound up in hospital in Liverpool, England with tuberculosis. "A hazard of the tropics," Chip had offered, indicating he was not put off by the diagnosis. "And my nursing sister, she was a colored girl from Cholo. She was an Oddy and told me anybody here would know that name," Ba concluded the story. "Remarkable coincidence," Chip commented, "We all know the Oddys."[252]

It wasn't long before Ba and Peggy became regular attendees of the 'flying club breakfasts' at Satemwa, where, on any given Sunday, Chip's flying club friends flew over the tea, landing on the Satemwa runway – conveniently close enough to Chip's house that a short taxi around a few curves and up a slight hill allowed pilots to park their planes, as if automobiles, at the front steps of Chip's house.[253]

One morning Chip raced out early with two white sheets and laid them on the lawn in front of his house to make a cross. The women didn't know what he was up to and just minutes later the roar of the Cessna 206 Skywagon harkened in the distance. The 206 was known for its ability to carry parachutists and was requested at air shows all over Central Africa as a result. On Chip's instructions, the four of them, Des and Peggy, Chip and Ba, gathered on the grass and watched as parachutists, "Knuckle Heads", jumped out of the 206, aiming for the crossed bed sheets in front of Chip's house. Four of the five made it within meters of the cotton slips, but one, the only woman – light as a feather – was carried on a gust of wind and disappeared into the tea fields below Chip's house. "I'm always telling Ingrid she needs to put on weight," joked Rick Tilley, one of her fellow jumpers who worked in the tea industry in Mlanje.[254]

Merilyn Ann Nichola Freeman, known only as Ba, stole what many thought could never be taken that night in Zomba - Chip's heart. He was crazy about her; he was madly, wildly, selfishly in love. The truth was he never had a good model for how to do marriage. His father and mother, although committed, were like partners who wrote accounts of business to each other across the continent, the eighteen years that separated them a gaping hole that only grew wider as time passed. But Chip was determined to give marriage a try and proposed quickly to Ba, marrying her just months after they met on the 6th of January 1963, in the All Saints Church in Cholo, with a reception at the Flying Club. Maclean supported the nuptials wholeheartedly, while Jean protested the union by wearing black the whole day. The success of the party in Zomba capped off two weeks later when Des wedded Peggy, on the 20th of January, 1963. The flying friends, each now married, forced themselves to find balance, although it was not always easy to do.[255]

Chip had a relatively small amount of time to organize a honeymoon since he had to be back in time for the wedding of Des and Peggy. He arranged a trip to Mombasa, thinking Ba would appreciate being back in Kenya. Flying out from Luchenza in Romeo Tango, his reliable Cessna 175 Skylark, they encountered rough weather just before touching down in Lilongwe for a re-fuel. Nancy Fenner, the Shell Agent at Lilongwe, filled their tanks and told Chip, "You're in for nasty, terrible weather heading north." But Chip pushed on to Mbewa where he got tangled up in a convergence and changed course. "How about Salisbury?" he asked Ba, who was slightly pale in the passenger seat. "Salisbury it is," she said. They downed the night back in Lilongwe and the next morning, the weather still pressing, set off for Salisbury. "I know every mango tree in Central Africa," Chip assured Ba, who still seemed nervous to be up in the dark, threatening skies.

When they made it to Salisbury, they drove Juliet's MG Magnette and headed for the old ruins of The Great Zimbabwe, a medieval city in relics, the Capital of the 'Kingdom of Zimbabwe' during the Iron Age. They hadn't made it far, when the MG splashed into a large puddle and water filled the old-fashioned engine and filters causing the car to stop right in the middle of the puddle, with Chip and Ba impounded inside. Ba looked at Chip with wide eyes as if to ask, "What else could go wrong?" Minutes later the MG fired up and they made it, late, to the old ruins and their hotel for a few nights. It was possibly the wettest January Rhodesia had faced, and it rained for three days straight, Chip and Ba holed up in their hotel with not much to do. "Blah!" said Ba on their third, boring day, laughing to herself, "What luck. I should hope this is not a precursor for our marriage…" They returned to Nyasaland a little soggy, but ready for the next party.[257]

Chip thought Des did a better job juggling his responsibilities at home and at work. Perhaps because he was older, he approached the unity of marriage with greater maturity, or perhaps it was because Des' family business, locally-based, brought his work and home close together. Chip couldn't put his finger on all the obstacles, but he felt torn whenever he was in Mozambique or Salisbury, knowing that his new wife was alone on Satemwa.

Ba assured Chip he shouldn't worry about the time he was gone but he still felt guilty. He told her he was unsure how to change his schedule and still keep everything afloat. A baby was due to the couple in December of the same year they married, and when Juliet Mary was born on Christmas day at Malamulo Mission Hospital in 1963, both Ba and Chip were ecstatic. "I think Juliet is a perfect name, Chip," Ba had said, agreeing they should honor Chip's sister if their first-born was a girl. Juliet was a lovely baby, soft coos at night, and a placid temperament, a firm jaw and a determined cry for milk, Cathcart Kay features evident at birth. Chip was more in love than he had ever been with a hobby, a plane, or a woman. He was smitten and spent hours tickling his baby's feet and kissing her cheeks. Juliet's birth made travel almost undesirable.

Yet travel was such a part of their life and Chip suggested a trip up to Kenya, accompanied by Ba's parents and combining business and holiday. Chip adored Ba's father, Mr Freeman and respected his work in education. He was glad for the Freeman's company and knew that the presence of her parents would put Ba at ease. They stayed near Nyere at the Izaak Walton Inn, an old colonial trout hotel established at the turn of the century. Chip had reserved a three-bedroom suite, a room for he and Ba, one for her parents, and one for baby Juliet, although she didn't spend much time in it. Gardens rolled out from the walkways around the hotel and bursts of color from the wildflowers scattered at the garden perimeter, contrasting the pruned and well-planned bushes in the interior where landscaped design defined the space. There was ample room for his family to enjoy daily walks, and the restaurant, offering the best cuisine, was sure to please them. He settled the family into the hotel, spent a few days with them, then, forgetting his regrettable travel itinerary, he flew out to India, leaving them behind at the Izaak Walton, presumably in great comfort for a few short weeks. "I'll be back in a fortnight," he told his wife, who by now was accustomed to his habits. What he didn't realize was that each time he left, she started to need him, want him a little less.

Andrew Yule and Company, a British tea empire, had organized a tour of India's tea districts, and Chip, eager to learn had signed on for the safari. He arrived at the Oberoi Grand Hotel in Calcutta through a mass of humanity which made the growing population of Nyasaland seem meager. Located in the central business district of Calcutta and unrivaled by other luxury hotels, The Grande Dame of Chowringhee as the Oberoi was often called, provided a welcome break from the bustling city streets. Upon entering the hotel Chip noticed an American Bar, very popular in India after the war, and a large sign above it that read, "NO DOGS OR SOUTH AFRICANS." Having gained their independence in 1947 just after the Second World War, India was finding a voice against apartheid policies upheld in South Africa, even if it was mainly in five-star hotels as conditions of entry into their 'American bars'.[258]

Three men escorted Chip to his room, one carried his bag, one his hat, and the other walked beside him with the key. When the door opened, the man with the key took Chip's jacket, the other undid his laces on his shoes, and the third man went straight to the bathroom to draw a warm bath for Chip. "Just a few inches of water, please," Chip called out to him when he heard the taps turning. It was something he thought very civilized about India, the bath. Where he had to look high and low for a bath sometimes in England, it seemed they were all over the place in India. "That's just five-star establishments," Ba laughed later when she heard the stories. He splashed in his three-inch bath, and dressed for a night walk, hungry to find the best restaurant outside of the Oberoi. He walked towards the hotel entrance and the 8ft heavy door which was guarded by a 6ft tall Sikh soldier donned in Indian Army apparel with a huge blush rose turban swirled on his head. His long black beard was rolled up to make a tidy fringe around his jaw from ear to ear and his black moustache, fiercely curled. "No Sire," the Sikh said as Chip approached. "Oh, good evening. I am going out for a walk," Chip said. "No Sire," the guard repeated. Disregarding the door he led Chip over to the cubbyhole next to the gate and placed a crate under the window for Chip to use. Once up on the box, having gained the height of the Sikh, Chip looked out through the small window to the streets surrounding the hotel. "They're all lying down," Chip told the Sikh, relaying his observations from his perch. "There's so many of them" "Yes, Sire…. Dead, Sire," said the Sikh.[259]

The following morning the newspaper arrived under the door in Chip's room. He picked it up and sat back in his bed, cover turned down and a hot pot of tea steaming on the nightstand. "One hundred and twenty dead from smallpox," read one side of the newspaper column, and opposite it, "One hundred and fifty die from cholera overnight."[260] He had never seen such an outbreak in Nyasaland. Cholera's active agent, vibrio el tor, entered India in March 1964 through the port city of Chennai, and spread slowly until an outbreak gushed through Calcutta a month later.[261] Now, in the middle of that outbreak Chip was terrified to think so many were dying while he slept in fine cotton sheets with a feather-down pillow under his head. The next morning, a 5 tonne truck circled the city streets with cleanup workers tasked with body removal. To the shouts of "pass the body" in the local Hindu language, they heaved the lifeless masses, feet first, into the bed of the truck.

A car arrived at the Oberoi to collect Chip and take him over the river Hooghly to the offices of Andrew Yule and Company. "I'm so sorry to hear about the tragedy overnight," Chip said to the manager, thinking of the mass deaths in the streets outside the hotel." The manager looked up puzzled so Chip said, "You did see the newspaper this morning, didn't you?" Catching on, the manager replied, "Oh yes, well I'm afraid that's every day, Chip, sometimes it's 150, other days its more." He continued, "You'll stay here tonight and the tour will begin tomorrow."[262]

By morning Chip had been re-assigned from the Indian manager he was paired with the previous day to a European one. "Mr Keith Waddhams has requested to be your host," said the manager, adding, "If that's ok with you of course." "Ok!" Chip mused, "It's perfect. He was my very first flying instructor at Luchenza. I didn't know he moved to India." "Flying?" the manager asked, fishing for details. "Oh yes, Tigers, and now Cessnas. It's very addictive you know, flying," Chip responded.

When Keith arrived expecting Chip, he shook his hand with gusto and Chip asked, "How did you know I was here?" "Well, when you left the Oberoi two nights ago, they gave me your room and I found your laundry list, and it had to be your list – who else has such a detailed list for the laundry staff?" he teased. "So, I asked the desk if it belonged to a planter from Central Africa, and they said yes, so I figured you were coming here. I made a call to the head office and here we are."

Assuming his interests still centered around flying, Keith skimmed over the tea tour and took Chip to an airfield under construction. It was littered with thousands of workers, some digging, some dumping and others moving the earth. "It has to be over a thousand yards long," Chip thought. "Have you never heard of CATS?" he asked Keith, slightly shocked by the numbers in the workforce. "You could do in a month what these guys do in a year." "Yes, Chip, but then who would feed the ten thousand?" Keith replied. Chip remembered his morning newspaper and suddenly went quiet.[263]

After his tour he left India, the smells of poverty, where crowded streets wreaked of death, the contrasting tea fields with beautiful green flushes, and his first flying instructor Keith Waddhams who had surprised him in the best possible way. Returning to Kenya, he found his wife, baby and in- laws at dinner, baby Juliet taking her first bites of solid foods, squealing with glee as Ba spooned mashed pumpkin into her mouth. Chip was delighted to see them all, and amused them with stories from his trip to India. He had a way of relaying events and information that put him on a sort of platform, his audience captivated by the layers in his tales and the enthusiasm with which he told them. Chip wanted to hear about their time too and asked, "Now, is there any real difference since Kenyatta?"

Kenya had gained its independence from Britain just months before their trip, and they were all curious to see what, if anything, had really changed as a result. "It's too early to say," Mr Freeman ruminated. Along with Kenya, Nyasaland was now poised for majority rule and they all wondered, quietly, how Nyasaland would adjust to independence on July 6th, 1964. With Federation busted, progressive movements towards self-governance were inevitable. However, the minority was skeptical of the timing and the tendency shown in other independent countries to forgo democracy and install an autocratic, belligerent state was worrying. No one, black or white, was ready for that.

'The winds of change' were upon them, and what they didn't want to face before – the end of the colonial way of life, of Nyasaland – was now staring at them, blindly, forcefully. "These are the happy days," Chip laughed, "before it all falls apart."

Change and Democracy: The demise of Nyasaland 1944-1964

*His Excellency the Life President of the Republic of Malawi,
Ngwazi Dr Hastings Kamuzu Banda*

The year before the Second World War ended, James Frederick Sangala revitalized Native Association movements from the 1920's and 1930's into The Nyasaland African Congress (NAC). The quickening pace of political change in West Africa during the war along with ideas from India and elsewhere promoted the idea of Nationalism. Sangala, educated by the European mission at Blantyre and falling into a civil servant teacher role when trained, was also part of cutting-edge clubs, such as the "Black and White Club," aimed at bringing educated Africans to mix with like-minded Europeans. He sent a letter in 1943 to "All Africans resident in Nyasaland Protectorate" imploring "Unity is strength...time is ripe now for the Africans in this country to fight for their freedom."[(264)]

The population of Nyasaland had very nearly doubled in over 25 years, estimated around 2,960,000 by 1962. In seventy years, Rhodesia had grown from a mere 400,000 Africans to over 4,000,000. The white man's influence on the continent was undeniable. Their warfare on slavery, eradication of disease through advanced medical interventions, and African education brought by the missionaries all contributed to extending life expectancy within the colonies. Therefore, increased African representation was a natural inclination of politics in Nyasaland, but the rate of integration was never quick enough for the Africans, and always too rapid for the Europeans. They were at loggerheads on many issues. And solutions needed to be quickly found.[265]

Chip was away in England at Millfield, "a boy in short pants" as he put it, while the undertones for National Leadership and an overthrow of Colonial Government stirred during 1944. As a teenager, he had given little thought to the challenges each side faced, and tended to rest with his father politically, whose interests remained with scratching the earth and doing it respectfully for all involved. It was clear he suffered from 'white privilege'. He remembered the first time John Humbiani had waved him off to school when he was 9. "Teach me to drive, Chippy," John had asked. That's when Chip really felt white privilege. What would happen to John and Nelson while he chugged off to Cape Town? Why couldn't they come with him? "It's just not possible," his father would say, "There's things about the way this world works, that you don't understand."

The NAC experienced tumultuous years leading up to the debate for Federation between Nyasaland and the Rhodesias which simmered in the late 1940s and intensified in the early 1950's. Leadership changes within the NAC (Sangala, Matinga, Chinyama), remote control from powerful members (Hastings Banda), embezzlement of funds (Matinga), and in-fighting stalled their momentum which had been promising following the two-man NAC delegation to London in 1948 where the Colonial Secretary, Creech Jones, had sympathized with Nyasa views. Dr Hastings Kamuzu Banda, who had both politically and financially bolstered the NAC, sometimes acted as a puppeteer pulling strings that crossed oceans. Banda migrated from Kasungu, Nyasaland to South Africa as a small boy and had the fortune of being taken in by the African Methodist Episcopal Church and later sent by them to America. By 1938 his education moved to Scotland where he completed his Doctorate in Medicine. Rejected by Nyasaland for work as a physician he found a post in London, Harlesden where he administered care to a mostly white population. Involved in British politics and casting a vote for the Labour Party which saw Creech Jones elected, Banda was doing his part for Nyasaland's freedom from his home base in Harlesden.[266]

In 1951, Dr Banda found support for his anti-Federation campaign from both blacks and whites when he projected that amalgamation of the three countries was a 'disguise' for the creation of a Settler-controlled dominion in Central Africa. Nyasaland, reasonably governed by British civil servants, contrasted with the Rhodesias who were swayed in force by farmers and white settlers whom Banda accused of regarding "the Africans as inferior beings, with scarcely any right to a dignified and refined existence."[267] He gained support, and his attitude of cooperation within the Government in England, and his contributions to the fight in Nyasaland, earned him respect on both sides. However, when Creech Jones lost in the 1951 election, the staunch voice of his successor, James Griffiths, squashed the ideas of Banda, and contributed to a swing in Banda's political attitudes. Where he had previously touted "tactics and diplomacy, lenience and understanding," when Federation swept into law in the December 1953 election, he agitated with policies leaning towards a one-man king-like state. The NAC believed "democratic accountability existed in Britain but was absent from her colonies." Following his disappointment, and Federation's 'win', Banda lost credibility at home, and the NAC membership fell from 5,000 paid members to only a few hundred.[268]

Initially, Banda's main difficulty in Nyasaland was that he lacked a 'strong man' authoritarian approach to politics. Other liberated countries were freed on the backs of men such as Kenyatta of Kenya, Nkrumah of Ghana, Balewa of Nigeria, all of whom were narcissistic rulers hiding under a false veil of democracy and whom the years would prove as dictators, preferring a military-like state. In these countries, one strong leader was ousted by the next strong man, the pattern continuing to create political instability in the freed countries for decades. Banda's people did not understand his pandering to the British in political discussions, which clearly had no use when Federation surged ahead in 1953 despite his efforts. In Africa, tribesmen accept strength as the ultimate reckoning, the man with the gun rules. If Banda was to succeed in winning the ear of his people again, and in fighting for his country's freedom, he would have to change tact.[269]

Complicating politics for Satemwa and other estates in and around Cholo was the 1953 August riots that bubbled on the simmering discontent of the NAC's attitudes towards Federation, which had not yet passed in a vote, and the British government's attempts to subdue their murmurings by imposing stricter taxes and agriculture laws on the people. There were two accounts that surfaced following an incident on August 18, 1953 involving the Tennett Family and their orange orchards in Luchenza.

The African's, imbued by the belief of chifwamba – white man's cannibalistic desire to eat African flesh – upon hearing two shots, and seeing Des and Basil Tennett in their orange grove carrying two large sacks over their shoulders, perspiring from the load, concluded that the brothers had shot and bagged orange thieves and were now about to eat them. The European planters, also having heard the shots, saw the Tennett brothers with bulging sacks over their shoulders moving through their orchard and assumed they had fired warning shots to scare off orange thieves, and then having retrieved the bags the thieves had filled, were now carrying them out of the orchard to their packing sheds.[270]

Tensions, already tight, heightened the following day when an angry mob gathered at the Tennett's house in Luchenza, involving police intervention, tear gas, and the accidental shooting of a protestor. Riots in the region ensued and disgruntled Africans rose in objection alongside all the issues that the NAC had broadcast. In Cholo, gangs of armed men blocked roads and cut telephone wires, isolating Europeans on their estates. Workers went on strike, refusing to pluck a single leaf of tea or till the fields for tobacco. European homes were vandalized, along with several area chiefs, and some tax collectors were caught and severely beaten. Considerable detachments of armed policemen from the Rhodesias and Tanganyika arrived to curtail the threat, but it wasn't until the spotter planes from Salisbury raided the skies, raining rifle fire and tear gas, rendering 11 Nyasa's dead and 72 injured that the riots finally ceased.[271]

Discontent among the Africans raged: they were defeated both in their complaints about taxes and in their voice against Federation. Nyasaland and the Rhodesias became officially federated just months after the Cholo riots.

It took years for the NAC to re-group and when they did a surprising choice emerged as their leader. Dr Hastings Kamuzu Banda had taken over the leadership of the Congress from Chipembere who warned him that, "There is on the whole not widespread knowledge of what you are or what you can be for us." In spite of this Banda was positioned as a "political Messiah" – the man who would save his people from the British, although even Chipembere doubted that he could liberate the country.[272]

Sangala was correct, "Unity is strength," and when Banda arrived at Chileka on July 6, 1958, greeted by a crowd 3,000 strong, the trajectory of Nyasaland's future as a British country changed forever. Backed by the Congress Youth League, the revitalized Women's League and the NAC itself, Banda gained confidence with each step, and followers with every word. Speaking throughout the three provinces, Banda solidified the position of the NAC to win independence through whatever means became necessary, inciting followers to believe in violence when their pleas to government were met with stalling and apathy. Despite Nyasaland's Governor Sir Robert Armitage conceding that, "The future of Nyasaland lies in achieving regional autonomy within the Federation and that, in the circumstances of Nyasaland, an African controlled government will eventuate and be welcomed," Banda and the NAC were appalled at the rate of response and grew impatient with each delay. Policies to "Hit Europeans or cut throat," emerged alongside "Sabotage and civil disobedience," although many believed the violent rhetoric of the NAC was not matched with an actual desire to cause fatal harm.[273]

Within nine months of Banda's arrival, a state of emergency was declared. Colonial Authority began collapsing all over the country, as mobs swarmed police and taunted Europeans, rioting in civil disobedience by burning bridges, cutting telephone wires and blocking roads. In March, 1959 "Operation Sunrise" was launched, taking 149 nationalists into custody, the real 'trouble makers' flown out to Khami Prison in Rhodesia, and Banda, Chipembere, and Chisiza, the leading NAC members sent to Gwelo Prison, 170 miles south-west of Salisbury. Guilty of breaking the new law where 'being a member of the Congress' was illegal they were subject up to seven years in gaol. Banda's imprisonment and a flurry of political skirmishes in England led to a shortened sentence and Banda was released just over a year after his imprisonment in a whirlwind of controversy surrounding the nature of his incarceration, projected political stability in Nyasaland upon his release, and unwanted interventions from Britain.

Seen by the British as their best chance at 'compromise', Banda went "out of his way to call on people to be peaceful and to leave the fighting to him."[274] Now a 'government in waiting', Banda conceded structural advantages to the Europeans who believed they were working together to create an independent democracy which would smoothly transition from British rule to the new Malawi under the Malawi Congress Party (MCP) which was the new name for the NAC. With independence imminent, the British built a new parliament building in Zomba for the new Government[275] and flooded £1,523,000 into Nyasaland Police services who would need the extra funds to create a transition of power.[276]

Considered an 'outsider' to some, and to others a black skinned 'white man', Banda had challenges to overcome in leading the people of Nyasaland to freedom. He presented his speeches in English and refused to eat nsima – a trait that made people question his nationalism. Yet despite these foreign habits, Banda was the people's choice, the MCP's choice and in a strange way, England's choice to lead the country to independence.

By the early 1960's Federation was crumbling and the strength of Colonial Law diminishing. It was just a matter of time before Banda would rule over it all. The day before independence, Chip and his friend, Dick Marley, went to Chileka to watch the Duke of Edinburgh arrive, almost magically, through a deep chiperoni mist. The Bristol Britannia had landed, and along with it, a new era. 'The Whispering Giant', Britannia's premier airplane, carried the promise of democracy on her wings. "What do you think about this 'freedoms'?" Chip and Dick asked an African policeman in Chi'Nyanja. "Ah Bwana, but this is very wondrous," came the reply. It was clear, the people believed that Banda would rescue them, that in his reign, his people had hope.[277]

On July 6th, 1964, six years to the day after Banda arrived at Chileka Airport to a welcoming crowd, Nyasaland, once the 'Cinderella of British Protectorates' fighting to free the natives from the Arab slavers became the independent country of MALAWI under the MCP and Dr Hastings Kamuzu Banda, a man on the verge of dictatorship. "Malawi", is a derivation of "Maravi" – the Chewa people – Banda's people, originating from the Congo and settling in the land around Kasungu.

"You can't fight progress," some of Chip's acquaintances told him as they packed up from their colonial government offices and headed home to England. Left in the new Malawi, with an estate to manage and a life to maintain, Satemwa was Chip's home, his only home. 'Progress' was the very thing Chip worried about.

When It All Falls Apart 1964-1968

Chip Kay on a road trip circa 1959

The cabinet crisis that Banda faced just months after taking office meant the initial changes within the country were small. Previously close allies, (including Chipembere who was responsible for getting him elected), opposed him and were forced into exile, giving Malawi and the world a glimpse into what would eventuate as a one-party, "president for life" government. Things such as shifting the language from Chi'Nyanja to Chichewa were tolerable. Among the changes, Chewa represented Banda's people from Kasungu and name variances such as Cholo becoming Thyolo, Mlanje becoming Mulanje, and The Nyasaland Flying Club becoming The Luchenza Flying Club were largely acceptable. However, in Thyolo and Mulanje where tea estates occupied large acreages and peasants were landless, 'encroachment' onto European-owned tea estates ended with Banda introducing what he called a "very, very controversial," Malawi Land Bill, giving the Government ultimate power, but to the surprise of the Africans, protecting the land owners from the "predations of the landless."[278] However, Banda through the Smallholder Tea Authority of Malawi encouraged African participation in tea growing, an industry where African grown tea had diminished following the tea slump in the early 1950's. Moreover, this was an area where, in the following decades, the issue of land ownership would surface again but where land bills would not favor the established estates.[279]

Reading the results in the paper, Maclean predicted to Chip, "Well, reason may prevail this time, but there is a snake waiting to strike." There was wisdom in Maclean's hesitancy to accept Banda's 'bone' that was thrown to the Europeans early in the new government while Banda, still conscious of British opinion, was only mildly tempered by it. Chip, with a young family at home, was trying to navigate a way to keep his businesses in Southern Rhodesia and Malawi afloat. It had been challenging since Federation ended, with new laws that affected his dealings. However, he still kept his flying schedule, Wednesdays out and Saturday's home.

In the northeastern province of Nampula in Mozambique Chip discovered his plane had engine trouble. "It's got to have something to do with my exhaust valve," he surmised. The mechanic, catching onto Chip's broken Portuguese mixed with English told him, "I've patched what I can, but you better get it fixed properly as soon as you can get to Salisbury." Chip walked around his plane and patted the metal belly of it, comforting the aircraft as if it were a wounded dog. "Let's get you fixed, Romeo Tango," Chip muttered under his breath, wishing he was closer to a decent repair shop.

The letters VPYRT were boldly printed on the tail and body of Chip's 175 Cessna Skylark, "VP" indicating Nyasaland, and "YRT" – Yanky Romeo Tango – of which the last two letters were the plane's colloquial name. "7Q" – seven Quebec soon replaced "VP" as the preface when official changes occurred after Nyasaland became Malawi.[280]

Chip loved the long spats which sat over the Cessna's wheels like a mudguard, and the gear-propelled engine which he had to keep at high rev's for an unusual light aircraft engine, but one that he had fully mastered. 'Limping' over to Salisbury on a patched fix, Chip was relieved to make the journey to Salisbury Fields who were the Rolls Royce and Continental Agents. They sorted out 'Romeo Tango' and told Chip, "Try to restrain yourself to 10,000ft".[281]

One hundred and seventeen miles from the repeater on Zomba mountain Chip radioed Chileka on his 2 watt transmitter, "Romeo Tango, at the Flight Information Region (FIR) leaving Salisbury for Blantyre." "Copy that, Romeo Tango, you are clear," came the response. Proud of his accuracy in delineating an estimated time of arrival, Chip told the Air Controller in Chileka the estimate of his anticipated touchdown.

Five minutes since his last safety check, Chip noticed the gauges in the Cessna changing. "Remember the creed," he told himself, "Always trust your instruments." Lights began flashing on his control panel, the pressure dropped to zero and the temperature gauge hit the top of its range. Chip looked out the window of Romeo Tango where oil was splattering the wings and when the wind carried it onto the glass, obscuring his vision, he knew he was in trouble. "Oh God, this is it," he thought. Taking the plane up into a stall, he cut the engine forcing the fan to stop. "MAY DAY, MAY DAY, this is Romeo Tango, a beam Chingara 8 miles, TOTAL ENGINE FAILURE, forced landing inevitable."[282]

With the roar of the engine eerily absent, the plane fell silently, floating through clouds as if lost in a dream, Chip's heart pounding with no escape from his chest. He thought about Ba who was pregnant again and about his sweet little Juliet who always looked for him in the sky. He fortified his attitude and told himself he was going to make it. He peered through the patches of glass where oil free blotches allowed a view of the earth below, watching for familiar landmarks. He focused on a dambo, a dry clearing of land just miles ahead, his best chance at a safe landing. Grateful for the hours he had spent learning to fly Tiger Moths, which naturally glided to landing, Chip sat in the cockpit of Romeo Tango, urging the plane into the flattest gliding angle possible. Cautious to avoid a nosedive, and wary of the tedious balance of the airplane's lift and drag, he gently guided Romeo Tango in a silent descent. A Portuguese Air Force officer picked up Chip's May Day signal and sent a report to the air control trackers in Beira who, along with Chileka, followed Romeo Tango until it disappeared, lost in the Zambezi valley.

Having maintained a level gliding approach, Chip landed Romeo Tango onto the dambo without a scratch. He bounced a little, as the wheels rolled over the cracked earth and the occasional stone, "Kangaroo Kay coming in for a landing," Chip joked with himself when he realized he had made it. Dust hung in the air around the plane as Chip opened the door. He saw the cause of his problems, a misplaced grommet, which had lasted one and a half hours and eventually wriggled free from the engine, causing oil drainage. He walked around it, the heat of the day making the leaked oil smell pungent, and then climbed back in to the plane to collect his blazer from where it sat folded over the back seat, along with his little black, 'James Bond' briefcase. He closed the door and set out on foot.

Having gained a position from the sky, Chip knew exactly where he was, and paced the 5 miles to the road through the crusty fields and the hollowed earth which tried to trip him up in places. A further 2 miles once he reached the road and he was at the Chingara border greeting the African Sergeant who recognized him immediately. "Where's your truck driver, Mr Million?" he asked. "He's at home," Chip replied. "Well, where's your truck?" he probed. "At home," Chip said, offering nothing further. Puzzled, the Sergeant continued, "I thought you stopped trucking. I thought you go by air now?" Amused, Chip said, "Yes, I go by air." "So, where's your plane?" the Sergeant kept digging. Finally, Chip told him, "I did go by air, but then I decided to walk, so I've left my airplane." "Oh. You better come see the Bwana," the Sergeant said, leading him to the office of the immigration chief who gave Chip forms to complete. "Complete," he said nodding at Chip. Under 'reason for visit', Chip cited, "health" and then asked the officer, "Please sir, can you take me to see the District Commissioner (DC)?"

The DC wandered into the room. Awoken from his afternoon siesta, he squinted to see the man before him whom he did not recognize. "I wish to report an aircraft incident," Chip told him. "I am a pilot and my aircraft, suffering engine failure, is now sitting in one of your fields nearby." "Ah, ok. And what is the registration of the plane?" the DC inquired. "It's VPYRT, let me write it down for you," Chip stated. Before he could find a pen and paper the DC shouted, "Victor Romeo Tango!! And you, are you Senor Kay?" Surprised Chip agreed, "Yes, I am, but how do we...." "Oh! We may not have met in person, but we have spoken so many times over the radio. I used to be the senior air traffic controller for Beira."[283]

Having cleared customs and reported his incident, Chip stood at the rail of the custom building, searching for a ride to Tete. He found one with a tobacco farming couple from Malawi who were happy to help him when they discovered him stranded. They arrived at the Zambezi Hotel in Tete, a building sited on a street corner, sturdy and simple, the only hotel along the Zambezi river in a province swallowed on three sides by other countries. Chip signed in at the front desk, "Chip Kay, Satemwa, PO BOX 6, Thyolo, Malawi." Even that signature was difficult to get used to, "THY-O-L-O", "How can that really be Cholo?" he thought, scribbling 'Malawi' with a wrinkled nose. He took his room key and closed the door behind him. Almost instantly there was a loud "knocking" on the other side of the door. "Yes!" Chip said, as he opened the door, revealing a large German woman, a 'giant' of a woman next to Chip. "You – Maclean Kay – Nyasaland?" she spoke in broken English. "Yes, me Junior Kay, Maclean Kay, my father," Chip returned, wondering how he might know this woman. "Kommen Sie," she said, motioning for him to follow.

She led him to the manager's quarters, past the small kitchen, through a pile of laundry waiting to be folded, and into what looked like her private bedroom. "Oh goodness," Chip thought, "What does she want with me?" She reached her bureau of drawers, and pulled one of them out, resting it on the floor. Frilly, lacy snippets of clothing fell out, and Chip wondered if he was caught in a kinky sun-cured German Colonial twilight zone. Frau Shultz, the robust German woman before him, married to the famous hunter Herr Shultz, explained that years ago, 34 in fact, Chip had slept the night in that drawer when his parents had broken down on the

Salisbury road. "Ah, I see," said Chip, "Well I'm a bit too big to sleep there now."[284]

Meanwhile, Des and The Luchenza Flying Club heard the May Day with no rescue reported and took off the following morning in search of Chip and the downed plane. From Makwasa airfield, Dr Jack Harvey acting on an errant message from Beira went south, experiencing his own forced landing near Sena when his club plane ran out of fuel. Des, Jack and the pilots searched for hours while Chip drove back to Blantyre. His attempts to phone home having failed, he was completely unaware of the rescue operation that was circling overhead.

When he did make it home to Satemwa, Ba and Juliet were waiting for him. Juliet was picking sheaths of grass from the front lawn and laying them flat to make a road. "Julie!" Chip called out to her, as he ran from the car to the lawn, plucking her up and swinging her high over his head. She squeezed his neck tight and pressed her soft cheek into his stubble, making a grimace when she got scratched. "Hello, darling," he said to Ba, giving her a kiss and rubbing her belly, "And how is our other little one? Boy or girl? What do you think now?" he asked her. "I don't care," she said, "Another girl would suit me just fine." Juliet was waiting now, patiently, knowing that every time her daddy went away, he always brought her something small when he returned.

The lady at the shop in Salisbury had insisted on wrapping it. "Is this a Christmas present?" she asked Chip, "Oh no. This is a 'daddy's been away three days' gift," he said, winking at the clerk. He had enrolled the help of the lady to purchase a Fischer Price 'post office box' for Juliet. It was a sturdy metal case topped by a red roof with cut out shapes, triangle, circle, square, diamond and oblong holes, perfect to occupy young children with stuffing the matching pieces into the shape on the lid, and then retrieving them to begin the process over again.[285]

Juliet rattled the wrapped package. She looked at Chip. "Open it," he encouraged, and she opened the package, released the lid of the box and shook out the shapes. Reaching first for the round ball and finding the circle on the roof, she pushed it through the hole to the animated clapping of both her parents. She took one of the pieces over to her mother's bulging tummy and held it close, "Baby wants to play", she said. "Soon, baby will," her mother replied, softly patting her head.

She didn't have to wait long before she had a sister, Patricia Rose Kay, also born at Malamulo Mission Hospital just down the road from Satemwa. "Tryshie," Julie tried saying again and again, each time the name sounding different. "She's a beautiful baby," Chip told Ba, cuddling their new little bundle and holding her out for Juliet to see. They viewed her birth documents, checking the spelling of the names and the dates indicated for birth. Both parents froze when they saw emboldened the word, "MALAWI" under 'country of birth.'[286]

For most babies born in Malawi in 1966, 'country of birth' would be a non-issue. For a European family however, it signified uncertainty and distress. Prior to independence the British had made provisions for families such as the Kay's and transient Africans who teetered on borders, by stating that Malawi Citizenship should be awarded to "everyone born in Malawi irrespective of racial origin as well as all those who had resided in the country for seven years or more."[287] However, once independence was achieved, Banda denounced this provision, essentially rendering babies such as Patricia Kay "Stateless." Only Africans or babies born to an African mother could qualify for Malawi Citizenship. And under British law, since her father was born in Nyasaland, and only her mother in England, Trysh didn't meet the requirements for British Citizenship either. "God, they're bloody ignorant!" Chip said, holding his newborn's 'stateless' birth documents. He was referring to both Banda and the Brits.[288]

It took months of negotiations and appointments with lawyers to settle the matter, and when Malawi rejected baby Patricia, despite being a second generation born in the country, Britain finally took her in. With the battle over, Ba told Chip, "The children and I need a little break, perhaps we'll go see some friends in Cape Town." "What a wonderful idea," Chip replied, thinking of how it would ease his burden of worry when he flew out every Wednesday. "I'll arrange the tickets and you can leave next week."

When Ba departed for Cape Town, Juliet was three and a half, and baby Trysh, six months old. "Bye daddy, see you next week," Juliet said. "This time, you can bring me a present," Chip teased her, tickling her belly to make her laugh. He waved them off, and quickly his mind fell back to work. There were business cards that needed updating, address labels to print, tea processes that required supervision, entries to mark in his diary and minutes from his new business "Leopard Air Limited" to run through.

A week passed swiftly, and Chip, buried in work, was looking forward to his family's return. He welcomed phone calls from Ba and his children during the week, but then suddenly, the calls stopped and his calls south went unanswered. Then on the day they were ticketed to arrive back to Chileka, Ba and the two girls failed to show up.

Ba had taken the girls, and at some point during her 'short' stay in Cape Town had decided not to return home. She fled from friend to friend, taking the girls along, until finally, she was untraceable. Chip called all his contacts and acquaintances, begging for information, pleading with them to help him locate his wife and babies. He was desperate and for the first time in his life, he had no solution. He was completely out of control. He spent days on the telephones, calling hotels, friends, family, frantic for information about Ba, Julie and Trysh. He spent nights in deep sweats, the lonely echoes in the halls of his house a constant reminder of the absence of infant cries. Sometimes he would wake, believing it all a nightmare, and expecting to see Julie racing down the polished cement hall, slipping on the over shined floors right into his arms. Their absence was a constant torment for eighteen long, anxious months.

In the early days of June 1968, working alongside Ba's father, Chip managed to contact his estranged wife. She had landed in Natal with what Chip assumed was a boyfriend of sorts. "I blame myself," he told her when they finally reconnected. "All those days away, and you at home, alone. It wasn't fair." But she didn't offer any reasons or excuses for what she had done, only agreeing to meet Chip in Salisbury so he could see the children again and they could plan a way forward. On the day America was grieving the loss of another assassinated Kennedy (Robert F. Kennedy) Chip was reconciling with his baby girls. Trysh, now 2 years old was looking at him with peculiarity wondering who he was, and Julie rushing to him, wondered why she hadn't seen her daddy for so long. Tears welled in Chip's eyes as he hugged her. His family was broken; he was on the brink of divorce, but he had found his babies again and now he would never let them go.

The courts awarded Chip full custody of Juliet and Patricia in an amicable settlement where Chip and Ba, behaving like well-educated adults, made agreements and concessions for shared time with the girls. "They should stay with you for school," Chip told Ba. "I'll pay, of course, but I think they should attend a Catholic school, the Convent in Salisbury would suffice. Holidays they must come home to me at Satemwa."[289]

Their 'trade-agreement' seemed to work satisfactorily, and the girls bounced happily between Rhodesia for school and Malawi for holidays. Juliet was always keen to see her pet rabbit on Satemwa who she named "Thumper". She often told the guests who came for Sunday lunch, (just loud enough for Chip to hear), "Daddy thinks I don't know that when I leave to go back to school he eats my bunny, and then he puts a new one in the cage, ready for when I come back for holidays…"[290]

One day, when Chip had taken the girls with him to Mashonaland Flying Club at Mount Hamton, Juliet stood with her hand horizontal on her brow shading her eyes as she stared into the sky. One of the flying members came over to her and asked, "Who are you little girl?" "My name is Juliet," she stated, still fixated on the sky. "And what are you doing?" he asked. "I'm looking for my daddy," she said. "What's he doing up there?" "Well, he's in an airplane, he's a pilot," she told him. "Where is he from?"

the man continued delving. "Oh, he lives in Malawi." "And how do you know which one is him?" Juliet took her eyes off the sky momentarily and looked at the man as if he had just asked a silly question, then she specified, "My daddy's got a yellow tail."

LEOPARD AIR from 1965

From left: Basil Tennett, Des Tennett, Bill Stone, Chip Kay, Poocho Conforzi, Bob Slade
circa 1965

The original logo for Leopard Air was a dark blue tail, with a golden leopard sitting on a rock at the center. However, owing to the fact that the leopard was Malawi's national animal, Banda's Government quickly informed Chip that he was not 'allowed' to use it for his company. As a result, "LAL" Leopard Air Limited transpired with a fully yellow tail and the letters "LAL" on it. If nothing but a consolation, Chip enjoyed the fact that the yellow tail, easily spotted from the ground, allowed his daughters to trace his movements in the sky.

LAL formed in 1965 at Chip's house, over dinner, with five of his closest flying friends who were also keen to incorporate their love of flying with a business venture. "We'll all get more flying time, and somebody else will be paying for it." One stated, "We'll be able to open up Malawi's natural beauty to visitors who don't have time to go by car." Another chimed in, "We'll get LOTS of flying hours…and train many more pilots." One more said, "Chartered air is not available, we'll be the first. We get to buy more planes and sell them to others – one of us should be a Cessna dealer." The ideas were zipping around the table, and each man threw 1,000MK (Malawi Kwacha) into the pot towards the dream of providing a fully functional charter airline service in Malawi. The night ended with Chip volunteering to be an agent for Cessna, the company who boasted the most sales for light aircraft in the whole world. From the humble beginnings at Chip's table and their contributions, Chip, Des and Basil Tennett, Bob Slade (who worked with Chip at PTA), Bill Stone and Poocho Conforzi (whom Chip had taught to fly) formed LAL and established Malawi's first charter airline, offering services around the country.[291]

The letters "YCSACSOYA" occupied a large space on the notepads distributed at the Cessna Dealer convention for Southern Africa held in Johannesburg. Chip had applied for and been granted dealership status to sell Cessna aircraft in Malawi under agreements with Comair Airways in South Africa. "Is this a particular reference?" Chip asked the Cessna presenter, pointing to the YCSACSOYA at the top of his notepad. "It's an interesting question. We were wondering if someone might ask... It's very simple. Everybody look at your notepad, and I'll 'sing' it for you," the man offered. "You Can't Sell A Cessna Sitting On Your Ass."[292]

"What a perfect saying," Chip thought to himself, never being the type of man who sat around waiting for others to make things happen. "I'll adopt it for Satemwa...You Can't Sell Satemwa Tea Sitting On Your Ass in Thyolo."

Soon Leopard Air acquired its first plane, a Cessna 150, but moved as quickly as possible towards their preferred plane, the Cessna 206, a single-engine, general aviation aircraft that was increasing in popularity for commercial use. Described as the "sport utility vehicle of the air," the 206 was a robust, rugged choice with a large cabin that could seat six adults. Since the release of the 206 in 1962, "Bush pilots" who could use the plane for a variety of functions preferred it to previous models. The LAL members, some of the best 'bush pilots' in Africa, solely ran the 206 for charter work, until collectively they decided to expand their services, adding two 172 Skyhawks , and two 150 Commuters, bringing their LAL fleet up to five airplanes.

Central African Airways (CAA), operating eight-seater DeHavilland Beavers, emerged as the main competition for LAL charter services boosted by the government who blasted LAL with the directive to only occupy a maximum of three seats in their six-seater plane, excluding the pilot. In silent protest, Chip hung a sign on the back of the last row headboard stating, "These seats are not allowed to be occupied by order of the Malawi Directorate of Civil Aviation, supported by Central African Airways."[293] It was a load of nonsense, and everybody knew it, but the newspapers – afraid of recourse from a harshening government – refused to highlight the disadvantaged LAL, despite several articles submitted by members objecting to the 'monopoly' situation CAA held.[294]

Within four months of taking office, Banda had announced his plans to move the old Colonial seat of Government in Zomba to a new, central location in Lilongwe, despite the new Government House erected specifically for his presidency by the British before Independence.[295] In a passive aggressive fight against the restrictions imposed on LAL, the charter airline poked at Banda's stagnancy, which had not come to fruition even five years after his announcement, by describing tours that flew over Zomba as passing "the present-day Capital." "I hope he's reading that notice," Chip told Des as they denied another request to fly four people together in their six-seater plane. "It's really baloney," Des continued, "Who travels in groups of three anyways?"

Offering two-day, one-day and half-day tours, Leopard Air proceeded with its charter operations despite setbacks from a finicky government who were proving more and more confused about what the term 'progress' meant for a country and not just a few elites at the top. The most expensive two-day tour cost £40 per person, flying up to Kasungu Game Reserve, north of Lilongwe, where lion, elephant, kudu and the largest antelope – the eland- presented in strong numbers. Another two-day tour took passengers to Cape Maclear Hotel, an area of the lake "famous for goggling", later known as snorkeling. One-day tours went to Monkey Bay, Salima or Cape Maclear, and included stops for lunch at local hotels, some passing by "present capital Zomba" and covering between 250-300 miles in the day at a cost of £20 per ticket. One hundred and fifty mile, £11 half-day tours stayed in the southern district, flying down to the hot Shire valley which caught the backside of Thyolo mountain as it spilled over the escarpment, above the Shire Highlands, with a particularly good view of the beautiful tea below, or passing the "present capital", returning by the Shire Valley.[296]

There were several pilots whom LAL employed, most of whom were either taught to fly in Luchenza, or who came with some prior skills and built on those with the Luchenza Flying Club. "One should never think they know all there is about flying from just one instructor," Chip and Des had agreed, evidenced by Chip having 27 instructors in his lifetime, and teaching 24 others to fly. "Although I can never actually remember if it was 27 pupils I had, and 24 instructors or the other way around," he later admitted. They made it easy for people to learn to fly, giving their planes over to the club for students who only had to pay £3 per session to cover the gas and insurance. "It's a flying revolution," Chip marveled with Des as they stood on the edge of the grass runway at Lunchenza watching plane after plane soar into the sky, each time with a different learner pilot.[297]

On one occasion, Leopard Air pilot – Sam Richman – had an opportunity to cement the reputation the flying club enjoyed, boasting some of the 'best bush pilots in Africa.' He had taken two tourists on a charter flight destined for Salima along the lakeshore on a docile day where the warm sun would make the journey pleasant. Ascending from Chileka in LAL 7QY-FB, "Fox Bravo" Cessna 206, Sam was barely at

1,000ft when the boss failed. The eight bolts holding the fan tight popped, each one flinging off the propeller with a terrifying 'zing', and within microseconds the windscreen was black. "Hold on," Sam told his passengers while he radioed the control tower he had just left, "MAY DAY Chileka, this is Fox Bravo below 1,000ft and declining quickly, propeller malfunction."[298]

Looking out the side window for a landing, he dropped the plane searching for a soft place to bring Fox Bravo down. Having viewed one clearing, he was preparing the cabin for impact when at the last moment a mud-bricked school emerged into his view, hundreds of little children screaming at the thunderous 'bird' that was chasing them. He pulled up on the controls, managing to scrape the plane over the thatched roof, before settling it in the middle of a field of maize, just on the other side of the school. It was a bumpy landing, but everyone survived. One of the men suffered an injured leg, but the only fatality was Fox Bravo who never flew again. "If it wasn't for Sam's expertise, we might have been planning funerals today," Chip told the investigators after the crash.

Leopard Air pilots and non-commercial pilots from The Luchenza Flying Club often went to the movies as a group on a Saturday or Wednesday night in Limbe. They bunched together on rows of seats where six were attached by a metal rod. Sitting in a section they had unofficially reserved for pilots, there were approximately 24 seats consumed by the 'flying community.' On show – a war movie called, "The Dam Busters", which followed the efforts of wing commander 'Guy Gibson' who led his squadron in the 1943 Ruhr dam busting raids over Germany. After Gibson had dropped the bombs into the dam from his mosquito airplane flying at a death-defying low level, he began a steep pull upwards to avoid hitting the wall of the dam on the incline. The flying section in the Limbe theatre all sensed the drama of the moment and urged Gibson's plane to fly above the wall by leaning too far back in their rows, willing the planes above the dam wall. Just as Gibson flew out of the dam, the entire flying community fell backwards in their seats, the connected rows of six, hurtling to the floor like dominoes. "Might I suggest a 'romantic' flick next week...," one member suggested, as the pilots turned their seats over and took their place again among the "hushing" of other theatregoers who didn't understand why an entire section had just fallen over.[299]

The Luchenza Flying Club was also growing during the time that Leopard Air had formed, and each member was charged with a project to enhance its development. Chip was to build the Luchenza Club Swimming pool, a long rectangular pool neatly edged by cement, with palm trees stretching through the landscape at one end. It was equipped with a diving board and bench seats surrounding it, and painted in the brightest blue available, a quality paint that would outlast the cement. It was ironic that the one person who didn't swim was in charge of building a pool, but he took to the task, applying his penchant for quality and produced a beautiful pool, with a proper 'deep' end for the flying club. On the official opening day for the Luchenza Flying Club Swimming Pool, models from the school for young ladies in Blantyre beautified the club as they strolled about in their bikinis and high heels, a thing that Chip thought would make his sister smile, even from the grave. Juliet would have been the first to dive into the pool, having developed a love for the water when she was just 'wee wig' with her mother and brother in Cape Town. Unfortunately, Chip had not taken to the swimming lessons his mother had pushed on him as a young boy in Cape Town, despite his father's concerns voiced in letters to Flora Jean about Chip's inability to swim. Now, as a grown man in the middle of his life, he was petrified of water, more than a few inches in his bath.[300]

A couple of the men at the Flying Club thought the guy who made the pool should be thrown in. After all, it was opening day and Chip should be the one to 'christen' the pool. They grabbed Chip from behind and with mighty laughter heaved him into the water, slapping each other's hands with jovial giggles as they turned towards the bar, unaware that they had left Chip behind drowning. Realizing he was about to be thrown into the pool, Chip had shouted, "I can't swim", but his voice was overridden by the laughter of the men. Those who knew Chip well understood his fear of swimming, even if he had joked about "just walking uphill" should he ever find himself in such a situation as he was in now. It turned out "walking uphill" was difficult. Below the surface of the water he was like a weighted tea chest, sinking as the air inside escaped to the light. Looking up at the sunshine which split the water into a thousand tiny circles each trickling down towards his heavy body, he saw a shadow appear into the light and felt the arms of a strong black man pulling him back towards the surface. Snowdrop, the barman at the club had seen Chip pushed in and watched the men who did it walk away while Chip disappeared. Fully dressed, shoes still on his feet, he had leapt into the pool to save Chip's life. "I must be the only guy here who can't swim," Chip told Snowdrop as they sat on the edge of the pool, soaked from head to toe. "And I might be the only barman who can," Snowdrop answered, pulling Chip to his feet and accompanying him back to the club.

Chip hated the thought of swimming so much, that despite the opportunity to see cichlids, the famous fish of Lake Malawi appearing in a rainbow of colors, he had never been into the lake. The Flying club had taken their Tiger Moths, along with a few more modern aircraft to Monkey Bay, landing in elephant grass, so tall it could conceal mostly anything. As not many planes used the landing strip at Monkey Bay, it had become a ritual between Chip and Des to 'mow' the runway shortly after landing, to clear a path for take-off. They would start the propeller on the Tiger, one of them sat in the cockpit and the other held the Tiger's tail up, tilting the blades at the perfect angle so the grass in front fell upon contact with the spinning fan. Up and down the grass strip, they sauntered until they mowed an area large enough for a clear take-off.

The Flying Club, along with skilled instructors and practising students had gone to the lake for a weekend of fun, flying low over the waters, finding hippopotamus' in the quiet bays tucked by Nkudzi and occasionally performing stunts, although more for their own enjoyment in the absence of a crowd. Dr Jack Harvey, the 'flying doctor' from Malamulo Mission Hospital, was a highly skilled acrobatic flyer, maneuvering Spit Fire planes in the war and after arriving in Nyasaland in the late 1950's, had become the Chief Flying Instructor (CFI) for The Nyasaland Flying Club. Missionary children whose parents worked with Jack at Malamulo often waited near the airstrip at the mission, hoping Dr Harvey would offer them a flip, one boy remembering how on take-off Jack coaxed his plane into a barrel roll over the top of village roofs as they soared up from the mission.[301]

At the lake, he had taken Les Shapiro as co-pilot up in Des Tennett's Oscar Charlie Tiger Moth and was flying low by the resorts along the lakeshore. He flicked the plane into a roll, as he had done a hundred times before, but something went awry. Oscar Charlie, out of control, plummeted into the waters just meters from the sandy shore. The Luchenza pilots who stood on the beach watching Jack and Les rubbed their eyes, the scene before them confirming every pilot's worst nightmare, and they ran alongside the shore towards the accident, fearing the worst. Forgetting that he didn't know how to swim, Chip dashed into the water, towards Oscar Charlie. Fortunately, the plane, rested on the lakebed, shallow enough that Chip's feet always found solid ground. He touched the wings, and shouted to the open-aired cockpits, "Are you fellows alright?" To which he heard the good news, "Both OK, just a little beaten up…."

It was the only time Chip even "swam" in the lake, and he liked to remind Jack about it when he asked Chip to come help him 'cure' whooping cough at the Flying club. Jack believed, because he had seen it happen, that taking a slow climb up to 12,000ft (approximately one hour), then a sudden drop acted like a decompression chamber, curing children of the dreaded whooping cough. Chip was happy to oblige and took children up in his plane with a Malamulo nurse holding onto the child. After several trips, he also began to think this method really did work.[302]

Dr. Jack Harvey was senior to Chip, not just in flying but also in years, and Chip always looked up to him as a mentor. He flew around the country giving medical care to those who couldn't reach a hospital, and even obliged house visits for Jean Kay, just twenty kilometers down the road at 'The Satemwa House'. One day, while Jack piloted a Tiger Moth at The Nyasaland Flying Club, thrilling crowds with his superior aerobatic skills, waving to his newly pregnant wife when he swooped low over the clubhouse where she sat sipping tea, before climbing up towards a final ascent, a loud 'boom' flooded the sky. Irene, Jack's wife, saw the plane dive nose-first towards the ground, where a haunting thud echoed towards her, rattling the teapot on the table. Friends held her back, not wanting her to see what most feared to be a fatal crash. Someone telephone Chip, "There's been a hell of a prang at the flying club, please come immediately – it's Jack."[303]

"Not Jack!" Chip thought, calling to Folloko Banda, his house boy, trained to help start both a Tiger Moth and a Cessna. "Fox Echo," Chip's 172 'horsebox' sat on the front lawn, with Folloko inside. Chip at the front of the Cessna, wound the fan and instead of waiting for Chip patiently, as he had done a hundred times before, Folloko opened the throttle, the tail lifted up, and the Cessna jumped the chocks. Narrowly, Chip escaped the whirring fan, and raced around the side of the Cessna, swung up on the arm, wrestled the wind to open the door and pulled Folloko Banda out. Together they stood on the lawn, watching as "Fox Echo" left the ground, not without paddle but without a pilot, bobbling through the sky before crashing into the trees just a few hundred yards from his front door. He had now lost two planes in the space of an hour. But, had he also lost a friend and a flying mentor?

He sped to the club by road and arrived to discover that his worst imaginings were reality. Jack had been taken by air to Malamulo, his pregnant wife driven to the house of friends on the mission. Jack's death was confirmed by the wail of women at the hospital, their cries trickling up the hill to where Irene sat, now a widow. "I don't want to go see his dead body," she told her friends, "I always want to remember him waving to me from the Tiger at the club."[304]

The flying community were like a brotherhood, looking out for each other, bonded by the common thread of piloting a plane. If one went missing, or had a problem, the whole group came to help. But it was often Chip who was called first or ended up being a bearer of bad news. One day, a pilot, trained by a Leopard Air Instructor, failed to check in on his flight plan. George Modesley – known to his friends as 'Jungle Jim' was on a standard flight path that he flew frequently. He had taken a job with Lunhro in charge of overseeing the transport of barges full of Molasses from Malawi to Holland. Once, on the airfield in Chikwawa in the seething hot Shire Valley, it was decided to slap the runway with Molasses to make it smoother. What the engineers didn't account for was the intense heat, which on a new runway, slathered with Molasses, holds onto wheels like glue. Unaware of the sticky trap, Chip's airplane got stuck for 3 days, and was a "hell of a mess to clean up afterwards." He couldn't help but think of that moment, with the tacky molasses when George Modesley's wife called him with the news, "George is missing Chip, it's been 5 days."[305]

Jungle Jim had gone to Mozambique and when Chip asked his wife for details of his route, she didn't have much to offer. Chip kidded her, "He's probably gone there to eat all my prawns - well, leave it to me, and I'll go find him," Chip told her, making plans to leave as soon as possible. He made inquiries by phone first, searching for details about George's flight path, where he had last checked in and where he had said he was going. He reached out to a network of flying friends stretching from Johannesburg to Nairobi, but no one had heard about George. Everybody said, "There's no record of him." Then one suggested, "I'd pop over to Nacala. He often goes that way." Nacala, in northern Mozambique sits on top of pristine white sands, over vivid turquoise waters on the deepest natural port on the East Coast of Africa. "Maybe he's checking on his molasses barges," Chip thought, as he traced a flight path to Nacala.

Chip radioed Chileka and informed the tower, "I'm going to Nacala, it's an emergency. One of my friends is in trouble and I need to go help him." "Inde Bwana, suuure, when you get back you can clear customs," said the traffic controller, 'suuure' a very African, English word that made Chip think of Nelson and his singing "Tweenkel Tweenkel Leetle Star." Arriving in Mozambique on a rescue mission, Chip wasted no time in seeking the most competent Air Traffic Controller in the region. "Ah, George Modesley," the man said, scratching his chin. "Yes, we remember George, his registration numbers are right here," he added pointing to a torn-off paper sheet which could have easily been lost in yesterday's rubbish. "And the flight plan?" Chip inquired, pressing them for details. "Ah, flight plan," he replied, fearing having misplaced it. "We know he was in Nacala, then he left Nacala...." "What time did he leave Nacala?" Chip queried. "Ah, but it was around seven in the morning, six days ago," the controller replied, pleased he had some information to contribute.[306]

"I'll need some help," Chip thought, finding an engineer from the customs office who was willing to join the rescue. "He should have been on his way to Bangula, and most likely experienced a forced landing somewhere en route," Chip told his new companion, as he slid his finger over the map of Mozambique. Commandeering a taxi for their mission, Chip informed the driver, "Listen, we are going to be stopping every few miles to talk to the natives, ok?" The driver took them all the way, eighty miles to Nacala, and when they arrived Chip remarked, "Thank you very much, you can go home now." The engineer looked at him strangely, as if he didn't sign up to go 'walking on foot'. However, the determination in Chip's stride gave the man hope and the two of them - carrying water and some bread rolls - set out on foot to find George. "Pilots fly with the railroad on their left, so we will follow the railroad and we shall find our man," Chip stated to his new friend. They passed village after village, each time with little more information, excepting that around the time of George's disappearance the weather had been terrible, enveloped with clouds and patches of heavy rain.[307]

Finally, a man in one village had seen George "flying very low" and passing "just over there…" So, Chip and his friend went by the railroad in the direction of the tip-off, walking through desolate countryside, the occasional tree looking out of place in the desert like terrain. "Eeeee, I don't like this country," said the man alongside Chip, "It's lion country, you can smell them…along with other predators," making both men a little uneasy, as they were clearly unprotected from the threats. There were boulders clustered into a small hill, forming little kopjes in the otherwise flat landscape. "Now I don't like this country," Chip added, thinking of the dangers of flying low in bad weather with rocks stubbing the ground, too small to mark a mountain on the map, too large to fly too low. Out of the dry, barren land, a little village appeared, with a forest of trees behind. "We saw such a thing, falling by those trees…," the curious people agreed, trailing behind Chip and the engineer as they walked closer to the site. By now, two or three villages had joined Chip as he searched the Mozambique countryside for the missing pilot. Most, unaware of what they were looking for, bumbled along in jolly tones, the dust from a hundred pairs of feet clinging to the search party in a dirty bubble. The children ran – like flag bearers – pushing rusty bicycle rims with sticks just ahead of the adults.

Scraps of plane glinted in the early afternoon sun, providing a path to the bulk of the wreckage, wedged between boulders in a small kopje just beyond the forest. The villagers who were following, turned around at Chip's request, allowing him some privacy to survey the crash and check for signs of life. Down by the pedals, George's hat lay stuck underneath the accelerator, torn bits of clothing strewn about the seat, and a logbook on the dash, which George had written in minutes after crashing. "Flying at 20ft, poor visibility, plenty of fuel on board." He had survived the impact, but the broken windshield breached the safety of the cabin, exposing him to the elements, and the remnants of his person were all but gone. "Hyena," the two men agreed, noting blood gushes on the ripped upholstery where not even a bone remained. "I imagine his legs were crushed when the plane collided with the rocks. He was a like a 'sitting duck', poor chap. What a way to go…" Chip shook his head and motioned to his companion that it was time to leave the terrible sight.

They stood by the railroad, waiting for a train. One came, traveling in the wrong direction and stopped so the conductor could ask Chip, "What on earth are you doing out here?" "There's a plane over there," Chip motioned to the kopje. "Is the pilot alright?" "Well, no not really. In fact, he's quite dead." The conductor nodded and pushed on. Chip and his friend sat under a mango tree and waited. Four hours later, another train came and took them back to the offices where Chip had left his plane. Chip thanked his traveling companion and flew back to Malawi on his own. He radioed Chileka, asking them to inform Satemwa of his flight straight to Sucoma, down in the Shire Valley. When he touched down, he met the General Manager and told him about George. "I don't think we ought to tell his wife anything, except to say that the body is missing," he suggested, knowing that she would want a body for the funeral, but not wanting to put her through the agony of knowing her husband's last moments were in the jaws of one of Africa's most notoriously creepy hunters.[308]

Timati Moyo Kukoma 1968
(Life Is Sweet)

Maclean Kay standing on the khondi of the Satemwa House circa 1965

In Malawi, certainly in the old Nyasaland, a person might inquire of another, "Moyo Kukoma?" (Life is sweet), "Ku siya chinachilichonse?" (Will you leave any cows?) Sometimes, when his workers were in heavy discussions that leaned towards self-indulgence and narrow perspectives, Chip invoked this saying as a combination of admonishment and a call to action at the same time. In English, the saying meant, "You might as well spend your money here; you can't take it with you (when you die)." He asked them, "Do you think you're so important, that you will leave behind many cows when you pass on?" The old saying, if used sparingly, had a way to quiet groups, and a way to incite individuals to deep thought about the future. Life is sweet - will you leave any cows?[309]

Ten days before his death Maclean at the age of 76 had been in his usual place – the Satemwa Tea Factory just below 'The Satemwa House', monitoring the processes of drying and inspecting the quality of tea as it sifted from the dryers. He sat on a tall tea table, his legs dangling with a gap of at least two feet between his heels and the ground. His workers gathered around him as he gave them updates and listened to their sign-offs. When he jumped from the table and reached the floor, awkwardly, his body shook on impact and shortly after he fell sick. Captain Knox, a chief Leopard Air pilot, flew the Kay's to Blantyre with Maclean laid out on a stretcher on one side of the plane, and Chip squashed beside him on the other, holding his father's cold hands, and tucking a blanket around his body as they flew.[310]

Doctors suspected a 'fractured oesophagus', as he hemorrhaged after the incident at the factory and landed in Blantyre General Hospital (Queen Elizabeth Hospital), never to recover. Dr Coffin, a name Chip thought very apt for the circumstance, signed his death certificate citing "hepatic failure."

Two years earlier, Maclean had suffered an attack of malaria while visiting London. Hospitalized, the Doctors began tests and told Maclean, "It's very odd that you should be from Central Africa, but you quite clearly have Malayan malaria today." It had been over 45 years since Maclean had left Malaya, and yet the malaria that he so vehemently fought while working for Guthries had remained with him, dormant for years.[311] "Given my father's unusual history with tropical illnesses, I would request that we send his liver to London for testing," Chip asked the Doctor at Blantyre Hospital who agreed and sent Maclean's liver hoping for further information into the cause of his death. With his father's liver on the way to England, Chip took the rest of Maclean's body to Salisbury, to a proper funeral parlor where the Scottish planter was cremated and then brought back to Malawi.[312]

Just over a decade after "wee wig" perished, Maclean joined her in the All Saints Cemetery in Thyolo, his grave within inches of hers. By no accident, his tomb was allocated in the center of the Kay family row. Once in place his black marble tombstone, with a substantial cross rising from the head would read, "To The Glory of God - Maclean Kay – born 4th July 1892, died 9th Dec 1968 – REST IN PEACE."

After all, he was the reason the family experienced the problems and privileges of the African continent. He was the giver of a colonial childhood to his children, a mixed life of opportunity and toil for his wife, and by his example and exertions he gave a legacy to his grandchildren and his great grandchildren. It was a legacy of hard work, perseverance and determination. What began in 1922 in the British Protectorate, Nyasaland, really started in 1892 when on Nithsdale Road, a Scottish family welcomed their last-born boy into the family. Over the years, Maclean battled drought, re-built burnt homes, nurtured fickle crops and raised a family amongst tropical perils. He triumphed with Satemwa – taking it from a fledgling tobacco farm in the Shire Highlands, to an estate sprawling with tea. He was a planter, through and through, from rubber to tobacco and

164

finally to tea; 'scratching the earth' was his passion. Delighted to watch plants grow and live off the land he taught the African people a new way – what he considered a better way forward – always advocating for nutritious food and improved conditions for his workforce. He was a true colonial pioneer. Fiercely loyal – he loved deeply and at times he lost more than he thought he could bare.

When Maclean (Mick) Kay died in the Blantyre General Hospital on the 9th of December 1968, he left behind more than a few cows. He gave to his family, "Satemwa" – an estate that Chip said "is a monument to human endeavor. Satemwa is my father's work, and me? – now I am the caretaker."

Maclean Kay in his tea factory on Satemwa circa 1955

Dolce Vita 1968-1970

Chip Kay in Captain uniform circa 1973

After his father passed away, it was Jean who – along with Chip – was in charge of maintaining Satemwa. It was a difficult time for Chip (now 37) and his mother (aged 59), set against a backdrop of political changes and uncertainty. Southern Rhodesia, watching members of their old Federation gain independence, decided unequivocally against the idea, the white settler government – a self-governing colony since 1923 -digging its heels into Africa and proclaiming a Unilateral Declaration of Independence (UDI) from Britain on the 11th of November 1965. However, the 'illegal' UDI, under Prime Minister Ian Douglas Smith, caught the ire of Britain, and the Crown opposed the 'rogue' settler country, imposing harsh sanctions against them when Ian Smith showed no interest in acquiescing. Many white settlers in Malawi, having already experienced a capricious new 'majority' government on the verge of autocracy and political close-mindedness, left and joined the UDI movement in Southern Rhodesia, believing that 'law and order' under a 'minority' leadership was the only way Africa – at least in the current climate - could survive.

If it wasn't for Michael Blackwood's (the family's lawyer) intervention Chip might have merged with the Rhodesian efforts, having already been offered a job with 'Sky Work' charter flights in Southern Rhodesia. With growing agitation between Chip and his mother, conflicting over ideas for running the estate, a new future in Rhodesia held appeal. At a family meeting with the Kay's lawyer, Michael Blackwood discovered the dispute between Chip and Jean, and Chip's ensuing plans to relocate to Rhodesia. Chip tried explaining, "It's very difficult because mother has got some strange ideas, and if you look at my portion of the estate I think it could even be described as the 'crown of Satemwa' yet she won't give me heed to do as I know best." "I understand you. But she is your mother, and this estate – Satemwa – is your heritage. I beg you not to give it up," Michael pleaded. As Michael spoke, the atmosphere softened. Jean, also convinced that working with her son was problematic, relinquished Satemwa to his control granting him 'full executive powers.' Relieved, Chip decided to stay in Malawi.[313]

Among those who departed was Chip's best friend and flying compatriot, Des Tennett. A few years before their exodus from Malawi, Des and his wife Peggy had lost a baby, just as Chip's parents had – to malarial complications. Then opportunities arose for the family in Rhodesia leading the Tennett's across the border to start afresh. Chip told Des, "It's no matter, I'm often in Salisbury and you can fly back here and still be a part of the Luchenza Flying club, whenever you like." But it was still a hurt, no matter which way Chip looked at it. He had lost his marriage, his best friend and his father within a few short years of each other and the trifecta plunged him further and deeper into work.[314]

His regular flying routes between Mozambique, Malawi and Rhodesia, now covered in part by Leopard Air pilots who transported goods and parts for PTA, subsequently released Chip to expand his flying routes north into Tanganyika, Kenya, Uganda, Kivu, The Congo, and Somalia.[315] He had bought and developed a building in Luchenza which operated as a tea factory of sorts, just opposite the railway station. The Luchenza factory was a magnet for tea, loose leaf spilling in from estates in Mulanje, Thyolo, and even Mozambique. Sorting through the leaf, Chip mixed varieties and hashed up the tea to create special blends, which he bundled into four 25 pound packages within a single tea chest. The materials for his tea boxes came from the forests on the Zambia side of the Rhodesian border before the Caprivi strip. Chip enjoyed the process of blending teas, but he also reveled in the art of trading his products, expanding tea consumption in Africa one sale at a time.

Off the coast of Dar Es Salaam in Tanganyika, the island of Zanzibar, which Chip had initially visited on his first annual leave from Satemwa, was emerging from its history as a hub for the African slave trade, to its present claim - the spice center of Africa. Under the flapping canvas of the entrance to Adam Juology's spice shop, where bags of cloves created lumpy cushions, Chip and Adam sat, drinking chai, laden with condensed milk. "Adulterated tea," Chip thought to himself and chugged the beverage before him. "Why spoil such an accomplished beverage with the thick proteins of milk?" It was something he never understood, always taking his tea black, with a slice of lemon, or a sprig of lemon verbena. The chai kept rolling in, with Adam and Chip drinking what seemed like bottomless cups, before reaching a deal.[316]

From Zanzibar he flew north to Mogadishu, the capital and port city of Somalia, "the white pearl of the Indian Ocean." Chip visited buyers for his tea, inquiring into the arrival of his products and the satisfaction of those who bought it. Shipping tea chests from land-locked Luchenza to Mogadishu was fairly uncomplicated, with a railway start, and a shipping system that functioned well, dropping tea chests at the Mogadishu port, dry and well transported. However, the 'coral-choked' Port Sudan was a different story. Around the horn of Africa alongside the Red Sea, large ships carrying the tea chests from Malawi to Port Sudan could often not dock, a problem that Chip solved by painting his hessian-wrapped banded tea bundles with tarmac. He would indicate the load to be taken by small dows off the main ship, where they were heaved into the water, and pulled onto the beach by Arabs drawing long ropes. Once on the sand, they were just meters away from the railroad, which came right up onto the beach and took the tarmacked tea on trains through Omdurman, a portion of the city of Khartoum at the confluence of the White and Blue Nile. Continuing north to El Said by road, the tea then traded to Arabs who showed up to purchase it on the backs of desert-born camels. Loaded onto the dromedaries, the tea moved west into Tchad, where Chip had secured the largest concession for tea in the country.

Visiting his Tchadian clients one day, he arrived at their leathered tent, pitched against the dry winds in the middle of the desert, large enough for four homes the size of 'The Satemwa House' to fit underneath. The Arab merchants planned a feast and Chip, caught in the middle, an on-looker, a business partner, was invited to participate. It lasted three days, endless catering and soft, cozy nooks in which to rest when a partygoer tired. Besides the location and the unusual style of hospitality, there was something very peculiar about the feast. Meandering among the Arabs, the wait staff, and the odd foreign visitor were slave girls. Their white skin and blue eyes indicating their abduction from European homes, a trail of the Barbary slave trade that bristled the region more than two centuries ago. Chip had never seen a white person enslaved. It was a strange confrontation and he immediately felt awkward. Catching the eye of one young woman, he turned to his Arab friend and inquired, "How does this work? Can anybody have her?" The man turned to Chip and laughed, "Oh no! Do you not see their pendants? They belong to someone already, and their owners don't like to share."[317]

Sometime later during his travels up in France with a PTA employee, Bill Stone, Chip was presented with an opportunity to own a home in Morocco, complete with staff - a butler, gardeners and a young girl slave - part of the purchase to be used however the owner deemed fit. Chip had taught Bill to fly, pulled him out of his role as a Federal teacher, and placed him with PTA, flying every week to Mozambique to retrieve tea samples, process them, and put them on a VC10, which flew to London every Wednesday. By Friday, Chip had a deal brewing at the auction floors on Mincing Lane. Once, when Chip and Bill had completed their business in London, Bill said to Chip, "I'd like to go see France." Thinking it a good idea, the pair rented a car and motored around France, heading south, winding up in the Algarve. They had been enjoying their tour so much that at certain villages, they had dallied with the idea of buying a vacation home. "We could split it between six of us pilots, and each one would get two months a year," Bill suggested, but when the Algarve opportunity arose, the weather closed in and reminded Chip of being stuck in a blistery chiperoni, "Too lousy of weather here, they should be growing tea," he commented to Bill and closed the subject.

Continuing through France, they drove to the point in Spain where a ferry runs the Strait of Gibraltar between Europe and Africa. "Let's go, come on," Bill suggested holding up a bottle and adding, "I've brought Port - it's anti sea-sick you know." Chip wasn't convinced about the alcohol taking away his nausea, but he did fancy a trip to Morocco, and soon the pair had landed across the waters, into the unsuspecting guidance of a local who immediately asked them if they would like to "see souq." "Souq" – meaning a marketplace – was where foreigners often liked to visit. "Yes, we would," said Chip and Bill following the man. After a while the man inquired, "Tomorrow, I'll show you a house?" "Yes, fine." The next day, the Arab man picked up Bill and Chip from their hotel and drove them down what looked like "millionaire row." They passed mansion-sized double-storied homes, with substantial fences, immaculate gardens and pristine driveways, pulling up at a gate marked "PRIVATE" and driving through as if they hadn't seen the sign. Chip turned to the Arab and told him, "No, we can't go in here, it says 'Private Property', and where I come from, we don't go on another man's land unless invited." The man smiled and assured him, "That's ok, but this house is for sale, so we can go in."[318]

"You should buy this house," the man said, even though they had only set foot on the path leading to the front door. "Right now?" Bill looked at Chip and chuckled, making light of the fact that business should never come so easy. "Let's see what's on offer," Chip responded to the man, as they walked together through the large glass plate doors that swung to reveal lavish marble flooring and a sweeping staircase with a polished wooden banister. Everything inside the house was spotless, free of clutter, and well maintained to the point that Chip wondered if they really were on the Continent. He could see several workers in uniform pretending to be busy, even with the absence of guests, and he inquired from the man showing them the house, "How much do you want for this place?" "Oh, it's £6,000," he stated, adding, "It comes with staff you know…." "Ok, who does it come with, how does that work?" "Well, there's the butler – he's in charge of all the staff, the two garden boys, the cook and the girl…" "The girl?" Chip asked. Without need for discrepancy, the Arab announced, "Yes, a 16 year-old virgin from the mountains – very white skin – very beautiful…," emphasizing the word 'white' and watching for a reaction from the two men before him. Curious, Chip clarified, "And suppose I don't like her. Suppose she's no good. Then what?" Clearly having heard this question before, the man said, "It's no problem. You buy her for £500 and you sell her if she doesn't satisfy you…"[319, 320]

The Moroccan house presented new terrain for Chip and Bill and with each additional detail of the prospective purchase offered before them, all their senses were tingling at the same time. The opulent house, in a faraway land, where seclusion and secrecy prevailed, tantalized their lives as single bachelors, where fantasy – their own mini-kingdom might reign. They could have it all. They could be incognito with every desire of a man's heart met, every need seen to, and every whim a prospect just waiting for the master's fingers to snap, calling his staff to attention. Ogled by the idea, their mouths fell open as they gawked at the lingering words of the Arab as if suspended in time, while their minds caught up to all the possibilities on offer. "£6,000 is doable, if we split it six ways…£1,000 each…we'll have a key club and we'll pick two months a year each…." Audibly now considering the proposition, they rationalized all the pros and cons back and forth until Chip realized, "I'll have to sell a plane to finance my portion, and I'm just not prepared to do that…"[321]

Flying was still more important to Chip than women. Perhaps more so than before, having thrown his hat into marriage only to have it end quite rapidly in divorce; he was more committed to the Flying Fraternity than ever. He was a 'bachelor' and never intended to marry again. "Marriage? – that institution is for fools," Chip told himself, "And I am no fool. I am bachelor daddy, and my two little girls are all I need to worry about."

The Dawn of a new Era 1970 – 1971

Dawn Cathcart Kay nee Fenner circa 1965

While Chip abandoned the idea of re-marriage for himself, he had not given up enjoying a good party, often finding himself the host of one, or loaning his house at Satemwa as a venue for fancy dinners and swaths of weddings. Flying types – the blokes from Luchenza Flying Club – often asked Chip if he could open his home for their wedding ceremonies and receptions.[322] He gladly obliged, giving his house staff directives to bring out the best wine, and set the tables with his finest silver and whatever remnants were left from his ex-wife, and her attempts to de-bachelorize the house before she left. The fireplace in the entrance room functioned as an altar, "with a pipe that goes straight to heaven," or so Chip liked to tease the brides and grooms moments before their nuptials. Bridal parties were photographed on the front lawn, meters from the main house, with the lush backdrop of bright green tea and soft rolling hills where Thyolo Mountain took center view. Celebrations that begun in the afternoon filtered into the early morning hours. On one occasion, long after the event was over and the soft glow from the rising sun warmed the grass, a guest's car remained in the driveway, but he was nowhere to be found. Chip, thinking the worst, gathered his staff and combed the property, only to find the man, within minutes of beginning the search, curled up in the sandstone alcove underneath the stairs that led to the second terrace off the front lawn, fast asleep.[(323)]

Owing to increased distance of travel, Chip's flight routes extending throughout Central Africa and into the North of the continent, the diversification of his products, and scheduling LAL pilots who could taxi trips on PTA's behalf, Chip's available time was minimal. And he spent his free time at the Luchenza Flying Club, surrounded by like-minded people who were crazy about planes. He missed Des, not seeing him as often as he thought he would, his calendar flinging him all over Africa. He was less tied to Rhodesia than he initially thought he would be. However, he made other friends, and was grateful for Dick Marley, who had witnessed alongside Chip, the Duke of Edinburgh flying into Chileka in 1964 on the "winds of change." Dick had become a member of the Luchenza Flying Club, a student pilot taught by Chip how to fly and later recruited by him to be the Satemwa Factory Manager. They developed a wonderful friendship, spending weekends in the sky, and weeknights at the theatre, both single, both happy to be so. It was Dick Marley, as a very young man, who had shown up on Chip's mother's farm – Elladale – in Southern Rhodesia, along with ten other British policeman seeking shelter for the night and pitching their tents on the farm pasture. Flora Jean had told Chip it was a very unusual occurrence, as the sergeants and constables played a bugle and sang the "Last Post," putting themselves to sleep at night with their portable flagpole stuck into Africa, flying the Union Jack with great pride.[(324)]

One Saturday night as Chip and Dick made their way through Limbe heading to a function at the Limbe Sports Club, two long-legged, "blonde bombshells", walking on the path ahead, seized their attention. Not recognizing who they were from behind, the friends made plans to talk to them. "You take the one on the right, I'll take the one on the left," Chip told Dick, pulling into the car park and watching as the women entered the hall. In pursuit, they rushed into the club, eager to find the ladies and make their acquaintance. But suddenly Chip slowed his stride and, recognizing their faces immediately, lost his nerve. "It's Dawn Fenner and her mother, Nancy," Chip whispered to Dick as if they were 'untouchables'. "She got married at Satemwa a few years ago, it was a hell of a party." "Who did she marry?" Dick asked, lost for memory. "I called him "Mr Colgate" because he sold their toothpaste here... now I can't quite recall his actual name...," Chip admitted, not embarrassed at all. "Well, talk to her – she's here alone, isn't she?" Dick prodded Chip, who took some liquid courage from the barman and strolled over to see about Dawn.[(325)]

She was standing near a cocktail table, her long silk dress sweeping the floor, a clutch purse under her arm, and her smooth blonde hair elegantly pinned high on her head. Her blue eyes outlined by dramatic lines and soft pink blush dusted her cheeks above her equally pink lipstick. Everything about her body was long and slim, toned and very attractive. She had the skin of an angel, and the poise of a Queen. Even without her fixings and "dolling up," she was easily the prettiest girl in the room. It was as if she had stepped out of a Vogue Magazine, right into the little country club in Limbe, and the awe-struck admiration of every man in the room. Next to Dawn, her mother, Nancy Fenner, a well-known agent for Central African Airways (CAA) out of Lilongwe, and a Shell fuel representative – was the lady who had filled Chip's plane on his first honeymoon and warned him of inclement weather. She was a markswoman, with a keen shot, taking down a leopard who was stalking her one night, proceeding with the dead animal slung over her motorbike's handles to the admiration/horror of the hotel staff where she was staying the night. She was a dance instructor, a tennis, golf and squash player – noted to excel in squash – and an all-around pioneering woman. Her accomplishments were not unlike Chip's own mother, whose sense of adventure had led her far and her responsibilities at times had been very large.[326]

Chip found Dawn and brushed up next to her, touching her shoulder with his fingers to announce his presence. They began conversing, although Chip felt he was doing most of the talking, but he was not unhappy – for his own sake - to learn that her marriage to "Mr Colgate" had ended only a few years after it had begun. "I'm very sorry," he told Dawn, trying to lighten the mood, "You know I never use Colgate, only Macleans…" She laughed a little and they spent the evening reacquainting. "Come to the Flying Club," Chip asked her, hoping to see her again after the night in Limbe. "We'll see about it," she replied, non-committal, not looking for another man to marry, especially one ten years her senior.[327]

The more Chip thought about Dawn, the more his sentiments of 'bachelorhood' became unstuck. He envisioned his life taking a new direction, with Dawn by his side, a loving companion, a business partner and a mother figure for his girls who he thought so desperately needed one on their Thyolo holidays. The only problem was convincing her. She seemed to appear at functions and then disappear mysteriously, a beautiful blonde enigma that haunted his dreams at night and evaded him in the day. Employing all his charm and resources, Chip persisted on the chase, Dawn hinting at times that she might be interested kept him hot in pursuit. One day, he leaned in to kiss her goodbye and she flinched at his coarse moustache, laughing when it prickled her skin, and then lifting the weight of it up, she found his lips underneath and kissed those instead. "Ah! You don't like the moustache," Chip mused, stroking it with a broad smile and telling her, "It's been with me for years, since 1953 when the Henderson brothers and I were all growing our first moustaches for the King's birthday holiday…should I shave it off?" he asked her, ready to do anything she might suggest. "Oh, heavens no! You have to keep something with such a vintage," she winked.[328]

Something between the two of them had clicked, compounding their chemistry, as if they had been missing each other their whole lives up until this point. Nothing about their relationship was forced, and Chip often marveled at Dawn's natural instincts for motherhood when his two girls visited and began calling her "Thyolo Mum" without his knowledge. She was the most peaceful, kind and devoted woman he had ever met. Wednesday and Saturday nights, the two nights during the week where he went to town to visit her in her Blantyre apartment, could not come quickly enough. Dawn was working as a secretary for a large cement company in town, skills that would transition well in the future when Chip asked for her hand in marriage. He had flown to Salisbury and procured a large solitaire diamond, although he was certain it could never match the beauty of the woman he hoped would wear it. When Dawn agreed to his proposal, the couple realized the next step in building their lives together was to inform their mothers of their decision to wed.

The long table in the dining room at Chip's house was shortened to create a cozy rectangle, with places set at opposite ends and two facing each other in the middle. A large bouquet of mixed flowers graced the center, wafting sweet perfume from the half-opened roses set between ferns. A pale laced-linen cloth covered the table, with settings of Wedgwood china and crystal wine glasses on top, flanked by Chip's King's Pattern Silver service cutlery. Candles atop tall, twisted golden holders shone soft light over the room, as Dawn believed women should always dine by candlelight. Chip sat opposite Dawn in the middle of the table, each one a little nervous about the news they were planning to break. Taking a seat at the head of each end of the table was Flora Jean and Nancy Fenner, neither aware of the reason they had been called to a dinner with just Chip and Dawn but each growing more suspicious by the minute. At some point during the low hum of conversation, Chip leaned towards Nancy and asked for her permission to marry Dawn, which she heartily agreed to. Emboldened by her approval and now seeking his own mother's he stood to his feet, raised his wine glass, and called for the wait staff to fill empty goblets around the table. Clinking the side of the crystal with his knife, he called the attention of everyone at the table to his announcement. He looked to his mother, who sat with her eyebrows slightly raised, "Mother, Dawn and I are getting married."

Jean acted as though she had just heard the most shocking statement of her life, second only to the news of Juliet's death. She looked straight at Chip, frowning through her eyes, her jaw gritted and her mind stern. "You can't do that," she said after several breaths of silence. "What on earth do you mean, mother?" Chip inquired. "Well, you are already married."[329]

Chip rolled his eyes as a child and responded, "Yes, I was married, but I am no longer. I have final divorce and custody of my two girls." "Nonsense!" Jean muttered. Sensing defeat in the subject she crossed her arms over her stiff body and pushed herself away from the edge of the table. Embarrassed and upset simultaneously Chip took charge, "Well, mother, you're going to have to get used to it. Nancy – your little girl is going to be my wife and everybody will just have to accept it."

"Well, do you have a date yet?" Jean asked. "Not yet, but we are thinking later this year, perhaps November?" Dawn entered the conversation, her manner relaxing the tension; she caught Chip's eyes as if to cry, "May Day! What do we do with your mother now?" It was a very frosty meal, and the cook's best dishes returned to the kitchen barely touched, the ox-tail in gravy, roast potatoes and crisp lettuce salad only poked about from guests who lost their appetite on the tails of Flora Jean's remarks. As the evening ended Chip walked over to pull his mother's chair back and asked her, "Would you like me to drive you home mother?" She huffed back at him, "No, thank you, I'm quite capable of driving myself."

His mother's over religious bent on his divorce and subsequent desire for re-marriage rattled him; she had been ungracious at a time when he had hoped she would choose love. She had allowed her Catholic roots to grow through her heart and blind her vision. How could she care so much for him and disregard his affections for Dawn so bluntly, so openly? Despite her objections, the couple proceeded with plans for a wedding, choosing The All Saints Church in Thyolo, only to have the clergy proclaim them 'unfit' for a Church wedding, seeing as they were both divorcees. "Disappointing! It seems the Church and mother are equally judgmental. Well, forget the Church – we will have it our way," Chip told Dawn, "We'll marry in Rhodesia at the Rock's house. It's just down the street from my Rhodesian home… Our mothers can come if they like, but we won't hold our breath."

Denise Rock, married to Mark Rock, used to be Denise Thorburn, a childhood friend of Chip's whose parents visited each other when either one visited from Mstitsiwire Estate or Satemwa Estate. When the Kays were at Mstitsiwire Chip was forced to play 'fairy gardens' with Denise, flying little sticks around the vegetable patch, pretending pixies were chasing the whimsical winged creatures who threw magic dust on a cabbage and invisibly sat on it, avoiding the pixie hunt. When the Thorburns came to Satemwa, she was obliged to play tea factories, digging in the mud and making little brick piles, burning them with wood, and then stacking them to form a factory which could process the tea they had plucked while running wildly through the fields. They were life-long friends and when Denise heard of Chip and Dawn's bungle with the Church in Malawi, she immediately agreed to host a wedding for them. "Yes, we'll do it at my house, by Mark's 300 year-old antique lamp post, with a proper pre-UDI officiate," she told Chip, aware that since Rhodesia's Unilateral Declaration of Independence, any official who got a license after 1965 might wed a couple whose marriage would fail to be recognized by Britain, making children born to those couples illegitimate.[330]

Chip and Dawn on their wedding day 1971

On November 3, 1971 Dawn prepared herself, dressing in a tailor-made candy pink fitted satin dress. Chip thought there must be a hundred candy pink buttons at the front of the dress, running from her neck down the center, ending near her mid-drift, and he wondered how long it had taken her to put the dress on, and how long it might take him to remove it. Her ash blonde hair was neatly swept into a wave, and pinned under itself, and each ear held a single pearl. She took Chip's hand tightly, as he walked her to their places by the vintage lamppost at the home of Denise and Mark Rock. Chip's patterned bow tie was the focal point of his black single-breasted suit and crisp white shirt. Juliet and Trysh were bubbling with excitement, stroking their hand-made pink chiffon shift dresses and waiting for the ceremony to begin.

Nancy had arrived tastefully outfitted in a light blue, white marbled midi dress. To the surprise of Chip and Dawn, Jean attended their wedding. Not wanting to be over excited, she donned her dull navy skirt suit, with fitted sleeves that stopped midway down her forearms, a small gap of skin showing between the end of her sleeves and the short white gloves on her hands. In one gloved hand she held her boxy white leather purse, and in the other she held onto Chip's arm, not wanting to let him go. Her hair was detained in a small bun at the base of her neck, and on her face she wore round, dark sunglasses, which she kept on not just for the ceremony, but also for all the pictures that followed. Sensing Chip was a little perturbed by his mother's cold presence, Dawn reassured him, "It's just nice she came now, isn't it?"

With very little pomp, Chip and Dawn married - by the old lamppost, in the home of their friends, with arches of fresh pink gladiolas, lilacs and deep pink bougainvillea lining the reception room. A white iced cake, made by Dawn's mother and set on a shiny silver stand, was cut under the watch of a few friends and family sipping champagne. This indicated that the ceremony was closing. Chip and Dawn were married - a joining that seemed to fit like a puzzle, a perfect match, a union made for life. Chip, beaming so wide his moustache curled at the ends, knew he was the luckiest man in the world, "Shall we away for our honeymoon Mrs Cathcart Kay?" "Yes, we shall Mr Cathcart Kay," she responded. With her arm tucked under his, they were ready to soar.

Paradise 1971

Chip and Dawn leaving their reception for honeymoon 1971

There was not a rain cloud in the sky when Chip boarded his new wife into the LAL plane, Fox Echo – the 172 "Horsebox". Setting off from Salisbury for South Africa, "the only navigational tool we need are the mango trees below…," Chip joked with Dawn, who was looking around the cabin for all the maps and briefcase of airplane supplies. Dawn was a fantastic navigator; she could pinpoint a location on the map, even after taking a nap, which made her a wonderful co-pilot. She trusted Chip, and felt completely at ease with him in charge. She didn't even inquire where they were headed on their honeymoon, although from take-off, flying south, it became quite obvious.

They flew from Salisbury to Pietersburg and The Ranch Resort, a family-run hotel opened a decade earlier. Designed as a stopover location for travelers coming from Rhodesia to South Africa, the hotel was the perfect distance from Salisbury and Chip, having flown there on many occasions, knew it well. There was a grass runway, where he plonked Fox Echo down, grateful for the perk of private air travel being the fast track of customs and immigration stops. He made his way to reception and secured a room for the night. They taxied the plane to their chalet, unpacked, dressed for dinner and headed to the bar. There was a young couple, "freshly dating," Chip told Dawn, guessing their situation from their body language and the 5 empty peanut bowls beside them. "Ah, I've heard a rumor in South Africa," said Chip to the barman, "that peanuts make you sexy…" He looked over at the couple who were now looking at their empty bowls. "May we have some peanuts?" he continued, but the humble barman had to admit, "I'm sorry Sir… all the peanuts are gone…"

Chip, stirring the pot, said to the young couple, "Now, you two have a good night, ok?"[331]

From Pietersburg, with no firm plans, they flew on, circling in the air at times, just looking for another suitable stop for the second night. Nearly eighty kilometers past Johannesburg, Chip spied a large dam and river system, "The Vaal Dams," he said, turning the plane again so they could both enjoy the gushing waters of the river and the enormous dam from the air. "Let's dump the plane down there for the night," said Chip pointing at a strip of cleared land indicating a runway which was owned by a nearby hotel. Similarly, to their first night, Chip checked them in, they taxied to their room, and prepared for dinner. Within half-an-hour of their landing, several motor cars zipped up to the hotel, a wake of dust evidence of their speed. Soon, several men were knocking on Chip and Dawn's hotel room door.

Years earlier, amid filthy weather too risky for flight to Satemwa, Chip had to abandon his plane at Chileka. The wind was howling around him as he bent over the wheels of his Cessna, tying it to the pegs which held airplanes in place on the cement parkway by the private hangars. The clang of a run-away tin can racing over the strip was heard, and bits of paper and plastic were hurled from their rubbish bins into the air by a gusty gale around him. With his plane secured, he found his driver, who had received his call to bring a car to fetch him at Chileka. Just as he was about to drive away, five planes appeared in the sky, battling the convergence and descending towards the Chileka pitch, looking drunk as the wind knocked them from side to side. Curious, Chip waited for them to land, noticing their South African licenses, he went right over to meet them. It was a large group of doctors who had been on safari to the lake, about eighteen in total, and with the inclement weather and their plans to push on to Johannesburg aborted, they were now stuck in Blantyre with nowhere to stay. Chip called Des, who agreed to host a few and then asked the group, "Would you like to stay with me tonight?"

At Chip's hotel door in South Africa, having recognized the bright yellow LAL tail from the ground, Chip opened the door to the applause of the travelers who had come to find him. "We've met before," one stated, "You're the man who rescued us one night at Chileka – you and your friend Des." Another inquired, "What are you doing here?" And Chip responded, "I'm on the second night of my honeymoon. How did you know I was here?" "Well, we saw this plane circling in the sky and we thought maybe you were lost. Then we saw your yellow tail and we all said, hey this guy comes from Malawi." They spent the early part of the evening together, reminiscing on their time at Chileka and staying on Satemwa, and enjoying a few drinks at the bar.[332]

The next day, Dawn and Chip flew southwest to the Drakensburg Gardens, a beautiful five-star hotel up in the Eastern portion of the Great Escarpment, where the mountains reach up to 3,482 meters. Drakensburg – meaning 'Dragon's mountain' or the 'barrier of spears' in the local languages - stretches over 300 kilometers and is touted as South Africa's premier mountain range. Here, Chip planned to spend several nights, hiking bush trails, snuggling by the fireplace, horse riding – at least for Dawn – and quiet romantic dinners under candlelight with the moon outside so round and so close they could almost reach up to touch it.

Stepping out of the plane, the crisp mountain air enveloped them, and Dawn reached for her jacket and swung a scarf to cover her bare neck. Chip asked the English couple who ran Drakensburg Gardens if they wouldn't mind lighting the fireplace so his wife could warm up next to it. They looked at him strangely, being that summer was around the corner and to them - having lived through much colder temperatures just months earlier - it wasn't cold at all. "Well, you see, we're coming from Rhodesia." Chip began trying to justify their request for heat turning to Dawn quietly, "The English! They only put fires on when the calendar says to." Dawn giggled and made a slight chattering noise to emphasize how cold it really was. "Oh right, we'll sort out some logs right away," the manager said as he motioned to his staff to load the fireplace. "I must tell you," he continued to Chip, "Our electricity is having a spot of bother. The thing is, we're a long way from anything and sometimes the poles fall, so we've got a standby plant but it's got a big problem…," the man informed Chip. "Well, what's the problem?" Chip asked. The English manager took Chip to the engine room where he showed him the Blackstone machine that was failing to turn over due to a piston part he couldn't find in Africa. "Right," Chip said, "Maybe I can help you. I run a small engineering firm. I'll contact them and see if we can get this part for you."[333]

Within hours, Chip had connected with his PTA branch manager and asked him to locate the needed spare, which he did by phoning the main shop in London, who then checked their records for suppliers in Africa and soon Chip reported, "There's only one of the part you require – in all of Africa. It's in Windhoek, Namibia and I've arranged for it to be sent to Durban. Tomorrow I'll fly down and pick it up and help you install it." It was only a three-hour return flight to collect the part, and he apologized to Dawn for taking time away to fix the broken machine, getting it started around midnight, puffing and chugging with a loud crack before settling into a rhythm and humming to the satisfaction of all involved. Dawn didn't mind at all, and settled with a good book in a hammock amid two trees at the edge of the forest. She happily read, stopping occasionally for a cup of tea or a bite to eat. "Proud of you Chip.

You have helped them so much – and I have just finished an excellent book, so we shall call it an all-around win." Dawn smiled at Chip as he lifted his moustache up, hoping for a kiss.[334]

Attempting to show their gratitude the following day, the managers from Drakensburg Gardens arranged a special day trip for Chip and Dawn into The Kingdom of Lesotho, an enclaved country within South Africa and a former British Protectorate. Lesotho's mountainous terrain, difficult to access in parts, made journeys on horse or donkey backs desirable. "Doesn't it sound fantastic?" Chip said excitedly, hoping his new bride was equally looking forward to the day safari. And she did seem keen until she looked into her purse and pulled out their travel papers and passports, "Yes, but there is one problem. Unfortunately my passport still has my divorced name on it, making it different from yours, and it would seem too embarrassing to check into a new country with miss-matched papers. It would appear very improper." She was disappointed and although Chip tried to convince her, "To hell with what other people think," it was too much, and they declined the offer and prepared for their next stop along their honeymoon tour.[335]

"Let's go somewhere warm…," Dawn suggested as she moved closer towards the newly lit fireplace. "Perhaps coastal," Chip responded, thinking about sunshine and prawns simultaneously. "Seafood and sunshine – what could be better, we'll leave in the morning for Lourenço Marques."

Flying over borders in his private plane allowed them ease with clearing customs, and when it came to Mozambique, they didn't have to clear customs at all. Chip reached for his 'immigration pass' that he kept in his black briefcase. Years earlier, the Governor General of Mozambique had issued him a wax-sealed envelope, tied with a ribbon, the contents on the paper inside stating, "The son of my friend, Maclean Kay, is no longer required to clear customs and immigration when travelling into Mozambique." He was even allowed to land his airplane directly on the beach, and along with his father had permission to eat the 'King's Game' – Oysters - in as large a quantity as he desired. After all, the Governor's wife had taught Flora Jean how to bake Oysters, which, delicious as they were, had hooked Chip and his family into a hopelessly oyster-addicted state.[336]

Situated along the southern coast of Mozambique just 120km from the South African border, Lourenço Marques – named after the famous Portuguese explorer - was Mozambique's Capital city, one bustling with life and brimming with buildings. Separating Marques Bay from the Indian Ocean, Inhaca Island with its irregular coastline, small aircraft runway, and selection of hotels was an easy choice for their next night's stay. Crossing the border into Mozambique, and greeted at the Inhaca airport by the hotel

Land Rover, Dawn and Chip were bumping along the sandy stretch of track between the airfield and the hotel when all of a sudden a cracking thud at the rear of the Rover indicated the back axle had fallen off. The vehicle was going nowhere, the back end sinking in the sandy soil. Accustomed to Africa, and pushing the apologies of the driver aside, they walked the distance to the hotel, hand in hand, a line of two or three men behind them carrying their luggage. Being fit and young, the only real danger was posed by loose coconuts, swaying in the ocean breeze meters above their heads. "If one should fall suddenly, I want you to know these are the best days of my life," Chip teased Dawn as they looked overhead at the leaning palms and the husky round coconuts bunched at the center of the trunks.[337]

Several days later, they flew up to Santa Carolina – also known as Paradise Island, a sort of half-way point between Lorenço Marques and their home in Malawi. It was Dawn's first time to see Paradise Island, the gem of the Bazaruto Archipelago, just five miles off the mainland coast surrounded by a ring of three pristine coral reefs and an ocean teeming with a variety of tropical fish and their predators. At high tide, the airstrip straddled coral, disappearing underwater, and having built the runway there himself, nobody knew how to navigate it better than Chip.[338]

They touched down on the lush green sliver of land on a day when low tide conditions rendered travel perfection. The land was framed by golden sands with the island just over 3 kilometers long and less than half a kilometer wide. "Wait until you see the hotel. It's right on the edge of the ocean," Chip told Dawn as they exited the plane and gave instructions to the airport crew to tie it down. The Paradise Island Hotel protruded in complete order from its surrounds. Its modern two-story rectangular design, stretching long across the stony shoreline – elevated upon the rocks just high enough that the bulk of the salty spray from the crashing waves below fell short of the hotel windows. Three sets of three arches on each level framed the hotel frontage, with a protruding circular appendage on the left side of the hotel. The round rooms housed a bar, with stools ready to welcome guests, and a decade-old fish mural splashed across the wall behind the bar; tantalizing the viewer towards the foaming ocean to experience the ample reef life for themselves.[339]

The few days they spent on Paradise Island were abundantly pleasant. Mid-morning walks along the perimeter which they could circumnavigate within an hour, and lazy afternoons in lawn chairs, watching the waves thump onto the reefs were always enticing. Sipping cocktails decorated with pineapple slices, amid bites of freshly prepared prawns or oysters were a delicacy. The island certainly lived up to its name - Paradise. Traveling back to Malawi via a stop in Beira, their honeymoon had circled South East Africa and to Chip, the last few weeks were an indication of the years to come. In fact, the entire honeymoon was so beautiful and so perfect, that Chip couldn't help but think of his previous rain-soaked Rhodesian affair that ended bitterly in divorce, and how if a honeymoon was to be an omen for a marriage, then his marriage with Dawn was destined to be full of peace, love and adventure.

It would surely stand the test of the changing African continent, the bush wars festering in their neighboring countries, the maintenance and growth of the legacy his father left - Satemwa, and heartaches large enough to rip families apart, which from the sands of Paradise Island they could never fathom.

Satemwa, Tea and Coffee 1971

The Satemwa tea factory circa 1973

In the Protectorate of Nyasaland, at the turn of the twentieth century, the prominent export crops were cotton, tobacco, groundnuts, sisal, rubber, beeswax, and coffee. Before the explosion of cotton, coffee had been the Protectorates most cultivated crop, noted for high quality taste and often fetching "very high prices" on the world market.[340] Coffee plantations spread throughout the Protectorate, including a substantial portion of the Mission land close to Thyolo, which before belonging to the Adventists under Malamulo Mission in 1902 was a Baptist run enterprise, using coffee sales to bolster their mission work. By 1908, coffee by weight had exceeded exports of any other commodity, outdoing tobacco, the second highest yielding crop by pound, by over 225,738 lbs. However, by value and acreage coffee ranked second to cotton, the Protectorates premier agriculture crop, grown on the tails of David Livingstone's dream to end slavery by undermining the American cotton barons through increased production elsewhere.[341]

However, even with the success of the early coffee plantations, it was a crop that settlers viewed as "fluctuating" - determined primarily by the first rainfall - where a late first rain caused the bushes to lose their blossoms, subsequently diminishing their yield. Arguably the most "speculative" crop of the early Protectorate days, affected by rainfall, soil fertility and susceptible to leaf rust, coffee was a win-win or lose-lose crop. Cementing its erratic reputation, coffee fell from favor dramatically when the coffee leaf rust - a type of fungus - knocked out the majority of coffee bushes in Nyasaland. Its acreage dramatically decreased in particular in the

Shire Highlands and where possible, many settlers chose to abandon coffee agronomy.

Over sixty years later, sitting in the head offices for Satemwa Tea Estate, Chip on one side of the desk and his mother, Jean, opposite, discussions began for diversification and growth of the estate. "I think we should consider coffee," Chip suggested, "although I don't drink the stuff, from all accounts, Malawi coffee is some of the best, and when the old settlers were farming it around here, if they looked after it – it did well." Not convinced, his mother took a while to buy into his ideas, eventually not wanting to give in to his 'bullying' about starting coffee, but also not wanting to be so stubborn as to throw a profitable idea away. "Might I suggest," she began, "that you run a coffee section on Mwalunthunzi, and I oversee one by 'The Satemwa House'." Since his father's death and the departure of George Holden, their General Manager, Chip found it increasingly awkward to parallel his ideas for growth with his mother's, and he thought the coffee compromise was the only way forward. "Fine, you will run your own section of coffee and I will do mine, but we will only need one factory. Might I suggest to you mother that you consider an all-female workforce. It certainly works for me." It surprised Chip when his mother agreed about the female labor. He wondered if she had remembered Maclean's stance on the subject when he instructed them both, "Women are the lifeblood of this society – no matter how bad times are - you must never lay off women, and everybody – male or female, working 3 or 6 days a week must have a hot lunch."[342]

Chip often thought of his father's advice, especially now - since the future success of Satemwa depended heavily on his decisions. His responsibilities with PTA, and Leopard Air – of which he was now the sole owner, having bought out the other members as they left the country one by one - spread him thin across South East Africa. It was difficult to keep an eye on all the business enterprises he managed, but particularly his beloved Satemwa, which he now felt overwhelmingly accountable for.[343]

Keeping his flying schedule, out on Wednesday, home on Saturday, he was pleasantly surprised when he discovered how well Dawn managed his absence. But he was more impressed by her aptitude for estate business, both in the office and in the fields. He found her working late, crunching numbers on his £73 calculator, assembling data for production lines, sales and estate records.[344] "Let's take a break, and go fish in Goose Dam," Chip said, closing the ledger book under Dawn's nose, encouraging she take time out of the office. Goose Dam was close by the main offices, and often just an hour from sunset, the newly married couple would set off with a picnic and a blanket spread out by the gazebo – which Chip had made specifically for their rendezvous. Next to their blanket, a basket filled with fresh sandwiches, hot tea and two slices of cake, and fishing rods, one each at the bank. Here, they talked about their future, their hopes and direction for life, the instability of investing in only the African continent, as the neighboring countries fell into civil wars, and they spoke of tea – tea and coffee.[345]

Together, following the patterns of the moon, and the cycles for planting, they figured out pruning systems that would allow the tea to flourish, all the while Chip marveling at Dawn's capacity for understanding the crop and for devising new methods to manage it. After their picnic, they would head back to the office, where the day's work concluded at 11pm, a glass of wine on the coaster beside Dawn, and Chip with his whiskey and ice nearby. When they finally left work to find sleep, Chip had to worry about Dawn's dog - a boxer called Major. Major did not like to share his master with anyone. Often, as Chip approached Dawn, he heard a low, rumbling growl, followed by a flash of white teeth bared in warning. Dawn would chase him off with a few claps and a stern "Ma-jor!" Once Major settled, they could hear owls hooting and insects flitting in the dark night sky, signaling the end of another long, satisfying day.

Dawn rode a horse since before she could walk, and it didn't take long before she had established a stables on Satemwa, just a few hundred meters from their home. She organized a paddock below the airplane parking terrace and rode every morning, afternoon, and on weekends for hours. The only conflict arose where she invited the 'pony club' for Sunday breakfasts, and Chip unknowingly double booked their kitchen for his Luchenza Flying Club breakfasts. The horses in the lower paddock, sensing planes overhead, snorted, and Dawn on the horse's back shook her head, "Excuse me ladies. I have to go speak to the cook about making some extra breakfast…"

With coffee now a secondary agricultural crop for Satemwa, Chip needed to build a factory to process the beans. He went to Rhodesia and took a camera and 5 films, snapping over a hundred photographs of coffee factory set-ups so he could design a proper factory in Malawi for Satemwa. Laying out the developed pictures across the desk when he got home, he made plans for a coffee factory with a 180-ton capacity, a figure he hoped they could attain if all the growing conditions aligned.[346]

Maclean's tea factory, built in 1937, was functioning well. With a few tweaks and some improvements in machinery, troughs and drying systems, it was the same at his father had built, but with modern upgrades. Chip's PTA building at Luchenza, with 100 meters of 40lb rail line, connected his warehouse to the main railroad, creating a thriving tea distribution center, particularly on weekends when other estate managers had all gone to the lake and the rail line was quiet. On those weekends,

Chip called the stationmaster and requested two covered bogies (CB) each one capable of holding 400 chests of tea, which would be sold at 1 and 6p a pound. Along with his team, they worked hard all Friday, Saturday and Sunday to hash up and box the tea into chests. Then taking a 6ft long crowbar, they shunted the covered bogies on Chip's rail line from the Luchenza warehouse to the main station, where it would catch the 8am or 2pm train down the escarpment to Beira, where it was loaded on a ship and sent to Mr Lipton in New Jersey.[347]

Years Later, when the railway systems in Malawi began to crumble and Mozambique was scattered with land mines where civil war threatened havoc for transport, Satemwa tea was sent on an 'orbital' route. It traveled through Thyolo, Lilongwe, Lusaka, The Caprivi Strip, down through Botswana to South Africa, where it was packed into tea bags, and then onto Lipton in New Jersey. On one occasion, the conglomeration of tea chests from around Africa arrived in the Unilever Pietermaritzburg (PMB) tea factory, teas from Malawi, Tanzania and Mozambique, sent to the PMB factory to be sorted into tea bags, destined for export. The tea was flying down the conveyor belts, packaged into tea bags when suddenly, a siren sounded and thousands of tablets started shooting out, covering the floor. The engineer and manager were called to assess the problem and discovered that illegal 'Mandrax' pills had been disguised in a tea chest which had come from Vat B, Satemwa, Bandanga and Espiranza tea estates in Malawi. In Vat B, the 'Mandrax' was traced to chest number 62, Pekeo Fannings, bought on the 10th of May from Satemwa.

It was not unusual for trucks carrying commodities to be tampered with on their journeys to South Africa. Many Nelson Mandela sympathizers in central African countries snuck weapons – land mines, AK 47's and ammunition onto southbound trucks, to aid in the fight against Apartheid. But they also tampered with the trucks, taking off chests of tea, emptying the sack and then filling it with drugs. They marked the new bag with an 'X', and when it arrived in South Africa, the bag with an 'X' would be removed, and the miss-count on tea sacks apologized for by stating, "lost in transit."[348]

By the time the 'Mandrax' crime had been reported to Satemwa, Interpol in France had already been contacted, and the situation dissolved because the drug cartel that had placed the illegal pills in the Satemwa sack, was notorious, and fortunately for Chip, the suspicion on him fell moot.

Since his mother seemed intent on leaving Malawi, perhaps an attempt to salvage her relationship with her son - thinking distance might be the answer - Chip moved his operational focus from PTA, employing general managers to run the company, and chose to spend more time with

Dawn on Satemwa, growing the estate and diversifying their assets. When Jean departed 'The Satemwa House' to own and live on a small vineyard in Cape Town in 1974, Chip and Dawn were left alone to run Satemwa, the effects of the 'executive' papers signed years earlier, now being easier to carry out without his mother nosing about. Jean's timing, as usual, was a little off given that Dawn had given birth to their first child, a boy – Alexander Cathcart Kay, on January 20, 1974. It seems Jean didn't mind leaving her family in Malawi and set her sights south in Cape Town. Nevertheless, the transition was rooted in wisdom, where distance made hearts heal and grow as the years would later prove.

Clouded with so many hobbies and a changing family life in the past decade, Chip decided to clear his head and dive into the business of tea production with passion, employing the knowledge he had gained from his father and the Nyasa Capitaos who had instructed him as an eighteen year- old returning to Nyasaland from England.

Chip naps with Alexander circa 1975

The tea fields of Satemwa were an eclectic mix of tea varieties, prompting one of Chip's friends years earlier to comment with great fervor from a plane 10,000ft above, "It's a million shades of green." "And that's just the problem," Chip had said sullenly, taking the wind out of her enthusiasm, "We grow from seed, each acre has 2,722 bushes in it, and just like you and me, there are no two humans alike, tea when grown from seed is the same – no two bushes are alike - therefore you get a million shades of green." Satemwa's acreage beamed with flushes of green tea, but as Chip told his friend that day in the plane, when they are all ripening at different rates, it makes plucking a "hell of a job."[349]

By the time Chip took hold of the reins for Satemwa, the entire planting process had changed so much from when his father began the first nurseries in 1924, planting the first field in 1926 with Camelia Senensis tea seed derived from China. When Maclean started in tea, nurseries were prepared with soil three feet deep. Tea seed germinated in sand with a wet hessian bag on top. Every now and then a planter would peek under the hessian 'blanket' to see if the seed had split. When it did, and the radical poked out, it was ready for planting in the prepared soil. Two and a half years later, after the plant had reached six feet in height, it was pruned to within six inches of the ground. Out in the fields, holes dug 9" round x 18" deep waited for the cut seedlings to arrive, and once placed in the opening, the hole around the seedling was filled with dirt. Planters would then come visit the new field and watch for the bud break – the first green leafy nodule to burst out of the implanted stick, indicating the seedling would eventually grow. The long drawn out process of tea field planting culminated 7 years after the seedling process began, when the first green leaf would be ready for harvest.[350]

The first Assamica tea seed from India was sent from Maclean's brother Alexander to Satemwa in 1928 and planted into field 3 two years later, following the same system of nursery to field as the original seed from the Camelia Senensis variety. Field 8 was planted in 1941 by Maclean with a hybrid seed, India cross China. Field 25 on Satemwa was a poly-clonal mish-mash of six different cultivars or clones, the seeds of which were sold to the Colonial Development Corporation in the early days, and forwarded to the African small holder contingency before they sold out to big businesses in the post-war tea slump leading up to Federation in 1953.[351]

Allowed to grow without pruning, a tea bush can reach heights in excess of 25ft. Satemwa's seed-bearer tea trees, lovingly referred to as the mother bush, provided tea seeds that supplied their two nurseries in the growing years when Chip re-planted fields 4,5,6, and 7 from the seed-bearer Satemwa stock. It was these tea seeds that Chip began exporting, making sales in South America, Argentina, Brazil and Bolivia, where Satemwa tea samples, flown personally by Chip were tested and approved for purchase on a large scale. However, the government in Malawi decided to clamp down on exports of tea seed, and after the first few sales, the international market that Chip had penetrated, collapsed.[352]

Tea processes by the late 1950's and mid 1960's began to change. In place of tea from seed, came tea from a cutting – or cultivar tea, where clippings from a 'golden bush' were planted into potties, producing roots and flourishing as if from seed; the benefit being that cultivars coming from the same bush produced tea with the same genetics, reducing the effects of a "million shades of green." Clonal, cultivar teas which were not from seed sprang out of research from Cambridge in 1957 which, picked up by the Mulanje Tea Research Station in the mid 1960's, produced the famous SFS (Swazi Field Selection) 204 and 150 bushes. Across the

Nswadzi river from Chip's home, the fields on the left heading up the hill were planted in Mulanje Tea Research 'Golden Bush' variety called the 204 and 150. The proclamation of a 'Golden Bush' was determined by its resistance to drought, insect attacks, the speed of true leaves after pruning or first rainfalls, and its ability to ferment.[353]

Many planters, including Chip, who were interested in growing better tea, walked around their fields with a cork-ended chlorine-filled test tube and a piece of cotton wool being a permanent fixture in their pocket-laden vests. In search of the 'golden bush' a planter would take a leaf from a plant which had budded first after pruning, place it inside the test tube – known as the chloroform test – and watch to see whether the leaf fermented or not. If the tea leaf turned reddish in color then it was a good fermenter, and a good fermenter produced an accomplished cup of tea.[354]

Some twenty years after the 'golden bush' discovery, planters realized they needed to go one step further and find a 'super root' on which to graft the 'golden bush' cuttings. Most often the Camelia Senensis from China produced the 'super root' after care was taken to nurture it in proper subsoil in the nursery. Very different to tea from seed which his father planted in 1924 into the nurseries, Chip and his contemporaries following the TRF were planting differently. Taking a bud, the unfurled leaf and the internode that sat between the leaf and the bud, Chip planted it in prepared subsoil potties in the nursery, where under the right growing conditions the clipping was forced to develop root structure by growing more down than up. After ninety days the dark shade that covered the nursery would be lifted a little each week, slowly allowing air, daylight and moonlight into the atmosphere, cool temperatures at night acting like soft rainfall when the dew fell from the plastic in the early morning.[355]

Slowly Chip and Dawn began the arduous task of selecting fields planted by seed many years ago, yielding less green leaf than their clonal competition. Once identified, the old tea bushes were pulled out by the roots, and the fields readied for the more modern, higher producing cultivars stemming from the research movement. However, one field that Chip would never replace was the very first one his father painstakingly planted in 1926 by the light of his kerosene lamp, seed at stake, alternating tea and tobacco. "That field right there is a legacy itself," he told Dawn as they footed about from the factory one day, "a legacy begun by my father."

However, after George Holden had left Satemwa and Chip and Dawn were charged with running the estate full-time, they managed to double the yield, applying principles of pruning and planting devised together. Chip gained a reputation as a planter who could 'make things happen' and soon his fame spread across the borders of Malawi into Mozambique.

The expansive tea estates of Villa Junquiero in Mozambique where years earlier Chip had risked his life flying onwards with nowhere to land until he saw the mountain rising behind the tea, now offered him a job. The managing director of Cha'Mozambique Tea urged Chip, "I want you, no, actually I NEED you to be my Visiting Agent (VA)." Running PTA, Leopard Air, and doubling Satemwa's tea production after taking over from George Holden, had Chip's time more than occupied. Besides, he did not want to work for someone else. He was a 'free man', and he liked his life because he could do things his own way. "I'm sorry, but I can't be your VA," Chip apologized to the director, "but thank you for thinking of me." The Cha'Mozambique director was not interested in Chip's refusal and pushed him further, "Anything you want, just name it." Chip scuffed the ground with his shoe, and still trying to get out of the offer he told the director, "There's a problem with your company that's very difficult to resolve." "Oh, and what might that be?" the director inquired. "It's really two things. But one of the things you will certainly find too great of an obstacle." The director was eager to learn and pressed Chip, "Tell me everything and I will do as you say."

Chip explained to the director that his pruning program was all messed up and that, "I will need the only key to your pruning knife store." "But why?" "Because nobody will prune a single bush until I am there. I will start the pruning, and I will end it." Chip detailed how the pruning program directly affected yield and how without understanding – what his father would have called 'reading' – the tea bush, the production would be affected. The director agreed and asked, "Well, what's the other thing?" Taking a slow, deep breath of air, as if bracing himself for delivering bad news Chip stated, "I can't work with your General Manager. Either he goes, or I don't come." There was a long silence, followed by a few elongated nods of the director's head as he absorbed the information. It was a tricky decision now, as the General Manager, the man who didn't know what he was doing with tea, was the Director's brother. "9am, tomorrow. Let's meet at your hotel, and I will have my decision."(356)

The following morning Chip sat on the khondi of his hotel eating his breakfast, waiting for the Director of Cha'Mozambique to arrive. He wasn't sure if the Director would take offense to his requests and approach him with hostility or if through the advice given, he would willingly move his tea company forward. Before he could reach Chip at his breakfast table, the Director broke into a smile, offering his hand to Chip, "We've got a deal. I've spoken with my brother, and he thinks he would like to go down to Lower Maputo (LM) and run our packeting plant for Kadshu. When can you start?" Chip caught the smile and promised, "I'll be back in a fortnight."(357)

Within five years, with Chip as the Visiting Agent, Cha'Mozambique prospered; their tea doubled in yield because of Chip's pruning programs and inputs into their operations. "Anybody who knows anything about tea could have done it," Chip said modestly when presented with the figures of their first boom in growth. Yet, everything he turned his hand to seemed to prosper, and he told Dawn, "It's because everything I do is fun."

Together, they were juggling responsibilities at home, alongside pressures at work. Juliet and Trysh were still visiting Satemwa when school breaks allowed, with each girl happy to have a younger brother to play with. Alexander, named after his Great Uncle Ally from Scotland, loved the estate, where he was riding horses before he could walk, and played on the lawn outside his parent's home, pushing his tricycle along with little legs, trying to keep up with Chip's plane as it left the lower terrace and taxied toward the runway. Chip noticed Alexander's penchant for scratching the earth, and thought he inherited Cathcart features, not just the physical attributes either. He loved the animals, whether they were horses, dogs or pigs, and particularly enjoyed the vegetable patch, although mostly the art of prematurely pulling out carrots. "You're going to be just like your old man, aren't you?" Chip often told Alexander, who was much too young to deny it.

Dawn gave birth to a second boy, who like his older brother, Alexander, was also born in Salisbury. The political climate suffocating the once functioning systems of Malawi, evidenced by a notice outside the Blantyre Adventist Hospital one night, when Dawn and Chip showed up for Lamaze classes. "We regret to inform you that clinical classes are cancelled henceforth without further notice." Banda's government caught wind of Blantyre Adventist nurses prescribing birth control measures for families, and he became outraged, deporting three of them that very night. "Salisbury seems a better bet for delivering the baby, wouldn't you agree Dawn?" Chip told her as they drove home to Satemwa without their lessons.[358]

Their second son, Maclean (Maxie) Douglas Cathcart Kay, was born in Salisbury on the 15th of August 1975. His blonde hair looked transparent at birth, just little wisps that gained color as they grew. His blue green eyes were so large they captured his face and demanded onlookers linger a little longer. He was a happy baby and smothered in love from his parents and brother at the same time. Chip enjoyed bringing both Maxie and Alexander into bed in the mornings, and in the daytime calling 'shotgun' for naps, as he dozed off in his lawn chair beside the infant Maclean in his pram. Maclean, baby "Maxie", was content to watch his older brother run circles around him where he sat in his yellow bubble car, kicking up his feet, as his legs were long enough to touch the ground.

Alexander and Maclean "Maxie" Kay circa 1977

When Maclean was inside Dawn's belly, Alexander dubbed his mother's 'bump' "Raisin", a name that no one understood but a name that nevertheless clung long after birth. Alexander refused to call his brother by any other name. "Raisin wants milk," or "Raisin is taking my car," he would tell his mother as Maclean crawled over to his pile of toys and picked out a metal truck, mimicking his older brother as he tried to make the "vroom" sound with his mouth.[359]

Chip and Dawn presented Alexander with a Jack Russell puppy when Maxie was born; a puppy also named "Raisin," which Dawn errantly thought might allow Maxie to reclaim his. "There's two Raisin's now," Alexander said as he picked up the terrier and introduced him to his brother. "Raisin, meet Raisin…" And that was it. For Chip, it was the busiest, most chaotic period in his life, but he loved every day, he savored every moment. "They grow so quickly," he said to Dawn, "Just look how Juliet and Trysh are practically young ladies now."

"Raisin" Maclean 1975

Maclean Douglas Cathcart Kay circa 1977

Sometimes Chip ran a mental stocktake on his life, always concluding he was a "millionaire of happiness's," pausing to absorb the beauty of his home on Satemwa, which since its inception as a three-room, mud-bricked home for a bachelor, had grown significantly especially under Dawn's classical eye for renovation and improvement.

An open-air courtyard graced the center of their home, decorated by bougainvillea, potted palms, and white orchids. There were tables and chairs enough to seat forty adults and the courtyard quickly became the preferred dining choice, weather permitting. A library with imbedded bookshelves skillfully carved by a local artisan had views onto the center courtyard, and the house spread out to the east, west and north with additional bedrooms. The kitchen, which fed a number of visitors each week, had been enlarged with a scullery, a butler's pantry, all decorated in brown tiles. The laundry room hummed with washing duties in the large garage.

They employed eighteen domestic workers, each tasked with various duties, and each allocated a home, in a compound, along with all their families, sometimes their children peeking out behind the stable walls, trying to catch a glimpse of Dawn as she led a horse out into the paddock for her morning ride. The stable workers, seeing the young children watching the Madam with fascinated eyes would chase them off, their giggles lingering in the wind, making Dawn smile at their curiosity. "They must have seen me a hundred times before, same riding pants, boots and hat...yet each time they appear, they act as though I'm something of a rare sighting," she told Chip one day, after a particularly large group of children were caught peering at her in the lower paddock.

Chip's work as a planter, entrepreneur, and pilot was satisfying but providing happiness in the greatest measure was his growing family, and the devoted love and companionship of his wife Dawn. He felt privileged to be born into the colonial life, a pioneering family, who had carved something out of nothing, of which the efforts of his father continued to abound under his guidance. He thought himself 'lucky' to have a taxi way for his planes right up to his doorstep, and a view on the top terrace, just twenty steps from his front door, overlooking Thyolo Mountain, where the sunset oscillated between fiery red and pastel pink and where the neatly pruned tea fields capped the foreground . It was a 'thousand cups of tea' vista, where visitors were welcomed to recline in lawn chairs and sip a hot cup of Satemwa Red served alongside an afternoon cucumber sandwich. Dawn was a premier host, timely pouring teacups before visitors could even think to fetch one themselves, which was against the etiquette of tea-time besides.

Alexander and Raisin filled the adult chatter with baby giggles and squeals and their Nanny was tasked to make sure neither fell off the stone steps to the second terrace where Chip parked his planes.

According to Chip, there was no better place in the world, and he made sure to tell people on his travels about his little corner of Africa, and the splendor that dwelled in the Shire Highlands, on 'Satemwa Free State' as he had taken to calling his property after Independence. However, as much as he enjoyed time at home, he was still actively traveling, employing the motto he adapted from his Cessna course years earlier, "You can't sell Satemwa tea sitting on your ass in Thyolo." He had friends dotted throughout the world, such as, "Jim Jim", who worked for the American Embassy and who ended up naming his property in West Virginia, "Satemwa West", in honor of Chip's 'free state' in Central Africa. "Jim Jim," always welcomed Chip and his family to stay, "however long you like," he told Chip, hoping it would be more than the usual two or three days. Once again business had taken Chip to America, signing deals and selling Satemwa Tea and Coffee. He had left his family behind to enjoy their home in Salisbury, complete with staff and a delightful swimming pool.

While he was away Dawn often moved between Malawi and Rhodesia, developing a network of friends in both countries and trying to maintain houses in each as well. Their home in Rhodesia was effortless in comparison to Malawi. Supplies were easier to acquire, despite the embargos imposed on Rhodesia, workmanship more reliable, and the children had friends close by and were happy to push tricycles around the cement pathways, and splash in the backyard pool. It was a small hacienda-styled house, with arches over the garage, decorated tiles, and a jellybean-shaped swimming pool surrounded by a child-proof fence and gate, and the exotic garden with plants from all around the world announced suburban living. With accounts to keep for Satemwa, two babies under the age of four to watch, and a globetrotter husband, Dawn was grateful for a little time away in Salisbury.[360]

"Take Nanny with you," Chip encouraged, "She needs a job, and you need a rest." The children's Nanny often accompanied the family, whether by car or plane, traversing to Rhodesia, or as far as Cape Town when the family visited Flora Jean. "I will," Dawn had decided, as she packed bags from Satemwa bound for their Salisbury home.

"Raisin wants to take his blue shoes," said Alexander authoritatively on behalf of his brother. "Blue," Maxie told Dawn, picking up one shoe and handing it to her. The boys ran down the hall into the drawing room, pushing the velvet cushions from their place on the landing in front of the fireplace and racing matchbox cars along the painted surface. "That's YOU!" Alexander said to his brother, lifting his chin up to the right of the hearth where an artist's impression of both boys hung independent from the other, mounted in a golden oval frame. From the artist's depiction, although exaggerated, it was easy to tell the brothers apart. Alexander's petite features centered around his grey-green eyes, his tidy blonde hair swept by the artists crayon behind his ears, a polo necked sweater hiding the skin on his neck, his outfit complete with overalls. Maxie's portrait was hung just a few feet away to the right of the crimson wall sconce. "There," Alexander turned the distracted head of his younger brother to view the drawing. "Raisin," he announced with great gusto, pointing at Maxie's picture and desperate for his brother's acknowledgement of it. With Alexander's refined features and Maclean's bold blue-green eyes set on a face "which could belong to an angel," it would be difficult for anyone to miss it, anyone other than young Maxie caught up with his matchbox cars. Both boys were beautiful, strikingly so, and Chip often told Dawn, not meaning to boast, "We should have more. Look at our good work."

Dawn and the two boys settled into their Salisbury home, where Chip had taken the brazen "Delgarva" name plate from Scotland, after his father's family had passed it along, and hung it on the gate to their home in Rhodesia. Nanny set to work busily unpacking their suitcases and preparing the rooms, while Dawn took the children around the garden, inspecting the rhododendrons, foxgloves, and bromeliads, which had grown considerably since her last visit. On her knees, around the edge of the garden where the freshly mowed lawn met the interesting plant life, Dawn pulled a few weeds that the garden boys had overlooked and tossed them into a pile. She was like Chip's mother in this regard, a keen sense for plants and an adventurous spirit which prompted her to smuggle seedlings into the country.[361]

Alexander and Maclean were nearby, content to pad about on the lawn, where Dawn overheard Maxie practicing the word "TWO" with his brother. "How old is Raisin?" Alexander asked, to which Maxie would say, "DOOO," holding up both his pointer fingers to indicate so. "And brother, me, is THREE," Alexander would respond, adding, "Almost FOUR."

It was a blistering October, where the mercury hit well above 35°C on the thermometer, and where from sunup to sundown almost the only reprieve from the repressive heat was a cold shower, or a dip in the swimming pool. "Our kids really do need to learn to swim," Chip had stated, "I never did. And it's a bit of a handicap, isn't it?" "I don't think we need to worry about the boys liking the water," Dawn responded, "They're both little fish, you know." Dawn enjoyed swimming, but not as much as Alexander and Maxie, whose magnetic attraction to the pool only intensified during the summer.

After breakfast Dawn took the children outside, and they rolled balls on the lawn, back and forth, chasing them into the garden, where Dawn reminded them to "tread lightly" amongst her Rhodesian flame lilies, which she hoped might bloom in early December. By mid-morning with sweat coating their backs, Dawn allowed the boys inside the pool fence, unlatching the child proof gate as she ushered them towards the steps, and holding tightly to one arm of each child, as she stuffed their arms into mouth blown floaties, before releasing them to play in the sparkling blue water.

There was no happier place for Alexander and Maxie, and they stayed in the pool until their bodies were completely water-logged, the skin on their fingers pruned into miniature ridges. "Raisin," Alexander called, before cupping water and flinging it towards him, "Watch out," he warned, spraying his brother with drops. They both giggled, and Maxie tried returning the 'favor' as he squirted water right back. "Okay, you two, time for lunch and naps," Dawn told her boys, lifting Maxie out by his hands, and wrapping him tightly in a towel. Alexander took his towel, wanting to do it himself, "self," he told his mother who had leaned over to assist him. She helped the boys through the gate, latching it firmly behind her and smiled to her gardener, Enoch, as he clipped the hedges nearby.

They ate pasta with red sauce and picked at their side salads before Dawn took them to the master bedroom, setting Alexander outside, just through the French doors, on the day-bed telling him, "You don't have to nap, but you must have quiet time." She took Maxie, whose eyelids were already half-closed with her and turned the bed covers down so their bodies rested on top of the cool cotton sheets, a ceiling fan working hard overhead. Dawn picked up Maxie and stretched out on the bed, tucking him under her arm and gently singing to him as his half-closed eyes shut. His little body was hot, and they were both sweating, blanketed in the heat of the day. Within minutes they were both in a heavy slumber. Alexander was quietly humming on the khondi, until he too, succumbed to the post-lunch tidal wave of sleep. He was napping when Dawn woke suddenly, her outstretched arm still wet from where her baby had been lying. She sat bolt upright and looked around the bedroom, noticing a little stool pushed close to the cracked door. She sprang to her feet and called to her boy, who was just on her arm, "Maxie! Maxie! Where are you?" But Maxie was nowhere to be seen.

Chip was far away. In fact, Dawn didn't know how to reach him. He was across the ocean, somewhere in North America and his flexible itinerary afforded him the inadvertent life of an incognito tea planter from Central Africa whose whereabouts were a mystery at times even to his wife. He checked in with her every few days, and usually this plan sufficed. While Rhodesia choked by a heatwave, America was cooling down, and fall was celebrated by pumpkin festivals, hot cider and cinnamon donuts and the middle of the National Football League's yearly season.

Chip had concluded his business dealings and surprised "Jim Jim" when he pitched up at his home saying, "I heard you were about, so I've come to make sure you're not up to any mischief." Jim was thrilled that Chip considered their friendship the kind where he could drop by and immediately suggested they go the next day, Sunday October 16, across state lines into Pennsylvania to watch the NFL game between the Philadelphia Eagles and the St Louis Cardinals. "Dick Vermeil is one heck of a gutsy coach," Jim informed Chip, "He's taken on a nobody player from last year, a guy called Vince Papale and still thinks he will help the Eagles win, somehow…"[362] Chip raised his eyebrows, indicating he wasn't up to date with American football, but was happy to go along for a guy's afternoon, and figured he could at least learn more about how the American's played ball. The friends were so busy from the moment Chip arrived that he failed to check in with Dawn in Salisbury, assuming 'no word is a good word,' forgetting that she didn't know where to find him.[363]

With thick woolen scarves and thermal gloves, that Chip thought might be over the top, they settled into their seats at Veterans Stadium where over 60,000 fans had gathered to cheer their teams.[364] The Eagles and Cardinals seemed evenly matched by half-time and not long after the second half kicked off, Jim nudged Chip and asked him, "Did you hear that? I think they just called me to reception." They both shut out the noise of the stadium and waited for the announcer to speak again. "Will Jim Farber report to the reception desk immediately." Jim told Chip, "Wait here, I'm sure it's just the office panicking about something. I'll be right back." Chip didn't know how many minutes he had been gone when he finally returned but appearing in the row of seats and excusing himself towards where Chip waited, Jim looked positively pale, like he had seen a ghost, or worse.[365]

The Eagles made a touchdown, and the stadium resounded with feet pumping the floor and shouting as the home crowd erupted with applause. Jim, returned to his seat, leaned in towards Chip and grabbed him under the elbow, drawing him close. "We've got to go, Chip," Jim began, "We really have to go." Chip, still thinking Jim had troubles at the office to sort out, replied, "Of course, if you need to tackle something, I can wait. I'm flexible." "Chip, it's Dawn. Well, actually its Max. I don't know how to tell you. Let's get out of here." He pulled on Chip's arm, leading him through the crowd and out into the corridor where the occasional vendor was hocking hot dogs and popcorn. "Maxie," Chip thought, not knowing what could possibly have happened, "Surely he's ok." Chip's heart suddenly dropped out from his chest. He could no longer hear the beat of life in the stadium, only the heavy thud of his own footsteps as he followed his friend. In the cold, empty mezzanine floor, with shouts of "hot dogs" in the distance, Jim held Chip firmly and relayed the message he received, "They called me to reception, Chip, because Dawn has been trying to get a hold of you for days. I don't even know how to say this…." He paused, "I was told Maxie drowned, Chip, he drowned in your pool in Rhodesia."

Chip closed his eyes and pressed his palms into his face. He let his head fall onto the shoulder of his friend who reminded him to breathe. "Could it really be true? Perhaps there was some mistake in the message as it traversed the cables around the world." He longed for a rewind, for any other news. A wave of grief sucked him down, along with heavy tears of anguish, instant sorrow, escaping his eyes again and splashing onto the grey floor at his feet. He had absorbed terrible news before, like when John Senior's brother-in-law told him his sister was killed in a plane crash, and even then, he wondered how he might carry on, but nothing, absolutely nothing could prepare him for the loss of his child. The death of a healthy, happy boy, who just two months earlier had celebrated his second birthday with a vanilla frosted cake, red roman numerals - one through twelve – written around the cake's circumference turning the top layer into the face of a clock. Two single red candles alight in the middle of the cake, and Chip could remember Maxie angling towards the flames, with a mighty huff and blowing until those two little red candles held nothing but hot wax from the drooping wicks.

He thought about his rapid departure for America, how he had wrestled both his boys, and kissed their cheeks, while Maxie held up his arms for "more", as Chip dashed away, towards his work and his travel. Now, those cheeks he had hurriedly passed by were gone; he could never kiss them again.

Quickly his thoughts turned to Dawn, and he desperately needed to contact her. "I'm coming, right away," he said, finally reaching her by telephone and aching at the distance that separated them. "I'm coming home…" It was all he could say, the miles between them and the torment of losing Maxie, too much to process from America. He needed to get back to Africa, to his wife - swiftly.

Ticketed through London, he stopped off to tell his mother who was staying in her English flat the bad news. If anybody could understand what they were going through, it should be her. Afterall, she had suffered twice over with the loss of a child, but when he relayed the news of Maxie, he couldn't tell how the death of a grandson affected her, the hollowness that she felt, crammed by religious duties and incantations, by that faraway look of a woman who had almost reached the maximum suffering one human can carry. He left his mother and hurried on, flying to Johannesburg and up to Salisbury on the next available plane. Arriving at their home on Lunnark Road he found Dawn and hugged her, with the kind of grip that spoke for the words that wouldn't flow out of either of their mouths. They sobbed together, with broken hearts until finally, Chip was able to speak assuring Dawn, "This is not your fault. I don't ever want you to blame yourself."

A string of unfortunate events led to Maxie's death, events they did not care to recount for many years. Enoch, who was distraught at the realization he had left the gate unlatched after cleaning the pool, and the haunting words of their Nanny who told Chip, "God made a terrible mistake when he took your little boy. He should have taken me instead." Chip told Enoch and Nanny they couldn't blame themselves either, after all, there was no point trying to change something as permanent as death.

Returning to Malawi they knew their life had changed forever. Pictures of Maxie sat in every room, and neither contemplated removing them for a minute. "He'll always be our baby," Dawn said stroking the frame with his picture in it. He was a special child, a gift that they had enjoyed for only a short time. His little character, which shone through in his cheeky grin and toddler swagger, would remain in their hearts forever. They would remember the moments.

At the All Saints Church in Thyolo, in a private ceremony attended by close friends and family, they buried their little boy, Dawn was dressed in black from head to toe, a color that dominated her wardrobe since Maxie's death, and Chip, holding her up, tried to be brave enough for them both.

When the white marble tombstone was placed, it read, "To The Glory of God and in Memory of Maclean Douglas Cathcart Kay, born August 15, 1975, died October 14, 1977 RIP."

His little grave, half the length of those nearby, rested on the right-hand side of his Aunty Juliet, whom he never met, both their lives lost too soon. The row reserved by the Kays for the Kays now had three graves. The patriarch, Maclean – Chip's father – at center, and plotted out from his right, his daughter, aged 22, and his grandson, just two years old.

The Cathcart Kay family row at All Saints Church Cemetery Thyolo

Hoodwinked from 1978

Alexander Kay on the lawn of House Number One with Chip's plane on the lower terrace circa 1976

Since Maxie died even the brightest days always cast a shadow. And the grieving never stopped, only changed from one day to the next. But even grieving people find happiness again, even grieving parents can laugh again, feel joy again. For Dawn, Maxie was very much present in her life. He would always be with her, and she wouldn't move on from him, only forward with him.

It was Chip's forty-seventh birthday, and Dawn, conspiring with her Doctor in Salisbury, Dr Hilliard, gave him the best gift any father could receive. "It's a boy," Dr Hilliard announced, grabbing the baby by his foot as he slipped out into the world, a world buried in conflict. In that happy moment, they didn't think of the bush wars that were wreaking havoc, in both Rhodesia and Mozambique, nor did it matter to them the sex of their new baby. They were simply delighted at the gift of another boy, a playmate for Alexander, who had been desperately lonely since Maxie's death. Dawn told the Doctor "We're naming him "Hilliard" – after you - because you have helped us in our happiest and saddest moments over the years and we hope this baby will do the same for others." The doctor was very humbled, and Chip stepped out into the hallway to make calls home to Malawi announcing the birth of their third son, Hilliard James Cathcart Kay, born September 25, 1978.

Outside of their daily routines, the world was again shifting. They were completely occupied with their home life on Satemwa, young Alexander to nurture, and all the pressing needs of a new baby. And their estate business was complicated by the increasingly fragile state of commerce in an African-run country, which at times seemed more interested in the idea of 'revenge against colonials' than in collaboration between all peoples to propel the country forward. They found themselves spending more time at the office, skipping picnics at Goose dam, and staying up later than ever, as they adapted to new business rules, a changing tea market and employment challenges – such as the difficulties in recruiting and maintaining European staff to manage portions of the estate.

They built a new head office, moving its location onto their home site, a double storied building attached to their garage with a sweeping wooden staircase which led up to a conference room, a work office where a secretary aided Dawn with her bookkeeping and sales, and a private office for Chip accessed through the space where Dawn sat. He proudly displayed pictures of his Leopard Air fleet on the wall, alongside his family, and the bookcase filled with genres from agriculture and machinery to planes and flight logbooks. His flying briefcase, always at the ready, with maps of his regular flight plans and copies of the Rhodesian Immigration forms for arrival in Rhodesia and when leaving Malawi, the "Report of Departure of Aircraft and Statement of Stores on Board" forms to help him transition through customs more rapidly. Filing cabinets in the corners housed important documents, and he was careful who had access to them. Dawn, really the one in charge of the office, held the keys.

Satemwa, in his father's day, had an unspoken policy for recruiting European staff from abroad. Maclean thought any bloke could manage life in the tropics, as his work would keep him busy from sunup to sunset, but to ward off loneliness or wanderings, Maclean said he would only hire a married man. And the wife of a potential employee for Satemwa or any other estate in Central Africa would have to be unique to survive life in the tropics. She must enjoy animals, grow vegetables, be independent, assertive, supportive, and find a way to get on with the business of life despite the extra challenges of living in a country that lacked the commodities of her homeland. "So, really son, you see, we are interviewing the wife," his father had said, explaining how he determined which engineer to hire.

"We need an accountant, a good one," Dawn reported to Chip after closing the books one night. "Can't you sort one out from England?" Moreover, Chip agreed that business dealings spread across his many companies needed the eye of a chartered professional and sent word to Price-Waterhouse in London to organize five candidates for interviews.

Once in London, he met with the applicants, one by one, asking them if they could please bring their wife for a lunch or dinner, adding, "Whatever suits you best, either the country club for lunch or dinner downtown." He had interviewed four of the men and their wives, without much separating the accountants, when on his last dinner, a man by the name of Ted Pickford whisked through the door, a gorgeous woman hanging on his arm. They became acquainted; 'Mrs Pickford' was the daughter of a sugar cane plantation owner in Jamaica and Chip concluded she would find life in the Shire Highlands a breeze, where mild temperatures would be more pleasant than where sugar grows in heat. She was a third cultured kid and Chip believed that she could last in Africa. He hired Mrs Pickford by telling her husband he had won the job and booked them on a flight to Malawi the following month.[366]

However, Ted arrived, alone, and proved a less than ideal employee for the job at hand. He promised that his wife would join them soon – a lie which he gave up on, shortly after arrival, when the ugly truth surfaced that he had hired the woman for the day, knowing his chances were better should he acquire the 'right type of lady' as his 'wife.' Dawn had words with Chip on his gullible sense of believing the best in everybody, not able to sniff out a bad apple from the bucket, and although it took some time, Ted eventually returned to England. "Well, that was a mess," Chip surmised, "I'm bringing you on my next interview trail," he told Dawn, closing the chapter of Ted Pickford and chalking it up to a moment in life where you just have to 'live and learn.'

A little while later, Chip decided he needed a Rhodesian Coffee manager, and went to Rhodesia to find one. "I'm sure they're not hiring wives in this country," he thought to himself as he remembered Old Ted Pickford with disdain. He met a man named Richard Klues, awarded 'planter of the year' for Rhodesian coffee, and Chip made his acquaintance and offered him a job. "We'd be delighted," Richard responded. "My wife and two children, we can start right away." Chip signed them on to Satemwa Coffee, and not having a chance to prepare their home, welcomed the family to his house and the lower bedrooms - temporarily - until their estate house was fixed properly. One night, while Dawn went to check on Alexander and Hilliard, she found something very unusual. She woke Chip up, "You've got to come see this," she said, a soft torch light in one hand and Chip's hand in the other, leading him down the hallway to where four bodies were fast asleep in the passage. "Oh, Rhodesia," Chip whispered in sad tones to Dawn, "What can the future hold?"[367]

Once the household was quiet, and due to a habit, which had formed during the Rhodesian bush war, Richard and his family had taken their pillows and blankets and made a little bed in the hallway at Chip and Dawn's home. They were safe from the crossfire, which at any moment of night might riddle the walls of a home in Rhodesia with a hundred bullets, and an ambush of angry guerilla troops, thirsty to watch white blood spill. Only now, they were in Malawi, and now, they could sleep in their beds. "We'll tell them in the morning," Chip suggested, his heart burdened for the suffering caused by war and the knowledge that Rhodesia was on the verge of complete collapse.

His routine of flying between Malawi, Mozambique and Rhodesia soon stifled, as each of the countries adjoining Malawi fell deep into civil war. Mozambique gained independence from the Portuguese in 1975 and was now consumed by Renamo guerillas supported by South Africa, opposing the ruling party Frelimo and their Soviet ideals of a socialist one-party government. And Rhodesia, whose declaration of Independence in 1965 unsettled the black majority and incited a wave of international sanctions against the 'rebel' white government, the effects of which would be long felt.

The WARS on Colonialism 1965-1980

After the Second World War, "Colonialism" especially in America and Asia became an "obloquy to describe the condition of dependence or of non-full self-government." Calls for "liquidation of colonialism" rang out across Asia, with leaders condemning Colonialism and promising they would never "tolerate domination, or threat of domination, or any behavior after the old pattern of Colonialism." Political sentiments in Britain pressed by a rapidly changing world echoed in the halls of their parliament where National delegations from British Colonies partitioned for their independence. The recently formed idea of "Nationalism" had taken root in a once tribal mindset, especially in Africa where a few educated tribesmen caught the flame of nationalism abroad and sought to spread the flicker to unite once sparring tribes in the 'western' formed concept of "Nationalism."

The Empire and it's far reaching colonies were now at the judgement table. In the Victorian age, pressures of industrialism and commercialism caused the English to look abroad for answers, annexing territories which were often sparsely populated, as they sought control of natural resources and a way for Britain to grow outside their over-stretched homeland. However, they also answered the calls from missionary explorers who begged them not to ignore the carnage against black humanity in Central Africa, sending government aid, gunboats, soldiers and strategy to win the war against slavery at a financial loss. All these actions were now held in the balance as ideas of nationalism grew and unrest under Colonial Law intensified. The British were often criticized for profiteering in the colonies. However genuine partnerships between the native peoples and the British often prevailed, evidenced by the undeniable improvement in mortality rates amongst the natives and their increased levels of skills and education as a direct result of colonial presence.

Preceding independence for many of the African colonies, Britain's Right Honorable A. Creech Jones forecast that Colonial Rule cannot be "suddenly revoked without inflicting confusion and possibly anarchy on the people concerned." The British never intended to force minority rule over their colonies forever, especially as the world became more closely knit. Self-governing policies became a part of Colonial strategies, where they encouraged the majority towards independence through provisions expanding their utilities and public services, giving them greater responsibilities until the day they were ready to collaborate and eventually self-govern as a majority rule. Six years after the Second World War, Creech Jones stated, "Nationalism has transformed Asia and is a strong influence in Africa, all underdeveloped regions are a matter of international concern, and the Imperial powers are enjoined to advance self-government."[368]

Rhodesia's Ian Douglas Smith agreed with the movement in Britain towards self-government, but he differed with them on majority rule. He had watched countries gain independence in Africa already and fall into the very anarchy that Jones had warned against. Even neighboring Nyasaland had suffered a cabinet crisis just four months after independence. Smith and the Rhodesians were not going to let their country - the breadbasket of Africa - fall into chaos. But the international watchdog was not going to allow Smith and Rhodesia their Unilateral Declaration of Independence (UDI), as it would undermine the authority of Britain and potentially create havoc among countries not yet liberated from the Empire. Pre-warned by Britain of the consequence of UDI, Rhodesia set up measures to ensure success against sanctions, becoming their own micro economy, producing most goods within the country, and exporting some with help from a few friends.

Chip and Juul's PTA business in Rhodesia was among many companies that formed a proud "Sanctions-busting" cooperative. It was white Rhodesia's way of saying, "You can't keep a good man down." And for a time, it really worked. In fact, under sanctions Rhodesia's economic prosperity matured. They had an infrastructure that could produce for its own needs, and the money that was retrieved from the economy was put right back in, partly because there was nowhere else to spend Rhodesian dollars. One company under the umbrella of PTA was K&G, who made reflective paint powder. Chip had found a mica 'dump' in Rhodesia and bought all 8 tonnes of mica waste. He invented a squashing wheel which crushed the rock bits until only a fine powder remained. When this powder was mixed with paint it shone against lights at night and was often used to line roads or barrier bumpers. A Swedish dealer took on partnership with K&G during the time of 'Sanctions', and when the Swedish government caught him importing Chip's K&G reflective powder, earmarked origin – Rhodesia – the Swedes temporarily threw the man into jail.[369]

Wives and children were running many of the companies and farms throughout Rhodesia with the men now occupied with a duty to protect and guard their families, their black workers and their assets. The companies included PTA's K&G paint company which didn't sit well with Chip when he saw the white men guarding the black workers in his mine and on the rail links to the factory. "They have more important work to be doing…," Chip thought to himself, "than guarding my assets. I have enough to keep me occupied with these other PTA companies and on Satemwa…" He told Juul, "We're closing K&G to support Ian Douglas Smith. Banda has ruined Nyasaland, and I can't bear the thought of one of these guerilla groups doing the same here." Juul agreed and they streamlined their businesses in Rhodesia, considering the available manpower and where those men could be better used in the bush war. They kept the aluminum smelting company open, making motor parts which contributed to the war effort. Their pre-fabricated building business, where quarry dust was used to create sheets of cement walls which could be transported easily and assembled on site was useful in the war, many Rhodesian military barracks employing PTA's services in various parts of Rhodesia. And through Mozambique alliances, the Sheik of Persia imported the pre-fabricated sheets, and Chip couldn't decide if it was the Sheik or PTA who bore the badge of 'sanction's busting' with the most pride.[370]

Two communist-backed black majority parties emerged in Rhodesia to oppose the Smith regime. Zimbabwe African National Union (ZANU) supported by China, created the Zimbabwe National African Liberation Army (ZANLA), while Soviet backed Zimbabwe African People's Union (ZAPU) formed Zimbabwe People's Revolutionary Army (ZIPRA). Friction was taught within the country, as both ZANLA and ZIPRA gathered support, propelling surface tensions into what became the Rhodesian Bush War following a ZANLA attack on white farms in the north of Rhodesia in 1972. Hostilities grew with each new attack and were answered in force by the ruling whites, plummeting the country into a hidden bush war.

Families on farms laid pistols on top of their khondi tables within reach of their fine china teacups so they would be ready should a gang of ZANLA or ZIPRA spring out of the fields undetected. Men who had been content farming a decade ago were rostered for patrol, keeping communities safe from sudden ambush. White Families drove around town with uzi's and rifles pointed out their car windows, often the wife driving and the husband and children at the firearm ready. Unease grew and Smith knew the Rhodesia he dreamed of protecting had already disappeared. He began talks with non-militant majority groups, working towards a joint black-white transitional government, set to take over in 1979 as Zimbabwe Rhodesia, subject to multiracial elections. But neither ZANLA nor ZIPRA agreed to compromise and Smith resorted to diplomacy 'undercover' hoping ZIPRA's Joshua Nkomo might prove a reasonable partner for a new administration.

Yet, the joint government never had a chance to administrate. Nkomo and Smith announced their 'secret talks' to a disgruntled ZANLA and ZIPRA majority, on September 2, 1978, and the very next day, a passenger plane, Air Rhodesian Flight 825 - the Hunyani – a Vickers Viscount airplane – was shot out of the sky by a soviet made shoulder heat seeking missile.[371] Co-piloting the Hunyani was one of Chip's Leopard Air graduates, Captain Beaumont, and together with Captain Hood they tried to belly land the Viscount. Even if the guerillas had made a mistake by targeting a civilian plane, when they realized what they had scored a hit on, they should have responded appropriately. Instead, they chased the Viscount as it flailed to the ground, catching a ditch and cartwheeling into a cotton field, torn into pieces. Only a handful survived the impact. Nevertheless, the VIPRA soldiers arrived on the scene, gathered up the ten visible survivors and mowed them down with automatic rifles, killing those who survived the AK-47 shower, including a mother and her 3-week-old baby, with bayonets shouting, "This is our land!" Passengers who had managed to hide in the scrub were terrified by the level of brutality and hate spitting out of the guerillas, watching quietly as they raided the strewn suitcases and dead bodies for jewelry and other effects. Nkomo claimed responsibility for the incident, denying the massacre that followed the downed plane, laughing as he spoke with BBC's Today programme about the event. His demeanor and his lack of empathy for the murdered lives unsettled both black and white Rhodesians alike.[372]

It was a somber incident for Rhodesia, not just because of the innocent lives who perished, but because the rest of the world seemed indifferent to their plight. Apart from articles run in various magazines, such as Time, overseas governments were apathetic toward Rhodesia's battle. As if America, Australia, and other 'settled' countries who fought over land with natives had forgotten what the struggle was like, willingly or unwillingly ashamed of their own past with conquering lands, and killing natives, the latter being a non-issue for Rhodesia who sought to encourage the natives towards Western ideals of prosperity and education. One thing became resoundingly clear, Rhodesia's bush war would have to be won or lost without help from the West, and against mounting strength from China and Russia who were flooding the guerilla troops with increasingly sophisticated weapons.

Five months after the Hunyani imploded in a cotton field, another Vickers Viscount, Rhodesian Air Flight 827 was picked out of the sky by the same Strela-2 missile, killing all 59 passengers on board when it fell into rough terrain by Lake Kariba. This was the worst aircraft fatality Rhodesia had seen, prompting the airlines to counteract heat seeking missiles with low radiation paint on their remaining fleet, and shrouding the exhaust pipes to reduce their infrared signature. The Smith government could not ignore the growing dangers on civilian lives and the 827 tragedy plunged the parliament deeper into political talks regarding the difficult road ahead.

Chip was still flying into Salisbury from Malawi when his friend Jim Farber, "Jim Jim", who worked for the American Embassy in Malawi, called him, "Chip, you're taking risks, flying out to Salisbury, you know." "Yes, I know about the bush war, Jim, I'm being careful," Chip responded, "You got any tips?" knowing that Jim had pertinent information from the Americans. "Well, let me tell you, fly low – they have heat seeking missiles and can catch you up to 22,000ft. Fly LOW Chip," Jim warned, emphasizing LOW and hoping Chip would take heed. "No problem for me," Chip returned, "I'll fly amongst the mango trees. I know every mango tree in Africa anyway," to which Jim replied, "Be careful my friend, these guys will hunt you out of the sky if they can see you." Miles before the Malawi Rhodesia border, Chip's nerves started tingling, and he steadied himself, "Don't let a silly bunch of terrorists shake your courage," he told himself, as the wings of his Cessna clipped the mango leaves below.[373]

But like so many Europeans born and raised in Africa, Chip and Dawn – owning homes in Rhodesia and invested in businesses through PTA, were not about to turn their backs on the country, despite the bush war. Like so many Africans, both black and white, they believed a future of collaboration was possible, and that anarchy might be preventable.

On one occasion Chip was driving Dawn in his old Green Mercedes, which had done "half a million miles" already, from Salisbury up into the Easter Districts to visit Troutbeck Hotel. They stopped along the road home to buy some trout from a little shop and returned to their car which would not start. Chip thought it best to take the trout back to the saleswoman and request she keep it on ice until they could sort out their car troubles. She agreed and Chip said, "Zikomo." "Ah, I am Malawian…are you from Malawi?" the black saleswoman inquired, prompting a long conversation in Chi'Nyanja well into the afternoon. The lady told Chip how the guerilla forces had raided her family's village one night, accusing them of collaborating with the 'quislings', the French, and without trial or pause she watched as they slashed the breasts off her mother's and sister's chests, before punching the same weapon through their hearts. She hid behind the clay water pots in the dimly lit kitchen and hoped her sobs would not rat out her presence. "Oh yes, we are all suffering with this bush war," she said, tears still fresh in her eyes as she thought of her wasted family.[374]

The bush war was ruthless and often indiscriminating. Chip's Honey business, led by a Kenyan, Jeremy Wakeford, closed due to the war. Jeremy produced Queen bees and sold them to shareholders who owned up to five hives each, which were dispersed in the forests. Harvesting hives at night by flashlight was possibly one of the deadliest occupations in Rhodesia during the war. Chances ran high that somewhere, crouched in the brachystegia, an armed man waited, and a light, no matter for what purpose was a target. Chip told the one hundred small-scale apiarists who were enjoying a living off the blue gum honey, that they should abandon their hives until the war ended. He knew their livelihoods would suffer, but the alternative was certain death. The sweet, sticky Marendelos honey that was sold all over Rhodesia, on the side of roads, in small village shops, and even supermarkets, would have to halt production, sending families into economic hardship, and leaving the African bees to solve their own over-production problems once the hives ceased harvesting.[375]

Land-locked Rhodesia faced several problems during the time of international sanctions. And when Mozambique gained independence and the Soviet backed ruling party of Frelimo entered power, Rhodesia's difficulties worsened. Together with South Africa, Rhodesia supported the opposing force of Renamo who began a guerilla warfare against the soviet ideals of socialism that the new Frelimo government was imposing. Rhodesia, already thick in war, now spread thin. But alternatives were lacking, and they needed allies in Mozambique, to strengthen their hold in Rhodesia and to support activities of sanctions busting. Tucked in between two countries at war, Malawi witnessed the breakdown of democracy and the very state of 'anarchy' that Creech Jones had forecast in 1951, the takeover of a once stable economy, crushing infrastructure and stability so that by the late 1970's both Rhodesia and Mozambique were in a complete state of chaos. Rhodesia had a war it couldn't win, although the internal veins of the country were still functioning, and Mozambique fell to pieces, both internally and externally. Twenty-two tea factories were destroyed, the beautiful tiled motifs that the Portuguese eloquently decorated their buildings with were shattered, and the tea fields leading up to the estates and factories were sprinkled with numerous land mines that made pluckers quit their jobs and escape to the hills. The owner of Cha'Mozambique told Chip, "We have to send goats through the tea fields to take out the landmines because they are everywhere."

The picturesque Villa Junquerio where Chip was the Visiting Agent, was targeted along with other estates who now looked like pre-historic cities scattered with ancient ruins, although the dust from the fallen buildings had not yet settled. One day, when Chip was flying into Mendala, he had not yet touched down on the grass runway when he looked at the large umbrella trees by the pitch.[376] Dangling from the strong branches, several lost black lives, strung by rope, wasted away in the afternoon shade. Walking around the tree of dead bodies, the labor force, at gunpoint, was marched as the hostile military prodded them with the butt of their rifles if they broke form. Chip had a reputation as a 'neutral' tea planter, who was sort of just a guy you could leave alone, which allowed him travel even during the war. One European farmer overheard troops talking one night about "the white tea planter who flies all over Africa, and has many planes." The Frelimo troops had surmised they could possibly just "pop over the border to Malawi and abduct one of his planes under the cover of night."[377]

Often Chip sat in the restaurant of his friend's hotel, Monte Vende Hotel, taking it upon himself to buy dinner for all the young Portuguese soldiers who at the age of 18 had been sent from Portugal to fight in the former state of Portuguese East Africa, alongside the rebel Renamo opposing the socialist government. "They don't even know what they're fighting for," Chip thought to himself, knowing that each week when one of them died in the war, another would be sent to take their place.[378]

It was difficult at times to believe that countries he once flew to regularly were no longer safe. And he didn't like the idea of 'grounding' himself in Malawi, just because of some unrest next door. He told Dawn, "We should still carry on with our regular lives, wherever possible, and just be a little more cautious when needed." He often took Dawn to Mozambique, driving by car across the border. They waited for the military convoy to escort them to the coast, although many of the hotels they had frequented before the war were now empty shells. If they had to sleep the night in the bush, they would find a Murrum – a gravel mine – and bunk down in it. There were too many landmines to risk wandering far; even a few meters from the roadside could prove fatal.[379]

Once, when Trysh was grown and married with a young baby, working at the Tea Research Foundation in Mulanje, she was shot at by two Rhodesian MIG's flying low near the mountain, confusing Mulanje for Villa Junqueiro in Mozambique. She tried to squeeze under her VW to avoid strafing but along with baby, couldn't fit. Fortunately, the MIG's missed them both, but her car suffered bullet holes along with the tree beside her.[380]

Although not in 'war', Malawi was experiencing its own form of oppression. Banda, "the conqueror of Colonialism", was rallying against the West, and 'protecting' his country from their influences. At heart, he was preferential to his tribesmen, siding with his Chewa people in the central region of Kasungu, ostracizing the northerners and southerners who made up the majority of prisoners in the jails. He arrested people for breeches of the Censorship and Control Act of 1968, which he passed to curtail 'corrupt' Western ideals. Wearing short skirts, bell-bottom trousers and long hair on men was suddenly 'illegal', and films and books insinuating even mildly passionate scenes banned and all offences were subject to imprisonment.[381] Chip, who often kept a playboy magazine and a bottle of Johnnie Walker Red Label whiskey in his airplane, "to aid in difficult border crossings," now had to be a little more secretive about his arsenal. "It's a foolproof plan," he had often told his friends who wondered how he cleared borders in Africa with such ease. "You just pull out the magazine while the immigration officer is reviewing the documents, and let them catch a glimpse of the centerfold, only a glimpse, before tucking it back away, out of sight," he told his friends one day, "Then, the officer will likely ask for a look, at which I say – you can have the whole magazine – if you just get me through this bloody post quickly." And, if the Playboy magazine failed, a bottle of Red Label was a solid back up and was sure to clear Chip and his plane through customs rapidly.

Although, there was a time when Dawn took Juliet and Trysh out of Malawi, without a passport, accompanied by her good friend Dottie Henderson and her baby Nikki, as Chip and Dottie's husband, Drew, drove to meet them in Mozambique. Exiting Malawi was no problem, even though Juliet and Trysh were not on Dawn's passport but entering at Maputo was difficult. Dawn thought about how Chip might have pulled out his magazine or offered a bottle of whiskey to the immigration chief, but lacking both, she was stuck and waited with the girls until Chip arrived by car to sort out the problem. "You see, both of these girls are on my passport," he told the officer, "Now, please, you have to let us all go, we are tired and hungry."

Dealing with immigration officers and border crossings became the least of Chip's worries, and soon, he would encounter Malawi's dictator, face to face. With his ire fairly up, Malawi's self-proclaimed 'President for Life' Dr H Kamuzu Banda summoned Chip to Zomba through the secretary general of the MCP, Mr Dick Matenje. Dick tracked Chip to his hotel in London, where he was preparing to fly to New Jersey to sign a big contract with Lipton Teas and ordered him to return to Malawi "immediately!" Chip told Mr Matenje, "Don't be absurd! I'm about to get on a plane and sell Malawi tea for dollars to one of the world's most notable brands, and you should be supporting that sale." Somewhat sympathetically, Dick stated, "When the President says you must come, you must come. Otherwise I have been told to arrest your wife and you will lose Satemwa." Defeated, Chip agreed to return to Malawi the following day, postponing his meeting with Lipton, and now worried beyond hope that the belligerent government might take his estate, or worse – touch his wife.

Government officials met Chip at Chileka and pushed him into a black Mercedes Benz which to Chip smelled like a thousand sweaty socks. Chip resisted letting his breath out, for fear of the next odorous inhale. Yet, sandwiched between two men, he had no control over the windows. "Where are we going?" Chip asked the one who had pushed him into the car. "Zomba." "Oh," Chip settled down, trying not to think of all the possible ways he might have offended the President. He did not let his mind wander to what the results of his indiscretions, whatever they were, might incur. "If my father could see me now," he thought, "it's best he is resting in the ground."[382]

Banda was in his palace in Zomba, one of eleven Presidential palaces dotted throughout Malawi. The black Mercedes climbed the bottom part of the hill that led to the Plateau, passing the Colonial Zomba Sports club as they drove. The heavy iron gates swung open as the car approached, and now Chip was inside the tall-bricked walls of the palace grounds. He felt desperately alone, maddened by his recall, but incredibly vulnerable at the mercy of the man responsible for Malawi's autocratic state. The only memory Chip had of Banda in person was when he had commandeered the Luchenza Flying Club for a rally and sat motionless on the podium while a man battered about Banda's face with a flywhisk and another polished his shoes. Now, he was about to meet the controversial President face to face.

Still unaware of the reason for his detainment, Chip waited for Banda to appear. He was a short man, unmarried, but accompanied in most circumstances by a woman known to the public as Mamma Kadzamira. "She's good company, isn't she?" Banda nudged his Doctor one day, as the Doctor waited in the halls outside his bedroom in case Banda's "tummy upset" worsened. Doctors were not the only people who Banda thought had nothing better to do than to wait on him. Every person in Malawi, if he said so, would have to arrive and depart at his command. And now Chip, instead of meeting with Lipton and signing contracts for Malawi tea sales, was sitting in the palace in Zomba, looking around the opulent room, when the President decided to enter through the carved wooden doors. Chip stood up to greet him, as he shuffled on the floor, his stature even less impressive in person, but his entourage so large, it filled the halls. He didn't have a chance to shake his hand or begin a civil conversation as Banda railed from the outset, "I will pull every tea bush out of Malawi. My people don't eat tea – they eat maize." This was afterall the man who had promised, "I will trade with the devil if it's for the good of my people." Chip was taken aback by Banda's aggressive approach, still unclear why he had been summoned to Zomba. Banda's eyes crossed when he angered, and it was difficult for Chip to concentrate on his face without trying to follow one of the Presidents wandering eyes around the room.[383]

"You have broken the law," Banda shouted at Chip, who was still in the dark about his sequestering. Banda turned his back in a great huff and one of the ministers explained to Chip the reason he had been detained. "It's about a maize mill, in Luchenza. We have been informed that your

Indian employee is using your electricity to run the mill at night, and that is against the law." It was true, not just that the Indian whom Chip employed to process tea was running a maize mill at night, but that it was illegal to do so. Banda had set up rules forbidding any non-black African from owning a maize mill, and he had also decreed that all Indian's who were the economic heart of many small towns around Malawi – must relocate into one of three cities, Mzuzu, Liliongwe or Blantyre, believing that their exodus from small towns would open up commerce for the Africans. Unfortunately, the opposite transpired, and once bustling towns, where Africans could enjoy imported goods, decayed, becoming ghosts of their past.

Banda started again, "I will pluck out every tea bush," when suddenly he stopped. Raising a single finger under Chip's nose he shook it and asked, "What's your relationship to Miss Maclean?" Chip responded, matching Banda's fire with a seasoned calm, "Miss Maclean is no longer alive." "I know that," Banda snapped, his eyes bulging with indignation. "She was my Grand-Aunt," Chip said, watching the news settle on Banda as he pondered the information. "And what do you mean by a Grand-Aunt?" the President busted with impatience. "Well, she was my grandmother's sister. My grandmother was Mary Maclean." Mary and her sister, who was only ever known as Miss Maclean had returned from Canada to Scotland, where Miss Maclean became like the Dowager of Glasgow. She was influential in the Scottish Kirk, which Chip never approved of, owing to their Sunday rituals of pulling all the drapes in the house, rendering it dark and gloomy and a perfect condition for the quiet, somber day of 'worship' – but - a day that never appealed to children.[384]

During Banda's time in Scotland, Miss Maclean had taken him in, recommending election of Banda to the post of church elder. He must have always remembered her kindness; because it was the only time he softened during Chip's visit. As soon as their discussion about Miss Maclean ended, Banda went straight back to "pulling tea bushes out of Thyolo." Then as eerily as the meeting began, it ended and Banda shuffled back out of the room, trailed by the clunks of his entourage.

Chip waited a few moments and then walked out the front door. Finding Dick Matenje on the khondi he told him, "Right, we're through now. I've got to get back to Blantyre and over to America. What do you people think I should tell these Americans anyways? What will they think of Malawi now, huh?" Dick looked at Chip unaffected by his chiding and shrugged. "We have the best tea, so tell them that." Irate, Chip declared, "We most certainly do not! And I know because I grow it." It hurt him a little to talk of his tea this way, but he was fuming, and wondered how to explain the arrogance of Banda, and the little country of Malawi to a large tea conglomerate in the USA who were expecting him days ago. But he knew anybody who stood up to Banda would face consequences and he wondered what his might entail. After all, the man who had summoned him, Dick Matenje, mysteriously died a few years later, part of the 'Mwanza Four' who were increasingly critical of Banda's totalitarian rule, and in the end, paid the ultimate price for speaking against him.[385] Ruled as a traffic accident, little was done to avenge the death of Dick Matenje and the other three ministers until Banda was put on trial in 1995, but was acquitted due to 'lack of evidence.'[386, 387]

His encounter with Banda only solidified his animosity over losing 540 acres of tea years earlier, when the government minister, "Gwanda" Chakuamba Phiri arrived one day on Satemwa declaring, "I'm here for the whole of the Nswadzi valley." "I'm afraid to tell you, Sir, that you can't have it. It's my purchase of land," Chip began, but suddenly realized he was fighting a battle he couldn't win. "Let's walk the boundaries together, and I'll show you what we can give you," Chip offered.

Government land grabs had become a common occurrence, especially if Banda's youth gestapo had tipped off the Government about unfavorable comments or events on foreign owned land. At Malamulo Mission, just down the road from Satemwa, an Afrikaner manager had unwittingly plowed up a field of maize which the villagers had planted on mission property so the mission could farm the land for its own needs. When the government discovered the offense, Banda flew out to the mission and ripped so many acres of land away from Malamulo, just a strip remained. Malamulo's 2,000 rightful acres decreased to less than 200. It was an enormous problem, which would only exaggerate as the villages pushed closer to the mission. As the hospital, which treated the surrounding poor communities, grew in staff and facilities, the struggle to house the hired nurses, doctors and support staff would prove a chief difficulty. Land that once belonged to the mission now flourished in maize, or mudded homes, whose tin roofs glinted in the sunshine, among the logged land - titled elsewhere.[388]

The 'land grabs' in Malawi were noted by the government as 'land sales'. However, the purchase price, determined by the government at £1 per acre, could be viewed as nothing but 'stolen' property by those whose land was forcefully 'sold'. It was difficult to see it any other way than a sort of retaliation against the partnership that Britain tried forming with the local chiefs when it established government in 1892 to 'Protect' the tribal people of the region from slavery. With improved conditions and access to medical care, the population continued to grow, and by the late 1970's exceeded more than six million people, six times greater than when Maclean arrived in 1922. The reliance on subsistence farming and the population explosion increased the strain on land ownership, and tensions ran high.

It was difficult for Chip to 'give' the land away to the minister when he arrived on Satemwa to claim property and even more difficult to watch the virgin forest being slaughtered, animals displaced, and crops of maize and patchy small-holder tea grown in the once lush jungle's thrashed boundary. Standing on the Mwalunthunzi estate and viewing the gradual descending hillside towards the Nswadzi River, it was easy to distinguish Satemwa tea, grown in neat nettings over the hills, from the small-holder's sparse, patchy shrubs, which dotted the stolen land.

"What kind of progress is this?" Chip thought to himself. "This eyesaw is the very thing wrong with this country." To him, it was a metaphor for the changes since Independence in 1964. It was an example of what happens when you turn something that requires attention to details, specialized skills and a passion for ownership over to someone ill-equipped to manage it. And again, Creech Jones' warning regarding the sudden withdrawal of European presence in Africa reverberated, and Chip believed it to be true, because he was beginning to witness with his own eyes that state of "anarchy" that the British had hoped to avoid.

Mischief and the Full Moon Jackals
(Mid 70's and 80's)

Daytime noises on Satemwa centered around the drone of tractors, pulling full loads of plucked tea towards the factory, or taking empty trailers to the sail cloth awning where it awaited pluckers to fill their baskets and emerge from the field to weigh their haul. Chip remembered the early days when they relied on trucks to cart the fresh tips of tea between the fields and the factory and felt proud of his suggestion to move the company towards tractor loads with multiple wagons. It certainly was a more efficient way to transport their commodity.

Sometimes, even above the hum of the tractors, the silvery-cheeked hornbills could be heard as they swooped into the vegetable garden by house number one – the common name given to Chip and Dawn's home - to peck on paw paws as they ripened on the tree. When spring brought new buds and a full-breasted flower repertoire in the front garden, the sound of bees buzzing as they pollenated Dawn's flowers might even at times drown out the clang of the trailer hitting the tractor hitch when it flew over the bumpy estate roads. And then, at ten in the morning and four in the afternoon, the creaking wheels of the tea trolley, rattling down the hallways of their home, with the promise of a hot cup of Satemwa Red, and a tea-time treat, was the most welcome sound of all.

But when the sun dipped low behind Thyolo Mountain, and the colors of twilight elongated from their front terrace with the bright colors of day cleaving to the tips of the tea and the ridge of the mountain, other noises took over, noises that were sometimes alarming. "Don't forget to bring the dogs inside," Dawn reminded the night watchmen. "It's a full moon tonight, and the jackals will be about." Opening the French glass doors onto the khondi in the evening hours, with the sound of a warming log fire crackling behind her, Dawn curiously watched as the side-striped jackals appeared, trotting along the front lawn, pausing long enough at the steps to the lower terrace that she could easily identify them. They were illuminated by the rotund moon which showered light into the garden and onto the night-time creatures lurking in the shadows. Chased off the lawn by the cackles of hyena, the disturbed jackals gave way to the dominant predator, and Dawn retreated inside to the glowing embers of the fire with Chip, who was sitting beside it, telling her "Not to worry about the hyena tonight. The watchmen have their orders, and there will be no trouble." He said this with all the confidence he could muster. Yet Dawn was not easily convinced.[389]

Years earlier, when one of her horses had died and required burying, she had walked back to the grave the following day only to discover clumps of dirt shifted into mounding piles, and the body of her horse, bones and flesh, consumed. "Hyena," said the garden boy, finding tracks nearby and following them to the eating ground, where not a morsel remained. "Savages!" Dawn retorted, telling Chip, "Next time we must put lime and big rocks on top of anything we bury here. What an awful way for my poor horse's body to disappear."

They often saw leopard in the garden too; their shiny spotted coats and strong tails that stretched long behind their bodies unmistakable. Bothered about their own business chasing rabbits, or larger quarry, occasionally picking off goats and chickens, the leopards were a more welcome night-time sighting. With little reason to fear them, Dawn often remarked to Chip, "Did you see that beautiful leopard last night? He was beside the cobblestoned fence and disappeared behind the shed…"

Sometimes, after such sightings Dawn thought about her cattle, collared just on the other side of the airfield a few kilometers from their house. Dawn managed the herd, roughly seventy in number, and they were protected , not as much by the watchman but by a donkey called Neddy. City thieves were beginning to emerge in the country districts like Thyolo, where they hoped to steal cattle, among other things, and targeting Satemwa's cows one night, they were in for a rude surprise. One thief managed to get under the wires, corralling the herd towards the gate where his friend was ready to open it, when suddenly a snorting sound startled him, followed by a forceful knock to his stomach, which sent him hurtling to the ground. Standing above him, and threatening further damage was Neddy, whose nostrils flared, and teeth bared with gummy donkey drool that dripped onto the grounded man's forehead, frightening the thieves back to Blantyre. Now awake, the 'watchmen' had seen Neddy in all his horrible glory and reported back to Dawn that her donkey was possibly the "bravest animal he had known."[390]

Occasionally, protecting their assets became a bloody affair, and when Chip discovered that city thieves were netting the dam which he had stocked with Tilapia for his labor force, he became cross. "These fish are for you guys!" he told the workers who reported the fish theft. "Do you like eating fish? Do you want to eat any more?" he asked them, boiling in outrage at the bold thievery. The dam harvested around seven tonnes of tilapia per year and provided needed nutrients to augment the labor's diet which was dominated by hot carbohydrates such as maize. Just like his father, Chip believed in feeding his workforce properly, taking care to give them a balanced diet and adequate portions. He rallied with his workers at their compounds and they all agreed to meet the thieves that night with fury.

Down the road, three box-body (pick-up) trucks rattled to a halt, their engines cut, leaving the night eerily quiet. "We'll wait here," Chip spoke in hushed tones to his Capitaos, "and listen for the whistle signals," he added to the group of estate workers huddling behind the hedges along the dam, ready to protect their fish. Chip's truck rolled out of view but with the key in the ignition, ready to flare at any moment. They waited, hearing nothing but the far-off drone of the factory and the occasional fluttering of a bat overhead. Then suddenly, a whistle pierced the night, and a second whistle bled out, followed by a third and so on until the whole line of guards had their mouths pressed to their metal noise makers, indicating trouble approached. Chip flicked the car into gear, thrusting his lights to high beam, and revealing fifteen men, knives in hand, dragging a net between them towards his dam. Already suspicious their cover was blown, the armed men, upon seeing Chip and his workers abandoned their net and prepared to meet the onslaught who had descended upon them shouting, "Go back to Blantyre, you are nothing but thieves." The intruders tried to stand their ground, clashing knives with pangas and battling Chip's labor until, completely overwhelmed they began to run, Chip's truck lights shining down the road and giving him a view of the ensuing chase.

The next morning, one of his Capitaos came to find him. "Bwana, we have found something most distressing," he said, presenting Chip with a severed arm, grey by now, with tendons and veins sticking out the cut end. "What should we do with it?" Chip looked at the arm, and asked him, "One of ours, or one of theirs?" to which his Capitao said, "Thankfully theirs." "Right, well leave it to me," Chip told him, asking his house boy to bandage up the appendage and place it in a plastic bag. He drove the arm to Thyolo District Hospital where he found Dr Lucas, a Dutch doctor, telling him the story of the previous night and leaving the arm with him, "in case the owner might show up."

However, the man with the missing arm never appeared, dead or alive, and the arm was burned in the hospital incinerator three days after Chip had donated it. Re-telling the story to Dawn over supper, he suggested they call it, "The Night of the Lost Arm," which they did forevermore.[391]

Another incident involving a Satemwa cow occurred during the years when Neddy was no longer around to "see them off." Rustlers, people trying to steal cattle, had been stalking the Satemwa herd, eyeing the fattened Jersey heifers, particularly a pregnant cow who would be ideal to take. Bungled at their attempt one night to lead the pregnant jersey out of the collar to their awaiting truck, they engaged now in a struggle with the watchman and the poor cow was cut a fatal blow that killed both her and her baby inside. Over the radio the voice of the watchman sounded,

"We are alert," bringing others to the cattle collar, the thieves narrowly escaping in their clapped-out truck. Chip was upset upon hearing of the pregnant Jersey and phoned the local police immediately to report the incident. He prepared the cow and baby so they would fit into his Rhodesian deep freeze. The farm freezer could hold half a ton of meat. It was made like a water drum, round with a flat top, and although a squeeze, the Jersey and her unborn baby fitted inside.

Bothered by the local police's apathy towards his situation, Chip phoned police headquarters in Zomba reporting a "murder on the Free State of Satemwa," for added effect. Within hours a team of two cars arrived, checking in at the main barrier in haste, and making their way to house number one where Chip awaited their arrival. "Thank you, officers, for coming," he began, "As I'm sure you can tell, this is a most serious problem." The lead officer, the detective in charge, asked Chip, "Do you have a body? Where is it?" Chip, taking the moment to pause for dramatic effect, breathed in long and deep saying, "Actually there are two. She was a pregnant female." The officers all looked at each other in disbelief, "Pregnant female! Who would do such a thing?" one mused, "Please take us to the bodies immediately." "Yes, where are the bodies?" the detective asserted, pressing closely and pushing his spectacles up on his nose with one finger. "Well, she is in my freezer," Chip said, squinting at the detective and waiting for his response. "The freezer! Well, open it." He was on the edge of shouting now and Chip, who had reported the murder, was now irritatingly slow at offering answers. "Right, the freezer, well it's locked," Chip said, proposing nothing more. "And where is the key?" the detective demanded. "With the cook," Chip replied. "Well, get the cook," he barked, clearly at the end of his tether.

Chip sent his garden boy to chase down the cook and bring him along with the key to the shed where they all gathered around the deep freezer. Unlocking it and lifting the lid, Chip revealed the body that had finally brought the police out to investigate his complaints. Looking up at the pack of men clustered around the rim of the freezer, the Jersey's large brown eyes, frozen solid prompted the detective to bawl, "Is this a joke?" "Oh, no detective, I can assure you this is no joke. If you look very closely, you can see where they originally cut her, where the thieves murdered her and her unborn calf. And to make it worse, she was my pedigree Jersey."[392]

"Ugh, murder," the detective muttered, realizing they had been somewhat duped. They returned to their cars and left Satemwa as quickly as they had arrived, closing the case before it was really opened and leaving Chip to mourn his dead cow by himself.

LOST – 1970-1988

Flora Jean Kay

The nursery room at 'The Satemwa House' had been empty for many years and before Jean moved away to Cape Town in 1974, she had designated a corner of the nursery as a chapel. A candle burned daily, and incense mingled with the little slips of wind that pushed through the opened windows. The same windows Chip - as a six year-old boy - used to escape from when the first rays of sunlight crept into the room, the same windows that Juliet, age 20 sat beside, as she contemplated her return from Madrid to Nyasaland, wondering how long she might last back in her parents' home. Jean found herself visiting the empty nursery room every day, passing the hall by 'father's room' as if watched by the ghost of Maclean, and kneeling beside the candles, where the flames consistently glowed. She spent hours praying, reciting prayers, staring at the beds where her babies once lay. The chasm in her heart, split like a canyon the day Juliet died, and now she was searching for something to save her aching, tired spirit, a way to push through the pain, which at times felt like it would consume her.

Introduced to Father Barrett of the Catholic order of Priests in Salisbury by Denise Rock, Jean felt an instant connection to the light inside the Holy man. He offered a way forward, he exuded strength with each step and 'hope' in every word. Father Barrett and his message captured her broken heart and for the first time since Juliet's death, she felt courageous. The gumption of the woman, who had hitched from Cape to Cairo during the Second World War, was returning with a new direction and a new focus. Bathed in the Holy Word, and dedicated to her newfound religion, she travelled to Rome, acquiring, as customary in the Catholic Church, a Godmother – Adrianna, who at the age of 24 was certainly her junior. In an official undertaking in Rome, she was devoted to the work of the Catholic Church, baptized into their ranks with a 'new' life of promise, of discipline and strict adherence to the faith.[393]

She returned to Malawi and built a side-wing chapel at the large Catholic Church in Luchenza, dedicating the wing to Juliet. Under the archway in the front of the chapel, a pulpit stood, illuminated by the arched window on the right, the sculpture of a Saint displayed in the arched alcove sunken into the wall directly behind the pulpit. In a circle, painted onto a teal square on the front of the pulpit was a white lamb with a Shepherd's rod, and in the right corner of the painting the words, "In Memory of Juliet Kay." She sent letters back to relatives in England, and to her Godmother in Rome, asking for prayers to be returned, and soon, all her communications, her thoughts and her energy was centered around the Catholic Church. She built an addition at 'The Satemwa House' – a full Chapel, jutting off to the right-hand side of the house, connected only to the khondi. The Chapel had vaulted ceilings, the highest in the house, and a large rectangular window over the tall wooden doors that led out to a private khondi overlooking the garden. 'Mother's Room', Flora Jean's bedroom, was situated on the same side of the house as the new chapel, along with the dining room, formal living room and kitchen.

Her life soon revolved around the Church. If she heard of a Catholic Priest stranded in a faraway town in Malawi, she sent a car and a driver to rescue him. If a Priest or layman was in need of bedding and food, she provided it. If a member of the Catholic Church was unemployed, she gave him a job. However, burdening Satemwa and her son Chip with her Holy Savings program caused problems, and Chip noticed that her favoring the Church was bleeding the estate. At one stage, there were eight Catholic Churches on the books at Satemwa. "We have to put some boundaries up for these people," Chip begged his mother one day, "They are taking advantage of your generosity."[394]

While many 'strays' seemed to descend on Satemwa to drink Jean's best Port and eat at her table just because she served delicious food, there was one visitor who could never be accused of sponging off her open-handedness. Father Barrett, who often came to Satemwa to visit Jean, was her staunch advocate and one of her favorite guests. On one occasion, when he was at 'The Satemwa House', Jean phoned Chip, "Hello Chip,

I've got Father Barrett here with me, do you mind if we come to see you? I'll make tea and then we will be up." "Forget making tea there. I'll have it made here. Come whenever you like," Chip responded to his mother who promised they would be over shortly.

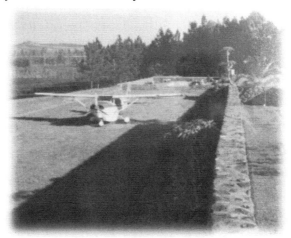

The terrace at Chip and Dawn's home circa 1975

When they arrived, Father Barrett immediately noticed Chip's plane, 7QYFF, "Fox Fox" parked on the second deck. He made a few comments to Flora Jean as they passed it, "Oh – it's got a yellow tail. I think I have seen it flying around Salisbury. Gosh, it sure would be fun to ride in a plane like that. He must really enjoy seeing Africa from a different angle." They settled down on the front lawn, looking towards Thyolo Mountain, a tea trolley beside them, and a hot cup of tea paired with a sandwich spread with cold butter and left-over chicken liver paté and served on a bed of crisp butter lettuce. Soon, Flora Jean looked at Chip and asked, "Please Chip, could you take Father Barrett for a flight in your airplane?" "Certainly, Mother, I would be delighted," Chip replied, "I'll go prepare the plane and then we can take off."[395]

They spent half-an-hour circling the skies above Satemwa, Father Barrett particularly enjoying the view of 'The Satemwa House' from the air. "I never thought of the house gardens as being so expansive," he commented to Chip, "and the mountain, that special picnic spot with the flat acacias, wow! I didn't realize that just beyond dramatically drops off to the Shire, it's simply stunning." It was an enjoyable scenic flight and although he didn't know it at the time, the half-an- hour he spent soaring above Thyolo with Father Barrett would one day be his connection with a crew of strangers.[396]

When Jean left Malawi in 1974 to own and run a small vineyard in Cape Town, Chip had to make the effort to connect with her, flying his family to her home in the Cape, or joining his mother on holidays in places such as Greece, where she inadvertently booked a villa overlooking a nudist colony. "Keep that boy away from the window," she told Dawn, horrified at the naked bodies jumping off yachts into the turquoise Mediterranean below and dreading the impact it might have on Alexander's young, impressionable mind. "If mother wasn't here, we could join them," Chip joked with Dawn after more prude remarks flew. Despite the awkwardness of Jean's religious bent, Chip recognized her hollow eyes, the distant searching of a woman who by all accounts was more beautiful than most, and on all accounts more lost than most. After the death of Maxie, he saw those same hollow eyes sometimes staring back at him in the mirror. And he saw that same distant wandering, the gaze of being 'lost' in Dawn's, sometimes when she was walking in the garden, and at other times, in the middle of a Christmas dinner, but especially in October, every year when Dawn spent the weekend alone, remembering Maxie.[397]

Jean Kay in the living room of the Satemwa House circa 1939

However, only close family and friends could see the bite of chronic sorrow with which Chip wrestled. Bred of the same stubborn character as his father, partnered with the resilience of his mother, he constantly pushed forward. He looked for ways to create synergy between his businesses and interests, and told Dawn one day, "We're going to spray our own crops, and we'll organize it for others too, through our new company 'Skysprays'. " He held out his arms and lifted his eyebrows the way a dancer does at the end of a recital, tapping a single foot on the wooden floors, indicating an "Ah-ha" moment. She looked up from the keyboard where she was typing, and not saying a word prompted him to explain. "I've just bought two new Aero Commander Thrush Airplanes," he informed her with unreserved excitement. "From America. One arrives next week and the other a month after." He looked at her, waiting for her approval which she gave in her customary quiet way. He had signed for the new airplanes on a five-year letter of credit with the Reserve Bank of Malawi, and a forex rate of $1.22 USD to one Malawi Kwacha. The Aero Commander, like most agricultural aircraft, was a single-seat monoplane, a conventional taildragger, which Chip felt he might be partial to, having learned to fly in a Tiger Moth. Either way, the arrival of the Thrush aircraft would be the kickoff for another business venture, one he was sure would succeed.[398]

Chip contracted a professional pilot by the name of 'Slim Bird' to fly his two Aero Commander aircraft from Portland, Maine to Malawi. Slim flew the first plane via the Azores, an archipelago near Portugal in the North Atlantic Ocean, comprised of nine volcanic islands. He was flying a straight line, between Maine and West Africa, arriving in Malawi with no problems. The second plane, however, he brought out in February, taking the 'northern route', because the winds were supposed to be favorable. He departed Portland, Maine on direct route to Reykjavik, Iceland, where winter reigned in fresh powder and temperatures so cold they froze the 1 ½ inch pipe that lead to the fuel tank of the airplane, causing Slim to 'dead stick' as he glided the aircraft to landing, just beyond the end of the Reykjavik runway. The plane slid into a soft snowbank, necessitating rescue by a tractor in the middle of the night. Grounded for two days, he waited, impatiently, while the airport crew de-iced the plane and cleaned out the fuel tanks. Once cleared, Slim hurried down the runway, soaring into the ascent climb and out of Iceland. However, halfway through his climb, the fan stopped working, the engine began to splutter, as if mucked fuel was creating a plug and he found himself engaged in a stall-and-glide, landing in a snow field, about thirty-two kilometers from the airport.

Slim grabbed his bag from behind the seat, and opened the door, climbing out of the cabin onto the low wing of the plane before landing in a foot of fresh snow. The plane was practically buried in the powder, and he shrugged his shoulders and thought, "Well, that's too bad," before finding a road and flagging down a car to take him back to the airport and a commercial flight home to Maine. He rang Chip reporting, "Your plane is stuck in Iceland, near the airport, but bugger me if I could get it out. Sorry for that, Chip, you'll have to make another arrangement." Left on the other end of the line, saying, "Hello, Come again What!" was Chip, wondering how to reclaim his plane, or explain the unexpected loss to the bank where he was deep in debt.

Meanwhile, thirty-two kilometers from the Reykjavik airport, Chip's plane was discovered by two local policemen, who happened to be interested in flying. "Abandoned ship," one wrote on his notepad; the other looking up with glee, "Yes, abandoned and under international law if there is no Captain or pilot to speak for it, well, finders – keepers." They winterized it, boarding up the glass, and roping the ailerons and tail flaps to secure them in case of a snowstorm. Then, when the weather improved, and the snow began to melt they disassembled it, towed it to the local airfield, screwed it back together and congratulated each other on their find - a quarter of a million dollar plane – and now the only thing left was to learn how to fly.

A court case opened into the missing plane, and it was agreed, after hearing from Chip in Central Africa, that the case would adjourn until June when the tea planter who owned the plane could fly to Iceland to dispute the claim on his plane in person. When the day arrived, Chip flew up to London, spending a few days on business before reaching Luton Airport, where the airlines were engaged in a strike. Chip checked the inside of his leather belt, searching the secret compartment, where an undetectable zipper enclosed foreign currency, illegal in some places he travelled, and therefore necessary to conceal. He didn't have enough pounds for a hotel, just a few Sterling which would afford him food to endure the strike.[399]

He slept two nights on the floor at the Airport, eating sandwiches from less than mediocre establishments, but relishing a hot cup of tea twice a day and with every meal, before the strike cleared and he was on his way to reclaim the lost plane in Iceland. Onboard the Icelandic Airways Flight, Chip found himself in the company of three other men, all up for a good time, which began when the stewardess in the First-Class Cabin served them 'take-off' champagne. The champagne starters was soon followed by whiskey and between the four passengers at the front of the cabin, a proper party developed. They began regaling each other with stories. An Italian man who was a police commissioner boasted he had his name printed twice in the London Times in one day. One mention was from a University that was honoring him, and the other had something to do with the Italian Government. "Good for you," another passenger said, motioning for all four glasses of whiskey to toast the Italian's achievement. They were all very merry, and the Italian then looked at Chip asking, "And you, what about you, who are you?"

Chip looked at them, not sure how to give them the 'nutshell' answer and offered, "I'm Chip Kay. I'm actually a tea planter. I'm a born and bred African, and I live in Malawi, Central Africa, and I am a pilot." "There, that pretty much gave them the picture," he thought, settling back into his leather seat. But they all wanted to know more. "Well, what are you doing in Iceland? Salmon fishing?" "Actually, no, I lost an airplane. It was being flown from America and got dumped in the snow fields..." This piqued the interest of the stewardess who asked, "Are you anything to do with a firm called, 'Skysprays?" Chip, wondering how she knew, replied, "Well, yes, in fact I AM Skysprays." The stewardess was excited, as if meeting someone famous she re-told the story of Slim Bird to the other passengers almost as if Chip wasn't present. "This American flew the plane, it had fuel trouble, landed in a snow field, now some guys have claimed it and have dragged it to their local club where they are learning to fly."

So, the three other passengers became interested in Chip, one leaning across the aisle to tell him, "Gosh, I once knew a Catholic Priest and he lived in Central Africa, but he was Rhodesian. You know, I think he had a lady friend somewhere in Central Africa who owned a tea estate." Chip realized that Father Barrett was probably their mutual friend, but he didn't let on, and the man continued blindly, "This lady, she had a son, and he flew all over the place. In fact, you won't believe this, but he kept an airplane on his front lawn. Anyhow, he does things in other countries, has a six seater plane and he took my friend the priest for a flight once." The man was so enthralled in telling his new 'friends' about this pilot that he kept going. "He drops parachutists from his plane all over Central Africa." Chip looked at him, seemingly just as interested as the other two men and the stewardess were to hear his stories and asked, "What sort of airplane was it?" The man admitted, "I don't actually know, it was white or blue, I forget...," and Chip prodded, "What do you know about the plane?" The man thought for a moment, "Well, it had a very distinctive tail, a funny, bright color with numbers on it, oh! And I'll tell you something about the owner. He's famous in the flying world because he only ever wears red socks." With that Chip lifted the legs of both trousers to reveal bright red cotton socks, pulled up above his calves. All the men finally caught up, "Oh!! You're the old lady's tea planting son. You have an airplane on your front lawn." Chip acknowledged, "Yeah, that's me."[400]

Arriving in Reykjavik Chip gathered his things and caught a taxi over to the local flying club, catching a glimpse of his plane outside the clubhouse. He found the man in charge and spoke about the two men who had rescued his plane, wanting to meet them. "Thank you for saving my plane," Chip told them both, "It seems a bit tricky that ownership is now in the courts." They looked up at him, "Well, yes Sir, it is," one responded. Chip sat and talked a while and then suggested, "Why don't you let me pay for your flying lessons, and you let me take my plane home to Malawi, alright?" They agreed, and Chip phoned his secretary at Satemwa's Head

Office, Maria Lampat Stoakes, who organized payment through the Malawi banks to Iceland so the two retrievers of Chip's plane could finish their Private Pilot's License.

"All's well that ends well," Chip chuckled with Dawn once home to Satemwa, and back on his favorite place in front of his house, watching the fading sun, and sipping a hot cup of tea. "Yes, it would appear so," she responded, handing him a slice of sweet, sticky teacake on his side plate, and a white cotton napkin edged in crochet, which he tucked into his shirt.

But sometimes, if "All's well that ends well," was to hold true, he wondered how things with his mother would turn out in the end. Since he was a child, he was desperate to please both of his parents, going out of his way in the latter years to help his mother whose independence was hindered by the process of aging. When she left Malawi in 1974 – buying a small vineyard in Cape Town, she never returned, living in the Cape a decade before moving to England, and a small flat, the last home where she would reside unassisted. Father Barrett, aging alongside Jean, remained in her life, a part of her story right up until the day she died.

Chip had flown to London, staying in the family flat for twelve weeks and visited his mother every day at the assisted living facility nearby. Cared for in a hospice, and deteriorating quickly, she sometimes recognized him immediately, speaking mostly in French, and other times she viewed him curiously. By coincidence, her evening nursemaid was Malawian, her mother's home in Mulanje, and when she brewed fresh tea for them both, Chip thanked the nurse in Chichewa. Flora Jean's face invariably lit up, "Zikomo", triggering her memory and launching her back fifty years to the home she built with Maclean. To the middle of a humid summer at 'The Satemwa House' where on her garden rounds alongside her eighteen garden boys she would review the progress of the plants, and when satisfied thank the gardeners with a hearty, "Zikomo, nchito ja bueno." And she smiled, thinking about the tree that Juliet planted outside the living room of 'The Satemwa House', which had grown so wide and so tall it moved the concrete khondi in places, and the two little potted trees that once sat on the khondi, released to the soil on the lawn, now stood tall like sentinels, an indication of the passing years.[401]

One evening as Chip walked along Pimlico, where a grid of residential streets gave heart to the Westminster City on his way to see his mother, a tall man, over 6ft, very handsome, bent over a walking stick, caught Chip's eye. The man had difficulty seeing, having mostly lost his vision, but he managed to shuffle along, navigating streets he obviously knew well. "Excuse me Sir," Chip motioned to him, "Are you Father Barrett?" He hadn't seen Father Barrett since the day they went flying over Satemwa and he had been taken with the view of 'The Satemwa House' from the air. "Oh yes," the man replied, straining to see Chip who was by now just under his nose. "In fact, I've been to see your mother, and I've just read to her - her last rights," Father Barrett said with compassion running through his voice. "Is she going to die tonight," Chip asked, hoping Father Barrett had the answer. And somehow when he responded, "Yes, she will," he felt comforted, like someone knew that it was going to be okay even though death was inevitable. "Okay then," Chip said, "I'd best go be with her then."[402]

Jean Kay never returned to Malawi, not even in death, willing her body to remain in England, her 'homeland.' Her grave, estranged from her family who rested in Blantyre and Thyolo, was oceans away from her father, her husband, two children and one grandchild, who together, lay under the African sun. Oddly, Chip understood his mother, obliging her wishes as he organized her burial in London. She was a third culture child, born in England and to her, England was always 'home.' However, for Chip, born at Namireme in the Shire Highlands, Malawi would always be his.

Old and Bold from 1983

Chip Cathcart Kay circa 1980

"There are old pilots and bold pilots, but no old, bold pilots."
E. Hamilton Lee (1949)

The Malawi Department of Civil Aviation "Personal Flying Log Book," which Chip kept in his James Bond flying briefcase experienced a decrease in entries, the hours logged in "Fox Fox" almost 'obligatory' hours, just the minimal amount required to keep an active license. It was something Chip tried to ignore for a few years, his reaction time in the cockpit, his delay in making decisions that required split-second judgments, overall, his ability to be the safest, best bush pilot in Africa, hampered by the inescapable aging dilemma. Echoing in his mind was the pilot adage, "There's no such thing as old, bold pilots," and he wrestled with himself over the painful, but unavoidable decision, the inner tension that ran through his veins, keeping him awake at night, knowing at this point the choice only he could make was the decision to ground himself. The last stamp in his logbook was dated 7 January 1983.[403]

Chip was in his early fifties when he piloted his last flight, a commemorative scenic flip over Thyolo, and he resisted the tears that he felt all those years ago when stepping off the Mauretania at Liverpool as a fourteen-year-old boy; the overwhelming tears that sprang from his eyes whenever he felt a transition skulking in the passage of time. In his heart, he was not ready to retire "Fox Fox" to the hangar on Satemwa, a hangar that took him twenty years to build, just opposite Dawn's horse stables. He was not prepared to give up his freedom, yet he knew his time had arrived.

He had seen too many aeronautical accidents during his life, and he was determined to remain a safe pilot, even if that meant not flying anymore.

He had accomplished many things during his 'flying years.' Having flitted between Mozambique, Zimbabwe and Malawi for most of his flying career, Chip had the opportunity to build a handful of airstrips in other countries, such as the shallow pitch he laid out on Paradise Island in Mozambique. During his years as a pilot, he had learned skills for flight from 24 instructors and taught 27 students to fly, with the disclaimer of the numbers possibly reversed. He was a pioneer of civil aviation for Nyasaland after the Second World War, and he would always remember how flying opened up the world for him, not just for business, but also for friendship. Des, across in Zimbabwe, had hung up his flying cap almost a decade earlier, and Chip decided they would always have each other to call whenever one needed to "relive the glory days."

He had built 28 airstrips in Malawi, including the Malamulo Mission Airstrip, ZOA tea estates that was only 350 yards long, and logged the first landing on Mulanje plateau, where he had helped Tony Gunn working for the mining company, Lonrho, to plot a straight runway on Luchenja where the golden mountain grasses stretched for miles.[404] When the Mulanje airstrip tested satisfactorily, Chip flew Dawn up to the island in the sky, landing in an afternoon shimmer of gold. He set a small table with a cloth beside the plane and retrieved hot flasks of tea and Wedgwood fine china teacups from the basket, pouring the hot tea and sipping quality mountain top brew.[405]

Chip missed flying but so did Dawn and she now had to wade through commercial lines and ticketing agents for her travel. She added humor to their commercial flights by recounting their memories from when Chip piloted them around Africa. "Remember when we came home from Maxie's christening in Durban?" she began one day, sitting next to Chip on a commercial flight just before take-off at Chileka. "We had Joy, and the two boys," and then Chip cut in, "And that Jet. Remember? It just went Whoosh across our path." "Oh yes, I remember, but I was too busy changing clothes after the baby spat up on me for the third time," Dawn added, to which Chip replied, "I seem to remember both you and Joy being out of clothes by the time we landed in Maputo."[406]

"Yes, but nothing could be worse than that drunkard that met us at the plane with a gun," she said, still shivering at the thought. The drunkard was a soldier, on duty, completely inebriated, waving his gun around as though it were a sparkler in the dark night. Suddenly the gun fell on the floor of the plane, and Dawn braced herself, shielding her two boys in case of accidental fire. "I was petrified," she admitted to Chip, who was chuckling at the thought, "but not as terrified as that bicycle Bambo the night at Madema."

The night at Madema was the time Chip had to make a forced landing, traveling back to Malawi from Salisbury in a tangle of foul weather. "We'll make it to Chileka," he had told Dawn, who wondered what he would do as the weather prohibited landing at Chileka. "We'll head for the Madema Road, it's straight and should be fairly empty this time of night," Chip told his passengers, as the tension in the cabin mounted. With powerful halogen lamps lighting up the whole countryside, Chip found the Madema Road, angling for the straight flat section he saw just ahead. However, between him and the landing was a man on a bicycle, pedaling furiously under Chip's spotlight, seemingly unaware of the looming danger should he remain on the road. Chip tapped his lights on and off in a desperate effort to communicate with the cyclist who was clinging to the road. He revved the plane's engine, wishing it were equipped with a horn. The plane was dropping lower and nearer the tarmac, and Chip looked at Dawn, "There's six of us, one of him…everybody brace yourselves." He wanted to shut his eyes, fearing impact with the Bambo on his bike. But at the very last minute, just as the wings of his Cessna would surely have clipped the man from his seat, he turned his bicycle at a sharp left angle and darted off the road into the ridges of the maize field, waving as he bumped along.[407]

Loading "Fox Fox" from the terrace at Chip and Dawn's home circa 1976

It wasn't only his achievements as a pilot that gave him a sense of accomplishment. Everywhere he looked around Satemwa he saw developments that he had helped to create. He had overseen the building of houses for managers, one on Mwalunthunzi estate, just near his own home, and its identical floorplan built in reverse, erected for the manager at Chawani. Twenty-two dams were dug and formed on the Satemwa properties during his watch. He had made improvements to his father's 1937 tea factory, despite his father's resistance, tearing down a few brick walls to allow for improved airflow. Holding one of the large, solid red bricks he couldn't help but wonder if it might have been one that he had patted into a mold, along with the labor, in the mid 1930's, as they made thousands of bricks from the estate soil, firing them in large piles with kuni (wood) burning underneath. Whether it was sentimentality or owing to the fact that those old bricks seemed sturdier than the modern ones made in haste, with decreased firing time, due to deforestation and therefore a lack of available wood, Chip instructed the workers to salvage bricks where possible. He had built a hangar for his plane, and Dawn had started a cheese factory underneath it, hoping the cool air would aid in the needed refrigeration. He had also overseen construction of a string of houses from the old administration block to the crossroads, referred to as 'upper tooting.' And of course, there was the new Head Office, attached to their garage, a magnificent two storied addition.[408]

In Luchenza, he had the flying club, which he and Des built with the kind of loving touch small children employ constructing castles and kingdoms out of play-doh or legos. They had created hangars, a clubhouse, a swimming pool, and a beautiful airstrip, where planes buzzed on a Sunday, and people gathered to marvel at flight. Across the main road from the flying club stood his Luchenza Factory, with 100 yards of railroad, right from the main line, through the gate and into his factory, "because the railways actually used to work." Despite the changing world and the difficulty in not only adding to his capital, but maintaining what existed, Chip still believed he was a "millionaire of happiness's", and apart from the physical showings of his toil, the more important, the more lasting, shone out through his family.[409]

With the implosion of Rhodesia, now Zimbabwe, families in neighboring countries stopped sending their children to what was now Harare for boarding school. "It's just too far away, in case something was to happen," Dawn told Chip, adding, "Green Acres, here in Thyolo is a decent start and then Hillview would keep them close to home, and close to us." Situated in the middle of the Conforzi Tea Estate, and just across the road from Satemwa, 'Green Acres' was run by a few of the wives from Conforzi and Namingomba Estates and provided estate children with the schooling basics. Forty minutes' drive from Satemwa, heading towards Blantyre, Hillview School educated many tea estate children coming out of nursery feeder programs such as Green Acres.[410]

Not unlike his father, Alexander had a certain desire to grow things, accepting packets of vegetable seeds from his mother who told him, "Remember to keep 10% of the crop for seed, because I'm only buying this once." He dug his own little vegetable patch in his mother's large garden, and watered, weeded and harvested some of the best vegetables Thyolo had seen. He began to sell them in the parking lot at Hillview, and parents would see his mother approaching in their Toyota station wagon, and begin calling out, "Is Alexander there? What vegetables does he have to sell today?" Alexander, along with being a vegetable gardener, was a successful pig farmer, acquiring the runts of the litter from Anne Pieman, who raised pigs in Zomba. He penned them in the animal sheds behind the carport, and nurtured them, until they were sizeable enough to sell. Anne always coded her pigs, which Alexander kept, adding an additional description to the original name. If Anne said it was pig L for Lulu, he would add Lulu – Lunch, if it was B for Betty he added Betty – Brunch, D for Dianna and Dinner, E for Elvis and Eat, and so on, feeling quite amused by his embellishments.[411]

When Hilliard, "Hilly" came of school age, he had already earned a reputation that would be difficult to shake. He was, "The Thyolo Terrorist", rambunctious, bursting with energy, not only cheeky in tongue, but a physical handful, and Dawn warned her friends, "Please don't give him any Coca Cola, or extra sweets," but of course, occasionally they did, which Dottie Henderson "regretted immediately." Hilly was always up to something, his mind ticking over with the next trick or practical joke. Once, when the adults were all sipping wine and dancing in the Thyolo Sports Club Ballroom, he sneaked around the carpark, unscrewed one tire valve cap on each car, allowing air to escape from the tires of every car in the parking lot. He stood for a moment when he arrived at his mother's car, contemplating her reaction, and decided to leave her valves intact. However, it was his undoing, and as Chip and Dawn drove carefree out of the lot, the suspicion immediately fell on Hilliard. Theirs was the only untouched vehicle, and unwittingly they left behind disgruntled club goers who forwarded messages of grievance to Satemwa the following morning. Chip teased Dawn that they should respond, "on behalf of the Thyolo Terrorist," Hilly's infamous nickname; "We are sincerely deflated to hear about last night's events, and we hope to put air in the situation as soon as possible."

However, being naughty also meant Hilly learned how to be resourceful. He was eight years old when his family, along with Hugh and Jill Kayes' family took a vacation up to the Nyika Plateau in the Northern districts of Malawi. The Nyika at 2,605m was not unlike some areas of Mulanje. Broad valleys and rolling hills intersected pine forests where little streams cut through the dell and where the Denhams' Bustard poked its large head above the golden grasses and the Roan Antelope stood aloof on the horizon. It was a destination where Chip, Dawn and the boys often spent a week each year, enjoying morning and afternoon walks and drives, and a large log fireplace that kept the cool temperatures bearable at night. The cook assigned to the chalet, made fresh bread in the wood-fired oven, and hot tea five times a day.

Hilliard (left), Dawn and Alexander (right) circa 1990

The children often traded seats between the caravan of two vehicles, the Kayes' Toyota double cab, and Chip's Khaki Range Rover. Hilly rode with the Kayes' and Alexander with his parents. It was around ten o'clock in the morning, and it was time for a tea break. Chip, the lead car, found a nice clearing along the roadside and pulled off. In the absence of house staff along, Dawn busied herself setting a table, complete with cloth, teacups, napkins and chairs that nestled around it. On a silver tray, biscuits offered a tasty morsel with the morning brew. Everyone was enjoying the reprieve from car travel, and Hilly, feeling the urge, wandered off into the bush to relieve himself.

In the meantime, the adults had finished their tea, and their roadside picnic was packed back into the cars. Soon, they were back on the road, Chip with his carload, and Hugh and Jill with theirs. They drove consistently until they found a nice lookout spot, along the Viphya range, and they pulled off to have their lunch. Exiting the vehicle, Dawn suddenly realized something was amiss. "Where's Hilly? Is he with you Jill?" she asked, worry covering her tone. "Not with us, we thought he was back in your car," Jill replied, "You're not joking, are you?" she added, wondering if Chip had put Dawn up to it. Chip and Dawn, realizing they must have left Hilliard at the morning tea break became frantic. "Right, we have to go back and find him," Chip stated, "He must be some 300 kilometers away." Chip and Dawn jumped back into their Land Rover, asking their friends to please wait there with Alexander, and took off at terrific speed, peeling out of the gravel covered road stop, and back onto the tarmac, heading south to find Hilly. They stopped at the nearest police station, sequestering a constable for their mission, and raced on towards where they last saw their son.

Meanwhile, Hilly, finished with his business had walked out of the bush to find his family and friends disappearing up the tarmac and giggled to himself, "Oh yeah, funny, funny, guys – I'll know you're just pretending to leave me here." He stood by the roadside, arms crossed, waiting for them to turn around and collect him. But as he kept watching, the cars got further and further away, until they disappeared completely around a bend. He waited several minutes, still anticipating their reappearance, and growing more agitated when they didn't show up, he thought, "Did they really just forget about me?" The reality was becoming plainer with each passing moment. He looked at his surroundings, sparse, scraggly shrubs clumped on the nearby terrain, large forests darkened the horizon, and a few three-stone village fires let off smoke ropes into the sky. He saw a lorry truck heading north and stepped closer to the edge of the tarmac, leaning into the road space and waving with large sweeps of his arms to the driver who curiously stopped, wondering why a little white boy was out in the middle of nowhere by himself. "Muli Bwanji," Hilly spoke to the man in chichewa, also a slight shock for the driver, "ndi parents alipo ahead, ndi ku funa ma ridey chonde?" "Ndi, bwela," the driver responded, motioning for Hilly to stand in the back of the truck and hold tight to the metal bar across the cab.

Traveling at speeds that made the constable nervous, his black knuckles turning white as he gripped the handle above the passenger door, Chip raced in his Range Rover, reaching 145 kilometers per hour in sections. "Slow down, Chip," Dawn requested, "What is that ahead?" Chip pressed the brakes, and the constable relinquished his grip on the handle, everyone glued to the scene traipsing up the road towards them. A white flash indicated the oncoming traffic was not all African and a closer look revealed Hilly, who at the age of eight had figured out a way to find his way about Africa. He had already spotted his parents and was waving frenziedly at the Range Rover, hoping they wouldn't miss him a second time.

****

Juliet's wedding 1990

Juliet and Trysh were very much young ladies by now, having met their potential life partners who both hailed from Malawi. Juliet would marry Hugh Saunders, a tobacco marketer from Lilongwe, and Trysh would marry Jim Henderson, also in the tobacco arena. Both the Henderson and Saunders families were long-standing settler families dating back to the early beginnings of Nyasaland and Chip couldn't believe his luck that both of his little girls would remain in the country. "To think so many of our friends have lost their children to England or South Africa, or even Australia," he mused with Dawn one night, "and here we are – the luckiest people – with both Juliet and Trysh just five hours away."

Alexander, who had taken to his studies with the same kind of aptitude he employed in pig and vegetable farming, did very well, achieving his high school certificate in Malawi, a Bachelors in Horticulture from the University of Nataal, and enjoyed a brief stint working as a game driver in South Luangwa National Park in between. He made his brother Hilly proud when he startled a Japanese peace worker inside her tent one night by playing pre-recorded lion roars just outside of the canvas, sending her screaming to the other corner of her tent. "I'm not the only 'terrorist' in the family after all," Hilly joked with his Dad upon hearing the tale.[413]

Alexander then returned, just like his father had, to Satemwa, and told Chip, "Right, I'm ready to work," adding, "I'll do anything, just tell me where I'm needed most." It was wonderful to have Alexander's help on the estate, his keen eye overseeing processes, his desire to learn more about tea renewed Chip's passion to grow it, and together, the family business prospered. With two men harboring a 'terrible desire to grow things,' they set out to propagate bananas, using tissue culture from South Africa and Israel. Their initiative took off, and soon fields of bananas sprang up, the best in the district. During this time, Alexander asked for a year out, where he attended Cape Town University, earning an MBA and nurturing friendships with like-minded people from all over the world.

Hilly had taken a different schooling path from his brother, having battled dyslexia, just like his father. Dawn searched and searched for the school, which might give him the best chance at learning. Finding Kearsney in Nataal, she enrolled Hilliard, and relied on their expertise to guide his education. Hilly blossomed at Kearsney, and although they missed him terribly in Malawi, Chip and Dawn knew they had made the best choice.

Kearsney was in the same district where years earlier Chip had taken Satemwa tea to sell to Five Roses, South Africa's big Tea company. He didn't have an appointment, but walked into the managing director's office, and waited for the secretary to confirm if the big boss would see him or not. "He will, but I'm afraid he's a grumpy old man," she told Chip, who had complimented her on making a very good cup of tea for him moments earlier.

When he was presented to the Five Roses manager, Chip told him, "Sir, I'm from Malawi and I've come to visit you to see if you would like the opportunity to buy any of our teas?" "No," he puffed, "We only buy Ceylon." Knowing this was false, Chip pressed a little more, until the manager stood up from his chair, "Well, its lunch time. Come with me." Chip obliged and they drove in the manager's motorcar off the main roads, passed where Hilly was now in school at Kearsney, arriving to a gate. "Open it," the manager said, motioning for Chip to get out of the car. The man drove through the gate and up the hill, and Chip closed the gate behind him and walked up to find the Five Roses manager overlooking "the valley of a thousand hills." Chip picked up a few leaves on his way up and began to chew on them. When he found the manager by his car at the top of the hill, he told him, "You know, we're surrounded by tea bushes." The Five Roses bwana cracked a smile, doubting if Chip would pass his test. "Don't talk nonsense," he told Chip, wondering if he could convince him otherwise, but Chip assured him, "No, these most certainly are tea," prompting the manager to reach for his hand, and congratulate him. "So, you really are a tea planter then."[(414)]

It was the same kind of confidence that Hilly produced when he stepped out of his house at Kearsney to find a tall tree beside the kitchen door. He recognized it immediately, running back in to tell his housemaster, "There's a tea bush outside the kitchen door." A few people came out to view it and told Hilly, "Don't lie, that is no tea bush." It upset Hilliard quite a bit, enough that he reported the incident to his father, and when Chip came down the following month to visit, he went to see the tree, walking back inside the house to confirm what Hilly had suspected. "Most definitely tea, Camelia Senensis – a native of China – imported here from Ceylon." In fact, Kearsney House where Hilly resided was the General Manager's house of the Nataal Tea Company seventy-five years before Hilly found the tree.[415]

Pursuing his interests in mechanics, Hilliard went for further training in Cape Town, enrolling and passing a variety of courses mostly to do with electrical engineering. Just like his father, Hilly loved all things mechanical and decided to move to England to work for Tesco in their refrigeration department. Also like his father and grandfather he desired to serve the Crown and signed up for the British Army, but upon enrolment he lost his chance when he had an unfortunate break in his leg.

Alexander, finished in Cape Town, returned to Satemwa. Satisfied with his training, he now dove into the estate business with a full head, making plans and running over books, looking for ways to modernize the 'old' systems. Like his father, and his grandfather before him, he had now bought into the privileges and challenges of the African continent. And his ability to adapt to political volatility, a crop whose value swung heavily on world markets, changing drinking habits around the globe, a fluctuating workforce, and a devastating fire that was just around the corner, would determine whether he would succeed or fail. One thing was certain, his parents were delighted to welcome him home, and hoped one day, Hilliard might join them.

Winds of Change – 2003

Chip and Alexander view the damage at the tea factory circa 2003

When Maclean Kay arrived in Nyasaland in 1922, tired from the long, arduous journey by boat, train and car, his future was uncertain. He had come to plant rubber for John Scott, a man who disappeared between the promise of employment and the time it took for Maclean to arrive in the British Protectorate. Maclean had little money with him, but through his brother's help, he purchased a 'piece of Africa.' The dominant crop on his new estate failed and he made the bold choice, swapping tobacco for tea. He lost two homes to fire and re-built on the original site a homestead at the heart of his purchase. 'The Satemwa House' was a 'modern' marvel, with its tin roof and high ceilings, additions throughout the years creating a large, spacious home and many happy memories. He had begun with almost nothing, and yet when he died in 1968, he left a thriving tea estate in the capable hands of his son, Chip.

Chip, the 'millionaire of happiness's' thought he was the lucky one. From his father's hard toil, he carried the torch, growing businesses across Africa, where everything he touched thrived, "because everything I do is FUN," he recounted, thinking of his own enterprises, his planes and PTA spread throughout Central Africa. But he knew, deep in his heart, he was the lucky one. His days were the carefree ones, the 'spend whatever you like' days, because money was easy, and business was good. Now, Chip wanted his children, all of them, to enjoy the same kind of whimsical life he experienced, the same kind of world where anything was possible. But if the last two decades in Malawi were any indication of the future, he would have to help his children 'buckle down' because things were bound to get worse before they could get better. Tea was declining on the international markets, with bumper crops in Kenya affecting their sales. PTA struggled to import goods under the eye of a suspicious, finicky government, and the explosion in population around Thyolo meant the local people felt burdened by the expansive tea fields, even though the tea was there long before most of them were born.

In the top right-hand drawer of his large wooden desk in his personal office, beside his old business cards, "Skysprays", "PTA Three Leaves", and "Leopard Air Ltd", Chip kept a momento from the Banda years. A newspaper clipping from 1994, "Malawi gets ready for life without Banda," detailing the one-party demise to a multi-party democracy.[416] Banda, "The Conqueror of Colonialism," left a country to ponder what that meant, and what exactly Banda had conquered. Were they better off before, or after? Banda's totalitarian government that "regularly tortured and murdered political prisoners,"[417] was ousted by a country tired of oppression and by promises Bakili Muluzi could never keep when he won the Presidency as the leader of the United Democratic Front (UDF) party. "The one promise Muluzi kept," Chip said wistfully from his front lawn chair as he looked at Thyolo Mountain in the distance. Campaigning in Thyolo, Muluzi had told the people, "I'll give you the Mountain if you give me your vote." He was ripping the land from the National Forest when elected, and turning it over to a jaunting crowd who believed they would all benefit from the land. Within a year, the surrounding villages had raped the Mountain of its virgin forests, trees with circumferences as wide as a car, falling under the saws of hungry men, fraught to plant maize. In reality, only a few shared the newly barren slopes, as ridges for maize, cassava and banana plants dominated the once dense jungle. The tree lined ridge of Thyolo Mountain, now desolate, revealed a large rock teetering on the apex.[418]

Accounts were tight but promising, and Alexander, monitoring the income and expenditure of Satemwa, knew they had to make some changes if they wanted to progress. They were managing, but he proposed there was room for growth. Besides, they needed to build a financial buffer – 'to save for a rainy day.'

Unfortunately, for Satemwa, the day arrived, not with rain but with fire. Chip and Dawn were working late, as usual, at Head office around 7pm when they heard the radio call from Rob Emmot, their General Manager, "Fire in the Factory."

Dropping their books and tasks immediately, Chip rushed out to his old Nissan Patrol, turning on the windshield wipers, hoping they would help to clear the thick Chiperoni that hung heavy in the air. He pushed through it, mostly by feel, knowing the estate roads better than anybody, and made it to the front of the factory where, through the deep mist, and illuminated by it, he saw his father's factory from 1937 engulfed in flames. "Are all the workers out? Is everybody safe?" he asked his manager who was standing beside him, "Yes, everyone is accounted for, everyone is safe."

It was a helpless feeling, especially for Chip, who was used to being able to 'fix' things. He watched the factory simmer, listening as the large 640-kilo fans fell from the ceiling, cracking the fermenting machine when they landed on its back. They heard the eerie noise of demolition as the flames spread through the factory, the sound of glass breaking as it imploded under the heat, and wood, stacked for the boiler, alight like a bonfire with dynamite at its base. Combusting under the blaze, the factory imploded, in an inferno that Chip told Dawn "couldn't have been stopped by the entire fleet of London's Fire Brigade."[419]

Alexander, who had joined his dad outside the factory, stood beside him, a quiet strength. At the time, his wife Anette was away, and he sent her a message which simply read, "Factory Burned."

The following day, Chip and Alexander walked around the factory site, stepping over chunks of charcoal, curiously viewing machinery that still stood, and wondering if it could possibly work again. A large piece of metal was bent in an unusual contour and a closer look revealed it shaped like a question mark. "How appropriate," Chip mused with Alexander, "That metal is exactly how I feel. Why?"

Without the Tea Factory, which was the center of productivity for the commercial estate, Satemwa would fail. Yet, re-building it, under limited insurance claims, was almost impossible. However, Chip was determined to have the factory operating at a level where it could function for all the basics of production within three months, and the entire workforce all moved towards that goal. He designed a new trussing system, installing twenty-eight 66-foot long beams. Bricks and wood were added where they had burned and soon, within three months, the factory was again processing Satemwa's green flush.

Finances had never been so difficult, and the factory re-build stalled due to the lack of available funds. Battling insurers proved futile and it became clear Satemwa would have a long road and a big battle ahead to recover what was lost the night the factory burned.

They needed help and Hilliard, sensing this, flew home to Satemwa four months after the fire, and began work for PTA, taking the burden off Chip and allowing him to focus on saving Satemwa. With all four of his children now in Malawi and Dawn as an ever-present source of strength by his side, Chip was determined to fight and protect the legacy his father began.

Selling company assets, and at times, "the family silverware", fine-tuning the labor needs, and watching their expenditure, they began to dig themselves out of debt. Alexander diversified the tea range, and experienced favorable reviews abroad, incentivizing him to continue. Their coffee competed on the world markets, shining among the best. The dairy herd was reduced to just a few cows, enough to provide milk, butter and cream for the estate homes. Dawn worked longer and harder in the office, finding ways to reduce spending. Every kwacha counted, because every kwacha mattered.

Sixteen Million and Counting 2003- 2013

Chip Cathcart Kay and his tea circa 2013

During the Banda years, Malawi experienced one of the highest Total Fertility Rates (TFR) in the world, averaging 7.6 births per woman in 1977. The population exploded and by the time Banda left office in 1994, there were nearly ten million Malawians in the country, six million more people than at Independence in 1964. Banda was proud of his people's fertility – because he thought of the people as Malawi's natural resource. Zambia was rich in copper, Botswana in diamonds and Malawi - Malawi had People. While education highlighted the problem of the growing population, a decline in the TFR was projected to take years before fewer births might ease the burden of the population boom, which exerted extreme pressures on land, education, employment and medical care. Malawi's ability to satisfy the most basic human needs was stifled by a population surging ahead towards a bleak future where deforestation, urbanization, housing, transport, and basic sanitation spelt disaster. Malawi, ranked as one of the world's poorest countries, in both GDP per capita and standard of living, welcomed an influx of Non-Government organizations, totaling 40% of the government's budget, "do-gooders" as Chip often said when he saw their brand new Landcruisers passing his estate, "The great white hopes, here to save Africa."

He didn't mean to be critical of their efforts or dampen their zeal for the 'mission at hand', but over the years, he had watched people – from outside – come and go. He had seen foreigners, well-intentioned; believe they had somehow 'saved' Africa, even after only two weeks in the country or contrarily leaving embittered and discouraged by their African experience. Even if he was alone in his thinking, Chip believed that foreign aid was not the solution to Africa's problems. And while he didn't pretend to know what was, he certainly knew the people, their mindsets, and their habits better than an outsider. He once told a short term missionary, who had come to sip tea on his khondi with friends, "I'm not racist, you people are," which puzzled the young "do-gooder" and prompted further explanation, "I accept the people, just the way they are. You – you come here to change them."

Chip, now in his eighties, white hair sprinkled over his balding head, a full beard of bristly snow colored whiskers covering his jaw and his wiry moustache as defiant as ever, still footed about the estate refusing the help of a walking stick. He was typically clad in his notorious khaki cotton 'uniform', red socks on his feet, a notepad, pen and cell phone, that struggled to pick up a signal, tucked inside the top left pocket of his collared shirt. Chip was heavily involved with Satemwa, even at his age, representing the company at the tea auction in Blantyre every Tuesday, visiting the factory every night, and ending his evening with a stopover at his childhood home, 'The Satemwa House'. Renamed by Dawn in 2007 as Huntingdon, and opened to the public as a luxury lodge. Since Maclean had purchased the deed originally from Mr Hunter, Huntingdon was a name that seemed to suit. The house and grounds became a venue for high tea, or an overnight stay in one of the original family member's renovated bedrooms. In the evenings at Huntingdon Chip found a variety of people who eagerly listened to his stories. Stories about his father who had started the estate and built the house where they were now enjoying their fillet steak with chili chocolate sauce, followed by the best macadamia pie in the country. He asked the guests which room they were staying in, "Oh nursery room," he would ruminate, telling them, "That is where I grew up." The guests looked curiously at Chip, as he proudly called himself a 'Colonial'. Some delighted to hear his tales, and others not sure what to make of them. He could see the word, 'Colonial' running through their brain. Was it a good word or a bad word? To him, it was part of his life. He was born a colonial and he would die a colonial. The years had somehow slipped by, and the 'winds of change' that had blown out 'Colonialism' and ushered in Malawi's first dictator now blew again.

The land of the "out-stretched hand", where children shouted, "Azungu!" (foreigner) at anybody with white skin, followed by a string of words in English, "Give me MY money," or "Give me MY bicycle," or "Give me a sweetie," irritated Chip. The people he knew in Malawi were better than a simple reduction to 'beggars.' In fact, he considered himself better equipped in understanding black people than understanding whites, certainly, if the case of Ted Pickford was anything to go on. He had spent most of his life immersed with blacks - most of his day spent with Malawians - a black driver, black house staff, black employees; he was comfortable around them, and they were comfortable around him. Although, wasn't he also Malawian, even though his skin was white? He noticed that as AID increased, more hands rose up in cries for help, help they could have provided for themselves and each other in many cases. Chip refused to wait for someone to drop out of the sky and solve his problems, and he wanted to encourage the African people to do the same. He began at home, on Satemwa, working alongside his people, asking them questions, "Now, come on chaps, how you can fix this problem of getting your maize to grow tall?" "Ah, Bwana, we are waiting for the fertilizer coupons," they would say, or "Give me some fertilizer, and then I can make it grow." "Well, how about I teach you to make compost, and then you can fertilize for yourself," Chip suggested, watching for the eyes of people who were willing to learn.[420]

He created a vegetable club among a group of ten women and he taught them to grow food, photographing the plants so they could visualize the progress. "Ninety days from seed. Isn't it marvelous?" he commented, watching as the women harvested their first crop of cabbages, reminding them to save enough from their sales to buy more seed. Word got out, as it does in Africa, and women from all over the estate begged inclusion in his vegetable initiative. "They are feeding their families and making sales," Chip said to Dawn, showing her the pictures of the women's gardens.

Investing in the Satemwa primary school, he encouraged mothers to send their children, and he invigorated teachers applauding them for their interests in education and imploring them to give the children a solid foundation. "If you can't get through to them, then what are their chances?" he asked the teachers. "Satemwa is here to support your work, so please, let's make it worthwhile for the children."

Chip held soccer tournaments at the football pitch on Satemwa, and attended the games, cheering for 'good sportsmanship' rather than a particular team.

He held monthly 'cleanest compound' awards for the estate homes, encouraging his workers to maintain a hygienic environment, giving awards for 'best sanitation', 'most wokongola' (beautiful) – which usually was awarded to the compounds who spent the most time gardening, and washing the outside of their homes, and 'best overall' taking into account a variety of factors.

Certain women employed at Satemwa, whom Chip had sent for further education, returned and now held meetings, educational programs for the Satemwa staff, teaching the female labor about child spacing, hygiene, drinking water and flys. "Eeeee, flys! The Bwana says flys are worse for you than mosquitos. They go chimbuzi (toilet) on your food, then you get the runs and the runs are bad."[421]

Driving to Chawani one day, he noticed two young girls, loitering about the gardenias near the Chawani Bungalow. He greeted them in English, and one ran behind a tree. He switched to Chichewa, instructing the girl who remained, "Tell your friend she mustn't be afraid of me." Moments later, having heard an old white man speaking in better Chichewa than her parents, the young girl emerged, "Ndi, Bwana, pepani (sorry) my rudeness." "Why do you not speak full English?" Chip asked them both, estimating them to be around fifteen years of age. "Because our teacher is no good," they responded together. "And what about your family? Does your father not speak, and your mother?" They shook their heads, "Eei." Chip practiced a few English words with them saying, "You're never going to learn if you can't speak English. What language are most of the books written in at the big libraries in town?" "English, Bwana," they replied, "Right, so every Sunday, I'm going to come here, and we're going to talk to each other in English. Alright?" They agreed, and every Sunday Chip found them waiting at the barrier by Chawani Bungalow, eager to see what lesson the Bwana Wonkulu had prepared for them and equally as thrilled to show him they had been practicing English with each other and were most definitely improving.[422]

Sometimes, he felt like he was making progress, and at other times, he felt stuck in the middle of 'tribal' warfare, where logic gave way to brutality, tele-porting the Africans back a few centuries, long before David Livingstone arrived. The half-Israeli, half South-African banana plants that he and Alexander had started, thrived in the field and after eleven months, yielded 40kg each of bananas, sweet, thick, creamy bananas, which he sold to the local economy and which the people all relished. One day, the manager of his banana crop, a Malawian Capitao in his mid-forties, alerted the Satemwa security of trouble in the banana fields at Sambankanga. He tried to scare off banana thieves, but had instead been caught by them and tied up, held on the estate, and threatened with his very life for 'chasing them off.' When Chip arrived, the people, a mob by now, refused to let his manager go. Despite negotiations and compromises, his manager was held, with a worsening situation and an increasingly agitated mob. "They are holding one of OUR people," he told his head security officer. "Radio Satemwa for a truck with twenty men and twenty pangas, and send them here immediately."

The truck arrived, along with the men and Chip told them, "These thieves have captured our manager, and have stolen our bananas. I want you to cut down EVERY banana tree in this acreage, and while you are cutting, you must shout, "Release the manager" and "Nobody eats stolen bananas". Twenty men descended on the field and within the hour the manager was released. Those who had held him begged Chip, "Don't slaughter the bananas, what will we eat now?" to which Chip replied, "You were about to harm, possibly kill a man for those fruits, now – every time you look at this empty field, you should remember to treat each other with respect."

Africans who worked for the Cathcart Kay family at their 'home' understood they should work hard, be loyal and responsible and that if they were willing, employment with the family was employment for life. Food and housing was provided along with medical care and education for their children. House employees could 'retire' knowing that someone was still looking after them. Juma, a man who worked for the Fenner's and put Dawn on a horse when she was two years old, stayed with the family until he died, and his daughter, Emmy, worked as Alexander and Hilliard's nanny, changing to household duties when the children grew but staying with the Kay's until she retired. The family dubbed Emmy, "the clever finder," because she always knew where things were. Within two minutes of Dawn calling out for lost keys, Emmy would invariably show up, "Alipo, Mamma," holding them in her hands. The children were close to Emmy, who was a natural caretaker, and managed to keep up with Malawian birth rates, popping out children and returning to work shortly after, as if nothing had happened. "We Nyasa's were all born colorblind," Chip often said, "I had a black nanny, and then I had a white nanny. Alexander had a black nanny. Hilly had a black nanny."[423]

When Emmy was old, and long retired from her duties at the Kay's home, she fell sick with cancer of the oesophagus. There was nothing that could be done to prevent her terminal diagnosis and Chip and Dawn grieved with Emmy, when she dropped by the house to inform them. It came to the point where the treatments she received were not helping, and Chip called the Doctor from Malamulo Mission. "I'm sending my girl – Emmy – to you. Please do what you can for her, and keep her in the Annex." The Annex at Malamulo was the private ward, and cost more for admittance than most people could pay, certainly more than a domestic worker could afford. One of the nurses, assigned to Emmy's care, saw Chip leaving the ward one day, and asked Emmy about the old white man. "My Bwana," Emmy said, struggling for words, "Ndi nchito ku Satemwa many many years." (I worked at Satemwa many years.) The nurse paused and smiled at Emmy and later told the doctor it was unsual for domestic help to be cared for in this manner. Certainly Emmy had a good Bwana.

Chip's childhood friend, John Humbiani, who was desperate to drive a motor car from the time he was small, earned his license in Chip's Morris Minor and drove for Satemwa Estates, staying with the company until he passed away. "Big-toe John," Chip sometimes teased him, causing both the childhood friends to laugh. Nelson Nagoli, on the recommendation of Chip's father, became a chief detective for the police force, and remained connected to Satemwa, visiting Chip at his home once a year, and writing letters, sending them via the post. One day he called Chip, "I'm coming for my job," to which Chip replied, "but you have a job," and Nelson said, "Yes, but I am coming to help you start a security force on Satemwa." Chip, content with his night watchmen, tried to reject the offer, but Nelson, determined, came anyway and began Satemwa's first security force. Maggie – Juliet's friend, disappeared from Chip's life around the time Juliet died, and he never found traces of her again, assuming she had married and long moved on.[424]

Sometimes he wrestled with himself over the dichotomy of emotions he experienced when looking at the country of his birth, the same sort of unease that shocked him on his twenty-first birthday celebration, gone wrong. There were more mouths to feed in a country bursting with people, sixteen million and counting, more men and women arriving every day to the factory pleading for work. Chip resisted the urge to tell them if they had not pillaged Thyolo Mountain of its virgin jungle, the rains would have come already, the tea would have sprouted, and he would have need for a plucker.

Dysfunction, corruption and egocentric reactions by politicians gave little hope. Malawi, burdened by a steady rise in population, faced a dilemma. And Chip, knowing he couldn't solve the pressures on land, employment, education, and health care by himself, contemplated the way forward. He and his family were not like other Europeans who resided in Malawi temporarily because when the going got tough – leaving was never an option. "Leave to where?" Chip would say, "This is my home." Returning from a visit with a local family in Thyolo, having sat with them in their home as women stirred a hot pot of nsima over a three-stone fire outside, Chip told Dawn, tears in his eyes, "There were eighteen mouths gathered around that fire, with nsima enough to feed three." Dawn held his hand, sensing his angst, "I can't help them all," he began, "But I can help one. And tomorrow I can help another."

Where There is TEA, There is HOPE

Dawn serving tea to her grandchildren at House Number One circa 2013

The rain fell in steady drops, long and hard, over the undulating hills of Thyolo. The tidy carpets of Satemwa tea, where bushes pressed together to form a tight green flush, burst in color. Shiny yellow raincoats dotted the fields, where pluckers hoisted the fresh tips into their baskets, trying desperately to pick as fast as the tea was growing. The red clay estate roads that cut through Satemwa were doused in water that dripped from the open sky with no sign of an end to the rain. Tractors, turning their large treaded wheels worked overtime, pulling trailers of fresh tea to the factory, dropping empty wagons at the fields where pluckers off-loaded their pickings. Cars and trucks, slipping on the saturated roads, sunk into the ditches and spun their wheels in a vain attempt to get out. "Glorious rain," Chip exclaimed from his front lawn, as he looked out over the terraces where the wet cobblestone gleamed and water seeped over the rims of the sodden potted plants. It was a beautiful March in Thyolo, and the acreages of tea answered the heavenly sprinkles with bud break that colored the whole district in green gold.

Chip and Dawn fell asleep to the sound of rain falling, dripping off their asbestos tiled roof and onto the vines and hedges that grew around their home. The air was muggy, and Chip opened the bedroom windows a little before settling into bed. The windows in their master bedroom opened onto the front khondi, enclosed with curly cue wrought iron bars soldered between large white pillars and secured at the gate by a chain and lock.[425]

Covered by the din of rain and a dull moon that dimly lit the sky, seven men, armed with knives, left the tarmac road behind them, and pushed through the tea fields and up the hill arriving under the arch by Chip's garage to find his watchmen huddled under the carport, escaping the rain. The intruders bound and gagged the guards and dragged them into the shadows as they scurried towards the main house. The motion sensor on the spotlight above the gate triggered and one of the men smashed it with the butt of his knife. Still no movement in the house. Even the dogs were silent. Another man snapped the lock with bolt cutters and the band of thieves gushed onto the khondi. The wooden French doors, usually locked, were ajar and the bandits turned the golden handle and gained access to the entry room. Instinctively, they moved to the master bedroom where Chip and Dawn lay entirely asleep.

One man flicked the lights on. Suddenly, Chip awoke, startled by the brightness in his room and the seven rain-soaked men that loomed over his bed. They were angry and shouted at him to "Get up!" It was half past one in the morning. Dawn, startled by the noise became alert, waking to a living nightmare. The thieves, barking at each other, almost as though they were waiting for one of them to make a plan, spoke in Chichewa amongst themselves and English to Chip and Dawn. "Clearly, they have no clue whose house they have entered," Chip thought to himself looking across the bed at Dawn, who also decided it was better not to let on that they knew Chichewa.[426]

The men stared at Dawn, dressed in a long white cotton nightie, shoulder length ash blonde hair falling softly, a beautiful 71-year-old woman. "Let's cut her titty off," one man suggested, licking his lips as he spoke. "No, better we rape her," another chimed in as they pressed closer to where Dawn now stood beside her nightstand with her arms wrapped about her chest. Chip, who always slept completely naked, told the lead man, "I need to find my trousers," and confidently walked to the sofa in his bedroom where his trousers lay and slipped them on. He added a thin white singlet on top of his pants and moved near to Dawn hoping to protect her.[427]

Speaking in English they turned to Chip and demanded, "We want to rape your wife," and Chip glared back at them, "Well, you can't because she is a very sick woman. In fact, she has been to Malamulo today for her medicines." Chip wasn't sure what he was trying to make the men believe, maybe that Dawn was infected with AIDS, or could pass something on to them. He continued, "Now, I am the one who can help you, so you need to let me take my wife to the other room, I will lock her in and then I will keep the key." Somehow, the men agreed, and Chip walked with Dawn through the hall past the drawing room into the guest bedroom where he locked her inside and put the key in his pocket. He felt a sudden relief.[428]

As soon as he turned around from the room in which Dawn was locked, the men rushed him and grabbed his shoulders and they bashed on his arms with the blunt edge of their panga knives. "Where is the money?" they shouted, hyping each other up as they spat the words into Chip's face. "I haven't got any money. I use checkbook," Chip told them, wishing he did have a stash which might have got rid of them faster. They shoved him to the floor, and one pinned him down, while the six remaining thugs rushed through the house, ripping drapes from their rods, emptying cases of their books, and smashing teacups in the pantry. They picked up the crystal decanter and threw it at the wall, enjoying the sound of a thousand shards splitting upon impact. They grabbed picture frames and displaced them, shouting, "Give me money!" as they sent family portraits tumbling to the floor. When the money didn't materialize, they switched to, "Give me a gun!" and Chip said, "I don't own a gun. There's no gun in this company." The lead man looked at the others and asked, "Company? Then what about wages, huh?" and Chip told him matter-of-factly, "There are no wages today. It's Monday and we pay on a Friday."

Capsizing the entire house, the intruders' outrage grew and when they found nothing of great value, they turned on Chip, slapping his forearms with the flat surface of the panga, the edges of the blade scoring his arms, because his thin skin could not tolerate the blows. They began knocking his head about and pinching one of his ears saying, "Do you hear me, old man, we will cut your ears off." The largest man in the group, a real brute of a guy, picked up the heavy Sealy bed in the main bedroom and tossed it over, like he was turning a leaf. "Nothing here," he reported before sweeping everything off the dresser and throwing all the drawers out of their holders, sending clothes flying around the room in a whirlwind of chaos. He cut the pillows and emptied the down feathers, shaking them all over the room, which now looked like a horrible winter storm.

One of the thieves peeked through the kitchen door, flung it open and yelled, "What's this building over here?" His buddy prodded Chip in the ribs with the butt of his knife, "The office," Chip said. "What kind of office?" "We sell tea." They pushed Chip towards the Head Office, rushing him on his wobbly legs up the slippery wooden staircase where they all suddenly ran into the conference room, thinking they had found something worth stealing at last. Chip saw the key dangling in the door and when the last of the men entered the room, he closed the door and locked them inside. He didn't have time to escape or radio out a May Day before the same brute who had tossed his bed, bashed in the door and he was again overwhelmed by them.

They started gathering computers, disconnecting the mouses and stomping on them when they hit the floor. The leader was constantly on the telephone, desperate to contact someone who wasn't answering his call. Chip figured they had planned to get away by car, but the driver wasn't picking up their call. Changing plans the leader found Chip: "Car keys," he shouted, and Chip showed him where to find the keys, as the others repeated trips in and out of the office, filling up his Nissan Patrol with computers, radios, and cameras, and when they found nothing else of value, they told Chip, "You drive."

Chip wanted to take the men away from his home, but more importantly, away from his wife. Forced to drive them he sat in his driving seat, with a thief in the passenger seat, one on the center pocket and five more crowded behind. The night was thick in a dense chiperoni, and he kept the Patrol in first gear, revving the engine as loud as he could. Approaching the main Satemwa barrier where he hoped his guards would provide help, he locked the doors to the car, and flashed his lights, keeping his engine on high revolutions. The night guard looked out from the shelter and saw the Bwana Wonkulu, surrounded by men, one hanging over his seat, and goods piled high in the back. He squinted as if caught in an apparition, and the thieves, having undone the locks, raced out of the car, and chased the guards off their post. Chip was stuck with the thugs and his heart sank as they jeered him on towards the main road. "Let's take him to Mozambique," they had discussed in Chichewa, making Chip nervous enough that by the time they reached the tarmac through thick slips of mud, he turned the faithful Nissan Patrol in the opposite direction from Mozambique and headed towards Blantyre. "Drive," the leader yelled, begging Chip to increase speed. "It's a very old car," Chip said, "and the weather is terrible."

Meanwhile back at the house, one of the house watchmen had freed himself and scampered across the airstrip down the embankment towards Hilliard's house. He arrived at the fence and woke Hilliard's guard shouting, "House Number one needs HELP!" Moments later, Hilliard, having learned of the attack and realizing that his Dad had been kidnapped, raced to their home, driving in his little bucky as fast as it would travel through the mud. He didn't know what he would find when he arrived. But he was ready for combat. The house was completely open, all the doors swinging on their hinges, and he saw his mother's favorite tea set in pieces on the kitchen floor. "Mum! Mum! Where are you?" he called, checking their bedroom, and wondering if she was hiding among the feathers. He saw blood covering the sheets on the upturned bed. "Hilly, I'm here,"

Dawn spoke, from behind the door, which Chip had locked. "They've taken your father, leave me here. Please find him," Dawn told Hilly, emphasizing, "Don't worry about me, find your Dad."[(429)]

Alexander had arrived at the house and they took his 4WD, realizing they may have to search off-road for their father. Hilly returned to his Mum, and not wanting to leave her locked in a room, kicked in the door and freed her. Together with his brother and their General Manager, they drove away to search for Chip. Two days prior to the robbery, Chip installed new Trekka tires on his Patrol, and Hilly, remembering this, picked up the tracks where the Satemwa road met the tarmac. "They've turned left, towards Blantyre," he reported on the radio. Hilly had sent out a "MAY DAY" call to the Satemwa Security Force, as well as Eastern Produce Tea Estates, and farmers scattered from Mulanje to Zomba, alerting them to Chip's kidnapping. Stopping at every junction, Hilly checked for tire tracks, hoping to find where the Patrol had turned. At Tsunga, he found Chip's tracks, and shouted over the radio, "Right at Tsunga, be alert." He organized a barricade at the Mulanje side exit from the backside of Tsunga, as well as a blockade from the Blantyre road. Now, the Patrol and the men inside would be obstructed from all three exits off that dirt road. Now, they just hoped to find Chip, and find him alive.

Hilly phoned the chief of Satemwa security every five minutes, "Anything, anything at all?" But even with spotlights shining out into the bush, through the thick chiperoni, it was difficult to see. He phoned the chief security guard again, "Anything now?" and the chief, distracted called out, "the Bwana's car," before he cut the line, with Hilliard on the other end crying, "Where, where is he?"

Satemwa Security, recognizing the Patrol, ran it off the road into a ditch and chased the seven thieves who abandoned the stolen goods and hurried through the bush to escape the guards. "The car has been recovered," came the call, "but the Bwana is not here."

A few kilometers away, bruised, bleeding, gagged, and bound with rope that cut into his skin, Chip lay in the fetal position, cold, wet, and alone. The thieves had pushed him out of the car, and taken command of the Nissan, crunching the gears as they peeled away. Relieved that he was no longer with them, Chip took a moment to hide himself, rolling his body about in the mud until he felt concealed in case they returned, looking for him. Once behind a tree, he wriggled his hands to reach his pocket and retrieve the penknife he always kept in his trousers. He cut himself free, releasing first his hands, then his feet and, ripping the cloth from his mouth, he breathed deep, a breath of freedom. He heard a car approaching and listened intently to the engine. "Buggered up engine," he thought to himself, "Native, probably," and he stayed hidden. Moments later, another vehicle rolled down the road, "Proper motor car," Chip thought, listening to the sounds it exuded. Feeling bitterly cold and recognizing he needed rescue, he crawled out onto the road, raising his arm at the oncoming vehicle. Two black men jumped out and Chip, obviously traumatized, flinched. "It's OK Uncle Chip, it's me, Ralph," came the voice from behind the wheel where Ralph Henderson and Dave Saywood sat in their pick-up before rushing onto the road to gather Chip, who felt like he might fall into a shivering heap at any moment. The radio calls rang out, "Bwana Chip has been rescued," followed by, "We are taking him immediately to the Police in Limbe."

When Hilliard and Alexander arrived at the station, they hurried to their father and hugged him. Chip looked up at them and asked, "Your Mum, is Pi ok?" "Yes, Dad, she is fine, Norah is there, and Dottie is on the way." "And the watchmen, are they alright?" "Yes Dad, no watchmen have been hurt." Realizing the police were dawdling about their duties, and seeing their father terribly cold and shaken, the boys told the Police, "We can sort out paperwork later today. We need to get Dad home to be seen by a Doctor."

Chip arrived home flanked by his sons and was ushered through the kitchen and hallway and given a comfortable padded seat by the fireplace in the entry room. They covered Chip in blankets, his body numb from the night's exposure. Hilliard went to make tea in the kitchen, passing the master bedroom, which no longer looked like a winter storm, the upside-down bed righted with fresh sheets neatly tucked under the mattress. The dresser held all its drawers again and was topped with unbroken ornaments with picture frames placed at the corners. The table in the dining room was set for breakfast, a cheery, floral tablecloth topped with mismatched plates and silverware. The broken china that covered the kitchen floor just hours ago swept up and disposed. Dawn, having bathed and dressed, her hair neatly rolled into a low bun, was instructing the house staff, who had rushed in early after hearing word of the kidnapping, what to keep and what to throw away. The kettle, whistling in the kitchen, signaled another round of tea was about to be served.[430]

Moments later, having driven the fastest twenty kilometers of his life, fishtailing in the sludge over the bridge at Kasembereka, the Malamulo surgeon, Dr Ryan Hayton, arrived, rushing through the kitchen, past the kettle, and into the entry room looking for Chip and Dawn. "Please check Dawn first," Chip told the Doctor, "You know, those savages punched her. They beat her." Dottie, who had been with Dawn for hours, having driven by feel through Thyolo in a thick blanket of chiperoni, had administered Reiki on her friend and by the time the Doctor checked on

Dawn, her blood pressure, heart rate and physical symptoms were normal. He checked her bruises and felt for broken bones, and when she was cleared, he went back to find Chip.

In the meantime, Chip had been warmed by a hot bath and seventeen cups of tea, "I know, because I've been counting," Dottie whispered to Dawn. "What's that?" Chip asked Dr Hayton, who was cleaning his wounds. "Dermabond, you can think of it sort of like super glue," the Doctor replied as he squeezed the product into the small gashes, pushing the skin together and sealing the wound. "Super, glue – I like that," Chip chuckled, "All these fancy things in the medical trade and my Doctor in Malawi uses super glue. I'll tell that to my Cape Town doctor next time I'm there."[431]

Chip's usual jolly tones and resilient countenance, which was momentarily lost along the cold, dirt road in Tsunga, began to reappear. Where hours earlier men had ripped the home apart, the atmosphere at the home now began to change. An angry family's rightful desire for revenge was lifted and a calming spirit fell over the home. "Do you feel that?" Dottie asked Dawn, who was pouring another cup of tea for a friend. Dawn looked up around the room at the family portraits replaced on the mantle, the rugs neatly lining the floor, the full-service tea trolley and responded, "Yes, there is no room for evil in this home, light will eventually drown out the darkness."

By lunchtime, word about the attack had circled around not just Malawi, but the world. An outpouring of support descended on Satemwa from near and far. One of the house boys was charged with manning the telephones, which rang off the hook for hours; friends and family calling to say "sorry," or "Are you ok?" or outraged, demanding, "Who did this?" All the responses were welcomed by Chip and Dawn, who were also flooded with visitors, the estate road leading from the tarmac was inundated by vehicles, all adding an extra rut to the already gashed road, and sliding through the mud, happily, to reach Chip and Dawn to say, "We care about you. We are sorry to hear what happened." Dawn greeted guests in the library, with a tea trolley beside her, offering a hot cuppa and a bite to eat. Many of the visitors were shocked at her graceful response to the night's events, and felt like although they had come to offer care for Dawn and Chip, it was now Dawn, in her quiet, loving way that was ministering to them, one cup of tea at a time.

The rain continued in steady drops. The sky, heavy with moisture, hung over Satemwa threatening rupture. Down in the factory, the machines chugged throughout the day, bright leaves, freshly plucked, rolling in by the trailer load, processed and packaged. The children, Chip's grandchildren, attended school. Emails streamed into head office, buyers in London requesting special blends, and banks sending statements of balance. The dogs ate their breakfast, cooked rice with meat and a few dry biscuits. The house staff counted china and reported to Dawn how many she could serve now with each set. The old blue "Poole" service from England remained with the most plates and Bester told Dawn, "Enough for twenty people." It was Tuesday morning, and the tea auction in Blantyre began, just as it did every Tuesday. Satemwa's bales represented not by Chip with his yellow briefcase but by the General Manager. "I'm sure I can make it," Chip told Dawn after the Doctor's visit and a short rest. But his family convinced him to take a day off and so he sat in the entry room, by the fireplace, reflecting. He thought about the events of the night: the seven writhing men, full of hate, seven men uninvited and unwelcome in his home.

He walked out of the entry room, onto the khondi, pausing at the front gate where the thugs had entered. He looked at the open windows, leading into his master bedroom, where welders now soldered bars. He wobbled through the wrought iron gate and down the front steps, his tired, old legs carrying him slowly, welcoming the mist that clung in the air and fell softly on his bruised skin. Shuffling along the cobblestone, over the driveway towards his favorite view, he found a lawn chair in his usual spot and reclined into it. While he sat, looking towards Thyolo Mountain, the dense chiperoni that had cloaked the morning lifted and the sun broke through the clouds, shining brightly on the tea trolley rolled out beside him.

He was alone on the lawn of a home he had built over sixty years ago, whose bricks were made from the earth just meters below where he now sat, forming a terrace – a perfect taxi way for an airplane. "Fox Fox," grounded along with Chip, collected dust in the hangar just a hundred yards away. The horses, which hadn't been ridden by Dawn in years, neighed in their stables opposite the hangar, waiting for the grandchildren to come with Dawn, "Pi", and a handful of sweet potato or carrots. The large swimming pool, on the second terrace, overflowed after the night's rain, a lock firmly guarding the arched gate.

In the distance he viewed the factory which had burned years earlier. Now re-built and re-furbished, it was now better than the original built in 1937. Progress had arrived, and Alexander had driven it. New machines and processes were implemented, and Chip admired the changes, the way his father – from 'The Satemwa House' – marveled when he saw electricity light the factory for the very first time. "We've come a long way," Chip thought, looking out over the terraces towards the fields of tea he planted in the 1950's as he drove expansion on the Mwalunthunzi portion of the estate. Bright green flushes of tea bursting in bud-break and ready for plucking.

Dawn joined him on the grass, pointing out the fluttering wings of the sunbirds who arrived in the garden to pollenate the hibiscus. She stood beside the wooden tea trolley where a gingham cloth was draped over the top tray covering the sandwiches underneath. She lifted the corner of the fabric to check on the fare; peeking under the silver lid of the sandwich dish, she informed Chip, "Cucumber and cream cheese." She picked up the silver teapot, which had survived the events of the night, a napkin wrapped around the handle that was equally as hot as the tea inside, and inquired, "Tea?"

"Oh, Yes! Please, Pi, yes…" Chip looked up at his bride of forty-one years, his hazel green eyes sparkling as the day she met him, his wounded eighty-one-year-old body 'glued' together, but the same mischief in his moustache which bristled with life.

She poured a hot cup of Satemwa tea into a 'Strawberry Fields" teacup that had also survived the squall of the night, lifting the strainer to catch the grounds as she poured. They sat on the lawn together, looking towards Thyolo Mountain and sipping "that hot, grateful beverage."

Tea – the brew that bolstered a nation during times of war, strengthened explorers to venture another day in the African Interior, and gave a Scottish pioneer the opportunity to create a monument to human endeavor. "Satemwa", with its neatly knitted carpets of tea, and planters who "talk with the tea bush" would carry on, the Cathcart Kay family driving its success, knowing, "Where there is TEA, there is hope."

Dawn with tea pot and tea cup circa 2013

Postscript

After a long health battle, which Chip fought bravely and tirelessly, he passed away in Cape Town, South Africa on January 24, 2020. He was 88 years old. His legacy extends further than this book could detail.

The extended Kay family at Christmas on Satemwa circa 2016

Acknowledgements

My deepest gratitude is to my parents, Kevin and Marian de Berg; my Dad for editing my manuscript with the kind of zeal he applies to his work as a scientist and my Mum for being the most famous author in the family. But above all, to both for their unwavering love and kindness which have been a lasting pillar in my life.

Thanks to Dawn Kay for copious cups of Satemwa tea and 'afternoon sundowners' at any time of the day; for taking in 'the strays' and including us for Christmas, every year; and for her grace and her trust in me to find a way to write the things too painful to be spoken.

Thanks to the Society of Malawi for a pristine collection of history, ideal for writing Kangaroo Kay.

Thanks to Jane Thorneycroft - rescuer, confidant, fierce protector, loyal friend, adopted Grandma. My number one 'phone a friend'. Her large collection of dogs always made my pack of five look small, for which I am grateful.

Thanks to the Naidoo and Graybill families for unmatched weekend warrior action. For speedy stand up jet skis, for 'any song's a winner', for Liwonde flash flood slick road driving and for hiking Mulanje Mountain, rain or shine.

Thanks to the Artie Farties – you know who you are, and you know why Monday nights were sacred.

Thanks to Anette Kay for homemade brownies, and mountain bike escapades. For her assistance in tracking down photos for this book. For being the founder of Artie Farties. For being kick-ass.

Thanks to Hilliard Kay, Dottie Henderson, Julie Saunders, Angela Kilner, Irene Harvey, Ron Mataya, John Marais and Alexander Kay for filling in the gaps and adding to the history.

Thanks to our friends in Malawi who opened homes and hearts to us. From Cape Maclear to Lilongwe, Zomba to Mulanje and Thyolo. You gave us needed respite. You helped us learn and helped us heal.

Thanks to the Malamulo Missionary Family for sharing the fishbowl, for potlucks, for Sabbath afternoon walks in the tea, for comradery, for understanding.

Thanks to Thoko and Susan for their care of our family in Malawi and for making food better than I could make it myself. For translating for this book and for putting up with my mess.

Thanks to Carolyn Rickett for instilling a love of writing in me in the first place.

Thanks to the old guard Avondale friends for knowing me in the awkwardness of my youth and for still loving me. For the four who flew a thousand miles to take care of me.

Thanks to our Michigan family; and the three ladies with the convertible.

Thanks to both Ryan's family and my family. For life-line endless support. For sending supplies to us at the mission, for visiting wherever we are, for cherishing our kids, for loving us with big warm hearts.

Thanks to my sister, Deanne de Berg - strong defender. For responsible big sister guidance and for sharing the spectacle of the sky-blue Volvo. For Bob Dufus antics and for knowing me better than anyone.

Thanks to my children for patiently waiting while this story was written. Benson, for blazing bravery in the face of challenges. Hudson, for feeling the things I feel and for keeping me honest. Jett, for cheeky grins and great mischief.

A heartfelt thanks to my husband Ryan who built a life with me in Africa. For his ethical care of the poor and his passion to provide equality in surgery around the globe. For being 'Google' on safari, or anytime for that matter. For being my memory-witness. For living as the 'get it done' man – not just for this self-published book, but for life. I am grateful to hold this love.

But especially thanks to Chip Cathcart Kay. For believing I could make sense of his butterfly thinking. For always being in possession of a fresh packet of Satemwa tea. For continually taking in 'the strays'. For carrying on after each heartache. For teaching me about Sanctions Busting. For trusting me to be his storyteller and for opening his story wide, even sharing with me tales that were "not for the book."

Kangaroo Kay: From Jungle To Teapot
Bibliography

Brief Historical Background To The Story

(a). Pachai, B. "In the wake of Livingston and the British administration: some considerations of commerce and Christianity in Malawi" The Malawi Journal. The Society of Malawi – Historical and Scientific. 1967, Vol.20 No.2 p40.

(b). The Colonial Reports – Annual. Annual Report of the Social and Economic Progress of the People of Nyasaland, 1934. H.M.S.O. London, 1934 No.1739

(c). http://historyhome.co.uk/europe/causeww1.htm Accessed 15 May 2017.

(d). Pakenham, Thomas. *The Scramble for Africa: White Man's Conquest of the Dark Continent From 1876 to 1912.* Avon, 1991. p204.

(e). Johnston, Sir Harry H. British Central Africa. Methuen & Co, London, 1897, p108.

(f). Goodwin, Dean. *Memoir of Bishop Mackenzie.* Cambridge University Press, 1865.

(g). McCracken, John. A History of Malawi: 1859-1966. Boydell & Brewer Ltd, 2012, p278.

(h). Dugard, Martin. *Into Africa: The Epic Adventures of Stanley & Livingstone.* Broadway Books, 2003, p33.

(j) Robertson, Olive H. "Trade and the suppression of slavery in British Central Africa." The Nyasaland Journal, Society of Nyasaland – Historical and Scientific, 1960, Vol.13 No.2 p16.

(j). Pachai, B. "In the wake of Livingston and the British administration: some considerations of commerce and Christianity in Malawi" The Malawi Journal. The Society of Malawi – Historical and Scientific. 1967, Vol.20 No.2 p59.

(k). Stuart-Mogg, David. *Mlozi of Central Africa: Trader, Slaver and self-styled Sultan. The End of the Slaver.* Central Africana, 2011.

(l). Robertson, Olive H. "Trade and the suppression of slavery in British Central Africa." The Nyasaland Journal, Society of Nyasaland – Historical and Scientific, 1960, Vol.13 No.2 p21.

(m). Baker, C.A. *"Nyasaland, the history of its export trade."* The Nyasaland Journal, Society of Nyasaland – Historical and Scientific, 1962, Vol.15 No.1 p8.

(n). The Colonial Reports – Annual. Nyasaland - 1922. H.M.S.O, London, 1922 No.1162 p4.

(o). Johnston, Sir Harry H. British Central Africa. Methuen & Co, London, 1897, p86,96.

A Colonial Childhood 1931-1945
(1). Kay, Chip (28 Dec 2015). Chip Kay Session 15 p8.
(2). Kay, Chip (15 Mar 2015). Chip Kay Session 3 25:31.
(3). Kay, Chip (23 Mar 2015). Chip Kay Session 4 16:59.
(4). Kay, Chip (23 Mar 2015). Chip Kay Session 4 16:59
(5). Kay, Chip (15 Mar 2015). Chip Kay Session 3 35:31.
(6). Kay, Maclean. (1938). Letters to Flora Jean Kay.
(7). Kay, Maclean. (8 August 1938). Letters to Flora Jean p2
(8). The Colonial Reports – Annual. Annual Report of the Social and Economic
Progress of the People of Nyasaland. His Majesty's Stationery Office (H.M.S.O),
London. 1938. No.1902 p38.
(9). Kay, Chip (15 Mar 2015). Chip Kay Session 3 54:38.
(10). Kay, Chip (15 Mar 2015). Chip Kay Session 3 25:31.
(11). Kay, Chip (23 Mar 2015). Chip Kay Session 4 25:31.
(12). Kay, Chip (15 Mar 2015). Chip Kay Session 3 35:31.
(13). The Nyasaland Journal. The Society of Nyasaland – Historical and Scientific.
1955, Vol 8 No2 p16. https://www.jstor.org/stable/i29545739
(14). Kay, Chip (23 Mar 2015). Chip Kay Session 4 38:49.
(15). The Nyasaland Journal. The Society of Nyasaland – Historical and Scientific.
1955, Vol 8 No2 p16.
(16). Kay, Chip (23 Mar 2015). Chip Kay Session 4 38:49.
(17). Kay, Chip (15 Mar 2015). Chip Kay Session 3 1:02:57.
(18). Kay, Chip (15 Mar 2015). Chip Kay Session 3 1:04:54.
(19). Kay, Chip (23 Mar 2015). Chip Kay Session 4 43:46.
(20). Mabel, Joe. "1940s Gilbert chemistry set" Wikimedia Commons.
https://commons.wikimedia.org/wiki/File:1940s_Gilbert_chemistry_set_02.jpg
Accessed 14 June 2019
(21). Kay, Chip (23 Mar 2015). Chip Kay Session 4 46:09.
(22). Kay, Chip (23 Mar 2015). Chip Kay Session 4 35:09.
(23). Kay, Chip (30 Mar 2015). Chip Kay Session 5 p2.
(24). Kay, Chip (23 Mar 2015). Chip Kay Session 4 13:03.
(25). Kay, Chip (30 Mar 2015). Chip Kay Session 5 17:16.
(26). Kay, Chip. (19 May 1941). Chip Kay Letter to Maclean Kay.

Maclean Kay, The Early Days 1892-1922
(27). Jackson, George. The Society of Malawi Journal. Society of Malawi –
Historical and Scientific, 1969, Vol 22 No.2 p74.
https://www.jstor.org/stable/i29778208
(28). Kay, Chip (2 Mar 2015). Chip Kay Session 1 35:10.
(29). Kay, Chip (9 Mar 2015). Chip Kay Session 2 29:46.
(30). "Guthrie (company)" Wikipedia The Free Encyclopedia.
https://en.wikipedia.org/wiki/Guthrie_(company) Accessed 2 May 2017
(31). "History of Seychelles" Wikipedia The Free Encyclopedia.
https://en.wikipedia.org/wiki/History_of_Seychelles Accessed 2 May 2017
(32). Kay, Chip (13 August 2015). Chip Kay Session 9.

(33). http://www.portofaden.net/en/site/page/16?slug=passenger-terminal Accessed 3 May 2017

(34). http://www.phrases.org.uk/meanings/port-out-starboard-home.html Accessed 3 May 2017.

(35). "Snifter" Wikipedia The Free Encyclopedia. https://en.wikipedia.org/wiki/Snifter Accessed 3 May 2017

(36). The Colonial Reports – Annual. Nyasaland - 1922. H.M.S.O, London, 1922 No.1162 p13. http://libsysdigi.library.illinois.edu/ilharvest/Africana/Books2011-05/469188/469188_1922/469188_1922_opt.pdf Accessed 4 May 2017.

(37). "Dona Ana Bridge" Wikipedia The Free Encyclopedia. https://en.wikipedia.org/wiki/Dona_Ana_Bridge Accessed 3 May 2017

(38). http://mikes.railhistory.railfan.net/r179.html Accessed 3 May 2017

(39). The Colonial Reports – Annual. Nyasaland - 1922. H.M.S.O, London, 1922 No.1162 p13.

(40). The Nyasaland Journal. The Society of Nyasaland – Historical and Scientific. 1955, Vol 8 No.2 p16. https://www.jstor.org/stable/i29545739

(41). Kay, Chip (2 Mar 2015). Chip Kay Session 1 p2.

(42). Johnston, Sir Harry H. British Central Africa. Methuen & Co, London, 1897, p6.

(43). The Society of Malawi Journal. Society of Malawi – Historical and Scientific, 1969, Vol 22 p23.

(44). The Colonial Reports – Annual. Annual Report of the Social and Economic Progress of the People of Nyasaland. H.M.S.O. London. 1939 No.1739.

(45). The Colonial Reports – Annual. Nyasaland - 1922. H.M.S.O, London, 1922 No.1162 p6.

(46). Johnston, Sir Harry H. British Central Africa. Methuen & Co, London, 1897, p221.

(47). The Nyasaland Journal. The Society of Nyasaland – Historical and Scientific. 1955, Vol 8 No2 p16.

(48). The Colonial Reports – Annual. Nyasaland - 1922. H.M.S.O, London, 1922 No.1162 p2.

(49). The Colonial Reports – Annual. Nyasaland - 1922. H.M.S.O, London, 1922 No.1162 p2.

(50). The Colonial Reports – Annual. Nyasaland - 1922. H.M.S.O, London, 1922 No.1162 p15.

(51). "Indian Scout (motorcycle)" Wikipedia The Free Encyclopedia. https://en.wikipedia.org/wiki/Indian_Scout_(motorcycle) Accessed 5 May 2017.

(52). Kay, Chip (2 Mar 2015). Chip Kay Session 1 p3.

(53). The Colonial Reports – Annual. Nyasaland – 1914-1915. H.M.S.O. London, 1915, No.883. https://libsysdigi.library.illinois.edu/ilharvest/Africana/Books2011-05/469188/469188_1914_1915/469188_1914_1915_opt.pdf

(54). The Colonial Reports – Annual. Nyasaland - 1922. H.M.S.O, London, 1922 No.1162 p7.

(55). The Colonial Reports – Annual. Nyasaland - 1922. H.M.S.O, London, 1922 No.1162 p10.

(56). The Colonial Reports – Annual. Nyasaland - 1922. H.M.S.O, London, 1922 No.1162 p14.

(57). The Colonial Reports – Annual. Annual Report of the Social and Economic Progress of the People of Nyasaland, 1934. H.M.S.O. London, 1934 No.1739 https://libsysdigi.library.illinois.edu/ilharvest/Africana/Books2011-05/469188/469188_1934/469188_1934_opt.pdf

From Jungle To Teapot, 1923-1945

(58). Kay, Chip (2 Mar 2015). Chip Kay Session 1 25:34.

(59). The Colonial Reports – Annual. Nyasaland, 1923. H.M.S.O. London, 1923, No.1204 https://libsysdigi.library.illinois.edu/ilharvest/Africana/Books2011-05/469188/469188_1923/469188_1923_opt.pdf

(60). Rangeley, W.H.J. "A Brief History of the Tobacco Industry in Nyasaland Part 1" The Nyasaland Journal, Society of Nyasaland – Historical and Scientific, 1957, Vol.10 No.1 p81. https://www.jstor.org/stable/i29545780

(61). The Colonial Reports – Annual. Nyasaland – 1914-1915. H.M.S.O. London, 1915 No.883 p11. https://libsysdigi.library.illinois.edu/ilharvest/Africana/Books2011-05/469188/469188_1914_1915/469188_1914_1915_opt.pdf

(62). The Colonial Reports – Annual. Nyasaland – 1914-1915. H.M.S.O. London, 1915 No.883 p11.

(63). Kay, Chip (9 Mar 2015). Chip Kay Session 2 48:36.

(64). "Wattle and daub" Wikipedia The Free Encyclopedia. https://en.wikipedia.org/wiki/Wattle_and_daub Accessed 18 May 2017.

(65). The Colonial Reports – Annual. Annual Report of the Social and Economic Progress of the People of Nyasaland, 1934. H.M.S.O. London, 1934 No.1739 p26. https://libsysdigi.library.illinois.edu/ilharvest/Africana/Books2011-05/469188/469188_1934/469188_1934_opt.pdf

(66). The Colonial Reports – Annual. Nyasaland – 1929. H.M.S.O. London, 1929, No.1489 p7. https://libsysdigi.library.illinois.edu/ilharvest/Africana/Books2011-05/469188/469188_1929/469188_1929_opt.pdf

(67). Kay, Chip (2 Mar 2015). Chip Kay Session 1 p10 00:55.

(68). Kay, Chip (2 Mar 2015). Chip Kay Session 1 p10 00:55.

(69). Johnston, Sir Harry H. British Central Africa. Methuen & Co, London, 1897, p41.

(70). Kay, Maclean. (12 Oct 1929). Letters to Flora Jean Kay.

(71). Kay, Maclean. (9 Nov 1929). Letters to Flora Jean Kay.

(72). Kay, Maclean. (9 Apr 1929). Letters to Flora Jean Kay.

(73). Kay, Maclean. (9 Apr 1929). Letters to Flora Jean Kay.

(74). Kay, Chip (9 Mar 2015). Chip Kay Session 2 21:30.

(75). Kay, Maclean. (10 Dec 1929). Letters to Flora Jean Kay

(76). The Colonial Reports – Annual. Nyasaland – 1931. H.M.S.O. London, 1931 No.1580. https://libsysdigi.library.illinois.edu/ilharvest/Africana/Books2011-05/469188/469188_1931/469188_1931_opt.pdf

(77). Kay, Maclean. (16 Oct 1935). Letters to Flora Jean Kay

(78). Kay, Maclean. (16 Oct 1935). Letters to Flora Jean Kay, p2.

(79). Kay, Maclean. (16 Oct 1935). Letters to Flora Jean Kay
(80). Kay, Maclean. (1938?). Letters to Flora Jean Kay, p1.
(81). Kay, Maclean. (1938?). Letters to Flora Jean Kay, p4 "Friday awoke at 1:30am…"
(82). Kay, Chip (1 Mar 2017). Chip Kay Session 29 p2.
(83). https://www.cooksinfo.com/british-wartime-food/ Accessed 5 Jan 2018

Educating Colonial Children 1945-1950
(84). Kay, Chip (30 Mar 2015). Chip Kay Session 5 p8-9
(85). Kay, Chip (30 Mar 2015). Chip Kay Session 5 p12.
(86). Kay, Chip (23 Jun 2015). Chip Kay Session 6 p6.
(87). Kay, Chip (30 Mar 2015). Chip Kay Session 5 p13.
(88). Kay, Chip (23 Jun 2015). Chip Kay Session 6 p7.
(89). Kay, Chip (30 Mar 2015). Chip Kay Session 5 p14.
(90). Kay, Chip (30 Mar 2015). Chip Kay Session 5 p15.
(91). Kay, Chip (23 Jun 2015). Chip Kay Session 6 p8.
(92). Kay, Chip (30 Mar 2015). Chip Kay Session 5 p16.
(93). Kay, Chip (30 Mar 2015). Chip Kay Session 5 p17.
(94). Kay, Chip (23 Jun 2015). Chip Kay Session 6 p4.
(95). Kay, Chip (23 Jun 2015). Chip Kay Session 6 p4.
(96). Kay, Chip (23 Jun 2015). Chip Kay Session 6 p5.
(97). Kay, Chip (6 July 2015). Chip Kay Session 7 p1.

When A Boy Becomes A Man 1950-1954
(98). Kay, Chip (6 July 2015). Chip Kay Session 7
(99). Kay, Chip (15 Mar 2015). Chip Kay Session 3 p7.
(100). Kay, Chip (6 July 2015). Chip Kay Session 7 p2.
(101). Johnston, Sir Harry H. British Central Africa. Methuen & Co, London, 1897, p218.
(102). The Colonial Reports – Annual. Nyasaland – 1948. H.M.S.O. London, 1948 No.1141 p10.
(103). The Colonial Reports – Annual. Nyasaland - 1922. H.M.S.O, London, 1922 No.1162 p13
(104). "War Against Wild Animals" The Nyasaland Times, 17 April 1950.
(105). Kay, Chip (6 July 2015). Chip Kay Session 7 p3.
(106). Kay, Chip (6 July 2015). Chip Kay Session 7 p2.
(107). Kay, Chip (6 July 2015). Chip Kay Session 7 p3.
(108). The Colonial Reports – Annual. Nyasaland – 1948. H.M.S.O. London, 1948 No.1141 p26.
(109). The Colonial Reports – Annual. Nyasaland – 1948. H.M.S.O. London, 1948 No.1141 p5.
(110). The Colonial Reports – Annual. Nyasaland – 1948. H.M.S.O. London, 1948 No.1141 p27.
(111). Kay, Maclean. (28 January 1939). Letters to Flora Jean Kay, p1.
(112). Kay, Chip (6 July 2015). Chip Kay Session 7 p5.

(113). Davis, F.E.W. "Women Workers" The Nyasaland Times Newspaper. 28 May 1951.

(114). Kay, Chip (6 July 2015). Chip Kay Session 7 p5.

(115). Kay, Chip (28 December 2015). Chip Kay Session 15 p12.

(116). Kay, Chip (6 July 2015). Chip Kay Session 7 p5.

(117). Kay, Chip (6 July 2015). Chip Kay Session 7 p7.

(118). Innes, J.R. "Leprosy in Nyasaland" East African Medical Journal, 1951, p9-17. http://leprev.ilsl.br/pdfs/1940/v11n1/pdf/v11n1a02.pdf Accessed 23 January 2018.

(119). Kay, Chip (6 July 2015). Chip Kay Session 7 p8.

(120). 26 July 1957 Ruth Kafere discharged by Dr. Harvey http://images.adventistarchives.org/AfricaMedicalIndigenous/source/51.html Accessed 23 January 2018.

(121). McCracken, John. A History of Malawi: 1859-1966. Boydell & Brewer Ltd, 2012.

(122). Kay, Chip (6 July 2015). Chip Kay Session 7 p8.

(123). Kay, Chip (10 August 2015). Chip Kay Session 8 p8.

(124). Kay, Chip (6 July 2015). Chip Kay Session 7 p8.

(125). Kay, Chip (6 July 2015). Chip Kay Session 7 p9.

(126). Kay, Chip (15 Mar 2015). Chip Kay Session 3 p7.

(127). Kay, Chip (15 Mar 2015). Chip Kay Session 3 p7.

(128). Kay, Chip (15 Mar 2015). Chip Kay Session 3 p8.

(129). Kay, Chip (15 Mar 2015). Chip Kay Session 3 p8.

(130). "Short Solent III Flying Boat" http://nonplused.org/panos/oam/index.html https://en.wikipedia.org/wiki/Short_Solent Accessed 30 January 2018.

(131). BOAC Takes Good Care of You. Nyasaland Times Newspaper, April 1950.

(132). BOAC at Cape Maclear. Nyasaland Times Newspaper, April 1950.

(133). "Citroën Traction Avant" Wikipedia The Free Encyclopedia. https://en.wikëipedia.org/wiki/Citro%C3%ABn_Traction_Avant Accessed 25 January 2018.

(134). Kay, Chip (23 Jun 2015). Chip Kay Session 6 p5.

(135). BOAC at Cape Maclear. Nyasaland Times Newspaper, April 1950.

(136). Baker, Colin. "Lake Malawi's First Flying Boat Visit" The Society of Malawi Journal. Society of Malawi – Historical and Scientific. 1988 Vol.41 No.2 p30. https://www.jstor.org/stable/29778599?seq=1#page_scan_tab_contents

(137). Saunders, Elizabeth. "For British Taste" The Nyasaland Times, 1955, July1.

(138). Kay, Chip (10 August 2015). Chip Kay Session 8.

(139). Launching of "Ilala II". The Nyasaland Times Newspaper. 1951, February 1 p7.

(140). McCracken, John. A History of Malawi: 1859-1966. Boydell & Brewer Ltd, 2012, p45.

(141). Withers, F.M. "A Sailor Who Did His Duty Belated Tribute to a Real Pioneer" The Nyasaland Journal, Society of Nyasaland – Historical and Scientific, 1951, Vol.4 No.1 p35-6. https://www.jstor.org/stable/29545632?seq=1

(142). Launching of "Ilala II" The Nyasaland Times Newspaper. 1951, February 1 p7.

(143). "Morris Minor" Wikipedia the Free Encyclopedia.
https://en.wikipedia.org/wiki/Morris_Minor Accessed 30 January 2018.
(144). Kay, Chip (10 August 2015). Chip Kay Session 8 p1.
(145). Kay, Chip (10 August 2015). Chip Kay Session 8 p1-2.
(146). Kay, Chip (10 August 2015). Chip Kay Session 8 p2.
(147). "Meikles Hotel" http://www.meikles.com/about/history Accessed 31 January 2018.
(148). Kay, Chip (10 August 2015). Chip Kay Session 8 p3.
(149). Kay, Chip (6 July 2015). Chip Kay Session 7 p14.
(150). Kay, Chip (2 Mar 2015). Chip Kay Session 1 p8.
(151). Kay, Chip (6 July 2015). Chip Kay Session 7 p5.
(152). Kay, Chip (6 July 2015). Chip Kay Session 7 p14.
(153). Kay, Chip (6 July 2015). Chip Kay Session 7 p15.
(154). Kay, Chip (6 July 2015). Chip Kay Session 7 p14.
(155). The Nyasaland Times Newspaper, 1955, March 25, p7.
(156). Kay, Chip (28 December 2015). Chip Kay Session 15 p7.
(157). Kay, Chip (23 Jun 2015). Chip Kay Session 6 p10.
(158). "Radiogram (device)" Wikipedia the Free Encyclopedia.
https://en.wikipedia.org/wiki/Radiogram_(device) Accessed 1 February 2018.
(159). Kay, Chip (8 Feb 2017). Chip Kay Session 27 p11.
(160). Kay, Chip (8 Feb 2017). Chip Kay Session 27 p11.

Elladale 1947-1953

(161). Kay, Chip (23 Mar 2015). Chip Kay Session 4 p9.
(162). "Federation of Rhodesia and Nyasaland" Wikipedia the Free Encyclopedia.
https://en.wikipedia.org/wiki/Federation_of_Rhodesia_and_Nyasaland Accessed
13 March 2018.
(163). Kay, Chip (23 Mar 2015). Chip Kay Session 4 p9.
(164). Kay, Chip (10 August 2015). Chip Kay Session 8 p4.
(165). McCracken, John. A History of Malawi: 1859-1966. Boydell & Brewer Ltd,
2012, p255.
(166). The Nyasaland Times Newspaper, 1955, April 19, p4.
(167). Kay, Chip (10 August 2015). Chip Kay Session 8 p4.
(168). The Nyasaland Times, 1955, March 29, p4.
(169). The Nyasaland Times, 1957, January 22, p5.
(170). Kay, Chip (10 August 2015). Chip Kay Session 8 p4.
(171). Kay, Chip (10 August 2015). Chip Kay Session 8 p5.
(172). Kay, Chip (23 Mar 2015). Chip Kay Session 4 p10.

The Wonder Of £85: From 1953

(173). The Nyasaland Times, 1951, April 9, p3.
(174). Reed, Douglas. The Battle for Rhodesia. Haum, 1966. p27.
(175). The Nyasaland Times Newspaper, 1953, December 8, p9.
(176). The Nyasaland Times Newspaper, 1953, December 18.
(177). The Nyasaland Times Newspaper, 1955, April 8.
(178). Kay, Chip (10 August 2015). Chip Kay Session 8 p7.

(179). Kay, Chip (10 August 2015). Chip Kay Session 8 p6.

(180). Hill, RW. "WW2 People's War" BBC, 2005.
https://www.bbc.co.uk/history/ww2peopleswar/stories/84/a4537884.shtml
Accessed 21 March 2018.

(181). The Nyasaland Times Newspaper, 1955, March 22, p1.

(182). The Nyasaland Times Newspaper, 1955, March 1.

(183). Shaxson, TF. "A Map of the Distribution of Major Biotic Communities in
Malawi" The Society of Malawi Journal. Society of Malawi – Historical and
Scientific. 1977, Vol.30 No.1 p46.

(184). Kay, Chip (10 August 2015). Chip Kay Session 8 p7.

(185). The Nyasaland Times Newspaper, 1955, May 12.

(186). Kay, Chip (10 August 2015). Chip Kay Session 8 p9.

(187). Kay, Chip (10 August 2015). Chip Kay Session 8 p7.

The Intoxication Of Flying 1954

(188). Kay, Chip (23 Jun 2015). Chip Kay Session 6 p13.

(189). Kay, Chip (23 Jun 2015). Chip Kay Session 6 p12.

(190). "de Havilland Tiger Moth" Wikipedia, the free encyclopedia.
https://en.wikipedia.org/wiki/De_Havilland_Tiger_Moth Accessed on 21 March
2018.

(191). Kermode, AC. Flight Without Formulae. Sir Isaac Pitman & Sons,
1955/1940, p80-1.

(192). Stevens, Arthur. Chileka Airport: The First Sixty Years. Montfort Press,
1993, p1.

(193). Stevens, Arthur. Chileka Airport: The First Sixty Years. Montfort Press,
1993, p14.

(194). The Nyasaland Times Newspaper, 1955, March 18.

(195). Kay, Chip (8 Feb 2017). Chip Kay Session 27 p4.

(196). Kilner, Angela Tennett. (21 March 2018). Phone Interview via WhatsApp.

(197). Tennett, Des J. "Luchenza Flying Club" The Society of Malawi Journal,
1989, Vol.42 No.1, p12. www.jstor.org/stable/29778607

(198). Kay, Chip (23 Jun 2015). Chip Kay Session 6 p12.

(199). Kay, Chip (28 Dec 2015). Chip Kay Session 15 p3.

(200). Tennett, Des J. "Luchenza Flying Club" The Society of Malawi Journal,
1989, Vol.42 No.1, p12.

(201). "H.J.C.'s Club Commentary: The Nyasaland Flying Club" The Aeroplane
Magazine, 1958, June 13, p832.

(202). Kay, Chip (23 Jun 2015). Chip Kay Session 6 p14.

(203). Kermode, AC. Flight Without Formulae. Sir Isaac Pitman & Sons,
1955/1940, p1.

(204). Kay, Chip (14 September 2015). Chip Kay Session 12 p3.

(205). "Chiperoni" Wikipedia. https://amp.blog.e-
hokkaido.in/28311421/1/chiperoni.html Accessed 15 November 2020.

(206). "Ab initio training: The vintage route." Australian Flying, 2010, April.
www.australianflying.com.au/news/ab-initio-training-the-vintage-route Accessed
23 March 2018.

(207). Kay, Chip (8 Feb 2017). Chip Kay Session 27 p18.
(208). Kay, Chip (23 Jun 2015). Chip Kay Session 6 p17.
(209). Kay, Chip (23 Jun 2015). Chip Kay Session 6 p17-18.
(210). Kay, Chip (23 Jun 2015). Chip Kay Session 6 p16.

Chasing Crocodiles 1955-1957
(211). Kay, Chip (20 June 2016). Chip Kay Session 22.
(212). Osborne, Frances. "The Bolter: The Story of Idina Sachville and "Happy Valley" Vintage Books, Random House, 2010.
(213). Kay, Chip (14 December 2015). Chip Kay Session 14 p3.
(214). Kay, Chip (20 June 2016). Chip Kay Session 22 p10.
(215). Kay, Chip (23 Jun 2015). Chip Kay Session 6 p8.
(216). Kay, Chip (23 Jun 2015). Chip Kay Session 6 p8.
(217). The Nyasaland Times Newspaper, 1957, February 8, p4.
(218). Kay, Chip (23 Jun 2015). Chip Kay Session 6 p8.
(219). Kay, Chip (4 January 2016). Chip Kay Session 16 p10.
(220). Kay, Chip (23 Jun 2015). Chip Kay Session 6 p9.
(221). Hartley, Saturday. "Two Rhodesians Killed in Air Crash: Light Plane Strikes High-Tension Wires" The Sunday Mail: The Rhodesian National Newspaper, 1957, February 10.
(222). Notice of Death. The Nyasaland Times Newspaper, 1957, February 15.

Kangaroo Kay 1955-1957
(223). Kay, Chip (16 November 2015). Chip Kay Session 13 p23-24.

Red lipstick and the largest Kasamba tree in Africa, April 1957
(224). Tennett, Des J. "Luchenza Flying Club" The Society of Malawi Journal, 1989, Vol.42 No.1, p18.
(225). Kay, Chip (14 September 2015). Chip Kay Session 12 p15.
(226). Kay, Chip (14 September 2015). Chip Kay Session 12 p16.
(227). "Mlanje Cedar" The Nyasaland Times Newspaper, 1951, June.
(228). Kay, Chip (14 September 2015). Chip Kay Session 12 p16.
(229). Kay, Chip (14 September 2015). Chip Kay Session 12 p17.
(230). "Troutbeck Resort" https://www.south-african-hotels.com/hotels/troutbeck-resort/ Accessed 11 April 2018.
(231). Kay, Chip (14 September 2015). Chip Kay Session 12 p18.

For Business And For Pleasure 1957-1962
(232). Kay, Chip (10 August 2015). Chip Kay Session 8 p7.
(233). Kay, Chip (10 August 2015). Chip Kay Session 8 p7.
(234). "Cessna 175 Skylark" Wikipedia. https://en.wikipedia.org/wiki/Cessna_175_Skylark Accessed 16 April 2018.
(235). Kay, Chip (10 August 2015). Chip Kay Session 8 p7.
(236). Kay, Chip (10 August 2015). Chip Kay Session 8 p8.
(237). Kay, Chip (5 September 2015). Chip Kay Session 11 p5.

(238). Dowling, Stephen. "The plane so good it is still in production after 60 years" BBC, 2017, March 2. www.bbc.com/future/story/20170302-the-plane-so-good-its-still-in-production-after-60-years Accessed 16 April 2018.

(239). Kay, Chip (8 Feb 2017). Chip Kay Session 27 p17.

(240). Kay, Chip (10 August 2015). Chip Kay Session 8 p8.

(241). Tennett, Des J. "Luchenza Flying Club" The Society of Malawi Journal, 1989, Vol.42 No.1, p16.

(242). Tennett, Des J. "Luchenza Flying Club" The Society of Malawi Journal, 1989, Vol.42 No.1, p18.

(243). Tennett, Des J. "Luchenza Flying Club" The Society of Malawi Journal, 1989, Vol.42 No.1, p18-19.

(244). Kay, Chip (14 September 2015). Chip Kay Session 12 p9.

(245). Kay, Chip (23 Jun 2015). Chip Kay Session 6 p18.

(246). Kay, Chip (23 Jun 2015). Chip Kay Session 6 p18.

(247). Kay, Chip (23 Jun 2015). Chip Kay Session 6 p19.

Madly In Love 1962-1964

(248). "The Visit of Her Majesty Queen Elizabeth the Queen Mother to Nyasaland 12th-15th July, 1957" The Nyasaland Journal, 1958, Vol.11 No.1, p12. https://www.jstor.org/stable/i29545804

(249). "The Visit of Her Majesty Queen Elizabeth the Queen Mother to Nyasaland 12th-15th July, 1957" The Nyasaland Journal, 1958, Vol.11 No.1, p7.

(250). Tennett, Des J. "Luchenza Flying Club" The Society of Malawi Journal, 1989, Vol.42 No.1, p17.

(251). Kay, Chip (23 Jun 2015). Chip Kay Session 6 p23.

(252). Kay, Chip (23 Jun 2015). Chip Kay Session 6 p22.

(253). Kay, Chip (5 September 2015). Chip Kay Session 11 p8.

(254). Kay, Chip (16 November 2015). Chip Kay Session 13 p5.

(255). Kay, Chip (23 Jun 2015). Chip Kay Session 6 p23.

(256). Kay, Chip (16 November 2015). Chip Kay Session 13 p12.

(257). Kay, Chip (16 November 2015). Chip Kay Session 13 p12.

(258). Kay, Chip (14 September 2015). Chip Kay Session 12 p4.

(259). Kay, Chip (14 September 2015). Chip Kay Session 12 p5.

(260). Kay, Chip (14 September 2015). Chip Kay Session 12 p6.

(261). Kohn, George C. Encyclopedia of Plague and Pestilence: From Ancient Times to the Present. Facts on File, Inc. 2007, p174.

(262). Kay, Chip (14 September 2015). Chip Kay Session 12 p5.

(263). Kay, Chip (14 September 2015). Chip Kay Session 12 p6.

Change And Democracy: The Demise Of Nyasaland 1944-1964

(264). McCracken, John. A History of Malawi: 1859-1966. Boydell & Brewer Ltd, 2012, p313.

(265). Nyasaland: Report for the year 1962. H.M.S.O. London, 1963, p25.

(266). McCracken, John. A History of Malawi: 1859-1966. Boydell & Brewer Ltd, 2012, p326.

(267). McCracken, John. A History of Malawi: 1859-1966. Boydell & Brewer Ltd, 2012, p327.

(268). McCracken, John. A History of Malawi: 1859-1966. Boydell & Brewer Ltd, 2012, p329.

(269). Reed, Douglas. The Battle for Rhodesia. Haum, 1966, p13.

(270). Kay, Chip (8 Feb 2017). Chip Kay Session 27 p5.

(271). McCracken, John. A History of Malawi: 1859-1966. Boydell & Brewer Ltd, 2012, p311.

(272). McCracken, John. A History of Malawi: 1859-1966. Boydell & Brewer Ltd, 2012, p344.

(273). McCracken, John. A History of Malawi: 1859-1966. Boydell & Brewer Ltd, 2012, p346.

(274). McCracken, John. A History of Malawi: 1859-1966. Boydell & Brewer Ltd, 2012, p364.

(275). McCracken, John. A History of Malawi: 1859-1966. Boydell & Brewer Ltd, 2012, p458.

(276). McCracken, John. A History of Malawi: 1859-1966. Boydell & Brewer Ltd, 2012, p446.

(277). Kay, Chip (16 November 2015). Chip Kay Session 13 p9.

When It All Falls Apart 1964-1968

(278). McCracken, John. A History of Malawi: 1859-1966. Boydell & Brewer Ltd, 2012, p456.

(279). Shaxson, TF. "A Map of the Distribution of Major Biotic Communities in Malawi" The Society of Malawi Journal. Society of Malawi – Historical and Scientific. 1977, Vol.30 No.1 p46.

(280). Kay, Chip (5 September 2015). Chip Kay Session 11 p8.

(281). Kay, Chip (5 September 2015). Chip Kay Session 11 p15.

(282). Kay, Chip (5 September 2015). Chip Kay Session 11 p16.

(283). Kay, Chip (5 September 2015). Chip Kay Session 11 p16.

(284). Kay, Chip (5 September 2015). Chip Kay Session 11 p17.

(285). Kay, Chip (23 Jun 2015). Chip Kay Session 6 p26.

(286). Kay, Chip (16 November 2015). Chip Kay Session 13 p9,

(287). McCracken, John. A History of Malawi: 1859-1966. Boydell & Brewer Ltd, 2012, p457.

(288). Kay, Chip (16 November 2015). Chip Kay Session 13 p4.

(289). Kay, Chip (16 November 2015). Chip Kay Session 13 p8.

(290). Kay, Chip (23 Jun 2015). Chip Kay Session 6 p25.

Leopard Air 1965

(291). Stevens, Arthur. Chileka Airport: The First Sixty Years. Montfort Press, 1993, p36.

(292). Kay, Chip (5 September 2015). Chip Kay Session 11 p4.

(293). Kay, Chip (5 September 2015). Chip Kay Session 11 p4.

(294). Kay, Chip (4 January 2016). Chip Kay Session 16 p2.

(295). Kalinga, Owen JM. "The Production of History in Malawi in the 1960s: The Legacy of Sir Harry Johnston, The Influence of the Society of Malawi and The Role of Dr. Kamuzu Banda and His Malawi Congress Party" African Affairs, 1998, Vol.97 Is.389, p523-549.
(296). Leopard Air Limited Tours of Malawi, brochure, 1969.
(297). Kay, Chip (5 September 2015). Chip Kay Session 11 p4.
(298). Kay, Chip (5 September 2015). Chip Kay Session 11 p4.
(299). Kay, Chip (16 November 2015). Chip Kay Session 13 p7.
(300). Kay, Chip (14 September 2015). Chip Kay Session 12 p12.
(301). Marais, Dr. John. (verbal stories from his childhood at Malamulo).
(302). Kay, Chip (14 September 2015). Chip Kay Session 12 p10.
(303). Kay, Chip (14 September 2015). Chip Kay Session 12 p15.
(304). Hellsten, Irene Harvey. (13 June 2018). "Crash at Luchenza" email.
(305). Kay, Chip (5 September 2015). Chip Kay Session 11 p13.
(306). Kay, Chip (5 September 2015). Chip Kay Session 11 p13.
(307). Kay, Chip (5 September 2015). Chip Kay Session 11 p14.
(308). Kay, Chip (5 September 2015). Chip Kay Session 11 p14.

Timati Moyo Kukoma (Life Is Sweet) 1968

(309). Kay, Chip (16 November 2015). Chip Kay Session 13 p3.
(310). Kay, Chip (5 September 2015). Chip Kay Session 11 p12.
(311). Kay, Chip (23 Jun 2015). Chip Kay Session 6 p28.
(312). Kay, Chip (5 September 2015). Chip Kay Session 11 p12.

Dolce Vita 1968-1970

(313). Kay, Chip (16 November 2015). Chip Kay Session 13 p14-15.
(314). Kay, Chip (8 Feb 2017). Chip Kay Session 27 p4.
(315). Kay, Chip (13 August 2015). Chip Kay Session 9 p11.
(316). Kay, Chip (13 August 2015). Chip Kay Session 9 p5.
(317). Kay, Chip (13 August 2015). Chip Kay Session 9 p6.
(318). Kay, Chip (13 August 2015). Chip Kay Session 9 p7.
(319). "Barbary slave trade" Wikipedia.
https://en.wikipedia.org/wiki/White_slavery "White slavery" Wikipedia.
https://en.wikipedia.org/wiki/White_slavery Accessed 2 May 2018.
(320). Kay, Chip (13 August 2015). Chip Kay Session 9 p8.
(321). Kay, Chip (13 August 2015). Chip Kay Session 9 p7.

The Dawn Of A New Era 1970-1971

(322). Kay, Chip (16 November 2015). Chip Kay Session 13 p9.
(323). Kay, Chip (23 Jun 2015). Chip Kay Session 6 p26.
(324). Kay, Chip (16 November 2015). Chip Kay Session 13 p9.
(325). Kay, Chip (23 Jun 2015). Chip Kay Session 6 p27.
(326). Nyasaland Portrait newspaper clipping and Picture Nancy Fenner (no date).
(327). Kay, Chip (16 November 2015). Chip Kay Session 13 p9
(328). Kay, Chip (16 November 2015). Chip Kay Session 13 p11-12.
(329). Kay, Chip (23 Jun 2015). Chip Kay Session 6 p27.

(330). Kay, Chip (16 November 2015). Chip Kay Session 13 p17.

Paradise 1971
(331). Kay, Chip (16 November 2015). Chip Kay Session 13 p19.
(332). Kay, Chip (16 November 2015). Chip Kay Session 13 p20.
(333). Kay, Chip (16 November 2015). Chip Kay Session 13 p20.
(334). Kay, Chip (16 November 2015). Chip Kay Session 13 p21.
(335). Kay, Chip (16 November 2015). Chip Kay Session 13 p21.
(336). Kay, Chip (13 August 2015). Chip Kay Session 9 p10.
(337). Kay, Chip (16 November 2015). Chip Kay Session 13 p21.
(338). Kay, Chip (16 November 2015). Chip Kay Session 13 p22.
(339). Kay, Chip (16 November 2015). Chip Kay Session 13 p22.

Satemwa, Tea And Coffee 1971
(340). Johnston, Sir Harry H. British Central Africa. Methuen & Co, London, 1897, p162.
(341). Nyasaland Protectorate. 1908-9 No.619 Colonial Reports-Annual. H.M.S.O. London, 1909, p7-9.
(342). Kay, Chip (16 November 2015). Chip Kay Session 13 p14-15.
(343). Kay, Chip (5 September 2015). Chip Kay Session 11.
(344). Kay, Chip (16 November 2015). Chip Kay Session 13 p15.
(345). Kay, Chip (28 Dec 2015). Chip Kay Session 15 p10.
(346). Kay, Chip (28 Dec 2015). Chip Kay Session 15 p10.
(347). Kay, Chip (6 July 2015). Chip Kay Session 7 p18.
(348). Kay, Chip (6 June 2016). Chip Kay Session 23.
(349). Kay, Chip (1 September 2016). Chip Kay Session 26 p1.
(350). Kay, Chip (11 January 2016). Chip Kay Session 17 p7.
(351). Kay, Chip (11 January 2016). Chip Kay Session 17 p5.
(352). Kay, Chip (11 January 2016). Chip Kay Session 17 p4-5.
(353). Kay, Chip (11 January 2016). Chip Kay Session 17 p4.
(354). Kay, Chip (11 January 2016). Chip Kay Session 17 p3-4.
(355). Kay, Chip (11 January 2016). Chip Kay Session 17 p3.
(356). Kay, Chip (13 August 2015). Chip Kay Session 9 p8.
(357). Kay, Chip (13 August 2015). Chip Kay Session 9 p9.
(358). Kay, Chip (24 August 2015). Chip Kay Session 10 p10.
(359). Kay, Chip (4 January 2016). Chip Kay Session 16 p4.

"Raisin" Maclean 1975
(360). Kay, Chip (4 January 2016). Chip Kay Session 16 p5.
(361). Henderson, Dottie. (6 June 2018). Dottie Henderson Session Audio Recording.
(362). "1977 Philadelphia Eagles season" Wikipedia. https://en.wikipedia.org/wiki/1977_Philadelphia_Eagles_season Accessed 6 June 2018.
(363). Kay, Chip (4 January 2016). Chip Kay Session 16 p5.

(364). "1977 Philadelphia Eagles season" Wikipedia.
https://en.wikipedia.org/wiki/1977_Philadelphia_Eagles_season Accessed 6 June 2018.
(365). Kay, Chip (4 January 2016). Chip Kay Session 16 p5

Hoodwinked From 1978
(366). Kay, Chip (30 Mar 2015). Chip Kay Session 5 p3-4.
(367). Kay, Chip (25 January 2016). Chip Kay Session 18 p11.

The WARS On Colonialism 1965-1980
(368). The Nyasaland Times Newspaper, 1951, April 9, p3.
(369). Kay, Chip (13 August 2015). Chip Kay Session 9 p2.
(370). Kay, Chip (13 August 2015). Chip Kay Session 9 p4.
(371). Kay, Chip (24 August 2015). Chip Kay Session 10 p8.
(372). "Air Rhodesia Flight 825" Wikipedia.
https://en.wikipedia.org/wiki/Air_Rhodesia_Flight_825 Accessed 23 May 2018
(373). Kay, Chip (24 August 2015). Chip Kay Session 10 p8.
(374). Kay, Chip (25 January 2016). Chip Kay Session 18 p5-6.
(375). Kay, Chip (24 August 2015). Chip Kay Session 10 p9.
(376). Kay, Chip (24 August 2015). Chip Kay Session 10 p7.
(377). Lockington, Maxine. (4 June 2018). Verbal stories and memories of Maxine Lockington.
(378). Kay, Chip (24 August 2015). Chip Kay Session 10 p6.
(379). Kay, Chip (24 August 2015). Chip Kay Session 10 p8.
(380). Kay, Chip (24 August 2015). Chip Kay Session 10 p7.
(381). Kalinga, Owen JM. "The Production of History in Malawi in the 1960s: The Legacy of Sir Harry Johnston, The Influence of the Society of Malawi and The Role of Dr. Kamuzu Banda and His Malawi Congress Party" African Affairs, 1998, Vol.97 Is.389, p523-549.
(382). Kay, Chip (1 February 2016). Chip Kay Session 19 p3.
(383). Kay, Chip (1 February 2016). Chip Kay Session 19 p4.
(384). Kay, Chip (1 February 2016). Chip Kay Session 19 p4.
(385). "Dick Matenje" Wikipedia. https://en.wikipedia.org/wiki/Dick_Matenje Accessed 16 November 2020.
(386). Kay, Chip (1 February 2016). Chip Kay Session 19 p6.
(387). "Confronting the Past: Accountability for Human Rights Violations in MALAWI" The Robert F. Kennedy Memorial Center for Human Rights, 1994, May.
(388). Matemba, Yonah. "Aspects of the Centenary History of Malamulo Seventh-day Adventist Mission, Makwasa, Malawi, 1902-2002" Chancellor College, University of Malawi, 2002, June 14, p20.

Mischief And The Full Moon Jackals – (Mid 70's and 80's)
(389). Kay, Chip (25 January 2016). Chip Kay Session 18 p13.
(390). Kay, Chip (25 January 2016). Chip Kay Session 18 p14.
(391). Kay, Chip (28 December 2015). Chip Kay Session 15 p9.

(392). Kay, Chip (28 December 2015). Chip Kay Session 15 p14.

LOST – 1970-1988
(393). Kay, Chip (1 September 2016). Chip Kay Session 25 p9.
(394). Kay, Chip (1 September 2016). Chip Kay Session 25 p2.
(395). Kay, Chip (1 September 2016). Chip Kay Session 25 p3.
(396). Kay, Chip (1 September 2016). Chip Kay Session 25 p3.
(397). Kay, Chip (8 February 2017). Chip Kay Session 27 p3.
(398). Kay, Chip (1 September 2016). Chip Kay Session 25 p5.
(399). Kay, Chip (1 September 2016). Chip Kay Session 25 p5.
(400). Kay, Chip (1 September 2016). Chip Kay Session 25 p6.
(401). Kay, Chip (1 September 2016). Chip Kay Session 25 p10.
(402). Kay, Chip (1 September 2016). Chip Kay Session 25 p9.

Old And Bold From 1983
(403). Chip Kay's Personal Flying Logbook 1983, January 7.
(404). Kay, Chip (8 Feb 2017). Chip Kay Session 27 p8.
(405). Kay, Chip (20 June 2016). Chip Kay Session 22, p3.
(406). Kay, Chip (14 December 2015). Chip Kay Session 14 p7.
(407). Kay, Chip (14 December 2015). Chip Kay Session 14 p9.
(408). Kay, Chip (28 Dec 2015). Chip Kay Session 15 p7.
(409). Kay, Chip (28 Dec 2015). Chip Kay Session 15 p4.
(410). Kay, Chip (4 January 2016). Chip Kay Session 16 p6.
(411). Kay, Chip (4 January 2016). Chip Kay Session 16 p6.
(412). Kay, Chip (8 Feb 2017). Chip Kay Session 27 p16.
(413). Kay, Chip (4 January 2016). Chip Kay Session 16 p12.
(414). Kay, Chip (4 January 2016). Chip Kay Session 16 p15.
(415). Kay, Chip (4 January 2016). Chip Kay Session 16 p14.

Winds Of Change 2003
(416). Young, Nick. Newspaper.
(417). "Hastings Banda" Wikipedia. https://en.wikipedia.org/wiki/Hastings_Banda
Accessed 13 June 2018.
(418). Kay, Chip (1 February 2016). Chip Kay Session 19 p8.
(419). Kay, Chip (28 Dec 2015). Chip Kay Session 15 p5.

Sixteen Million And Counting 2003-2013
(420). Kay, Chip (1 Mar 2017). Chip Kay Session 29 p5.
(421). Kay, Chip (11 January 2016). Chip Kay Session 17.
(422). Kay, Chip (11 January 2016). Chip Kay Session 17 p9.
(423). Kay, Chip (1 Mar 2017). Chip Kay Session 29 p10.
(424). Kay, Chip (15 Mar 2015). Chip Kay Session 3 p6.

Where There Is Tea, There Is Hope
(425). Kay, Chip (13 June 2016). Chip Kay Session 21 p8.

(426). Kay, Chip (13 June 2016). Chip Kay Session 21 p9.
(427). Henderson, Dottie. (6 June 2018). Dottie Henderson Session Audio Recording.
(428). Kay, Chip (13 June 2016). Chip Kay Session 21 p8.
(429). Kay, Hilly. (7 June 2018). Hilly Kay Session Audio Recording.
(430). Henderson, Dottie. (6 June 2018). Dottie Henderson Session Audio Recording.
(431). Kay, Chip (13 June 2016). Chip Kay Session 21 p8.

Buchanan, John. *The Shire Highlands.* Blantyre Printing & Publishing Co, 1885.
Eidhammer, Asbjorn. *Malawi: A Place Apart.* ABC Printers, 2017.
McCracken, John. *Politics & Christianity in Malawi 1875-1940.* Montfort Media. 2008.
Pakenham, Thomas. *The Scramble for Africa.* Random House. 1991.
Westrop, Arthur. *Green Gold.* Cauldwell, 1966.

Printed in Great Britain
by Amazon

54808832R00177